THE INTEGRAL ENNEAGRAM

A *DHARMA*-BASED APPROACH FOR
LINKING THE NINE PERSONALITY TYPES,
NINE STAGES OF TRANSFORMATION &
KEN WILBER'S INTEGRAL OPERATING SYSTEM

SUSAN RHODES, PH.D.

THE INTEGRAL ENNEAGRAM

A *DHARMA*-BASED APPROACH FOR
LINKING THE NINE PERSONALITY TYPES,
NINE STAGES OF TRANSFORMATION &
KEN WILBER'S INTEGRAL OPERATING SYSTEM

GERANIUM PRESS
Seattle, Washington, USA

ISBN 978-0-9824792-2-3

SUSAN RHODES, PH.D.

Acknowledgments

GRATEFUL THANKS to Deborah DiMichele and Carl Marsak for reading through the first draft of the manuscript and giving invaluable early feedback; to Charmaine Sungy for her always enlightening commentary; to Alexandra Hepburn for stimulating conversations and asking the questions that needed answering; to Judith Bouffiou for her thoughtful inquiries and feedback; and to Pamela Silimperi, Laura Rivendell, and Rev. Alia Zara Aurami-Sou for the daunting and difficult task of copy editing the final draft; to Jack Labanauskas & SueAnn McKean for their ongoing encouragement to develop my enneagram ideas; to the Thompson family (Norm, Adél, Norman & Hanna) and Sheela, Chiri, and Tilotoma Word for their love and personal support.

Other Geranium Press books by Susan Rhodes :

The Positive Enneagram (2009)
Archetypes of the Enneagram (2010)

To my dear friends Debbie & Pam
for their loyal support
and many hours reading
and proofing manuscripts

CONTENTS

PART I
AN INTEGRAL APPROACH

WHAT EXACTLY IS AN INTEGRAL APPROACH? *It's an approach to living that promotes **integration**: the harmonious meshing of diverse energies. True integration can be hard to achieve, whether we're talking about an individual seeking inner balance, partners seeking greater intimacy, or a group of people trying to make their neighborhood a better place to live. The more elements we have to harmonize, the greater the challenge.*

Integral systems are designed to support integration by providing a workable approach for reconciling differences in viewpoint or levels of functioning. The enneagram is such a tool; so is Ken Wilber's Integral Operating System (IOS). When we study each in relationship to the other, we begin to see the parallels between them—and to realize the advantages of a combined enneagram-IOS approach for inner work.

Part I introduces both systems, as well as a context for interrelating them. We start with an Introduction, followed by a look at the advantages of a dharma-oriented *approach (Chapter 1); a description of holarchy and why it matters (Chapter 2); an introduction to the personality enneagram (Chapter 3); and an introduction to IOS (Chapter 4).*

INTRODUCTION

THE ENNEAGRAM AND KEN WILBER'S IN-
TEGRAL APPROACH are two powerful systems for understanding human nature. The
enneagram unveils nine personality types
based on diverse core motivations; Wilber's
Integral Operating System (IOS) provides
a meta-framework for conceptualizing the
development of human consciousness. Although these two systems have developed independently of one another, each has a lot to
offer the other. IOS brings to the enneagram
a brilliantly-reasoned and progressively-oriented framework that can form the basis for
enneagram studies; the enneagram brings
IOS a methodology for examining how differences in temperament affect human development. So bringing the two together represents a "win-win" proposition.

Historically, the enneagram has mainly
been used to describe the enneagram types as
nine ego defenses that cut us off from our essential being. To those who have worked with
the enneagram, this description will sound
familiar. To those who have not, it may sound
a little odd (as it did to me when I was first
introduced to the system). I never got over the
sense that it was strange to think of personality as some kind of problem. To me, person-

ality is a marker of individuality—and individuality is our most precious gift.

So I searched for a way to work with the
enneagram from a more positive perspective.
However, I found no framework within the
field from which to work, no teaching presenting personality as an asset rather than a
liability. I finally realized that if I wanted to
work with the types from a positive point of
view, I would have to devise an approach myself, drawing inspiration mainly from sources
outside the field.

Wilber's IOS was one of the main sources of inspiration and support, although it
took me a while to realize its potential. But
the more I got into Wilber's ideas, the more
I saw the usefulness of his approach, an approach which championed individuality and
depicted transformation as a progressive
(transcend-and-include) process of creating
ever more refined structures of consciousness—not as a regressive, ego-annihilating
process of stripping away the structures associated with rational consciousness. Or as
Wilber himself so eloquently puts it,

> "Kosmic consciousness is not the oblit-
> eration of individuality, but its consum-
> mate fulfillment."[1]

The reason it took a while to grasp the potential of Wilber's system is that his system is vast; it also includes five major phases traversed over 40 years of work. Nevertheless, as I slowly worked my way through his books and articles, I kept running into ideas with which I resonated; my Wilber books ended up with extensive annotations in the margins, many of which started with "Right" and "Yes!"

I was also attracted by Wilber's interest in Arthur Koestler's holon theory, which describes a way of characterizing healthy hierarchical systems (Chapter 2).[2] Thus, although I drew from a variety of sources in formulating my approach to the enneagram (including my own work in cognitive psychology and research in the related field of positive psychology), Wilber's ideas increasingly came to play a pivotal role in my enneagram work.

A lot of my research involved writing, because I always seem to absorb ideas best by writing about them. So I wrote a lot. At first, the ideas were fuzzy and the work contained many holes. But eventually, key themes emerged and the writing became more fluid. Soon I began to post the articles on my website (www.enneagramdimensions.net). In 2006, after volunteering to generate a subject index for the *Enneagram Monthly* (*EM*)—a paper which has published enneagram articles since 1995—I became friends with the owner and chief editor, Jack Labanauskas. One day, I happened to mention that I'd written some articles. Jack took a look and asked to publish them; a couple of months later, I became the staff reporter for the *EM*.

My work has since been published in the *Enneagram Journal*, the research journal associated with the International Enneagram Association (IEA), and on the website *Integral World* (www.integralworld.net). I've also written two books, *The Positive Enneagram* (2009) and *Archetypes of the Enneagram* (2010), further described at the end of this introduction.

Since Ken Wilber's work was such a pivotal influence on my approach to the enneagram, I've probably written more articles exploring the link between Wilber's IOS and the enneagram than on any other topic. In fact, the second article I wrote for the *EM* was a two-part theoretical piece, "The Enneagram and Ken Wilber's Integral Kosmology," (Dec. 2006–Jan. 2007). In the same issue, I wrote a favorable book review of Wilber's then-new book, *Integral Spirituality* (2006).

The main purpose of this first article was to demonstrate how IOS could provide a theoretical justification for working with the enneagram from a depathologized perspective. But I also touched upon ways in which the enneagram and IOS could inform one another, topics to which I returned in future *EM* articles—and which became the basis for *The Integral Enneagram*:

- "The Retro-Romantic Ideal and the Enneagram," about the negative impact of retro-Romanticism on the enneagram field (Sept. 2010); see Chapter 5.

- "Ken Wilber's 8 Hori-zones & 9 Enneagram Types," on the uncanny parallels between the nine enneagram types and Wilber's eight hori-zones as described by Wilber in *Integral Spirituality* (June 2011); see Chapter 10.

- "Integral Living and the Enneagram," on the idea that transformation involves not only ascent but also descent (Oct. 2011); see Chapters 9 & 12.

- "Personality, Process & Levels of Development," on the parallels between Wilber's nine levels of development, the process enneagram's nine stages of development, and the personality enneagram's nine points of view (Dec. 2011–Jan. 2012); see Chapter 11.

- "An Enneagram-based Model of Integral Transformation," on using the process enneagram to fill in missing gaps in the current model of integral transformation (June 2012); see Chapter 9.[3]

After generating the first few articles, I realized I probably had a book in the making. So these articles form the basis for *The Integral Enneagram*. However, the book goes beyond the articles in a number of respects. Because during the writing process, new patterns emerged. And that's a good thing, because it would otherwise make converting articles to books an extremely tedious process!

Depathologizing the Enneagram

I originally described my enneagram perspective as a *positive enneagram approach*, in order to distinguish it from the usual *ego-versus-essence approach* of seeing the nine personality types as departures from our essential nature. (As we will see, Wilber associates the ego-versus-essence idea with what he calls a *retro-Romantic* philosophy of life and says it is based on a faulty premise about the nature of transformation; see Chapters 4 and 5 for a discussion.)

But a lack of positivity is not the only problem associated with the ego-versus-essence approach. In the first *EM* article I published, "Let's Depathologize the Enneagram!" (Oct. 2006), I listed four complaints about this

approach, noting that it is (a) unnecessarily negative, (b) insufficiently coherent, (c) psychologically divisive, and (d) overly narrow in focus.

The problem of **negativity** is rooted in the widespread belief that it is beneficial to focus our attention on negative type traits because it will allow us to curb the pernicious effects of those traits, such that at the moment they start to arise, we can "catch ourselves in the act." Over time, this kind of practice is believed to denude the ego of its power to delude us, thereby allowing our spiritual essence to rise to the fore. Unfortunately, there is plenty of research in psychology to suggest that eliminating a negative does not create a positive (as I shall argue further in Chapter 5, based on Martin Seligman's work on depression). Also, focusing too much on the negative aspects of personality can distract us from developing its positive qualities.[4]

The **lack of coherence** problem concerns the fuzzy logic involved in arguing that our personality type develops in such a way that it is unavoidably neurotic (see Chapter 5). It was easier in decades past—when infants were considered a *tabula rasa*—to make the claim that personality is largely the result of behavioral conditioning. It's much harder now, because there is such a large body of research showing that personality structures exist in nascent form at the very beginning of life.[5] Nevertheless, the belief that personality is mainly the product of environmental conditioning lingers on, especially in the minds of those raised during the pro-"nurture" phase of the ongoing nature-nurture debate.[6] However, the fact that type seems to be a permanent structure within the psyche makes it extremely improbable that it's the result of conditioning, since that which is the result of conditioning can often be re-conditioned, which our enneagram type cannot.

The problem of *divisiveness* (duality) concerns the way that enneagram theory divides the self into upper and lower halves, locating the personality self (with its "emotional vices" and "cognitive fixations") in the lower half and the Higher Self (with its emotional virtues and Holy Ideas) in the upper half.[7]

Dividing the self in half might not be such a problem if the goal were simply to integrate the halves (as A. G. E. Blake suggests it ought to be; see Chapter 5). But integration is *not* the goal in personality enneagram work; instead, the goal is to help people minimize the effects of the "lower" half, thus starving it of energy and attention. So the current enneagram model is in that sense quite similar to the model of human nature traditionally adopted by ascetics seeking to starve their baser impulses by ignoring or denying them. Only now, instead of targeting the body as the source of trouble, we target the ego.

Compare this dualistic approach with Jung's more transformationally-oriented vision of the psyche, where even the very worst qualities are viewed as the *prima materia* for transmutation—a transmutation that brings about not just the resolution of conflict but the transformation of consciousness. When viewed from this perspective, transformation becomes the process of reconciling the opposites within us, allowing us to gradually lay down the burden of dualistic thinking.

Or compare it to Wilber's "transcend-and-include" approach, where each stage in development is regarded as a foundation for the next, such that pre-egoic development forms the basis for ego development, which in turn forms the basis for trans-egoic development. As with Jung's model, the emphasis here is on integration, not separation.

Last but not least, the *narrowness-of-focus* problem concerns the fact that placing so much attention on the "negatives" of the types means placing much less attention on the "positives." Even when people allude to gifts of the types, they seldom speak of them with conviction. But this makes perfect sense; why would we associate a personality fixation with inner gifts?

Once we have come to associate the types with fixated functioning, it becomes tough to envision them as positive influences. While we may speak in theory of transforming emotional vices to virtues (or cognitive fixations to Holy Ideas), the habit of focusing on negative traits—once established—is hard to break.

Nonetheless, this narrow vision seems to be gradually giving way to a broader, more open-ended approach to working with the types (especially among coaches and consultants, whose business clients demand a "can do" approach). This trend will probably become even stronger in the future, as new enneagram generations develop new ways to work with the system.

Take the recent upsurge of interest in linking the enneagram and integral approaches—a development I had definitely not anticipated when I began writing this book in 2010. The interest in bringing these two systems together is pretty sudden and dramatic—which means that in the near future, Integralists are likely to be hearing a lot more about the enneagram and vice-versa.[8]

So it's particularly critical at this juncture to reflect on ways that we might broaden (and perhaps deepen) our view of the nine types, so that we see them as more than simply barriers to transformation. As I hope to demonstrate in future chapters, it's when we can envision the enneagram as a *potential-oriented system*—and its nine points as the diverse potentials that animate that system—that it becomes a potent tool for the transformation of human consciousness.

An Integral Enneagram Model

It's a tribute to the power of the enneagram that despite the above-mentioned limitations, it remains a useful tool for inner work. But for myself, it was impossible to work with the system as I found it. While the ability to identify type-related blind spots (if painful) was initially liberating, it wore thin after awhile. I began to feel trapped within a system that is supposed to be about inner freedom. It was only by separating the enneagram from the interpretive milieu in which it is embedded (which is based on the premise that ego obscures essence) that I was able to develop an approach to enneagram work that I could live with in the long run.

As mentioned above, I originally thought of this way of working as a positive enneagram approach. But as the result of my integral work, my original positive enneagram approach has been morphing into an integral enneagram approach that can generate an *integrally-oriented model of transformation.* This book is about that model.

The model is built on the premise that—although we all have within us diverse ener-gies that pull us in different directions—it's possible to integrate those energies in a way that allows us to function much more harmoniously in life. While the personality enneagram serves as its touchstone, it is heavily influenced by four complementary approaches: (a) Ken Wilber's Integral Operating System (IOS); (b) G. I. Gurdjieff's process enneagram; (c) Arthur Koestler's holarchic approach to living systems; and (d) the foundational idea that there is a central thread or theme that gives purpose to our lives, a theme I refer to as the *dharma.*

We'll take a brief look at each of these approaches below.

- *Wilber's IOS* provides an overall theoretical framework for enneagram work that is impressively comprehensive, optimistic in focus, and entirely progressive. Its *comprehensiveness* is embodied in the rich body of work created by Wilber over the last four decades, work discussing the nature of human states/stages of consciousness, lines of potential development, normal versus pathological development, the value of perspective-taking, and the need to integrate previous stages as we develop. Its *optimism* makes it congruent with current research on positive psychology conducted by Martin Seligman and similarly-minded colleagues. And its *progressive focus* means that the differentiation of psychic structures is viewed as the foundation for continued growth towards higher consciousness (rather than as an obstacle hindering that growth).

- *Gurdjieff's process enneagram* is geometrically identical to the personality enneagram developed by Oscar Ichazo. However, the process enneagram delineates the cyclical nature of transformational processes and the nine stages that are part of each cycle. As we will see, there's a direct link between the nine stages of transformation and the nine enneagram personality types—which means that understanding the process enneagram can help us understand the nature of the nine types.

- *Koestler's holarchic approach* speaks to the way that energy flows between the levels of a living system. When the system is healthy, this energy flows freely, creating energetic links between all the levels and allowing them to optimally function. Understanding the nature of a healthy living system helps us understand how to create a healthy psyche that can connect with all parts of life.

- *A dharma-based focus* emphasizes the idea that individual transformation never occurs in a vacuum but always in relationship to life's larger purposes. When transformation occurs in the context of the *dharma* (our purpose or path in life), it brings about a shift not only within our individual consciousness, but within the larger fabric of the living Kosmos.[9]

My purpose is thus to describe an approach to enneagram work that integrates the purposes of the individual with the purposes of life. For it's only when the two come into alignment that life becomes worth living.

While this is a fairly complex book, it assumes no prior familiarity with either the enneagram or IOS. Thus, those with a sincere interest in personal transformation and a willingness to reflect deeply on these ideas can probably find something here to spark their interest.

Organization

The book is organized into three parts, delineated below.

Part I. We are already into Part I, which includes this introduction. Chapters 1–4 present the ideas that are foundational to the concept of an Integral Enneagram. *Chapter 1* introduces the idea that "life is alive": that it has an innate order in which human beings play a purposeful or *dharmic* role. This perspective is the guiding principle that informs our exploration of transformation. *Chapter 2* explores the nature of the order that governs the created Kosmos, which is *holarchic*, i.e., composed of holons—entities that are by nature both *wholes* containing subsidiary parts and *parts* that are contained by larger wholes. In a healthy holarchy, all levels in a living system are interconnected and interdependent. *Chapter 3* introduces the personality enneagram and its basic elements: the nine types, 18 wing types, 27 subtypes, the two connecting points for each type, and the three energy centers (each of which contains three of the nine types). *Chapter 4* introduces the main tenets of Ken Wilber's Integral Operating System (IOS), including his five elements: states, levels, AQAL, types, and lines of development. It also introduces the idea that transformation is an essentially progressive (rather than regressive) process.

Part II. In Chapters 5–8, the focus is on the enneagram, particularly the significance of its geometry. The enneagram can be interpreted in one of two ways: as a tool for (a) exploring personality and (b) describing transformational processes. *Chapter 5* focuses on the personality enneagram and how personality development came to be seen within the enneagram community as an obstacle to spirituality (an approach Wilber would term *retro-Romantic*). *Chapter 6* introduces the transformationally-oriented process enneagram unveiled by Gurdjieff a half a century earlier than the personality enneagram. The process enneagram is usually considered to be more fundamental than the personality enneagram, which was introduced 40 years later by Ichazo.[10] *Chapter 7* demonstrates how the nine personality types/points of view can be mapped onto the nine stages of the process enneagram, a mapping that supports the idea of seeing them more as "transformation types" than "fixation types." *Chapter 8* describes ways of dividing up the enneagram circle into zones of influence and how this can help us devise a "one-enneagram" or *Integral Enneagram* model of transformation.

Part III. In Chapters 9–13, we explore the parallels between the Integral Enneagram model and Wilber's IOS. Not surprisingly, these chapters are longer and more complex. They also contain some novel theoretical ideas that arose as part of my ongoing reflections on the two systems. *Chapter 9* focuses on *vertical integration*: how using the process enneagram allows us to develop a bi-directional, enneagram-based model of transformation that includes descent as an intrinsic part of the transformational process without violating Wilber's pre/trans fallacy (the latter is described in Chapter 4). This model also generates eight transformational moves that are part of the embodied life cycle, moves that are also described in brief for each of the nine enneagram types.[11] *Chapter 10* focuses on *horizontal integration*: how we

can use the enneagram to map Wilber's four AQAL quadrants, eight hori-zones ("zones of arising") and "Big Three" value spheres. This chapter also includes a discussion of three conclusions I reached as a result of these juxtapositions, conclusions that (if accepted) would change some aspects of integral theory.[12] *Chapter 11* brings the horizontal and vertical axes together, allowing us to look at a number of additional parallels between the enneagram and IOS. *Chapter 12* focuses on integral living, exploring the nature of "win-win" (integrally-oriented) groups, the potential of limitations to stimulate us to live more creative lives, and the advantages of a receptive approach to spiritual ascent. *Chapter 13* sums up the previous chapters and provides point-by-point summary comparisons of IOS and the enneagram. It ends with further observations on *dharma* and how it facilitates a more integral approach to life.

A Quick Summary

Below is a description of the key premises underlying the Integral Enneagram model:

- All living systems are inherently purposeful in nature.

- Our purpose in life is to fulfill the *dharma*, which is in turn the means by which we attract the experiences that transform us.

- Our enneagram type is a vehicle that supports both the transformation of character and the fulfillment of *dharma*.

- Juxtaposing Gurdjieff's process enneagram with Ichazo's personality enneagram yields an *Integral Enneagram model* that allows us to better see the relationship between temperament and transformation (thus helping us to discover our transformational path).

■ Juxtaposing this Integral Enneagram model with Ken Wilber's Integral Operating System (IOS) gives us a way to relate to the dynamic interactions between the vertical and horizontal dimensions of life, which can in turn make us feel more at home in the Kosmos.

This is the book in brief. Although this description makes it sound like a polished treatise, it's really more like a leap into the unknown. Many of the ideas presented here are still in "seed" form—the analogy is exact, in that new ideas kept spontaneously arising, like little plants popping up out of the ground. I've done my best to tie up the loose ends, but there are a number of ideas that beg for more development, either by me or future writers.

A Progression of Ideas

The Integral Enneagram represents the third in my series of enneagram books.

My first book, *The Positive Enneagram* (2009), introduces the enneagram and the nine types from a positive perspective. It also introduces the link between (a) the personality and process enneagrams and (b) type limitations and creativity.

Archetypes of the Enneagram (2010) is a deeper and more theoretical work that delves into the rationale underlying the positive enneagram approach. It's here that I first introduce the idea of *dharma* as a focal point and use film examples to describe 27 life paths related to the 27 enneagram subtypes.[13]

The Integral Enneagram expands upon the *dharma*-oriented approach to explore how IOS and enneagram can be integrated in a way that takes advantage of the strengths of each system.

Evolving Insights

In the process of seeking integration, several surprising insights emerged concerning the nature of transformation (Chapter 9), the usefulness of adding an "include-and-transcend" component to Wilber's existing "transcend-and-include" approach (Chapter 9), and the possibility of reducing the number of elements necessary to fully specify Wilber's IOS from five to four (Chapter 10).

While I was not expecting this exploration to lead to these suggested revisions, when I could not square two conflicting ideas, I did my best to come up with a solution that amicably reconciles them. Whether you as a reader agree or disagree with the suggested revisions to both enneagram and integral theory, I hope you at least find them stimulating food for thought.

From the foregoing discussion, it's obvious that *dharma* is the unifying theme for the book. Chapter 1 explains why. In a nutshell, it's been my experience that the fulfillment of *dharma* not only transforms us, but transforms us in a way that naturally brings us into a more harmonious relationship with life. In the following chapter, we'll take a closer look at the nature of *dharma* and why it is the polestar for our ongoing discussion.

Notes

1. *A Sociable God* (1983/2005), p. 37.

2. Arthur Koestler is a prolific writer on a number of fascinating topics, such as the relationships between science, consciousness, and creativity. See Koestler's *Bricks to Babel* (1980) for an autobiographically-oriented tour of his many works; see Michael Scammell's *Koestler* (2009) for a thoughtful and well-researched biography.

3. An updated version of "An Enneagram-based Model of Transformation" is the basis for much of the information in Chapter 9 and is available at the Integral World website (www.integral-world.net).

4. Adopting a positive approach to enneagram work does not preclude focusing on either our psychological or spiritual deficiencies; it just means embracing the idea that nothing about our enneagram type is *inherently* deficient. There is a saying in Sufism: "First, remember your faults. Then forget them." We remember our faults in order to identify areas to work on. The next step is to do the work, not to keep ruminating on our faults, because too great a focus on deficiency is self-defeating. Over the long term, it can become a highly debilitating habit.

5. Parenting Science, an online resource for parents wanting to know what science knows about child development, has an excellent summary of neonate abilities (www.parentingscience.com/newborns-and-the-social-world.html; accessed 10-20-12).

6. If we embrace the idea that type is both universal and fixated, then we either have to embrace one of two equally noxious ideas: that fixation is a universal feature of our genetics or that it's a universal feature of human development.

Even during the mid-20th century (around the mid-1920s–1950s) when the pro-"nurture" camp in psychology was extremely dominant, the idea that personality develops in a way that is inherently distorted or that virtually everybody grows up traumatized is *not* part of either behaviorist or neo-Freudian thought. Donald Winnicott spoke of "good enough mothering" and his colleague John Bowlby went on to develop attachment theory, which has been subsequently tested using scientific methodology to demonstrate that small children vary greatly in the degree to which they feel confident and secure. However, research consistently shows that the majority of children (about 55–65%) are securely attached, a measure strongly associated with psychological well-being.

7. See "On The Nature of the Enneagram Subtypes," originally published in the *EM,* Oct.-Nov. 2009, for details on how the current enneagram paradigm can be divisive, available at my website (www.enneagramdimensions.net/articles%5Con_the_nature_of_subtypes.pdf#start).

8. When I speak of a dramatic upsurge of interest in integral ideas among enneagram teachers, I'm not exaggerating. Although I've been publishing articles on the enneagram and integral theory for six years, I received feedback on those articles from only a handful of individuals, such as Peter McNab, a founding member of Integral Institute who also uses the enneagram in his work. I had also spoken briefly to a well-known enneagram teacher, Terry Saracino, some years ago about our mutual interest in Ken Wilber's work.

But in April 2012, I became aware of a workshop given mainly to members of the Integral community by Enneagram Worldwide teachers Helen Palmer, Terry Saracino, Renee Rosario, and Leslie Hershberger in Boulder. In October 2012, I had the opportunity to attend a workshop by Leslie in Seattle, shortly after it was announced that the theme of the 2013 International Enneagram Association (IEA) conference—to be held in Denver—would be "Mile High and Integral"; the keynote speaker was announced as Jeff Salzman, the director of the Integral Center in Boulder. In the same month, Palmer released *Where the Narrative Enneagram Meets Integral*, a video of the nine-hour Boulder workshop. Two weeks later, Palmer was announced as the keynote speaker at the 2013 New Year's What Next conference sponsored by Integral Institute.

In response to these rapid changes, I wrote "The Harmonic Convergence of the Enneagram and Integral," for the Jan. 2013 issue of the *EM*, about the unfolding relationship between the two fields. As of January 2013, my proposal to give a talk at the IEA conference was accepted; I was also asked to participate on a panel on integral theory and the enneagram. And as of today (5-24-13), I was contacted about participating on a panel with the intriguing title, "Spotlight on Type: Creative Thoughts and Applications of the 'Marginalized' AQAL Element," at the 2013 Integral Theory Conference, sponsored by the MetaIntegral Foundation, to be held this July.

9.   In referring to the Kosmos (not the Cosmos), I am adopting Wilber's use of the original Greek spelling to denote not only the physical cosmos, but the Cosmos on every level of reality.

10. Oscar Ichazo has described the origins of the personality enneagram in many different ways; at times, he has said it came to him as an inner realization; at others, it was said to be the teaching of a mysterious (but unrevealed) teacher; a third story was that he more or less invented it based on his study of Gurdjieff's process enneagram. Which story is true? We don't know. What we *do* know is that, whatever its origins, the enneagram is a powerful tool for inner work.

11. Generally speaking, descent is seen as regressive and ascent as progressive, which is why Wilber does not include descent as an embodied aspect of the transformational process; see Chapter 8 in Frank Visser's *Ken Wilber: Thought as Passion* (2003) for a discussion.

12. Sometimes I capitalize "integral" and sometimes I don't, depending on whether the emphasis is on integration in the generic sense (small "i" integral) or on Wilber's IOS or the community surrounding it (capital "I" Integral).

13. For each enneagram type, there are three possible variants (subtypes) based on which of three arenas in life is most attractive to an individual: the self-preservation arena (focusing on self-responsibility and independence), the sexual arena (focusing on creativity and intimacy), or the social arena (focusing on networking and group standards); see Chapter 3 .

1
A DHARMA-BASED APPROACH

I don't know what your destiny will be, but one thing I know, the only ones among you who will be really happy are those who have sought and found how to serve.
– Albert Schweitzer

WHEN I WAS VERY YOUNG, the world was a magical place. My family lived in Beverly, Massachusetts, a town full of rambling old houses, small shops, and little lakes surrounded by woods. Our house was a dark green semi-Victorian on the corner of busy Dodge Street and not-so-busy Arlington Avenue, a cobblestone street lined with tall trees which made the sidewalks pleasantly cool on hot summer days. I liked to look out on Dodge Street from my bedroom window and count the passing cars.

There were lots of kids in the neighborhood, all slightly older than me. They adopted me as their mascot and showed me fun places to play. This was before the modern obsession with driving kids to lessons all the time, so we spent most of our free time exploring.

And there were plenty of places to explore: the dry swamp full of exotic black sand, the butterfly field, the train tunnel (scary but exciting), the seven small lakes separated by little strips of land, and the ancient water filter at the end of the street with its roaring machinery below a metal grid floor. The filter also had a dimly lit room with a large goldfish pool that reminded me of the one in Peter Rabbit. I loved to watch the fish move endlessly around in the tank, with the shadows of the water flickering on the wall—almost as much as I liked to visit the "bounce" tree in the forest, which featured a low-lying branch that was a natural trampoline for small children.

But when I turned seven, things changed. Dad got a job transfer and we moved to Baie D'Urfee, Canada, a suburb of Montreal. It wasn't a real town like Beverly, but a brand-new, amazingly sterile tract featuring "shoebox" houses arranged along treeless macadam streets on an orderly rectangular grid. Every street and every house looked almost exactly the same; the only good thing about the place was that it was flat (good for bike-riding).

Things were never quite the same after that. Although we only lived in Canada for two years (where everything cost ten cents more, adding insult to injury), we never again lived in a place like Beverly—or in a house with nooks and crannies and crazy angles. The houses were more expensive but also more forgettable; the neighborhoods weren't real neighborhoods but the kind created by urban planners, with carefully curved streets and safe-for-kids cul-de-sacs. The schools were safe but uninspiring. And the nearby clubs where my parents golfed seemed a lot less interesting than the butterfly field or the black sand swamp.

To make a long story short, I got lost during those years of later childhood and adolescence. The magical world of my early years disappeared, and I could find nothing to replace it. I had no religious upbringing, so the material world was all I knew. Although I attended college, no career really interested me. So after graduating, I gave up on seeking a career and looked for a job—any job, just to pay the rent.

I tried many different things, hoping to somehow hit upon something worth doing. I worked as a maid, laundress, dishwasher, factory worker, landscape assistant (read "manual laborer"), sales assistant, office worker, gas station attendant, tree planter, and short-order cook. What I mostly learned from these trial-and-error ventures was what I did *not* like to do. And that's a tough way to learn.

Life is Alive

The problem in a nutshell was that I lacked any sense of inner purpose. I had lost my innocence ("inner sense") and therefore felt not only lost and alone, but secretly angry—angry that life was bereft of joy. Eventually, I began to realize that it wasn't life that was the problem—it was *me*, more specifically, my inability to relate to life in a joyful way.

I thought of life as an inanimate object that was there to satisfy my personal needs. I wanted to use, control, and manipulate it (it was, after all, "my" life). But I never looked at life as something with its *own* needs, needs that it might need *me* to fulfill. I didn't realize that by treating life as an object, I was treating myself like one, too. To regain a sense of aliveness in myself, I had to see life as alive, too.

That life is actually alive might sound strange, but it's actually an ancient idea. It shows up in Plato's idea that the world is alive, that it is "endowed with a soul and intelligence...a single visible living entity containing all other living entities, which by their nature are all related."[1] Sufi teacher Llewellyn Vaughn-Lee says that the ancient philosophers and medieval alchemists saw the world "as a pure ethereal spirit diffused throughout all nature, the Divine essence that embraces and energizes all life in the universe."[2] G. I. Gurdjieff explains that "everything in its own way is alive, everything in its own way is intelligent and conscious...there are simply different degrees of animation and different scales."[3] A. G. E. Blake, author of *The Intelligent Enneagram* (1996), speaks of the "implicit order" of the universe,[4] and notes that the burning question for Gurdjieff was "What is the purpose and significance of life on earth and human life in particular?"[5] Maharishi Mahesh Yogi observes that "life is dynamic, not static. It is energetic, progressing, evolving, and developing."[6] And Ken Wilber observes, although life may look prosaic, *something else is going on here*: behind the happenstance drama is a deeper or higher or wider pattern, or order, of intelligence."[7] Elsewhere, he speaks of the role of purpose in evolution, noting that human beings do not behave randomly but are rather pulled purposefully towards an omega (end) point of their evolution.[8]

Although insights such as these have traditionally come from philosophers and mystics, by the mid-20th century, some scientists had begun to break out of the mold of scientific reductionism, which is built on a mechanistic model of life. One of the leaders in this movement was Ludwig Von Bertalanffy, a biologist who founded the discipline of systems theory, based on the idea that biological organisms do not exist in isolation but in relationship to other organisms. So in order to understand their nature, we need to look at the interactions between them.

In systems theory, "the emphasis...shifts from parts to the organization of parts, recognizing [that the] interactions of the parts are not 'static' and constant but 'dynamic' processes."[9] This focus on dynamism gives rise to the idea that in order for a system to prosper, it must be open to energy and information from outside the system; hence, Van Bertalanffy's statement that "living systems are open systems."[10]

Another leader was cognitive psychologist Jerome Bruner who—along with his colleagues George Miller and Ulrich Neis-ser—sought to break out of the rigid mold of mid-20th century behaviorism. The new discipline of cognitive psychology was originally designed "to establish meaning as the central concept in psychology."[11]

A third influential figure was Arthur Koestler, creator of the theory of holons (see Chapter 2), who also sees intention as central to systems and life processes. Koestler argues against the idea that evolution is a matter of "blind chance," observing that life processes are directive (goal-oriented) and therefore purposive in nature. He cites others who take a similar position, e.g., Herbert J. Muller (who avows that purpose "is not imported into Nature...it is simply implicit in the fact of organization") and Tolman and Krechevsky, who made the claim that rats learn to run a maze by forming hypotheses.[12]

In 1968, Koestler invited some of these visionary thinkers to explore a non-reductionist vision of scientific discovery in Alpbach, Switzerland, among them Victor Frankl, Jerome Bruner, F. A. Hayek, Ludwig Von Bertalanffy, Jean Piaget, Barbel Inhelder, J. R. Smithies, and C. H. Waddington. (Piaget couldn't attend, so his paper was read by Inhelder).[13] The focus was on both presenting scientific evidence which casts doubt on reductionistic hypotheses in the life sciences and on discussing the significance of intangibles, such as meaning and purpose, that cannot be easily measured using the methods of science.

Frankl in particular emphasized the importance of meaning as our primary motivator in life, going so far as to propose the "will to meaning" as an alternative to Freud's will to pleasure and Adler's will to power (p. 400). In reply, Waddington observed that the search for meaning seems to be taboo in our culture. Frankl replied that the reason for such a taboo may be because science has no adequate mechanism to account for it (p. 419).

The implication here is that modern culture has become so shaped by scientific reductionism that the greatest motivator in life—the quest for meaning or purpose—is now repressed, denied, or ignored. According to Frankl, this is why there's so much alienation and frustration in modern life.

An Unscientific Idea

The Alpbach conference was controversial, because of the anti-reductionist stance of its participants. However, their stature was such that they were more or less immune from attacks within the academic community. But those who have gone a step further—by challenging the objectivity of science itself, looking for links between science and spirituality, or daring to investigate paranormal phenomena—have not always been so fortunate. Many of them incurred the wrath of the scientific skeptics in response to their ideas:

- When psychologist Anne Wilson Schaef remarked several decades ago that the scientific method was "nothing but a religious belief system," she discovered to her dismay that the reaction to that statement "was so violent that I kept my mouth shut...for over twenty-five years."[14]

- After biologist Rupert Sheldrake published *A New Science of Life* in 1981, in which he posited a new theory of morphic resonance (the idea that there is a mysterious connection among organisms in nature and a collective memory within species), he was rewarded for his efforts by a senior editor at *Nature* ob-

serving that *A New Science* was "a book for burning."[15]

- Gary Schwartz, a Yale professor of psychology and psychiatry, had a related insight into the nature of universal memory but waited to publish it for 14 years—he admits to being afraid of the storm of criticism that was sure to follow. In the book he eventually authored with his wife Linda Russek, *The Living Energy Universe* (1999), the frontispiece of the book bravely states "Everything is alive—and remembers." As Schwartz anticipated, not only the book but Schwartz's subsequent work on *psi* at the Veritas Research Program at the University of Arizona has been mercilessly attacked by what one articulate commentator called "super-skeptics," despite Schwartz's impeccable scientific credentials.[16]

- As recently as 2011, when social psychologist Daryl Bem managed to get a mainstream research journal (*The Journal of Personality and Social Psychology* or *JPSP*) to publish a study showing support for the existence of precognition,[17] it made national news.[18]

So we are not quite yet at the point where the media and scientific establishment are willing to throw in the towel and admit that "there are more things in heaven and earth, Horatio, than are dreamt of in your philosophy."[19]

Nevertheless, a number of polls have shown that the American public is surprisingly resistant to reductionist claims. For example, approximately half of all Americans answer yes to the question, "Do you believe in ESP?" And when presented in a Gallup poll with a list of ten kinds of paranormal phenomena from which to select, three-fourths of respondents affirm that they believe in some form of paranormal phenomena.[20] Gallup also found that between 1990 and 2001, there was a 8% jump in the number of people who believed in "psychic or spiritual healing or the power of the human mind to heal the body," from 46% to 54%.[21]

According to *Time*, 69% of people believe in angels;[22] and 55% answered affirmatively to the statement, "I was protected from harm by a guardian angel."[23] The latter response is impressive in that it indicates not simply mental belief, but the kind of deeper conviction that comes from real experience. According to IANDS (the International Association for Near-Death Studies), about 13 million adult Americans have had near-death experiences.[24]

Conversely, only 4% of Americans are confirmed atheists; moreover, this figure has remained constant since 1944. And in former Soviet bloc countries—where atheism was drummed into the entire population from an early age and believers were commonly punished with imprisonment or execution—the average is 3.72%.[25]

It's remarkable that—in spite of an almost complete lack of support from both the media and scientific establishment—so many people stubbornly persist in embracing non-materialist beliefs. No wonder Randall Balmer, chairman of the religion department at New York's Barnard College, says that "there is a much broader uncharted range of religious experience among the populace than we [might] expect."[26]

So despite the claims of well-publicized atheists such as Richard Dawkins, Daniel Dennett, or Christopher Hitchens, people are not becoming less spiritually-inclined over time; if anything, the opposite is true. Additionally, there has been a glacially slow but perceptual shift within the scientific community as concerns research into the link between science and non-material phenomena, especially after the Dalai Lama began in the 1990s to take an active (and well-publicized) interest in promoting scientific research into the effects of meditation. The scientific studies on meditation indicate that it not only produces a sense of inner well-being and calm, but even physically thickens the dura of the brain.[27]

The 2011 publication of Bem's article in the *JPSP* is just one of the signs that the old materialist tactic of destroying their critics' credibility with ridicule alone is no longer working. When asked by the media why he allowed the Bem article to be published, senior *JPSP* editor Charles Judd observed that "it is not my job to decide what hypotheses are good or bad," that "it's...[the] responsibility [of an editor] to look at papers and give them a fair hearing, even if they fly in the face of conventional wisdom."[28]

No Purpose Allowed

Philosopher Michael Polanyi (1891–1976) was always skeptical about the reductionist program in science, especially the idea that life is purposeless. He observed that while science eschews teleology (purpose) in nature, it is impossible to look at how a being functions without considering its purpose: "Everyone knows that you cannot inquire into the functions of living organisms without referring to the purpose served by them...yet we must pretend that all teleological explanations are merely provisional. The story goes round that teleology is a woman of easy virtue, whom the biologist disowns in public, but lives with in private."[29]

And it's not just the biologists who traditionally eschewed purpose, but also psychologists, according to Lawrence LeShan. In *The Dilemma of Psychology* (1990), LeShan complains that when psychologists design experiments as if human beings have no consciousness, purpose, or meaning, they (no surprise) find their hypotheses confirmed (p. 83). He flatly refutes this idea, saying that "all behavior has a purpose" and says that psychology ought be defined as "the study of the individual's consciousness...and meaningful behavior" (p. 134).

If the current gatekeepers of American culture—the media and scientists—tell us life has no purpose (although implicitly sneaking it in when it suits *their* purpose!), those of us who take their pronouncements seriously are going to find ourselves in conflict, caught between our outer beliefs and inner *gnosis*. That's pretty much what happened to me: I spent years trying to reconcile the messages I was getting from the culture with my own intuitions, and it just didn't work.

One of the key things that helped me get beyond this impasse was my enrollment in a Ph.D. graduate program in cognition and perception, where I spent years studying the scientific method, doing research, and reading psychological studies. I had been interested in psychology since high school and would almost certainly have majored in it as an undergraduate, but for the fact that it was the 1960s and the cognitive revolution that swept out behaviorism had not quite reached my college, which was still a bastion of behaviorism.

Within another decade, behaviorism had been almost entirely upstaged by the new discipline of cognitive psychology, which focused not just on outer behavior but inner processes. And I found those processes intriguing. So when the opportunity to study cognition appeared, I took it.

I learned a lot in graduate school—not just about cognitive processes, but about the scientific method: its techniques, applications, and limitations. My participation in a research group was particularly illuminating, because it allowed me to see on a day-to-day basis how a study is planned, carried out, analyzed, and prepared for publication.

What I discovered is that the process is both messier and more interesting than most people imagine. It's very suspenseful—as well as exciting—because you never know exactly how the experiment is going to turn out. It's also exacting, because it must be properly designed and analyzed to yield valid results. And it's deeply absorbing, because it involves so many decisions at each point in the process of planning, execution, and analysis.

While some of these decisions are made on the basis of solely objective factors (e.g., deciding which statistical tests are most appropriate), many decisions are subjective, especially when it comes to interpreting the results. There are any number of personal, social, and political factors that enter into this decision-making process, such that the final report is inevitably a synthesis of both objective and subjective factors—however elegantly objective the published prose might sound! Beneath the objective facade of those tersely-written research articles is a longer and messier "story behind the story," but one that is seldom revealed to the public.

Understanding how science actually functions freed me from the belief that "science knows best" and allowed me to develop a more nuanced, less polarized approach to exploring the relationship between science and spirituality. Soon after graduating, I began a meditation practice that also supported this exploration. And the pieces started to fall into place; life began to make sense.

Changing Perspectives

Although reductionism is still extremely influential, non-reductionist ideas appear to be making gradual inroads into the scientific mainstream (albeit oh-so-slowly) as evidenced by an upswing in the number of studies on topics once considered totally taboo, e.g., the nature of near-death experiences (NDEs), the effects of meditation on the structure and functioning of the brain, and the effects of alternative healing modalities on physical and emotional health. Witness the number of recently-published books designed to demonstrate that science and spirituality need not be at odds with one another:

- *The Heart's Code: Tapping the Wisdom and Power of Our Heart Energy* (1998), by Paul Pearsall

- *Entangled Minds: Extrasensory Experiences in a Quantum Reality* (2006), by Dean Radin

- *The Spiritual Brain: a Neuroscientist's Case for the Existence of Soul* (2007), by Mario Beauregard & Denyse O'Leary

- *The Intention Experiment : Using Your Thoughts to Change Your Life and the exWorld* (2007), by Lynne McTaggart

- *Extraordinary Knowing: Science, Skepticism, and the Inexplicable Powers of the Human Mind* (2007), by Elizabeth Lloyd Mayer

- *The End of Materialism: How Evidence of the Paranormal is Bringing Science and Spirit Together* (2009), by Charles Tart

- *The Power of Premonitions: How Knowing the Future Can Shape Our Lives* (2009), by Larry Dossey

- *Evidence of the Afterlife: The Science of Near-Death Experiences* (2010), by Jeffrey Long & Paul Perry

- *The Science Delusion: Freeing the Spirit of Enquiry* (2012), by Rupert Sheldrake

- *The Science of Yoga* (2012), by William J. Broad

These are all thoughtful, well-researched monographs by credible authors (both scientists and journalists), and their publication reflects the development of greater tolerance for forms of inquiry once considered taboo.

As Ken Wilber has pointed out, any integrally-oriented approach to epistemology cannot rely on one single method, because there is not one right view of truth but a plethora of views, each of which has something of value to offer. (Interestingly, exactly the same thing can be said of the enneagram points of view—and as we will see in Chapter 10, a case can be made that the nine enneagram types bear a direct correspondence to Wilber's eight hori-zones or "zones of arising." But I'm getting ahead of myself here.)

Enter the Enneagram

In graduate school, I studied not only perception, cognition, and decision making, but "interaction effects" that are designed to provide insight into how differences in, e.g., sex, age, or mood affect the way people process information. I found the effects of personality of even greater interest, but discovered that—because of its complexity—personality was almost impossible to study using currently available statistical methods. For that reason, most of the psychological literature on personality was theoretical, written by such seminal figures as Sigmund Freud, Carl Jung, or Carl Rogers. While some work had been done to generate an empirical basis for personality (such as the factor-analytically based "Big Five" personality factors), most of this work was decades old. So there was no easy way to study personality using empirically-oriented methods.

Nevertheless, I never lost my interest in individual factors or personality. It was towards the end of my Ph.D. program that I first became aware of the enneagram—not from school but from seeing some enneagram books in the local spiritual bookstore. I was too busy at the time to do more than leaf through them, but even a brief perusal revealed a system that inexplicably characterized personality as some sort of neurosis. I already knew and admired the MBTI (Myers-Briggs Type Indicator), Jungian-based personality test, for its thoughtfulness and value-neutral approach to describing personality; I was also familiar with the MMPI (Minnesota Multiphasic Personality Inventory), a not-so-neutral personality test whose main purpose was to detect mental pathology.[30] The enneagram reminded me more of the MMPI than the MBTI in its orientation, so I decided to give it a pass. But funnily enough, after that first visit to the bookstore, the enneagram kept popping up in my life. People would ask me whether I'd ever heard of the enneagram or if I knew my type; one friend even put a list of type descriptions in front of me and asked me which one

fit the best! So a year or two after graduation, I decided to take a second look.

By that time, with a Ph.D. under my belt and a meditation practice, I was feeling less adrift than before. But it was when I began to study the enneagram that a lot of things really fell into place for me. Despite my early misgivings, something about the system somehow drew me in, and I soon became an admirer of its power and depth, each new insight acting as the impetus for further work. Not only was the work yielding specific insights about personality, relationships, and motivation, but the process of working with it was making me feel more alive, happy, and peaceful.

In my twenties, I worked at any job, trying to find myself while paying the rent. During my thirties and forties, I began teaching and also discovered the fascinating world of scientific research. But it was not until I was fifty that I found the enneagram, a system that has tied together all the separate threads of my life to create a living tapestry. Once I started working with it, all those disparate elements of my crazy-quilt life—from the magic of early childhood, to the loss of that magic, to the years of graduate school, to the beginnings of an inner life—came together to create a coherent whole. I knew I'd found my life's work.

A Unifying Thread

Every life has a central thread: a unifying design, pattern, path, or theme that makes it coherent. Robert Johnson thinks of the same idea in the plural, speaking of the "slender threads" that "give meaning to our existence...[and which are] the mysterious forces that guide and shape who we are."[31]

Meaning is central to life. With it, we flourish; without it, we die. I read a little study recently in which deliberately inflicted pain is rated as more subjectively painful than the same pain inflicted by accident, leading the authors to conclude that "the meaning of a harm...influences the amount of pain it causes."[32] In another study, subjects' recall of landscapes was worse when they had been previously asked to count trees in the scenes versus when they had been asked either to rate their pleasantness or contemplate the meaning of life while initially viewing them. So meaning matters; its positive benefits can even be objectively measured![33]

But it's easy to lose our way in life and begin to feel like "I don't matter," that I'm a very small person in a big world. This is the theme of the classic film *It's a Wonderful Life*, where the protagonist George Bailey—who feels discouraged by his seeming insignificance—comes to realize how greatly he would be missed if he never existed. It's a memorable film because it's based on a fundamental truth: that each life has inestimable value—and that if even one of us were not here, life would be the poorer for it. Put in another way, *life would miss our presence.*

This is why Sufis say that we come to the spiritual path not because we long for the Divine but because the Divine longs for us; and why they liken mysticism to a love affair with God; and why Kahlil Gibran tells us "the earth delights to feel your bare feet and the winds long to play with your hair." We are not the products of blind chance inhabiting an indifferent universe; we are sovereign beings who are completely loved and valued for who we are. Without that understanding, it is difficult to notice those slender threads that link us to our life's purpose.

Dharma in the *Bhagavad-Gita*

In Eastern philosophy, those slender threads are the indicators of the *dharma*: our life's work. The same idea shows up in the West as the concept of having a calling, vocation, or destiny. However, while the latter terms are often used to point to something special or unusual (thereby suggesting that only the favored few have a genuine calling in life), *dharma* is not for a small elite but for everyone.

In the classical Vedic work, the *Bhagavad-Gita*, Arjuna, a member of the warrior caste, is challenged to a fight against an army that includes friends, teachers, and members of his family. As a warrior, it is his duty to fight to protect the social order when it is challenged. But his nature is soft-hearted; it grieves him to think of taking up arms against those whom he loves and respects.

When the Supreme Personality, Lord Krishna, appears on the battlefield, Arjuna asks Krishna why he must fight; to him, killing his kinsmen would be to perpetrate a grave injustice. Krishna replies that it is because Arjuna is a warrior. So it is both his nature and obligation to fight.

But Arjuna remains distraught; to Arjuna, it seems better to beg than to continue to live at the expense of the great souls who have been his teachers. He confesses that he is confused about his duty (*dharma*) and asks Krishna to instruct him. It is this instruction that forms the substance of the Bhagavad-Gita.

Krishna begins by saying that Arjuna is grieving for something that is not worthy of his grief, because life is not confined to the physical dimension: "All created beings are unmanifest in their beginning, manifest in their interim state, and unmanifest again when annihilated. So what need is there for lamentation?" (2:28). Here Krishna speaks of the nature of life, which is vast, mysterious, and eternal—and also our nature, which changes form but is also eternal. So whatever happens in life (even physical death), it is only a temporary manifestation of something eternal. It should not thus be a source of fear or anguish.

Krishna explains to Arjuna more about the nature of duty, observing that it is done for its own sake (without regard for the outcome; 3:19). So the *dharma* is fulfilled if we act in accordance with it, whether or not we achieve the desired result. Krishna tells Arjuna that we never become so great that we outgrow the *dharma* (3:22). This speaks to the idea that there is always something in life that is greater than us and to which we are in some way responsible.

Krishna also stresses the individual nature of *dharma* when he says that it is always in accordance with one's nature (3:33), and then warns Arjuna that he must fulfill the true *dharma*, and not the *dharma* of another: "It is better to discharge one's prescribed duties, even though faultily, than another's duties perfectly" (3:35).[34] When the teaching is almost complete, Krishna once again stresses the link between one's nature and one's *dharma*, telling Arjuna that even if he should try to resist, his very nature will compel him to fight (18:59).

Sarvepalli Radhakrishnan, a former president of India, expresses the same idea when

he says of a person that "if he misses his destiny, Nature is not in a hurry; she will catch him up someday, and compel him to fulfill her secret purpose." The concept of *dharma* is so important in India that Hindus do not refer to their religion as Hinduism, but as *sanatana dharma* ("eternal duty").[35]

Dharma is also critically important in Buddhism, where it refers to "the universal law which governs the physical and moral order of the universe." Revered Buddhist monk Thich Nhat Hanh says that "the true *dharma* is revealed through our life and our practice... to take refuge in the *Dharma* is to choose the doors that are most appropriate for us."[36]

In Sufism, as in Hinduism and Buddhism, the *dharma* is also all-important (although it is not referred to as such). In response to a student who says he has forgotten something, the great Sufi teacher, Jalalludin Rumi, replies:

> One thing must not be forgotten. Forget all else, but remember this, and you will have no regrets. Remember everything else, but ignore this one thing, and you will have done nothing. It is as if a king sent you on a mission to a foreign land to perform one special task for him. If you do a hundred things, but not this appointed task, what have you accomplished? Human beings come into the world for a particular purpose, and if they forget it they would have done nothing at all.[37]

Rumi is very specific about what matters in life—and it's not simply living in harmony with one's nature or adhering to a set of moral precepts. It's the fulfillment of the specific purpose for which we were born. Another esteemed Sufi teacher, Radha Mohan Lal, stated his own life's purpose by saying "for me, there is nothing but duty [*dharma*]."[38]

And *The Cosmic Doctrine*, a book of higher wisdom received by esoteric teacher Dion Fortune, speaks of the Law of Limitation, a law defining the boundaries imposed on an embodied soul which "delimits the destiny to be worked out...[during that soul's] incarnation."[39]

Dharma versus Duty

In the West, there is no easy way to talk about *dharma*. Terms like "calling," "vocation," and "destiny" sound grandiose and therefore suggest a path that is larger than life. When we use such terms, it becomes hard to avoid dividing people into two groups: ordinary folk (who have no special calling) and extraordinary or heroic individuals who are called to fulfill some great purpose. There is no way to speak of destiny in a way that allows us to include both the little and great events of life (or to see all human beings as equal participants in its fulfillment).

The term most often used to translate *dharma* into English is "duty." But "duty" has a whole raft of connotations that distinguish it from *dharma* in many ways. Historically, "duty" is a specifically religious word that was originally used to describe an individual's religious obligations. Thus, in the Old Testament, we are admonished to "fear God and obey His commandments for this is the whole duty of man."[40] The New Testament tells us "When ye shall have done all those things which are commanded you, say: 'We are unprofitable servants: we have done that which was our duty to do.' "[41] In Barnes' commentary on this passage, the observation

is made that God "needs not our aid, and His essential happiness will not be increased by our efforts."[42]

So duty as described in these passages is quite different from *dharma*, in that it refers to prescribed tasks of a religious nature that are performed in obedience to God's command. In the latter passage, the term "duty" connotes "mere duty," as in doing the bare minimum to get by, which scripture (not surprisingly) tells us is not all that commendable.

What is missing here is the idea that duty is something we do not only to comply with outer standards but to bring about some sort of inner alignment, healing, or balance. Modern psychological research has enabled us to understand the difference between intrinsic and extrinsic rewards, and how too much focus on the extrinsic (whether it be the reward of social acceptance or the promise of reward in the afterlife) can inhibit the development of our ability to act because it is intrinsically rewarding (i.e., meaningful).[43] What empirical psychology cannot give us is the understanding that meaning arises out of the ability to be aware of our "still, small voice" and to translate its messages into purposeful action.

Carl Jung understood the importance of developing our inner discernment in a way that leads to the fulfillment of *dharma*, which is why he wrote that "a human being is charged with an individual destiny and destination, and the realization of these alone makes sense of life."[44] Elsewhere, he spoke of vocation along similar lines, noting that the word is directly related to the idea of an inner voice, and observing that "vocation acts like a law of God from which there is no escape."[45] So Jung takes the idea of *dharma* very seriously. But notice how he uses terms like "destiny" or "vocation" to describe it (not "duty"). This is because he wants to stress the value of listening to our inner voice, not the value of acting in response to the dictates of social or religious convention.

But if the biblical sense of duty has fallen out of fashion, its influence lingers on. One of its legacies is the ongoing but hard-to-pin-down sense that we are never truly worthy (no matter what we do) and that our inner self is therefore not worth developing. In the enneagram community, this sense of basic unworthiness is reflected in the belief that personality (as expressed through an enneagram type) is inherently fixated, i.e., motivated by a combination of savage survival instincts and distorted ego defense mechanisms. In the culture, this belief shows up as a sense of pervasive discouragement—with ourselves, with our relationships, and with life itself. It also shows up as the inability to take ourselves seriously, which makes it hard to truly grow up and become responsible adults. This unwillingness to grow up leads to further feelings of low self-esteem.

The way out of this vicious cycle is to affirm our basic self-worth, develop our inner life, and cultivate good outer habits in a way that does not do violence to our inner nature—and to understand that there exists somewhere within our being an aligning principle based on our life's purpose, destiny, or *dharma*.

To connect with that purpose is a powerful experience:

> When you are inspired by some great
> purpose, some extraordinary project,
> all your thoughts break their bonds:
> Your mind transcends limitations, your
> consciousness expands in every direction,
> and you find yourself in a new, great,
> and wonderful world. Dormant forces,
> faculties and talents become alive, and

> you discover yourself to be a greater
> person by far than you ever dreamed
> yourself to be.

This quote is attributed to Patanjali, the great Indian mystic and compiler of the ancient Vedas who is also considered to be the father of modern yoga. What Patanjali is describing is not just a psychological shift but a shift in our entire being—the kind of shift we experience when we begin to fulfill the *dharma*.

Dharma in Real Life

In a recent interview with Oprah on TV's *Super Soul Sunday*, intuitive Caroline Myss said, "If you have life, you have purpose." She said that everybody has a path in life, no exceptions. When Oprah asked, "But how do you know you're on the right path?" she replied, "You know you're on the right path when you don't betray yourself, [when] you don't have to compromise who you are. It *feels* right."

In her bestselling book, *Sacred Contracts* (2003), Myss talks about the concept of *dharma* by reference to a sacred agreement we make with life before we're born, an agreement to fulfill our Divine potential by learning to recognize key "choice points" in life and making choices using not only our intellect but our intuition. Myss acknowledges that it can be harder to do this than it sounds, because once we are incarnate, we think using earthly logic, and "Divine order and Divine logic are different from earthly logic" (p. 19).

Consequently we have to make many decisions using our intuition, in order to bridge that gap. If we are too stuck on understanding everything from a rational viewpoint before making any moves, it's going to be hard to fulfill our contract. We may just need to try something out and see what happens. Because as Myss reminds us, it takes practice to act appropriately on our intuitions. The mistakes we make help us develop better discrimination.

This is a key point, because we so often judge the worth of our actions in terms of success or failure. But as Krishna reminds Arjuna, we must not be attached to outcomes. From a *dharmic* perspective, what matters most is not the results of our actions, but the *quality of our engagement* with what we are doing. In a very real sense, we succeed to the extent that we take responsibility for our decisions, whatever they may be. If—having made the utmost effort to do everything possible to deal with a difficult situation—we are still unable to overcome whatever obstacles exist, that supreme effort may pave the way for help to emerge from other levels of life (assuming we are open to that help). This exemplifies the principle that making the supreme sacrifice "calls down the grace."

My favorite story illustrating this idea is about Marie Avinov, the wife of a Russian aristocrat exiled to Siberia during the Stalinist era. After a difficult winter trip on a freezing freight train, she was summarily deposited, along with a wily young criminal, in a tiny hamlet in the middle of nowhere. Marie and her criminal companion trudged from house to house, seeking shelter from the bitter cold. But the villagers were afraid; there was no shelter to be found. As night fell, the temperature plummeted, and a thick fog rolled in. Totally exhausted, Marie could walk no more. So she told her companion to take her last ruble and see if he could find shelter in a rough drinking house nearby. He protested, but finally took it

and ran off. Marie sat down and prayed to St. Seraphim, steeling herself for death.

But this was not her time to die. No sooner had Marie begun to pray than a figure suddenly appeared in front of her. It was a woman she had not yet met, who lived on the outskirts of town. The woman proceeded to loudly scold her for loitering about in the road at night. The woman then said she'd like to help—that she knew someone who needed a boarder—but she was late for dinner and had to go. As she began to walk away, another figure approached: the daughter-in-law of the very woman who needed the boarder! In this serendipitous manner, Marie came to live with this woman for the next two years. But her surprises for the day were not quite over, because when she learned the woman's name, it was Seraphima!

(There's an interesting epilogue to the story, too: the crafty criminal somehow managed to turn his fortunes around to the point where he not only survived but thrived by making black market deals. With his street smarts, he managed to procure whatever his patroness needed in order to live. And this is how Marie survived her years in exile.)[46]

This story illustrates the mysterious principle of synchronicity—how being in sync with life can powerfully "draw down the grace." Grace is the gift that comes in response to our need, assuming we are open to help from other levels of life.

And speaking of synchronicity, at the exact same time I was writing the last paragraph, I turned on the TV to see an example of the same principle—the idea of "drawing down the grace"—unfolding on my TV screen.

Luke, a deaf contestant on TV's *The Amazing Race*, is in India with his mother, his partner on the race. His task is to identify by smell a tea he'd drunk earlier in the day. However, he has to find the one right cup of tea amid hundreds (thousands?) of similar cups of tea set on tables in a large hall. Can he do it?

Well, not very easily. After hours and hours of trying without success, Luke begins to unravel. Falling into his mother's arms, he begins to cry. She hugs him tight, but then looks him firmly in the eye and says, "I know you can do this."

That is clearly not what he wants to hear. He looks completely anguished, torn between his desire to quit and his desire not to disappoint his mom. Eventually, he musters up the will to try again, to no avail. This time, he is so discouraged that he falls to his knees, in extreme distress. His mother looks pained but again encourages him.

So after a time, he goes back to try again. But it's obvious that something has changed. His anger and frustration is somehow gone, replaced by a kind of resigned acceptance. Instead of trying to discern which tea is correct, he calmly resolves to try out every single cup of tea, one by one, no matter how long it takes.

The first cup he tries is not a match, so he randomly tries a second. Unbelievably, it's the right cup. His face lights up in delight. The Indian attendants explode in applause and joyfully lift him up on their shoulders in congratulations—definitely an *Amazing Race* first! It was amazing to watch as a viewer, too, because it was a real-life example of how one person's resolution can not only transform an impossible situation but lift the spirits of everybody around him. It shows us the spirit of *dharma* "abroad in the land," the spirit of gracious acceptance—of service, surrender, and receptivity to life.

Dharma Can Be Anything

It's tempting to think, because the word "*dharma*" sounds spiritual, either that fulfilling the *dharma* means living a specifically spiritual life or that a spiritual *dharma* (vocation) is the best or only kind. But to pursue a path because it appeals to our spiritual imagination (or even vanity) is more likely to end in spiritual materialism than enlightenment.[47] As Buddhist leader Thich Nhat Hanh observes that, "to take refuge in the *Dharma* is to "enter the path of transformation, the path to end suffering."[48] Robert Hall, co-founder of the Lomi School, thinks that the point of spiritual work is to "fulfill the time that is allotted in this earthly journal in some way that has meaning."[49]

Tenzin Palmo, a Buddhist nun who meditated in a cave for 12 years, says that *dharma* is not about seeking a specifically spiritual path but about seeking an appropriate path:

> We should look and see what in this lifetime we are called to do. It's ridiculous to become a nun or a hermit because of some ideal when all the time we would be learning more within a close relationship or a family situation. You can develop all sorts of qualities through motherhood which you could not by leading a monastic life. It's not that by being a mother one is cutting off the path. Far from it! There are many approaches, many ways.[50]

I once met a young woman who was an earnest spiritual practitioner. But she was also a mom with a year-old baby whose demands made it hard to fit in much spiritual practice. This made her unhappy, so she sought guidance from her spiritual teacher. He looked at her for a moment and then gently told her that raising her child *was* her spiritual practice. This was the last thing she wanted to hear. Her real problem was finding some way to embrace her role as a mother, so that it actually fulfilled her, rather than seeking spiritual practice as a means of escape.

Later, I met an older women who had never learned that lesson. Her kids were now grown but not very happy. She saw them as "needy" and wanted only to meditate. When she tried, it didn't really work out, because she too was using spirituality as an escape from the *dharma*.

The *Bhagavad-Gita* makes it clear that *dharma* is not about being more conventionally spiritual, because the instruction concerns the need to fight, to engage in warfare—which is not usually considered to be a spiritual activity. So the use of this example really gets across the message that the *dharma* can be virtually anything.

If so, then how can we find it? This is seldom an easy question to answer. It certainly helps to understand the nature of *dharma* and possible paths of fulfillment (see Appendix A for additional resources for self-discovery). But while we can listen to Patanjali's wisdom, Myss' explanations, or inspirational stories of synchronicity, they are not likely to give us all the answers we seek.

Sufis would say that we don't find the *dharma*: it finds us. This is why the emphasis is on receptivity in Sufi teachings: so that we can recognize the subtle signals life sends us and respond to them appropriately. As Myss points out, we don't have to be perfect receivers; we can practice our skills, getting better with time. We can also ask for help (not to mention proof that what we are experiencing is real, not just a figment of our imagination).

Embracing the *Dharma*

Embracing the *dharma* is always a transformative act; avoiding the *dharma* blocks our ability to transform—or at least to transform in the way that matters. If we think of our life as a process of "transformation through experience," then we can think of the *dharma* as the alchemical vehicle, container, or platform that makes this transformation possible. But *dharma* implies duty, the idea that we have a responsibility to something beyond the self, a responsibility not only to other people or organizations, but to life itself.

In a *dharma*-oriented approach, what we are trying to reconcile are our own energies with the energies of all that lies beyond ourselves. When the two are in sync, we come into a dynamic relationship with life, a relationship that becomes the basis for the unfolding and fulfillment of our life's purpose.

But it's not always easy to develop such a relationship. And this is not just because of the materialism of modern culture. It's also because many of us find it hard to really come to terms with the idea of subordinating ourselves to some larger purpose, cause, or will, perhaps because we have done so in the past and been disillusioned as a result. Ken Wilber has tried to come up with a more balanced way to relate to the Divine by formulating three distinctly different ways that we can view God:

- **God in the 1st-person** (the idea that "I am God" or "God is within me")

- **God in the 2nd-person** (the idea that "Thou art God" or that God is a personage with whom I seek a meaningful relationship)

- **God in the 3rd-person** (the idea that "That is God" or that God is an impersonal force or set of laws)[51]

Relating to God in all three ways means seeing the Divine within ourselves, the Divine in others (and in God), and the Divine as embodied in the laws and principles that govern the Kosmos. It thus gives us a highly integrated way of relating to Spirit.

There's only one problem here: that people who seek a more integral approach to spirituality are often far more attracted to 1st- and 3rd-person concepts of God than to a 2nd-person concept of God. In other words, we like the idea that "God is within me" and that "God exists as an impersonal force," but balk at the idea that "God is a personal entity with whom I can have a relationship" (especially if we think of that entity as bigger, more powerful, and more authoritative than we are).

I saw this firsthand when attending an Integral event a couple of years ago that began with a guided meditation that asked participants to meditate on God from all three perspectives. This was followed by a discussion on our response to the meditation.

When it got to the 2nd-person perspective on God, many people said they felt themselves shrink back; they just didn't feel comfortable relating to the Divine in an "I/Thou" fashion. Either it made them feel like children (dependent and weak) or afraid (because it conjured up the idea of the Divine as a harsh authority figure). Not one person talked about this I/Thou relationship in a positive way.

While it was good that people were open enough to express their feelings, the discussion never reached the point where people felt they had any real insight on how to work with that aversion. Worse, I didn't get the sense that it was any sort of priority.

But what if we could get beyond our fears and conditioning, and become open to the idea that we are not spiritual practitioners operating in an impersonal Kosmos, but rather, participants in a great Kosmic drama—a drama in which every sentient being in the Kosmos plays a role, even God? Imagine envisioning ourselves as individuals who play a unique but essential role in an incredible production of epic proportions. What would it be like to know that we are not just co-creators in some vaguely positive (and emotionally reassuring) sense, but co-creators in a project designed to bring about not just our own transformation, but that of the entire Kosmos?

To think of ourselves in that kind of role is pretty awe-inspiring. Of course, it's also a little scary. But wouldn't it be nice to know that we are part of something that really matters?

A common alternative for spiritual seekers—which is to construct a spiritual life of pure fantasy—is not so inspirational. While we may experience spiritual states, such states are not quite real; they are literally something we dream up. If we take them to be a sign of spiritual progress, it's easy to start feeling satisfied—even smug—about our spiritual status. We may even think we're in a position to help those whom we judge to be less spiritually advanced. Perhaps we then decide to come together with others of a similar disposition so we can work as a group. But such a group doesn't usually get much real work done (other than to reinforce the shared belief in the spiritual goodness of its members).

There are many benefits of focusing on the Divine from an I/Thou perspective. The first is that it helps us develop the habit of inwardly *listening*, because it allows us to think of Spirit as an inner voice with the power to inform us. The second is that it allows us to *receive the love of the Divine* (Agape), because we understand it to be more than a theoretical abstraction. A third is that it discourages narcissism, because it makes us aware of the existence of intelligences other than our own. A fourth is that it provides a personally compelling reason to move towards Spirit, because it enables us to see ourselves as individuals with a unique destiny in life.

Oprah Winfrey relates the story of the time she tried out for a role in *The Color Purple*. She was in love with the book, which tells the story of a childhood marred by rape, poverty, and unwed pregnancy. This was also *her* story, so she wanted this part more than she'd ever wanted anything in her life. But initially, it didn't look like she was going to get it. She was told flat out by someone in a powerful position that she was just too inexperienced as an actress. But she was so certain she was destined for this role (even the character's husband, Harpo, was "Oprah" spelled backwards) that she prayed incessantly for it.

Time passed and nothing changed. She did not hear from the casting director. It looked like nothing was happening. But because she prayed so deeply, she eventually realized that she was praying for the wrong thing. Instead of praying for the part, she started praying for acceptance. But that did not come either. She was feeling ripped apart by these two conflicting desires. Finally, it reached the point where she was in a state of complete despair.

Still, she prayed. One day in prayer, something strange happened. She heard herself spontaneously singing, "I surrender all to God." It was as though somebody else was singing. She realized suddenly that she wasn't just saying the words but feeling them in the depths of her being. Although she still wanted the part, she was no longer consumed by her desire for it, much to her amazement. Almost before she could take in what this shift signified, Steven Spielberg phoned, telling her the part was hers.

Years later, looking back on that experience, she says that

> when you have done all that you can do, give it up to that thing that is greater than yourself. Let it then become part of the flow...I have never wanted anything as much as *The Color Purple*—and the wanting of it and the surrendering of it is what taught me how to live in the space of letting go...You can dream this much—but God has a bigger dream...The bigger question is, "What would God—the Universe—have me do?"

"What would the Universe have me do?"

This is the question that opens the door to *dharma*. In Oprah's case, she arrived at a critical point in her life, when she had to decide whether to cling to her goal or to "let go, and let God." She chose to let go—and got the role that launched her career in a way that she probably could never have imagined, even in her wildest dreams.

Thus, in many ways, a *dharmic* perspective is very much the same as an I/Thou perspective, because both rely upon our ability to cultivate a meaningful relationship with life.

Another way to think of an I/Thou relationship with the Divine is in terms of the "I" representing the self as an autonomous whole and the "Thou" representing that which is greater, higher, and more expanded in life—a relationship that can also be characterized as *holarchic*.

Chapter 2 explores this holarchic perspective in detail. For now, it suffices to observe that if the thesis in Chapter 1 is that "life has purpose," the thesis in Chapter 2 is that "life has order." These two ideas work together such that it is the ordered structures of consciousness that provide the framework which allows the purposes of life to be fulfilled through each individual.

Notes

1.   Plato, Timeus, 29/30; 4th century B.C.

2.   "Anima Mundi: Awakening the Soul of the World," (www.goldensufi.org/a_animamundi.html; accessed 4-19-12).

3.   Ouspensky, P. D. *In Search of the Miraculous: The Teachings of G. I. Gurdjieff* (1949/2001), p. 317.

4.   The Intelligent Enneagram (1996), p. 266.

5.   Ibid., p. 7.

6.   *The Science of Life and Art of Living* (1966/1975).

7.   *SES [Sex, Ecology, Spirituality]* (1995/2000), p. 3; *emphasis* his.

8.   Ibid., p. 84.

9.   "Systems Theory," Wikipedia article (en.wikipedia.org/wiki/Systems_theory; accessed 4-25-12).

10. "The Theory of Open Systems in Physics and Biology," January 13, 1950, Vol. 111 *Science*.

11. *Acts of Meaning* (1990), by Jerome Bruner, p. 2.

12. *Bricks to Babel* (1980), pp. 440–442. Here Koestler cites Muller's *Science and Criticism* (1943), Tolman's *Purposive Behavior in Animals* (1931/1964) and Krechevsky's (later known as David Krech), "Hypotheses in Rats," (1932).

13. See *Beyond Reductionism: The Alpbach Symposium* (1969).

14. *Beyond Therapy, Beyond Science: A New Model for Healing the Whole Person* (1994).

15. Not everybody saw Rupert Sheldrake's ideas about morphic resonance as crazy; he got positive reviews from *Brain/Mind Bulletin*, *New Scientist*, *Utne Reader*, and Arthur Koestler.

16. www.spinvestigations.org/Schwartz.pdf; accessed 4-22-12.

17. Daryl Bem's study on precognition is available at Bem's website: http://dbem.ws/FeelingFuture.pdf (accessed 4-22-12).

18. www.abcnews.go.com/Technology/extrasensory-perception-scientific-journal-esp-paper-published-cornell/story?id=12556754&page=2#.T5NxcNWvjk8; accessed 4-22-12.

19. *Hamlet* (1.5.166-7).

20. www.gallup.com/poll/16915/three-four-americans-believe-paranormal.aspx; accessed 4-22-12.

21. www.gallup.com/poll/4483/Americans-Belief-Psychic-Paranormal-Phenomena-Over-Last-Decade.aspx; accessed 4-26-12.

22. www.near-death.com/angels.html; accessed 4-22-12.

23. www.time.com/time/nation/article/0,8599,1842179,00.html; accessed 4-22-12.

24. www.near-death.com/faq.html; accessed 4-26-12.

25. See Chapter 14 in Stark's *What Americans Really Believe* (2008).

26. www.time.com/time/nation/article/0,8599,1842179,00.html; accessed 4-22-12.

27. www.hms.harvard.edu/hmni/On_The_Brain/Volume12/OTB_Vol12No3_Fall06.pdf; accessed 4-25-12. It should also be noted that the foundation for this recent work was laid by research on the effects of Transcendental Meditation; see especially Robert Wallace's *The Physiology of Consciousness* (1993).

28. abcnews.go.com/Technology/extrasensory-perception-scientific-journal-esp-paper-published-cornell/story?id=12556754&page=2#.T5NxcNWvjk8; accessed 4-22-12.

29. "On the Modern Mind," *Encounter* 24 (May 1965): 12–20, cited in Mitchell's *Michael Polanyi* (2006).

30. I have never liked psychological tests that focus mainly on detecting pathology, because they can too easily be used in a destructive way, to slot people into boxes with labels like "unfit," as was done during the early 20th century by the eugenics movement. And it's not just eugenicists who misuse such tests. A few years ago, I discovered that my own father—a highly competent and responsible CPA—had once been required to take the MMPI when being considered for a routine

promotion. He was very disconcerted by the many questions focusing on his mental balance.

31. *Balancing Heaven and Earth* (1998), p. *xi*.

32. Gray & Wegner's "The Sting of Intentional Pain," (2008). *Psychological Science* (www.psychology.uiowa.edu/faculty/mordkoff/Methods/section/intentional_pain.pdf; accessed 4-23-12).

33. Loftus, Greene & Smith's "How Deep is the Meaning of Life? (1980). *Bulletin of the Psychonomic Society*.

34. *Bhagavad-Gita, As It Is*, 2ⁿᵈ ed. Bhaktivedata Swami Prabhupada (1989), p. 202.

35. Sansonese's *The Body of Myth* (1994), p. 180. On the same page, Sansonese, writing of karma, says that "karma is not sin, though sin is always karmic. The karma that is not sin is called *dharma*, duty (especially by Buddhists)."

36. *The Heart of the Buddha's Teaching* (1998), p. 164.

37. *Signs of the Unseen,* Discourse 4 (www.khamush.com/discourses.html; accessed 4-24-12).

38. Cited in Irina Tweedie's *Daughter of Fire: The Diary of a Spiritual Training with a Sufi Master* (1995), p. 254.

39. *The Cosmic Doctrine* (1949/1995), p. 157.

40. Ecclesiastes 12:13.

41. Luke 17:10.

42. bible.cc/luke/17-10.htm; accessed 5-1-12. Regarding the passage that God "needs not our aid, and his essential happiness will not be increased by our efforts": Although this commentator and a number of others see it as warning us not to become inflated just because we have done a good deed (which is a valid point), such an observation does little to make us think of duty as something inherently noble and worthwhile.

43. See, e.g., Deci, Koestner, & Ryan's "A Meta-analytic Review of Experiments Examining the Effects of Extrinsic Rewards on Intrinsic Motivation," in *Psychological Bulletin* (1999), (http://files.meetup.com/1789648/Review%20on%20Effects%20of%20Extrinsic%20Rewards%20on%20Intrinsic%20Motivation.pdf; accessed 4-29-12).

44. "Dream Symbolism in Relation to Alchemy," from *Psychology and Alchemy*, in *The Portable Jung* (1971/1976), p. 455.

45. "The Development of Personality," in *The Development of Personality* (1954/1981).

46. *Pilgrimage Through Hell* (1968), by Marie Avinov & Paul Chavchavadze, Chapters 17–20.

47. See Caplan's *Halfway Up the Mountain* (1999) for a discussion of various ways in which people come to falsely believe that they are more spiritually advanced than they really are.

48. *The Heart of the Buddha's Teaching: Transforming Suffering into Peace, Joy, and Liberation* (1998), p. 162.

49. *Halfway Up the Mountain* (1999), p. 60.

50. *Cave in the Snow: Tenzin Palmo's Quest for Enlightenment* (1998), by Vicki Mackenzie, p. 197.

51. For a lengthier discussion on God in the 1st, 2nd, and 3rd person, see Chapter 7 of *Integral Spirituality* (2006) or Chapter 7 of *Integral Life Practice* (2008).

2

HOLONS UP AND DOWN

The Kosmos is the unending All, and the all is composed of holons—all the way up, all the way down.
– Ken Wilber

Our task is to learn how to cooperate with higher intelligence.
– A. G. E. Blake

MODERN LIFE IS COMPLEX: things move fast, change quickly, and interact in ways that can leave us dizzy with fatigue and aching for the simple life. Everything in life can seem to conspire to divide us into little pieces. By the 1960s, the fragmentation of life associated with modern industrialism had given rise to a deep-seated yearning for union, wholeness, and oneness: holistic health, whole foods, and the desire for a whole planet. (Stewart Brand's *Whole Earth Catalog* was launched in 1968; the first Earth Day was celebrated in the spring of 1970).

Another result of this new yearning for wholeness and simplicity was a "back to the land" movement in the 1970s. I was caught up in it, too. After graduating from college, not knowing what else to do with myself, I bought a book called *Finding and Buying Your Place in the Country*. Then I set off with my best friend, her two kids, and her cat on a jour-

ney in search of affordable real estate (singing songs like Buffy St-Marie's "I'm Born to Be a Country Girl Again" along the way.) It was a real adventure.

We found our dream in Cheshire, Oregon, a small town about 14 miles northwest of Eugene: a bare but largish farm house with 2.3 acres of land and a cottage we could rent out to tenants. It had drafty baseboard heating, but we decided to rely instead on a wood stove, perhaps because it appealed to our imagination. We bought a beautiful Quick Meal stove made in 1893 and collected wood for that winter from the forest. Although work was hard to come by, we were lucky enough to join the Hoedads, a local tree planting co-op, from which we earned a variable but living wage. I found an old Crown trailer for only $250 that I hooked up to my pickup that gave me a place to sleep when we worked in the woods. We made our own bread, bought our food from the co-op and our milk from the local commune. That first summer featured goat roasts and potlucks at the home-built cabins of our friends. Life was good.

It was especially good for the first couple of months, the "honeymoon period" of our move to the country. But as the months wore on, the disadvantages of our new lifestyle became apparent. The wood we collected was green, so our chimney caught fire; fortunately, it didn't spread to the roof, but we realized that the "free" wood from the forest had cost us more in repairs than it was worth. The house was against a steep hill and turned out to be pretty cold and damp—and our classic wood stove was a lot better for cooking than heating; it had to be stoked every 20 minutes.

My trailer was so old that the propane tank had no safety release valve, which meant that only gas station attendants with a daredevil streak would agree to fill it. (I guess that's why I got it so cheap.) And I didn't know how much oil to put in the oil burner in the trailer and like the chimney, it too caught on fire. I was lucky it didn't explode. The house next door had to be tended; and we often had tenant problems. Soon after we bought the house, my girlfriend hooked up with an old boyfriend, who moved in; unfortunately, he and I didn't get along (too much alike!). So after a year and a half, he bought me out, and I moved into town.

I have to say, by the time he bought me out, I wasn't all that sorry to go. I had got the place of thinking that life in the country would be simpler. But it wasn't. I had to drive long distances to get to work, do a lot of physically-demanding labor, make do with less money, and deal with the slower pace of country life. It wasn't working out quite the way I'd planned.

In retrospect, it was a great learning experience, because it allowed me to live out the fantasy of recreating the simpler, less complicated life of an earlier era—and discovering that it's not really possible to turn back the clock. I saw firsthand that any effort to promote wholism via oversimplification doesn't work: there is no quick fix to the problem of complexity. The only way to gain wholeness is to become more aware of our "partness"—and to figure out how to make them complements instead of opposites.

Wholism versus Holarchy

Arthur Koestler was also interested in the nature of wholeness. As we saw in Chapter 1, Koestler was an early advocate of systems theory and opponent of scientific reductionism. He was interested in how the different elements within a system relate to one another. So it's little wonder that he took more than a passing interest in Jan Smuts' *Wholism and Evolution* (1926), the book responsible for the idea that the whole is more than the sum of its parts.

In *Janus: A Summing Up* (1979), Koestler notes that although the book created a temporary public sensation when it was first published, it failed to unseat the atomistic paradigm within the scientific community, probably because both positivism and behaviorism were then so dominant. It took another four decades before wholism caught on, at least in the popular culture, such that people became interested in whole foods, holistic healing, and "whole systems" approaches to problem-solving. (It is still not widely embraced within the empirically-oriented scientific community, because the traditional scientific method relies on separating things into independent groups.)

Although Koestler was interested in systems theory, he was not a follower of wholism because it has little to say about the interactions between wholes and parts—and it is these interactions that fascinated Koestler. So he developed a theory of his own, a theory of holons or holarchy. The central tenet of Koestler's approach is that virtually nothing in a living system exists entirely on its own, but always exists within some larger context; conversely, every entity in existence consists of parts at different levels of its being, ranging from higher-level entities (such as the companies that are part of a multinational corporation) to medium-level entities (such as the divisions within each company) to lower-level entities (such as the work units within each division).

So whatever system we consider, everything within that system simultaneously plays two roles: that of an *autonomous whole* and that of a *participant* in some larger entity: it is a *holon*. To describe the nature of a living system consisting of holons arranged at different levels of the system, Koestler coined the term *holarchy*, which is basically a healthy, functional hierarchy.

The idea of holarchy is deceptively simple. But like many simple ideas, it has a lot of explanatory power. And that is why it became a central pillar of Ken Wilber's approach—and of mine, as well. To find out why, we need to take a look at the origins of holarchy and its potential for describing integrally-oriented systems.

Koestler's Early Life

To understand the deeper rationale underlying Koestler's approach, it's useful to look at his life and times. Koestler was a brilliant thinker whose ideas on political thought, creativity, systems theory, and philosophy are still cutting edge despite the fact that he wrote about them many decades ago. But perhaps he was more than anything a mystic, despite the fact that he barely alludes to his mystical experiences in much of his writing, perhaps because he felt it would damage his credibility in intellectual circles. It could also have been because he was a restless spirit who didn't like to be categorized in any way. Nevertheless, Koestler had many experiences of expanded awareness starting sometime in childhood, and they appear to have played a pivotal role during key moments of his life, as did the "slender threads" of Robert Johnson (see Chapter 1). And these inner experiences may account for why Koestler was so prescient about so many ideas, events, and trends.

Koestler (1905–1983) was born in Budapest, Hungary, to parents of Jewish descent, the only child in a household in which children weren't the first priority. So he was often left alone to fend for himself, which made him feel lonely and scared. It also caused him to feel rather distant from his mother later in life. (Although his father died in 1937, when Koestler was still in his early thirties, his mother lived another 23 years, until the ripe old age of 90.)

Although Koestler's family had a number of financial ups and downs, he was nevertheless able to enroll in Vienna Polytechnic University in the early 1920s to study engineering. But a year before he was due to graduate, he emerged from a late-night discussion with a fellow student with an "oceanic" feeling, a state he describes as one in which "all values are reversed."[1] According to his own account in *Bricks to Babel*, he became intensely aware of the non-rational and chaotic nature of life (decades before anyone was ever talking about chaos theory) and was seized with the conviction that "to embark on a reasonable career in the midst of chaos was madness" (p. 20). He found himself taking a match to his Index, a critically important matriculation book containing the only record of all the courses passed, without which he could never obtain his degree: "The burning of my Index was a literal burning of my boats, and the end of my prospective career as a respectable citizen and member of the engineering profession." (His biographer, Michael Scammell, says that he was also in danger of failing at this point, so Koestler may have had an additional reason for burning his Index!)

However, the subsequent events in Koestler's life seemed to point to some kind of deeper logic that was guiding his actions, because his writing career soon took off, and he did not find the absence of academic credentials to be a problem.

From this point on, despite the often harrowing events of the first half of his life, Koestler seemed in some mysterious way to be in sync with his own destiny, which may explain why—despite landing himself in a number of extremely dangerous situations in Israel, Stalinist Russia, the Spanish Civil War, Nazi Germany, and occupied France—he managed to cheat death many times, living long enough to pen over 30 books (both fiction and non-fiction) exploring the nature of life, evolution, and the creative process.

Koestler's first adventure was on a kibbutz in Israel. The kibbutz movement was a new quasi-Socialist experiment in living and it appealed to Koestler's desire (in his own words) to "till the soil of Utopia" (p. 21). Unfortu-nately, his desire to till the soil turned out to be more metaphorical than actual; as a young man with a grand passion, he really didn't like farming very much although he tried to hide it from his fellow communards. But they saw that he was not really suited for kibbutz life and booted him out after his probationary period. Writing about his experiences 40 years later, he says that it would be impossible to set up a society based on the kibbutz model because it's a rare individual that can live this kind of sacrificial life. But he remained an admirer of their pioneering spirit and the inspiration they provided to the budding state of Israel.

After being rejected by the kibbutz, Koestler became something of a wanderer for the next few months, taking odd jobs here and there around Israel, living a life of semi-starvation. Then he landed a job as a correspondent for a prestigious European newspaper chain and suddenly found himself as an accredited journalist with a decent salary and comfortable accommodations. He remained a journalist for the next couple of decades, although he also began to write the books and novels for which he is known today.

Koestler's youthful idealism led him to become a card-carrying communist who taught himself Russian and traveled around the U.S.S.R. during the early 1930s. Because he was sympathetic to the communist cause, he was not supervised during his travels. As a result, he was a first-hand witness to the violently repressive measures associated with the rise of Stalinism (most notably, the "holodomor," the state-created famine designed to wipe out the Ukrainian kulaks, the prosperous peasant class, in which between 1.8 and 12 million people are said to have died).[2] When traveling through the area by train, he saw desperate crowds in every station, who would sell anything they had (which wasn't much) for food. However, at the time, his zealous embrace of the ideals of revolutionary communism allowed him to overlook such depredations and to somehow minimize the significance of what he was seeing—which is why he later refers to himself as a "blinkered traveler" who saw only what he wanted to see.

The Hours by the Window

In 1936, Koestler was still a staunch communist, although few people knew about it. So he was sent as a journalist to cover the Spanish Civil War but also secretly functioned as a communist agent. Captured and sentenced to death in Feb. 1937, he was placed in solitary confinement. The atmosphere was unbearably tense; at night, the men in adjoining cells were taken to execution, never knowing exactly when they would be summoned. One night, Koestler saw the lock in his cell begin to turn, and he knew his time was up. But then it stopped; the jailer had opened the wrong cell by mistake. His life was spared, at least for the time being.

During this time of tense waiting, Koestler found himself in an altered state. He occupied himself by deriving formulas to esoteric math problems. One of those times, he experienced what must have been a remarkable shift in consciousness, because he later described it as the sudden understanding that mathematics represented a way to express the infinite nature of life within the finite logic of math. He found himself in the same kind of oceanic state he experienced when he burned his Index.[3] His exaltation was such that he literally did not care that he was on death row waiting to be shot. He describes

the experience as "floating on his back on a river of peace": "It came from nowhere and flowed nowhere. The 'I' had ceased to exist" (*The Invisible Writing*, p. 429).

This state persisted off and on for weeks—a period which he later called the "hours by the window." It was intense but also confusing, a period full of "oscillation between new certainties and old doubts...sudden illuminations followed by long periods of darkness, petty resentments, and fear" (*Bricks to Babel*, p. 143).

Meanwhile, journalist friends in England (most of whom were unaware of Koestler's political affiliations) raised a hue and cry about his innocence, and managed to forestall his impending execution. He was suddenly released three months after his capture and sent home to England.

After the hours by the window, Koestler's interest in communism faded, although it took some time for him to completely reject it. As he observes, "a faith comes into life through a spontaneous act, like the bursting out of a butterfly from its cocoon. But the death of a faith is gradual and slow" (p. 474). However, by 1936–37, the Great Terror in the U.S.S.R. was in full swing, which must certainly have accelerated Koestler's process of disillusionment, since scores of former comrades had by then been scooped up, jailed, interrogated, tortured, and finally either executed or sent to Gulag concentration camps where the conditions made survival improbable. The charges were inevitably fabricated; the goal was simply to instill terror in the population and silence anyone with potential leadership skills. However, many of those interrogated confessed to these trumped-up charges, including high Party officials. And these confessions puzzled onlookers in the West, especially those who had looked to the great Soviet experiment with high hopes. No one understood how so many innocent people could be made to confess their guilt, not just in the interrogation chamber but in open court.

One of Koestler's female friends (of which he had many during his lifetime) was among those interrogated. So he came to know precisely the methods by which these confessions were obtained and why they were never renounced. In Dec. 1940, he published his most well-known novel, *Darkness at Noon*—a fictionalized but extremely realistic account of the ongoing interrogation of a high communist official and the brutal but effective psychological methods used to ensure that the interrogatee would not later recant.[4] He said he wrote the book to repay his debt to all those who had worked so diligently to free him from his death-row cell in Seville.

Although Koestler calls the hours by the window a turning point in life, like Carl Jung, he seldom spoke of his mystical experiences in any detail. Nevertheless, these experiences obviously played a major role in shaping his ideas and values during the second half of life.[5] The books written during this period—books with titles like *The Yogi and the Commissar*, *The Act of Creation*, *The Roots of Coincidence*, and *The Ghost in the Machine*—hint at the fact that his writings were deeply inspired by transpersonal realizations. After Koestler's death in 1984, the full extent of his commitment to understanding other levels of life was revealed when it came out that he designated the proceeds of his estate to be used for the establishment of a university center to scientifically investigate paranormal phenomena. While both Oxford and Cambridge politely declined the offer, the University of Edinburgh accepted, establishing the Koestler Parapsychological Unit in 1985, a unit that remains in operation today.

"Father of the Holon"

Koestler is one of those imaginative thinkers in whom the burbling up of creative ideas is so prolific that it would be possible to spend a whole lifetime working with them and still not reach an end. Nevertheless, his ideas about the nature of life and how it is organized (i.e., holarchically) are among his most fruitful. They provide us with a way to reconcile two very different views of life.

The first view (the atomistic) focuses on the movement from small to big and those who embrace it tend to think that things are no more than the sum of their parts. This is the view of reductionistic science and forms the basis for "bottom-up" approaches to evolution, such as neo-Darwinism.

In both *The Ghost in the Machine* (1967) and *Janus: A Summing Up* (1978), Koestler explains his reason for rejecting scientific reductionism, including the idea that reductionism makes no place for values or purpose in human existence. Unfortunately, he notes, the reductionism of modern science is not confined to scientific exploration, but has "cast its shadow far beyond the confines of science, affecting our whole culture and even political climate" (*Janus*, p. 25). The result is a culture in which a number of educated people in influential positions see humankind as "nothing but" some form of mechanism.

Koestler has no real objection to seeing humanity partly in mechanistic terms (in that he sees that much of our behavior can be described in terms of automated routines).

But he has a very strong objection to seeing humanity *only* in mechanistic terms, either from a neo-Darwinian or behaviorist perspective, because he is deeply committed to Smuts' view that the whole is more than the sum of its parts, a view likely reinforced by his own mystical experiences.

So it's little wonder that he took more than a passing interest in Smuts' *Wholism and Evolution*, as noted above. But Koestler felt that neither atomism nor wholism were exclusively true, although each was true in its own way. He found a way to reconcile them by positing the idea that all elements in a living system play two roles—(a) a (semi-) autonomous whole and (b) a part within some greater whole—and calling them *holons*. An example would be an organ within the body, which is a specialized entity with a unique function. It is composed of cells, each of which are also autonomous entities but also members of something larger (the organ). In turn, the organ is a part of something greater than itself (the body) (Fig. 2-1).

Koestler's main purpose in formulating holon theory was to offer an alternative to scientific reductionism, wherein everything in a living system exists at the same level and there are no intermediate levels between the top and bottom (see his discussion in *Ghost*, p. 47–49). In consequence, he focuses very much on demonstrating the existence of these intermediate structures (levels) and the properties of the entities (holons) that create them:

> The members of a hierarchy, like the Roman god Janus, all have two faces looking in opposite directions: the face turned towards the subordinate levels is that of a self-contained whole; the face turned upward towards the apex, that of a dependent part.

One is the face of the master, the other the face of a servant (p. 48).

According to Koestler, holons maintain their roles as parts via an integrative or *self-transcendent* drive[6] and their role as wholes via a *self-assertive* drive (Fig. 2-2):

- The **self-transcendent drive** helps us become receptive to that which is transcendent in ourselves, but if it becomes too dominant, the result is an unassertive, ungrounded individual whose over-receptivity makes her open to all manner of suggestion.

- The **self-assertive drive** helps us function as a (semi-) autonomous individual, but if it becomes too dominant, the result is an

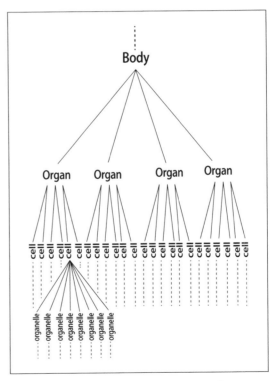

Fig. 2-1. An example of holarchy.

aggressively domineering, tyrannical individualist intent on controlling her "parts" (and presumably unaware or unresponsive to the role she plays in relation to a greater or higher self).

It is the over-suggestability that comes with too much self-transcendence that made Koestler view it as a greater hazard than too much self-assertiveness: because it potentially leads to the swallowing up of individual identity, as we strive to identify instead with some Great and Glorious Ideal that we usually believe to be more important than ourselves. He cites the religious sacrificing of 20,000–50,000 captives *per year* by the Aztecs to their gods as an example of what can happen when self-transcendence utterly outstrips self-assertiveness.[7]

Thus, the goal is for a living system to strive for a state of dynamic equilibrium, where the self-assertive and self-transcen-

dent tendencies are in balance with one another, equilibrium being specifically defined as "the relations between parts and whole (the whole being represented by the agency which controls the part from the next higher level)."[8]

Koestler also distinguishes individual holons from social holons. If we think of a human being as an individual holon, it can participate in groups with other human beings. But the group is not senior to the individual in the holarchic sense, because it's a different sort of holon. This is an important distinction, because it means that holon theory cannot be used to justify the trampling of individual rights by an exploitative government, using the argument that society is at a higher level in the holarchy.

While most of Koestler's focus is on the nature of the structures that create the holarchy (rather than the dynamic interactions between them), he does briefly allude to these interactions in his discussions of "fixed structures and flexible strategies," where he observes that the structures define the parameters of the system and the strategies are the activities that take place within those parameters. He gives the example of a pianist playing variations on a theme in which the variations in key, rhythm, syncopation, and phrasing nonetheless exist within the structure of that piece, such that they do not alter its essential identity (pp. 43–44).[9]

We'll return to this topic in Chapter 12, when discussing the role played by limitation (structure) in fostering creativity (strategy).

Wilber's Holarchic Approach

In the early 1990s, three decades after Koestler unveiled his holarchic model, Ken Wilber was working on his next book—*Sex, Ecology, Spirituality* (abbreviated as *SES*)—a work that he hoped would serve as the foundation for what he was

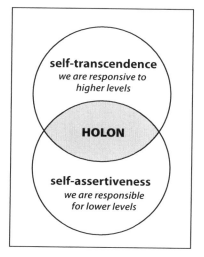

Fig. 2-2. Self-transcendence vs self-assertiveness.

beginning to call an integral view of human consciousness. But Wilber had a big problem: he had no general framework big or comprehensive enough on which to "hang" his ideas.

Although Wilber saw life as existing on multiple levels (thus implying the existence of hierarchies), he had no way to discuss the idea of hierarchy in a way that was equally applicable to all hierarchies. When Wilber realized the implications of Koestler's theory of holons, he realized that he'd found a way to present the idea of hierarchy that was compatible with an IOS perspective. Wilber says that once he realized that the universe is composed of holons, "all the way up, all the way down...with that, much of *Sex, Ecology, Spirituality* began to write itself" (p. *xiv*);[10] the book was finally published in 1995.

To say that the discovery of a particular idea enabled a book to "write itself" is pretty extravagant praise. But Wilber really means it: he comes right out and says that the book—all 851 pages of it—is about holons (p. 4). So it's not surprising that he develops 20 detailed tenets that set forth his formal approach to working with holarchy, an approach that serves as the uniting thread of *SES* (Table 2-1).[11]

We'll come back to Wilber's interpretations of holarchy below. For now, it suffices to say that the early chapters of *SES* introduce the concept of holarchy and the advantages of seeing life from a holarchic perspective, one in which both wholes and parts matter.

Wilber explains that the current cultural focus on wholeness can be problematic, because it potentially promotes the sort of wholeness that can be "totalizing and dominating" (p. 44) in which one's preferred vision of wholeness can be set forth as the only one that matters.

In political terms, "if the 'whole' is primary, and we are parts of the State, then clearly we exist to serve the State" (p. 87). Obviously, the same thinking can create religious cults and other structures that Wilber refers to as domination hierarchies. Robert Masters echoes the same idea in *Spiritual Bypassing* (2010), where he notes that too much emphasis on the whole (oneness or unity) can lead to the denigration of all that is seen as *less than whole*: all that is painful, distressed, and unhealed (p. 5).

It is obviously possible to focus too much on the parts, as well—to see things only in isolation, apart from the context in which they exist. When this happens, we lose the big picture perspective, which leads to an atomistic (reductionistic) view of life, as discussed in Chapter 1. Wilber speaks of context as "inescapable" (*SES*, p. 38), but notes that it is easy to become "disconnected from those contexts that are beyond...[our] own perception," which leads to alienation (p. 85).

So both perspectives—holistic and atomistic—are necessary for a balanced view, because both wholes and parts are necessary to a balanced Kosmos. And this is why the holarchic perspective became central to Wilber's emergent IOS.[12]

Two Views: Wilber's and Koestler's

When Koestler created his theory of holons, he did so over a period of years, eventually publishing an eight-page list of properties in the appendix to *The Ghost in the Machine* (1967); see Appendix B. When Wilber adopted Koestler's holarchic framework for his own use in *SES*, he also developed a list of his own—the 20 tenets shown in Table 2-1. While

TABLE 2-1. KEN WILBER'S 20 TENETS.*

1. Reality is not composed of things or processes, but of holons, which are wholes that are simultaneously parts.

2. Holons display

   a. self-preservation (agency)
   b. self-adaptation (communion)
   c. self-transcendence (self-transformation)
   d. self-immanence (formerly self-dissolution)**

3. Holons emerge.

4. Holons emerge holarchically.

5. Each holon transcends and includes its predecessors.

6. The lower sets the possibilities of the higher; the higher sets the probabilities of the lower.

7. The number of levels which a hierarchy comprises determines whether it is "shallow" or "deep;" and the number of holons on any given level we shall call its "span."

8. Each successive level of evolution produces greater depth and less span.

9. Destroy any type of holon, and you will destroy all of the holons above it and none of the holons below it.

10. Holarchies co-evolve. The micro is always within the macro (all agency is agency in communion).

11. The micro is in relational exchange with macro at all levels of its depth.

12. Evolution has directionality:

    a. increasing complexity
    b. increasing differentiation/integration
    c. increasing organization/structuration
    d. increasing relative autonomy
    e. increasing telos

*We obtain 20 tenets (not 12) by counting number 2 as four tenets and number 12 as six.

**In *SES*, Wilber presents the descending drive as self-dissolution but later retracts this interpretation (see wilber.shambhala.com/html/interviews/interview1220_2.cfm/; accessed 4-20-12), observing that self-dissolution refers solely to the pathological form of descent.

there is some overlap between the two, there are significant differences, as well.

The biggest single difference is the focus of these two theorists. Koestler wanted to develop a model that could reconcile wholism with atomism in order to describe the hierarchical nature of healthy living systems. So his focus was on demonstrating the multi-leveled nature of living systems and describing the means by which energy and information flows between the levels.

In *SES*, Wilber wanted to develop a hierarchical model that would (a) convincingly justify the idea of hierarchy as an organizing principle (especially to post-modernists and web-of-life advocates, both of whom tend to be anti-hierarchy); (b) describe holons not just vertically but horizontally; and (c) highlight the transformational potential of a particular holon: the holon we call human consciousness (especially its ability to transcend its current level—which for Wilber means moving upwards in the holarchy).[13]

Since human beings can also be characterized in terms of holarchic perspectives, the addition of a horizontal component enables Wilber to discuss the relationship between individuals and groups (i.e., social holons),[14] particularly large-scale social holons, such as cultures.[15] However, it also added a level of complexity that created unforeseen theoretical problems, thus drawing fire from a number of quarters. As Jeff Meyerhoff observes, "To enter the holarchic, holonic and four quadrant debates is to enter a thicket of intricate argumentation."[16]

However, at least a short discussion is necessary, if only to explain my preference for sticking with Koestler's original approach. I'll try to keep it relatively brief and pain-free.

Wilber's *goal a* of justifying hierarchy as an organizing principle does not stray much from Koestler's original formulation and as such is uncontroversial. However, when it comes to *goal b* (describing the horizontal and vertical nature of holons and the relationship between them), Wilber's approach not only makes the model more complex, but also introduces several concepts that subtly shift the meaning and/or emphasis of holon theory (see the first three points below); it is also not very systematic (point 4). Regarding *goal c* (to highlight the potential for holons to move upwards), the focus on upward movement is bought at the expense of the original focus on system integration (point 5).

So let's take a look at each of these points.

First, when describing the properties of a holon, Wilber speaks in terms of its *drives*, not just its functions. But drives are usually associated only with certain forms of biological life (especially humans) whereas the original idea of a holarchy does not require us to think only in terms of biological systems.

Second, instead of retaining Koestler's terms for the respective roles of holons (i.e., self-transcendence and self-assertiveness), Wilber re-defines *self-transcendence* to mean the move of a holon to a higher level. Similarly, Wilber jettisons the term *self-assertiveness* in favor of *self-dissolution* (because downward movement is seen as a move in the wrong direction). Although he later changes this terminology in response to feedback from Fred Kofman (see Table 2-1; see also Chapter 9), the term he switches to—*self-immanence*—has little to do with the self-assertive function of a downward-facing holon, as originally described by Koestler. Definitional changes like these reflect a very different approach to holons and holarchy.

Third, when introducing the horizontal functions/drives of a holon, Wilber speaks of *self-preservation* (agency) and *self-adaptation* (communion or "participatory bonding")— drives that are said to describe the relationship of the individual holon to the social holons (groups) in which it participates. Wilber regards these two drives as mutually antagonistic, such that the more agency we have, the less communion—and vice-versa—a view that is unfortunately not very integrative because it defines the relationship between groups and individuals as inherently adversarial, rather than potentially cooperative.[17]

Fourth, by focusing on the relationship between individual holons and social holons, Wilber makes not one leap but two, because he is describing not only a horizontal relationship (instead of a vertical relationship), but a horizontal relationship between *two entirely different kinds of holarchies* (individual and social), with no provision made for describing the horizontal relationships *within the same holarchy,* i.e., the different horizontal perspectives available to an individual's consciousness at a given level of development. So this explication of horizontal relationships is not really complete.[18]

Fifth, with regard to Wilber's **goal c** (which emphasizes the ability of holons to move up the levels): the net effect of describing holarchy in terms of holonic *movements* (as opposed to holonic *functions*) is that the integrative role of the holon basically disappears (drops out of the model), leaving a holarchic approach with no way to characterize the interactions between holons at different levels of a living system.

This shift in emphasis may suit Wilber's purposes, however, in that he has a passionate commitment to promoting higher levels of consciousness (a topic he and Andrew Cohen have discussed for over a decade)[19]—a commitment embodied in the following passage from *SES*, where he states that

> the great quest of postmodernity...is...[to arrive at] body-mind integration...[at the level of] worldcentric vision-logic.[20]

Although he also favors integration (as reflected in this comment), the fact that he has virtually eliminated it from his holarchic model sends a mixed message. If integration really matters, it must be an intrinsic part of the holarchy—as it is in Koestler's model. Koestler's holons are Janus-faced—gazing simultaneously up and down—precisely because this image depicts the means by which a system maintains its ability to function as an integrated entity.[21]

Perhaps Wilber would not have felt the need to change Koestler's theory to this extent, had Koestler explicitly incorporated a way to explain transformation into his original model, which he did not. Nevertheless, it seems evident that *healthy systems are balanced systems, and balanced systems are the kind most ripe for transformation.* Thus, the conditions that create inner balance also facilitate transformation.

The reverse scenario, however, is not necessarily true: if we focus primarily on transformation—seeing it as the main goal—integration may or may not be incorporated into that goal (or may not be incorporated very deeply). Historically, it has been the ascendent ideal that has predominated, not the integrative ideal. Thus, if we want to *ensure* that integration is part of the picture, we have to make it a priority. And it is Koestler's approach (not Wilber's) which does so.

This is why, in spite of Wilber's intriguing and provocative additions to holon theory, I prefer Koestler's original formulation: both because of its simplicity and its unambiguous focus on integration. So this is the approach used in future chapters of the book.

However, Wilber's efforts to introduce a horizontal component to holon theory highlight the importance of understanding horizontal processes (whether they involve processes within the psyche, one-to-one interactions between individuals, or one-to-many interactions). But it's possible to explore such interactions without making them a formal part of holon theory. As we will see in the next chapter, the enneagram can account for many kinds of horizontal influences and interactions; so can Wilber's quadrant perspectives (see Chapter 4). And in Chapter 10, we bring the two together to see how they can mutually inform one another.

Holon Theory in Real Life

There are two assumptions I make when doing practical work using any holarchic model. The first concerns the nature of a vibrant, cooperative holarchy; the second concerns the role of holons in creating such a holarchy. Let's take a look at each in turn.

Assumption #1: A healthy holarchy is one in which all levels play an important and intrinsically respectworthy role. Essentially, this means that no level within a holarchy is undeserving of respect, support, or care. Bluntly put, this means that "up" is not better than "down"—that the higher levels are not better than the lower levels. While they may be more *inclusive*, they are not more *whole*

(because holons are, by definition, always parts/wholes). So if the wholeness increases, so does the "partness." Neither are the higher levels more valuable; they are simply different. The fact that evolution involves the movement to higher levels of consciousness does not make higher levels intrinsically better, even if we tend to see them as conferring greater freedom, power, light, purity, morality, etc.

In taking this position, I depart from Wilber, who does make certain value judgments based on hierarchical distinctions, defining a holon's *intrinsic value* as determined by its level in the holarchy (i.e., higher holons having greater intrinsic value) and its *extrinsic* or *instrumental value* as determined by how basic it is to the holarchy (lower holons having greater extrinsic value). According to this approach, a human being has more intrinsic worth than a cell, but a cell has more extrinsic worth that a human being.

I understand what Wilber is getting at here, but this approach makes me nervous; it is just too easy to see intrinsic worth as "better" and to use that judgment to justify all manner of preferential treatment for higher-level holons. (Not to mention the problem of deciding who gets to make that kind of determination and on the basis of what value system.)

Fortunately, Wilber does discuss a third kind of value—*ground value*—which refers to the value that all holons possess, simply because that they are equally perfect manifestations of Spirit.[22] I wish he had decided to equate the ground value with intrinsic worth, though.

Ground value is what I emphasize in my life and in my work. Why? Because when I do, it tends to put me into right relationship with life. It specifically helps me look at a holarchy in its entirety, as a living system, whether we are talking about an individual holon (a human being, tree, or flower) or a social holon (a family, ecosystem, or culture). To understand the levels of a system is useful, but only when it helps us to better understand its functionality *in toto*. This is the essence of what holarchic ecology is about.

It's especially important to exercise care when it comes to placing ourselves or others we know on some scale of development. Comparisons may be odious, but that does not stop us from making them. But if we place too great a premium on our "height" within some personally-valued scale, we may be apt to treat those holons we regard as "junior" with subtle (and sometimes not-so-subtle) disrespect. We may also be unwittingly resistant to input from higher aspects of our being (or to advice from individuals who actually know more than we do). It can be hard to avoid seeing our relationships in a competitive light, sizing up other people in terms of who's at a higher level (rather than looking at what we can do to help one another or to work together for some shared purpose).

We might think we know how to recognize those who are "above" or "below" us. But *do* we? Who among us knows how to recognize a truly great soul?

Himalayan teacher Swami Rama once pointed out that the mentally compromised sister of one of his students was actually an advanced soul who had come back to help her sister learn how to serve others. Swami Rama himself related the story of when he was a brash young teacher with a small group of students. One day, a new pupil arrived who didn't seem very promising—and was treated poorly as a result. The new pupil turned out to be a great teacher sent by Swami Rama's teacher to give him a special blessing. But Swami Rama missed this opportunity because he was too arrogant to discern the true identity of the visitor.

The Sufi teacher Ibn Al-Arabi once had a dream where he saw the Pole of the Age—the greatest Sufi teacher alive—in a dream, only to see that same Sufi teacher in a gathering of Sufi sheikhs the next day. The man was unassuming and had a withered arm; the other sheikhs seemed to regard him as someone of little consequence. When Ibn Al-Arabi told him of the dream, the man said to him, "Do not say what you have seen." He was content to do his work totally without acknowledgement; Ibn Al-Arabi never saw the man again.

Morally, when we emphasize the sacredness of all levels of all holarchies, we foster a reverence for life that is otherwise missing. I am reminded of the scene in *Seven Years in Tibet* where Heinrich Henry Harrer is asked to build a movie theater by a youthful Dalai Lama—and told he must do it without harming any living creature, including the worms in the earth. Although Harrer initially balks, he eventually submits to this directive (which entails having an army of monks rescuing the hapless worms, so that the theater can be built without a loss of life). The whole idea of "reverence for life"—especially as originally promulgated by the great humanitarian Albert Schweitzer—is that it is critical to look beyond our superficial ideas of what constitutes "value" when devising a scale of development—and to continually question the belief that it is possible for any human being to devise a scale that is the ultimate measure of spiritual development.

The truth is that any scale we can devise—including a spiritual scale—is intrinsically subjective. Therefore, any value judgments made on the basis of scale position are morally questionable (especially when made by those who are particularly eager to devise such a scale).

Assumption #2: Holons act as "energy nodes" for the flow of energy and information throughout the holarchy. The Janus-faced nature of holons means they are designed to function as way stations for the flow of energy and information between levels of the holarchy. The upward-facing aspect of the holon serves primarily as a receptor for higher-level information that is descending down the planes while the downward-facing aspect serves primarily as a transmitter of information down the planes. At the same time, the upward-facing aspect of each holon must maintain its receptivity to higher-levels in a way that nevertheless retains its essential integrity (so that it does not become a "doormat" to overly-assertive higher level holons)—while the downward-facing aspect of the holon must exercise its responsibility in a way that nevertheless allows it to be receptive to feedback from the lower levels for which it is responsible (so that it acts responsibly rather than tyrannically).

When these conditions are met, energy can flow both up and down the holarchy, which allows it to function optimally. This up-and-down energy flow is implicit in Koestler's idea that systems encompass "fixed structures and flexible strategies." Although his discussions tend to focus more on the former than the latter, the structures alone are not the whole system (see Chapter 12 for a discussion on how the limitations of structure can stimulate creativity).

To understand the significance of these two principles (how they work in real life), try watching TV's *Undercover Boss*, a program in which a CEO or other high-level corporate manager visits the lower levels of his organization to discover what's going on. It's very illuminating to see what transpires.

Although their experiences vary, these CEO's share a common bond: they are all deeply touched by their undercover experiences. In the vast majority of cases, what they find is a group of hardworking employees striving to do their best in spite of limited wages, insufficient resources, and less-than-ideal lines of communication with higher-ups. Even in well-run companies, there are problems, simply because it's so easy to have communication breakdowns at various points in the process—sort of like playing telephone, where messages easily get garbled as they pass up and down the lines.

For the executives, the experience of going undercover is like undertaking an abbreviated form of the "hero's journey." They start out thinking they are just going to work within the ranks to assess the company from a managerial standpoint. However, with virtually no exceptions, they are transformed by the experience. And what is it that transforms them? It's the people they meet, the rank-and-file workers who take pride in their jobs, despite the many challenges in their lives, both on the job and at home. To a person, the executives come away with the strong conviction that *people are what matters most* in their organization. And often, it's the ones at the bottom of the totem pole—the people who scrub the toilets, install the fixtures, or prepare the fast food—who make the greatest impact.

For example, one British executive came back with a new appreciation for the dedication of the cleaners at his holiday camps, because he saw firsthand that it's their dedication that makes the company successful. Another saw the importance of finding ways to make even minimum-wage employees know their work is valued. Yet another CEO heading a company hard-hit by the recession (and having to make employee cutbacks) hung his head in anguish at one point, saying, "It's humbling to realize that my lifestyle is built on the labor of these workers."[23]

A second theme that emerges is the critical importance of fostering open lines of communication. Over and over again, the boss discovers that many problems he witnesses are completely unnecessary; they are just the result of communication breakdowns of some sort. It's funny just how many problems disappear once the communication channels are re-opened.

From a holarchic point of view, the descent of the boss to the bottom of the holarchy does two things: (a) enables him (or her—but there are definitely fewer female execs!) to gain a renewed appreciation for "holons" on levels far removed from the top and (b) creates much improved lines of communication, so that there can be a better flow of information within the company.

These stories reveal the interdependence of all the elements within a living system like a successful company—and how understanding that interdependence can help that company to operate in a way that makes it not only more efficient and effective, but more vibrantly alive.

Spiritual Work: A Company Job?

It may seem funny to think of transformational work as analogous to working in a company, but it can be a useful exercise to imagine transformational work as a "spiritual career." Anyone interested in inner growth needs to determine the framework for that growth, which is rather like finding the right company for which to work.

There is actually quite a bit of research to be done if we are to succeed in our spiritual career: we have to find out what sort of company (tradition) best suits us, how we need to prepare for our work there (what attitudes to cultivate), and how to show those in charge (the teachers or facilitators) that we are the right person for the work. We also have to be prepared to walk away from those situations that aren't a good match.

Once there, we need to learn how to function in a way that allows us to work at our current level as well as we can—even when we yearn to advance to a higher level (whether inwardly or outwardly). If we place too much importance on upward advancement, we may either advance too fast (becoming spiritual bypassers or spiritual materialists) or disdain our current work (because it seems mundane, unspiritual, etc.). Too-fast advancement may actually disrupt the "company" (whether this means the spiritual community or our individual psyche) because it can be unbalancing. Of course, the opposite scenario can also prevail (little or no advancement due to laziness, resistance, etc.). So the goal is to strike a balance between the work we're doing right now and the long-term goals we seek to realize.

If we are part of a spiritual community, we also have to ask ourselves how our individual work affects the work of others within that community. Even if we are ready to advance, we might ask ourselves whether the community is ready to *have* us advance.

There's a story about American Baul teacher Lee Lozowick and one of the students at his ashram, who—having a big appetite—was in the habit of consuming the leftovers from each meal. This individual had been doing this for some time; it was a habitual practice. One day, the student (apparently having decided to turn over a new leaf and exercise a more disciplined approach to eating) did not consume the leftover food. Lozowick asked her what she thought she was doing. The student told him she didn't want to eat leftovers anymore. Lozowick informed her that it was not appropriate for her to stop eating the leftovers, because it was actually a job that was important for sustaining a certain energy balance within the community. She was told to resume her former role until somebody else became available to take it on!

Another story involves a friend of mine who occupied a high position in a spiritual organization, where she was working directly with the teacher. One day, the teacher told her without explanation that she needed someone to clean the rooms and toilets; would my friend please take on this job? While the perfect aspirant might not have minded, my friend certainly did. Although she couldn't refuse, she was fuming inside! She had been sent "down the ranks" and did not like it one bit. (Later, she said she realized she needed to be taken down a peg; she worked as a cleaner for six full months before she was summoned back to her previous job.)

A third story involves an eight-year-old boy who was suddenly and permanently el-evated to a high level of consciousness by a Sufi master, to the extent that the little boy could recite Persian Sufi verses (he did not previously speak the language) and dispense Sufi wisdom far beyond his years. How this was possible is not related, but it was cited as an example of a teacher conferring certain abilities upon someone he felt was ready to be spiritually elevated.

In these three stories, spiritual aspirants are respectively asked to stay where they are, to move down, or to move up—not so much for their personal benefit but to fulfill some need that transcended their own preferences. While we may presume that our personal advancement is part of the work, the emphasis in these teaching stories is more often on our ability to be in sync with the need of the moment, so that our actions are not just for ourselves but in service to something beyond the self—something that is literally "transpersonal."

Only if we see ourselves within a larger framework will such stories make sense. But that is precisely why a holarchic approach potentially facilitates transformational work: because it provides us with such a framework by reminding us that everything in existence, exists within a larger Kosmological context. We are not simply free agents, operating without reference to any sort of orienting framework.

On a related note, it's critical to realize that—no matter how high we rise, however compassionate, unattached, or enlightened we become (or how ineffable our experiences)—*we never reach the point where we are only a whole and not a part.* This idea requires further discussion because in modern spiritual work, we hear so much about "ultimate" states or stages (enlightenment, realization, *satori*, emptiness, nothingness, Brahman, etc.). Although the problem is that it's hard to talk about such states/stages from such a limited perspective (because we can't really grasp the experience from this level), many of us are secretly attracted by the idea of getting to a place in which we will experience no sense of limitation, i.e., a state in which we will exist in complete and unmitigated *wholeness*.[24]

Given the dynamic nature of life, I'm skeptical about that idea. Additionally—whatever the true nature of such ultimates—it is clearly dangerous to aspire to them in a literal sense, because such aspirations become a breeding ground for hubris. (It has been said that Lucifer's real sin was not that he wanted to dethrone God but that he wanted *to be just like Him*—and just look where it got him!)[25] If an Archangel can't handle that kind of aspiration, neither can we. Unless we want to end up like Lucifer, Icarus, and others in the "melted wings" club, it's of practical value to think in terms of excelling as a *holon*, rather than questing to become a *whole*.

Holon theory is still in its infancy, especially in terms of its use in inner work designed to facilitate psychic integration. Using a systems-oriented approach to holon theory (i.e., Koestler's), we can summarize its main elements as follows:

- All elements in a living system have within them the dual capacity to function as both parts and wholes (= *holons*).

- As *parts*, holons assume a receptive role, opening to the energy and information that come to them from superordinate levels (= *self-transcendence*).

- As *wholes*, holons assume an executive role, appropriately filtering and passing along

that energy and information to holons at subordinate levels (= *self-assertiveness*).

- Holons retain their integrity by maintaining a balance between these two roles.

- Systems retain their integrity based on the ability of their constituent holons to work cooperatively, maintaining a balance between their own needs and the needs of the system as a whole.

Although holon theory can initially seem a little abstract, it provides a wonderful tool for understanding how living systems develop, prosper, and give birth to new systems, spinning them off in bursts of intense creativity, thus "growing" the Kosmos.

In the coming chapters, we'll revisit these holarchic principles again and again, in a way designed to bring them to life. Even in the next chapter—which mainly focuses on the personality enneagram, which is mainly horizontal—an understanding of holarchy makes it easier to understand how personality is both a receiver of input (from transcendent levels of the self), and an initiator of action (based on higher-level input).

Notes

1. *Bricks to Babel* (1980), by Arthur Koestler.

2. For more on the Ukrainian famine, search on "holodomor" on the Internet or see Robert Conquest's *Harvest of Sorrow*: *Soviet Collectivization and the Terror-Famine* (1986).

3. After his mystical experience in prison, Koestler observed that "solitary confinement is a spiritual hothouse," p. 142.

4. The method used in Stalinist Russia for breaking the spirit of prisoners was simple but effective: break the subject down using isolation, starvation, and sleep deprivation, and when he is completely disoriented (a process usually taking several months), tell him he can save his family from receiving similar treatment only if he confesses. If

the individual is a former Party member, the pot can be sweetened a little by telling him this confession is for the long-term good of the Party—so it can be seen as an act of nobility, not desperation.

5.   See the "Hours by the Window" chapter in *The Invisible Writing* (1954/1998) for a more detailed account of Koestler's mystical experience.

6.   Koestler sometimes refers to the self-transcendent drive as an integrative drive. However, in modern parlance, integration tends to refer to some form of synthesis or reconciliation of the opposites (as opposed to receptivity, submission, or openness to a greater whole). To avoid confusion, I use only his term "self-transcendence."

7.   See the discussion in Chapter 15 of Koestler's *The Ghost in the Machine* (1976).

8.   *The Ghost in the Machine* (1976), p. 347; see also Appendix B in this book, property 9.2.

9.   Koestler's example of a pianist playing variations on a theme is fruitful for considering the nature of creativity and the central role played by limitation in fostering it. It's no coincidence that Koestler was extremely interested in the nature of creativity; his book *The Act of Creation* (1964) is a classic on the topic. In the last chapter of *The Positive Enneagram* (2009), I discuss the role played by our enneagram type in limiting the scope of our attention in such a way as to foster greater creativity within the fixed (but not fixated!) structure of our enneagram type.

10.   By the time Wilber began to compose *SES* in the early 1990s, he was already at least marginally familiar with Koestler's work, because he mentions Koestler and holons on p. 83–84 of *Eye to Eye* (1983/1996). My guess is that he had yet to realize in 1983 the implications of holon theory or the central role it would come to occupy in his IOS.

11.   It is interesting that Wilber has devised his own list of tenets instead of using Koestler's tenets (see Appendix B), which are listed at the end of three of Koestler's books: *Janus: A Summing Up* (1978), *Beyond Reductionism* (1969), and *The Ghost in the Machine* (1967). However, the two lists emphasize different aspects of holon theory. While Koestler focuses primarily on the nature of the living systems in which holons operate (and thus on self-regulation, openness, and the relationship between "fixed structures and flexible strategies"), Wilber focuses mainly on the formal properties of holons and what they imply about the nature of human evolution.

12.   See Wilber's discussion on holarchy in *SES* (1995/2000), pp. 44-45 and 467-469.

13.   Human consciousness is a holon, because a holon can be virtually anything more or less sentient existing at any level of life.

14.   *SES* (1995/2000) p. 49.

15.   When discussing the context that affects our individual actions or perspectives, Wilber tends to focus on the influence of large social conglomerates (e.g., national, Western or global culture), perhaps as a means of addressing the concerns of an academic post-modern audience (especially in *SES*; see particularly his discussion on p. 197, where he speaks of the lower-left AQAL quadrant perspective in terms of cultural meanings, collective identity, and intersubjective ethics). However, context is not defined solely by large-scale socio-cultural influences. The context in which we act is influenced by many other factors, including our intimate relationships, family values and responsibilities, personal health, temperament, physical appearance, personal gifts, habitual acts and attitudes, abilities/disabilities—not to mention Kosmic influences, forces of nature, and Acts of God.

16.   See Chapter 1 in Meyerhoff's *Bald Ambition*, at www.integralworld.net; accessed 10-2-12.

17.   See *SES* (1995/2000), pp. 49 and 52. In Chapter 12, I discuss the "both/and" idea that more agency can actually lead to more communion (not less), citing several real-life examples to support that idea.

18.   Wilber's discussion of the holon's "participatory bonding" is clearly designed to describe the horizontal relationship between individual and social holons. Although Koestler and Wilber both speak of holons as being either individual or social, Koestler does not attempt to specify the precise relationship between them, as Wilber does in *SES*. Had Koestler made this attempt—as Wilber does—he probably would have run into the same problem, because it turns out to be quite difficult to simultaneously describe the vertical and horizontal relationships both *within* an individual holon and *between* individual and social holons.

But however admirable the attempt, it is fraught with complex theoretical problems. If we search on the term "holon" on Integral World (www.integralworld.net), the chief open forum for discussions of Integral ideas, we get 247 hits! The major players in this arena include Fred Kofman, Brian Eddy, Mark Edwards, Andrew P. Smith, Jeff

Meyerhoff, and Gerry Goddard; see especially Eddy's "Spectral Reflections" and Edwards' seven-part "Through AQAL Eyes."

While the critiques by these authors have not been totally ignored by Wilber, neither have they been systematically addressed. The main change Wilber made to his initial formulation of holon theory was to change his definition of downward movement from *self-dissolution* to *self-immanence* in response to feedback from Kofman in "Holons, Heaps, and Artifacts (And Their Corresponding Hierarchies)," (www.integralworld.net/kofman.html; accessed 6-18-12). As a result, this revision is often referred to as the *Wilber-Kofman model.* (Wilber's comments on these changes are available at http://wilber.shambhala.com/html/interviews/interview1220_2.cfm/; accessed 6-20-12.)

Despite Wilber's choice not to respond to most of critiques directed at his approach to holon theory, with the publication of *Integral Spirituality* (2006), Wilber clarifies his current position that—at least when discussing the horizontal quadrants/hori-zones delineated by his AQAL model—he is focusing on the horizontal perspectives *available to a single holon*, rather than the relationship between individual and social holons (see his footnote on p. 34).

It should be finally noted that, to their credit, regarding the Wilber-Kofman model, both Wilber and Kofman are aware of the dangers of inappropriately mixing individual holons with social holons; see Kofman's paper and Wilber's comments in *SES*, p. 49. However, Kofman's suggested revisions do not solve all of the problems regarding the nature of self-dissolution versus self-immanence; see Chapter 9 for a detailed discussion of the confusion surrounding the nature of transformational descent and a proposed solution to the problem.

19. See an introduction to the Wilber-Cohen guru-and-pandit dialogues at www.enlightennext.org/magazine/j21/gurupandit.asp; accessed 4-3-13.

20. *SES* (1995/2000), p. 548; *Vision-logic* refers to the level of development where transpersonal consciousness begins to emerge (see the discussion of Wilber's Spectrum model in Chapter 11).

21. Imagine thinking of the expansion of consciousness not just in terms of moving upwards, but in terms of enlarging our inner "range of reso-nance," e.g., developing our ability to attune to an ever-increasing range of frequencies, both high and low, depending upon the need of the moment.

22. *SES* (1995/2000), pp. 543–547.

23. This *Undercover Boss* CEO had just talked with a group of workers who didn't know how long their jobs would exist but carried on bravely, nonetheless. Naturally, the CEO—quite a decent guy—found this experience heart-wrenching. But it also gave him the determination to find ways to help the employees he could not retain by setting up programs for helping them transition to another company or line of work.

24. It would be hard to overemphasize the importance of the idea that inner work is not about becoming less of a "part" and more of a "whole." As Koestler observes, the role of a "part" is to be the servant of that which is higher; the role of a "whole" is to be the "master" of all that is lower. But implicit in this role of master is the necessity of maintaining an openness to input from higher levels. So in a very real sense, increasing wholeness implies ever-increasing responsibilities to the holarchy. This bears mentioning, because it's all too easy for the idea of wholeness to become divorced from the idea of responsibility. When this happens, people see wholeness as an escape from "partness." They want the light but not the responsibility it entails. But from a *dharmic* perspective, higher consciousness cannot be procured "on demand" (at least not in the long run), no matter how assiduous our efforts or how powerful our practices.

25. Transformational teacher Drunvalo Melchizidek once went searching with a companion for a crop circle in England. But even though they had very good directions, no crop circle appeared. He became very puzzled, because the directions to the site had seemed so straightforward. After thinking about it for awhile, it suddenly dawned upon him what was wrong: "We forgot to ask permission!" He and his companion found a nearby roadside chapel in which they prayed for guidance. When they emerged, they found a farmer who told them exactly where to find the crop circle—about 200 yards down the road! This idea illustrates the principle that real spirituality, guidance, or knowledge is always a gift.

3

ENNEAGRAM BASICS

We're not broken; we don't need fixing...The key to unlocking who we are is acceptance.

– Panache Desai

Psychologism is frequently combined with...pathologism. There is a tendency to go out and detect neurotic flaws and sexual symbols and so forth...But it must stop where the man who does the unmasking is finally confronted with what is genuine and authentic within a man's psyche.

– Victor Frankl

THE ENNEAGRAM IS SAID TO BE many things: a geometric figure, a personality system, and a means of mapping the nine stages in a transformational process. It's a universal symbol with mysterious origins yet practical applications.

The geometric figure looks deceptively simple, consisting of a circle enclosing two figures (an equilateral triangle and a six-pointed hexed). Where the figures touch the outer circle, they form nine points which are traditionally referred to by number, as either Point 1, 2, etc., or Type 1, 2, etc. (Fig. 3-1).

The enigmatic mystic, George I. Gurdjieff, was the first to publicly unveil the enneagram, describing it as "the fundamental hieroglyph of a universal language," "perpetual motion," and "the philosopher's stone of the alchemists." Above all, he sought to convey the dynamism of the enneagram, commenting that "a motionless enneagram is a dead symbol."[1] A. G. E. Blake says that "the prin-

ciple of the enneagram is a great secret. It is through this principle that we can work our way into reality...It is the way through which true value is added or realized. It is God, the guru and the disciple united in harmony."[2] Sufi teacher Idries Shah calls the enneagram a system of ancient origin and stresses its import as a hidden symbol.[3]

Comments like these are intriguing. They tell us that the enneagram has garnered the respect of individuals seriously invested in spiritual work. However, as originally taught by Gurdjieff, it was not an easy system to comprehend; although his hints enable us to see that the enneagram describes or represents a dynamic process that is transformational in nature, it's hard to know much more from his comments as reported by P. D. Ouspensky in *In Search of the Miraculous*, which do more to whet our curiosity than to satisfy it. This is probably why only Gurdjieff's students initially took any notice of the system.

However, several decades later, a teacher of esoteric studies, Oscar Ichazo, found a way to work with the enneagram from a more accessible angle. He spoke of the nine points on the circle as barriers to personal transformation and taught his students the characteristics of these barriers, which he called *ego fixations*. In 1970, when Ichazo held a long-term retreat in Arica, Chile, these enneagram-based teachings were a key part of the curriculum.

The idea of identifying ego fixations would have sounded appealing to the attendees, because the retreat was held during that cultural period in which anti-war, anti-ego, and anti-establishment attitudes were just coming to a peak. Ichazo's approach to the enneagram completely embodied the idea that ego development acts as a barrier to spiritual development:

> We have to distinguish between man as he is in essence, and as he is in ego or personality. In essence, every person is perfect, fearless, and in a loving unity with the entire cosmos…Every human being starts in pure essence. Then something happens: the ego begins to develop; karma accumulates; there is a transition from objectivity to subjectivity; man falls from essence into personality (p. 9).

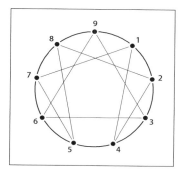

Fig. 3-1. The enneagram.

This "fall into personality" lands us on one of the nine enneagram points of view, each of which is associated with a particular form of cognitive distortion or fixation.

The Nine Types as Fixations

The idea of using the enneagram to identify individual differences in personality was sheer genius; the idea to envision personality as the enemy of essence was not. It lands Ichazo squarely in the camp of those who idealize infancy while denigrating any kind of personal development.

One of the more influential attendees of Ichazo's Arica retreat was Claudio Naranjo, an MD, psychoanalyst, and Gestalt practitioner closely associated with Fritz Perls and Esalen Institute. Naranjo later became the main disseminator of Ichazo's enneagram teachings. Most if not all of the first generation of enneagram teachers learned the enneagram from him, directly or indirectly; this group includes Helen Palmer, Don Riso and A. H. Almaas. Although Don Riso recently passed away, his work is preserved by the co-founder of Enneagram Institute, Russ Hudson. Palmer, Almaas, and Hudson remain extremely influential figures in the enneagram community, especially in the U. S.

Although these influential teachers have each emphasized different aspects of enneagram teachings, what they have in common is an inherited paradigm—derived from Ichazo and imparted by Naranjo—based on the premise that the nine enneagram types represent nine ways in which people become cut off from essence. And although the language used by these first generation teachers and those who follow them has become softer—and the type descriptions less negative as a result—in my experience, it is difficult for anyone steeped in this ego-versus-essence paradigm to entirely step away from the idea that the nine types are inherently flawed.

However, as the years have passed and new generations have come along, people have increasingly grown weary of seeing the types from such a negative perspective. During the early 2000s, articles began to appear in the *Enneagram Monthly* calling for a different approach to enneagram work, one less overtly negative. One writer, Paula Raines, specifically mentioned the then-new positive psychology movement and wondered whether we couldn't apply the lessons of that field to our own.

She is right, we can. But the move from a negative to a positive view is not so easy to make, as I found out when I started publishing articles on this topic. While readers initially liked the idea of a more positive approach, many balked when it came to the idea of a 100% positive approach (i.e., seeing the types as essentially positive centers of consciousness).

I believe this is because of the deeply retro-Romantic ego-versus-essence paradigm that has so influenced the enneagram field from the outset, a paradigm based on the premise that personality development obscures our essential being. We'll look at what Wilber has to say about the problems inherent in such a view in Chapter 4. And in Chapter 5, we'll discuss how Romanticism affects the way we view the enneagram types.

For now, it suffices to say that the descriptions in this chapter are based on a view of the nine types as *nine dynamic energy potentials arising out of an archetypal or core motivation that is the chief factor shaping our perspective, values, and preferences.*

It is a testament to the power of the enneagram that despite the widespread focus on fixation, the enneagram is used not only to identify blind spots and pathologies, but for more positive purposes, as well:

- inner work *(to better understand our personality and path in life)*
- relationship work *(to develop better relationships)*
- organizational work *(to promote team-building & conflict resolution)*
- family counseling *(to understand deep interpersonal dynamics)*
- coaching *(to determine leadership styles)*

While I have absolutely no objection to the idea of using the enneagram to identify type-related biases, blind spots, or areas of inadequacy, I cannot help but object to describing the types in such a way that it's all but impossible to avoid seeing them as pathological—or to depicting type development as a process that inevitably obscures our essence as a human being.

A New Phase in Enneagram Work

Despite my comments above, a lot of credit is due to those who have developed the enneagram field during the last 40 years, such that a system that was virtually unknown during the 1970s has now spread to the four corners of the globe.

At the same time, there is a definite need to move forward into a new phase of enneagram work based on the premise that the types are designed to facilitate our evolution, not to impede it. And it is to this end that I have been developing what I have previously called the positive enneagram approach, an approach that is now generating what is more properly termed an *Integrated Enneagram model.*

As mentioned in the Introduction, Ken Wilber's IOS has been pivotal in this work, especially in terms of providing a solid theoretical justification for a depathologized approach (see Chapters 4 and 5). My goal is to use this model to facilitate a new phase in enneagram work that emphasizes

- the positive role of type in transformation
- how type serves as a pointer to *dharma*
- why different types transform in different ways
- how understanding the types leads to greater integration and more creative living

So the material in the current chapter is designed to support this approach to the personality enneagram. The types are thus portrayed as energetic potentials whose development allows us to come into a deeper understanding of self and more intimate relationship with life. However, this does not preclude the idea that we can use the energy associated with our type in either a balanced or unbalanced fashion.

This chapter includes a brief introduction to all the key topics associated with the personality enneagram, including

- the three energy centers (*each of which contains three of the nine types*)
- the nine enneagram types (*also known as the nine points of view*)
- the 18 wing types (*the two types on either side of a given type*)
- the 18 connecting points (*the two types connected to each type via the inner lines on the circle*)
- the 27 enneagram subtypes (*the three arenas of life x nine enneagram types*)

Although the discussions below are necessarily brief, we will return to the types repeatedly in future chapters, focusing on them from different perspectives. (For expanded descriptions of the types and other basic concepts, please see my first book, *The Positive Enneagram*, 2009).

The Nine Types

Table 3-1 shows the deeper (core) motivation that serves as the impetus for each type, along with the behaviors associated with that motivation. One thing that can be hard to grasp is that, although we are speaking of nine personality types, the types are not simply *personas* (masks)—social roles we adopt to fit into our surroundings. *They are something present from the beginning of life that is part of our very nature as individuals.*

At birth, our type is like a seed based on an archetypal pattern infused with purposeful intelligence; its effects are a major factor in the diversity we see in the behavior of even day-old infants. Variations in the outer behavior of individuals of the same type are the result of finer-grained variants in temperament, environmental circumstances, and the choices we make in life, starting from a very early age. These three factors—temperament, environment, and choice—interact to produce unique individuals, as opposed to cookie-cutter stereotypes (see Chapter 7).[4]

It should be noted that until recently many people within the enneagram community had a vague sense that type was something that developed during infancy and early childhood, rather than something that is present at birth. This was due to the lingering influence of the extreme "nurture" schools of thought regarding the nature of personality

TABLE 3-1. ENNEAGRAM TYPE PROFILES.

	CORE MOTIVATION	SNAPSHOT DESCRIPTION
TYPE 1: THE PERFECTER	To embody transcendent ideals in a less-than-perfect world	**Ones** are preoccupied with "doing things right." As serious people, they are unusually exacting in their work, preferring to toil until they achieve precisely the results that meet their high expectations; but they find it harder to relax, so they can particularly benefit from loosening up & having fun.
TYPE 2: THE PEOPLE PERSON	To discover the self through personal relationships	**Twos** are sociable & sympathetic helpers who rally around good causes & people or animals in need. They are usually keen to find amiable companions to share their lives but are particularly apt to fall into co-dependent relationships if they do not first learn who they are & how to help themselves.
TYPE 3: THE SELF-TESTER	To develop the self through aspirational achievement	**Threes** are practical, cooperative "Type A" team players who are motivated to pursue goals that allow them to exceed their personal best. But they can find it hard to stop scheduling their every move or to set aside time for intimacy or other "non-doing" activities (e.g., meditation).
TYPE 4: THE DEEP SEA DIVER	To incarnate the authentic self	**Fours** are intensely passionate individualists who need a channel for their creative impulses, as well as the discipline to perfect their creations. They can be self-preoccupied or self-dramatizing & thus benefit from cultivating a positive attitude, "other-orientation" & service ethic.
TYPE 5: THE PUZZLE-SOLVER	To understand how life really works	**Fives** are seekers of wisdom who wish to deeply understand how things work, whether intellectually, artistically, physically, or politically. They are shy but adept thinkers with unusual perspectives who benefit from opportunities to share their understanding & emotionally connect with others.
TYPE 6: THE STEWARD	To find the self-trust that makes stewardship possible	**Sixes** are sensitive intuitives with strong analytical skills and an attraction to underdog causes. They have a strong service ethic but can find it hard to allay their anxieties, so they benefit from the support of loyal friends who can encourage them to trust their intuitions & pursue their dreams.
TYPE 7: THE IMPROVISER	To discover a vision worth emotionally committing to	**Sevens** are high-energy, mentally adaptable individuals with a zest for life & high tolerance for sudden shifts in their environment. It can be harder for them to settle down or focus on a single activity or a relationship for a sustained period of time, especially during the first half of life.
TYPE 8: THE MASTER	To honor and lead via the path of inner mastery	**Eights** are full-bore natural leaders who have the strength & power to become masters of their craft; they are motivated by big goals & a personal code of honor but need to learn how to curb their energy and exercise self-control if they are to be effective in a leadership role.
TYPE 9: THE STORYTELLER	To tell their own story in love & delight	**Nines** are natural mediators and lovers of nature who so identifiy with everything around them that they often remain unaware of their own interiority (and sense of identity), which eventually creates feelings of anger & resentment—until the moment when they realize that "I matter, too!"

development, both Freudian and behaviorist. However, one of the leading theorists in the field, A. H. Almaas, has always acknowledged the presence of type at birth.[5] This has always been my understanding, as well. The idea that type is present at birth has always made sense to me, because it is consistent with several decades of research by developmental psychologists. As a result, it is no longer possible to empirically justify either the view that we are at birth nothing more than (a) a collection of instinctual needs or (b) a blank slate whose personality is primarily a conditioned response to environmental stimuli.[6]

But the main thing someone new to the enneagram wants to know is not where the types came from, but "What type am I?" And this is not always an easy question to answer. One of the trickier things about determining our own type (or anyone else's) is that the same core motivation can produce diverse behavioral patterns. If we take the example of Type 6, the Steward, one person of this type may exercise that stewardship by becoming an extremely conscientious office manager while another may join the military in order to defend the country—and yet another may become a parent completely devoted to the welfare of her family. On the surface, the behavior looks different—but the underlying motivation is the same.

By the same token, different type motivations can produce behaviors that look the same. Both Type 9 Storytellers and Type 5 Puzzle-solvers can both seem impassive, but for entirely different reasons. In a Nine, impassivity often arises out of an innate desire to harmoniously blend in with his environment while in a Five, it's more likely to arise out of the tendency to stand back and take

stock of incoming percepts before determining how to respond to them. Similarly, a Type 7 Improviser may play racquetball every day because it's fun while a Type 3 Self-tester may play to give himself a workout or to become a competitive athlete: although the behavior is similar, the motivation is not.

It's for reasons like these that enneagram typing is as much of an art as a science: because differences in motivation can be subtle and therefore challenging to discern. But it's also the same reason that the system is of such value: because it can elucidate subtle differences that are based on inner motivation, not just outer behavior.

Ironically, the deeper our understanding, the less adequate we find the generic type descriptions used to introduce the enneagram to newcomers. So while the nine type descriptions provide a good starting point for studying individual differences, they should always be taken with a grain of salt; the same can be said for type labels and tests to determine type.

The Three Energy Centers

Nine types: that's a lot of categories to sort out—especially if we have no sense of how they might be related. Looking at each type in terms of its energy center gives us a starting point for understanding it, especially in terms of its underlying energy.

There are three energy centers: the Heart, Head, and Body/Gut centers. Each center has a highly distinctive energy signature, although it manifests somewhat differently according to which of its members we are discussing. Table 3-2 describes the nine enneagram types by energy center; Table 3-3 gives a detailed account of the properties associated with each center). Fig. 3-2 maps the energy centers onto the enneagram.

If we think of them in terms of *functionality*, the Heart center governs feeling, the Head center governs thinking, and the Body/Gut center governs action. If we think in terms of *gender* (polarity), the Heart center is feminine, the Head center is masculine, and the Body/Gut center is androgynous. If we think in terms of the *elements*, the Heart center is water, the Head center is air, and the Body/Gut center is fire.[7] If we think in terms of *temperature*, the Heart center is warm, the Head center is cool, and the Body/Gut center is hot.

Here's a quick summary:

- **Heart Center**:
  feeling–feminine–watery–warmth

- **Head Center**:
  thinking–masculine–airy–coolness

- **Body/Gut Center**:
  action-oriented–androgynous–fiery–hotness

Each of the centers contains three enneagram types; below is a more detailed look at the types within the centers.

HEART CENTER TYPES (2-3-4). The energy of this center is flowing, watery, and challenging to contain; it requires personal expression. Heart types want to know, "Who am I?", and seek out opportunities to understand themselves via their interactions with others. They can bring others into relationship but can find it hard to cultivate detachment or to fully attune to their physical needs. Typically: *Type 2* is particularly warm & extroverted; Twos like to be with other people and place particular value on their personal relationships. But they can become overly invested in others and in need of greater self-reflection.

Type 3 is also sociable but more business-like; Threes are more inclined to become preoccupied with work and to show their caring by financially providing for others. They can find emotional intimacy more of a challenge, because of its lack of structure and potential for too much self-revelation. *Type 4* is the most individualistic type—and also the one most preoccupied with personal authenticity; Fours value friendship but tend to have fewer but deeper relationships. They become conflicted in situations where they must choose between authenticity and group loyalty, and sometimes find themselves painfully "on the outs" when choosing the former over the latter.

HEAD CENTER TYPES (5-6-7). The energy of this center is light, airy, and quick; it requires solid grounding. Head types want to know "What is the nature of life?"; they are curious and mentally agile, but tend to worry about things they don't understand. While they have an analytical bent, they can get lost in their head or become overly-detached; they benefit from calm surroundings and closeness with those they trust. Typically: *Type 5* is rational, cool, and reflective; Fives are knowledge-collectors who like to delve deeply into topics that they find intriguing. But they are particularly detached and can easily become socially isolated unless they make the effort to find common ground with others. *Type 6* is also analytical but more edgy, nervous, and restless in disposition; Sixes have a "quicker" energy and can find it hard to avoid jumping to conclusions—a tendency for which they compensate by adopting a skeptical mindset. They are very sensitive to threats in the environment and thus tend to be more aware of fear than other head types. *Type 7* is high-

TABLE 3-2. NINE TYPES BY ENERGY CENTER.

HEART CENTER: "Who am I?"	
TYPE 2: PEOPLE PERSON, HELPER, CONFIDANTE, LOVER	**Twos** seek self-understanding by establishing meaningful emotional ties with people so they can see themselves through the eyes of others.
TYPE 3: SELF-TESTER, COMPETITOR, ACHIEVER, "TYPE A"	**Threes** seek self-understanding by seeing what it is possible for them to achieve, especially in comparison with previous achievements or with the performance of others.
TYPE 4: DEEP SEA DIVER, ARTIST, ORIGINATOR, INDIVIDUALIST	**Fours** seek self-understanding by plumbing the depths of their being in an effort to get beyond their superficial self-image so that they can find the authentic self.
HEAD CENTER: "What is the nature of life?"	
TYPE 5: PUZZLE-SOLVER, SCHOLAR, OBSERVER, SHAMAN	**Fives** understand the nature of life via minute observation, detached reflection & flashes of insight spontaneously arising out of their ability to see things from a completely different angle.
TYPE 6: STEWARD, SKEPTIC, SCIENTIST, SERVER	**Sixes** understand the nature of life via a healthy skepticism, systematic analysis & developing the courage to trust their innate awareness.
TYPE 7: IMPROVISER, JUGGLER, INNOVATOR, ENTREPRENEUR	**Sevens** understand the nature of life by cultivating curiosity, following up on their fascinations and allowing themselves to become completely immersed in new and unusual experiences.
GUT CENTER: "What values really matter?"	
TYPE 8: MASTER, LEADER, TOWER OF STRENGTH, EXEMPLAR	**Eights** measure value in highly personal, embodied terms, thus esteeming personal honor, comradely values, courage under fire & the determination to protect the weak & helpless.
TYPE 9: STORYTELLER, DREAMER, MEDIATOR, NATURE LOVER	**Nines** are motivated by values that further universal principles such as peace, brotherhood, harmony, oneness, simplicity & the preservation of nature.
TYPE 1: PERFECTER, DETAILER, ARBITER, RULE-MAKER	**Ones** see values as compelling ethical abstractions reflecting some sort of natural order and thus creating moral imperatives that require codification as rules, codes & enforceable laws.

TABLE 3-3. ENNEAGRAM ENERGY CENTER ATTRIBUTES.

	BODY/GUT CENTER	HEART CENTER	HEAD CENTER
ELEMENTAL ENERGY	fire	water	air
ENERGETIC NATURE	grounding	creating	drying
DOMINANT MODALITY	sensing	feeling	thinking
ASPIRATION	integrity	authenticity	truth
PRACTICAL GOAL	upholding standards	personal expression	objective understanding
DOMAIN	natural world	social world	mental world
REFERENCE POINT	moral perspective	subjective perspective	objective perspective
POLARITY	neutral	yin/feminine	yang/masculine
MODE OF EXPRESSION	being	appreciating	knowing
EVOLUTIONARY ROLE	originating	involving	evolving
SOURCE OF INSPIRATION	eternal values	personal values	objective values
EMOTIONAL TONE	hot	warm	cool
ACADEMIC FOCUS	law/theology	arts/humanities	science/logic
PLANE OF EXISTENCE	physical/spiritual*	emotional	mental
PATH TO INNER SELF	right action	self-discovery	understanding
SPIRITUAL QUALITY	presence	devotion	contemplation
SOUL DESIRE	oneness	ecstasy	awe

*The Body/Gut center is located at the place between heaven and earth; see Chapter 9.

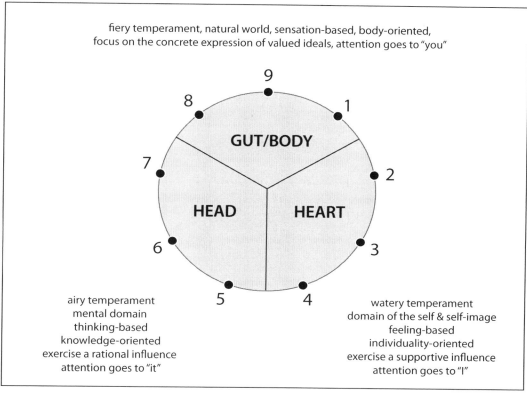

fiery temperament, natural world, sensation-based, body-oriented,
focus on the concrete expression of valued ideals, attention goes to "you"

GUT/BODY

HEAD   **HEART**

airy temperament
mental domain
thinking-based
knowledge-oriented
exercise a rational influence
attention goes to "it"

watery temperament
domain of the self & self-image
feeling-based
individuality-oriented
exercise a supportive influence
attention goes to "I"

Fig. 3-2. The three energy centers.

energy, enthusiastic, and curious; Sevens are the most extroverted of the head types, seeking out new relationships and experiences in life. But they are also easily bored, so it can be hard for them to finish what they start.

GUT/BODY CENTER TYPES (8-9-1). The energy of this center is hot, fiery, and combustible; it requires judicious containment and inner refinement. Body types are action-oriented, and actions are informed by values. So they want to know, "What values really matter?"; they tend to be idealistic but practical, and it's important for them to "ground" their idealism via regular exercise, time in

nature, or other experiential activities. Body types can serve as a grounding influence who remind others to stay in touch with their gut instincts; but they can find it hard to be self-reflective or fully attuned to the feelings of others. Typically: *Type 8* is a commanding leader with the ability to lead by example; Eights will step into any power vacuum and take command of the situation. They tend to be blunt, decisive, and action-oriented, and have little patience with half-hearted action or indecisiveness. They can seem intimidating to others and must take care to cultivate a supportive (rather than domineering) demeanor. *Type 9* is a natural mediator with the ability to make peace between warring factions; mild, receptive, and unassuming (at least in appearance), Nines would rather follow than lead, but often make excellent leaders if pushed into that role by necessity. But they can have a hard time changing gears or making decisions, and can easily lose sense of time or fall into the habit of accumulating "stuff" if they don't structure their lives by adopting a regular schedule. *Type 1* is orderly, self-disciplining, and perfectionistic; Ones often have an ascetic or minimalist streak that comes from their need to compartmentalize their inner fire, so that it does not leak out in a way that is inappropriate or hurtful. But if they can find a way to constructively channel that fire (and perhaps to allow its warmth to inform their hearts), they can become inspired leaders who are admired for their ideals.

The Wing Types

Each of the nine enneagram types can be further broken down into two wing types, creating 18 wing types total (Fig. 3-3 & Table 3-4). One wing type is more influenced by the neighboring type to the right while the other is more influenced by the type to the left. (Arguably, there are actually three divisions, because some individuals seem to be "bi-winged": equally influenced by both wings. Bi-winged individuals will share the characteristics of both wings.)

Breaking down the types by its wings gives us a finer-grained way to characterize each type. It also allows us to see the relationship of the types on the circle—the fact that we are dealing with a progression of linked energies rather than unrelated categories. This ability to link adjacent types reflects the fact that the

personality and process enneagrams are in fact two interpretations of one enneagram—something we'll discuss at greater length in Chapters 6–8.

The wing types are described as, e.g., 1w9 (for a One with a Nine wing) or 1w2 (for a One with a Two wing). For each type, there are two wing types (summarized in Table 3-4 and described below).

TYPE 1: The Perfecter. While most Ones have a serious disposition, high standards and ethical focus, the *1w9 Definer* is more reserved, precise, and inward (almost in a mystical sense) while the *1w2 Reformer* is more extroverted, outspoken, and apt to get involved in activities involving political action, the legal system, or the setting of social standards.

TYPE 2: The People Person. Although Twos tend to be emotional individuals who enjoy social interaction, the *2w1 Social Worker* is a more serious individual that prefers to work with people within a structured setting (like a school, social agency, or animal shelter) while the *2w3 Socializer* is more light-hearted, informal, and attracted to participating in fun social events, such as parties, fund raisers, or film openings.

TYPE 3: The Self-tester. Here we have high energy, industrious people looking for opportunities to exceed their "personal best"; however, *3w2 Managers* are more sociable, organizationally-minded, and adaptable team players while *3w4 Professionals* are more independent-minded individualists who work best in an unconstrained environment (e.g., as real estate agents, consultants, or marketing experts).

Type 4: The Deep Sea Diver. Most Fours share a common attraction to the deeper or artistic aspects of life, as well as a tendency to moodiness; however, *4w3 Specialists* are better at meshing their artistic skills with worldly practicalities (as designers, actors, or workshop leaders) while *4w5 Artistes* are particularly unyielding when it comes to personal authenticity (artistic and otherwise) and can find it quite trying to adapt to social norms.

Type 5: The Puzzle-solver. Fives are the classic image of the shy, "nerdy" type of individual with an extremely mental orientation; however, *5w4 Iconoclasts* are more apt to have an emotional streak and unusual opinions and lifestyles while *5w6 Thinkers* are more detached and analytical (and also more receptive to making some effort to at least nominally adapt to social conventions).

Type 6: The Steward. Sixes tend to have a strong service ethic and the desire to create a stable environment around them (whether in the home, in their community, or at work), in order to allay anxiety and feel safe and secure. But *6w5 Servers* are more reserved, overtly dutiful, and cautious in their demeanor while *6w7 Wits* deflect anxiety with wit and humor, although sometimes in a self-deprecating way.

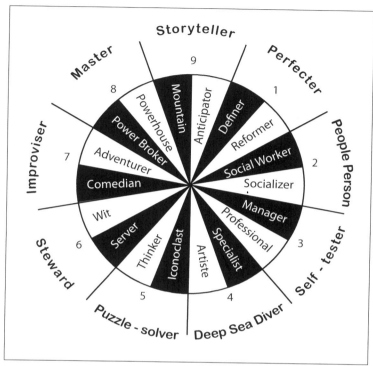

Fig. 3-3. The 18 wing types.

Type 7: The Improviser. Sevens are arguably the most adaptable, novelty-seeking, and entertaining type on the enneagram because so many of them have an uncanny ability to turn work into play and to make people laugh at their troubles. But the *7w6 Comedian* tends to be zanier, less grounded, and more apt to adopt a "life of the party" persona while the *7w8 Adventurer* is a high-energy entrepreneurial type who channels his desire for novelty into new inventions, ideas, or business ventures (often involving exotic travel).

Type 8: The Master. The mastery cultivated by Eights tends to put them in positions

TABLE 3-4. ENNEAGRAM WING TYPES.

1w9: **THE DEFINER**	A reserved, detail-oriented individual who may not say much but still has a definite idea of how things should be done
1w2: **THE REFORMER**	A decisive, impassioned upholder of standards who is committed to whatever cause attracts his concern
2w1: **THE SOCIAL WORKER**	A sympathetic helper with a serious concern for the weak & disadvantaged
2w3: **THE SOCIALIZER**	A warm, gracious & sociable friend, hostess, or family member who thoroughly enjoys interacting with others
3w2: **THE MANAGER**	A friendly multi-tasker with polished manners, good social skills & an innate knack for "rolling with the punches"
3w4: **THE PROFESSIONAL**	A hard-working, independent individual with tremendous drive & the ability to take the initiative
4w3: **THE SPECIALIST**	A high-powered but sensitive individualist with a distinctive style who "goes her own way" rather than stick with the crowd
4w5: **THE ARTISTE**	A highly-sensitive, artistic personality with an intense desire for depth, authenticity, and meaning
5w4: **THE ICONOCLAST**	A retiring but unconventional individual with a penetrating mind & great sensitivity to outside stimuli
5w6: **THE THINKER**	A reflective & self-contained philosopher with great observational powers & the ability to think out of the box
6w5: **THE SERVER**	A reserved, thoughtful & conscientious friend or employee with a scientific bent & skeptical disposition
6w7: **THE WIT**	A nervous but clever thinker with a respectful attitude but an off the wall (and often self-deprecating) sense of humor
7w6: **THE COMEDIAN**	A funny, edgy, high-spirited person who loves to play and make others laugh
7w8: **THE ADVENTURER**	An adventurous, high-energy explorer with an inventive mind & entrepreneurial spirit
8w7: **THE POWER BROKER**	A confident, blunt & assertive leader with the ability to take charge, no matter what the situation
8w9: **THE POWERHOUSE**	A calm, deliberate individual with great gut instincts who is well-suited to exercise tremendous but perhaps unseen influence
9w8: **THE MOUNTAIN**	A steady, impassive observer of human behavior who has the ability to gradually move in the direction of desired goals
9w1: **THE ANTICIPATOR**	A dreamy, idealistic person who likes to blend in and "go with the flow" but can get antsy in anticipation of new experiences

of leadership and power; however, the *8w7 Power Broker* is a flashier, more visible operator who enjoys public acclaim (and is usually charismatic enough to pull it off) while the *8w9 Powerhouse* is more like the "power behind the scenes" Force Majeure who understands that the greatest power is subtly wielded, and who thus prefers to conduct her affairs discreetly.

TYPE 9: The Storyteller. Nines tend to have a naturalness about them that creates an aura of peace and calm, enabling those around them to let go, relax, and imagine the possibilities. The *9w8 Mountain* is (as the name suggests) particularly impassive and grounded in a way that helps calm those around them; their ability to "just *be*" reminds us how to accomplish something without actually doing any physical action; the *9w1 Anticipator* is more of a dreamer with a certain restlessness and the need to translate their dreams into some kind of concrete activity.

(See "Wings Around the Enneagram" in Chapter 6 for a description of how we can use the wing points to see the relationship between all the types on the enneagram circle.)

The Enneagram Subtypes

So far, we've looked at the three centers, the nine enneagram types, and the 18 enneagram wing types. Each of these approaches enables us to move from a very general way of categorizing individual differences (by center) to a more specific level (by type) to another yet more specific level (by wing type). However, there is an even more detailed way of breaking down the nine types: into 27 subtypes. These subtypes are based on an individual's preference for one of three arenas in life, which I call *subtype arenas*: the self-preservation arena, sexual arena, or social arena.

I'll describe the defining features of the subtype arenas below, but I have to first note that my approach to the enneagram subtypes departs significantly from that used by many enneagram teachers. Why? Because the most influential enneagram teacher of the 1970s and 80s, Claudio Naranjo, portrayed the subtypes as instinctually-based modes of expression that are inevitably corrupted by the "cognitive distortions" and "dominant passions" associated with each type.[8]

It is unfortunately impossible to reconcile such a pessimistic interpretation of the subtypes with a depathologized approach to enneagram work, since it virtually defines human motivation (based on a primarily Freudian approach) as the product of distorted thinking, feeling, and instinct. It is one thing to note that distortion is possible; it is quite another to view it as inevitable (i.e., as a defining feature of the types and subtypes).

The approach I take is to define the subtype arenas very simply: as three arenas of activity in life. However, for a given individual, some arenas will be more attractive than others. And the ones that particularly attract us probably have something to do with our natural path or *dharma* in life. This is why I was interested enough to write an entire book on the topic (*Archetypes of the Enneagram*). Anyone interested in an expanded discussion can find it there.

Here our goal is simply to describe the three arenas and list the characteristics of the subtypes to which they give rise (Table 3-5):

TABLE 3-5. SUBTYPE PROFILES.

	SELF-PRESERVATION	SEXUAL	SOCIAL
TYPE 1	Precise & careful workers with a detail orientation & a serious outlook on life	Fiery evangelists with the courage of their convictions	Rule-makers, judges, & social activists who are more fair than flexible
TYPE 2	Loving nurturers who like to personally care for the young, sick or helpless	Sentimentally-inclined romantics who sometimes over-adapt to their partner's needs	Outgoing socializers who support those in need & excel as diplomats & organizers
TYPE 3	Type A strivers who make financial security a priority	Charismatic "stars" that capture the mood of the times	Image makers who like the public eye & excel as "first among equals"
TYPE 4	Independent creators who often work alone to manifest their creative vision	Intense, self-dramatizing & high-strung individualists with a competitive streak	Self-conscious but discriminating critics who are sensitive to public opinion
TYPE 5	Shy, detached thinkers who set personal boundaries but appreciate company	Secretive individuals with a few special contacts & unique powers of perception	Investigators of curiosities & teachers with unusual insights who enjoy recognition
TYPE 6	Warm & supportive family protectors who make their homes a haven	Feisty skeptics who often see a strong offense as the best defense; often counterphobics who challenge authority*	Loyal upholders of traditional values & enforcers of community norms
TYPE 7	Joyful celebrators of life & sensual pleasures who embrace unconventional family styles	Appealing wanderers with a charming air & "love 'em & leave 'em" tendencies	Imaginative thinkers with unconventional ideas & big plans who at times sacrificially limit themselves to fulfill their plans
TYPE 8	Strong-minded survivors who "secure the perimeter" to protect their space	Hot-tempered but honorable upholders of truth & protectors of the weak	Powerful leaders who know how to enlist loyalty from others & lead by example
TYPE 9	Calm & steady homebodies who love to putter around & do things at home	Receptive lovers of nature & harmony who seek oneness with their surroundings	Harmonious participants who enjoy blending into the energy of the group

*While the sexual subtypes for all the types are often more florid, intense, and passionate than other subtypes, this intensity shows up particularly for Sixes as the counterphobic tendency to confront fear by deliberately putting themselves in dangerous situations that force them to overcome fear with courage.

- the **self-preservation arena**, where the focus is on the self, self-reliance, home & family, personal safety & responsibility
- the **sexual arena**, where the focus is on intimacy, creativity, stimulation, excitement, intense experiences & sexuality
- the **social arena**, where the focus is on relationships, social interactions, community, politics, laws, status, manners & social action

Nine types × three subtypes yields 27 subtypes. Note that—just as with the types—subtypes are not just different personality types but different perspectives *within* each type, such that although we each have a dominant subtype, we each function in all three arenas (because they are all part of embodied life). So although a given person may identify herself as, say, a Sexual Eight, she will to some extent identify with the traits of a Self-Preservation Eight in survival situations or a Social Eight in social situations.

The Connecting Points

The connecting points are those points which are linked to one another via the inner lines of the enneagram. Each type has two and only two connecting points (see Tables 3-6a & b).

Like the wing points, the connecting points provide us with resources upon which we can draw, in addition to the resources associated with our dominant point of view. While the wing type energy tends to be more immediately accessible (because it is right next door), the energy of the connecting points is also accessible, but often in a less direct fashion.[9] While we may draw upon the energy of the wing point by a slight shift in perspective, it usually requires a bigger shift to draw upon the energy of a con-

necting point. It is for this reason that people may be said to "jump" or "go to" a connecting point, almost as though they are "leaving" their home point of view. And indeed, when individuals go to their connecting point, it can sometimes seem as though they are adopting an alter ego, at least temporarily.

Let's look at a few examples of how this works, starting with Point 5. Fives are normally shy, inwardly-oriented individuals. This inwardness can be an asset in situations requiring concentration, study, etc., but it's not such a big asset in social or conflict situations. However, Point 5 is connected to both Points 7 and 8. Point 7 can provide the Five with a certain charm, as well as the ability to think quickly while Point 8 can provide assertiveness and authority. Fives who know how to access these resources have an advantage over those who don't.

The same "backup resources" are available for all the types, although the nature of the resources varies by type. For example, a usually confident Three may respond to failure by "going to Six" (3 → 6), becoming more cautious and careful in his approach; alternatively, he may "go to" Nine (3 → 9), taking time off to re-evaluate his options. Similarly, a professional Four dancer can gain discipline by "going to One" (4 → 1), enhancing her artistry; she can gain greater empathy by "going to Two" (4 → 2), allowing her to better connect with her audience.

An understanding of the connecting points is also helpful for discovering a person's type. People experienced with the enneagram can use their knowledge of the connecting points as a form of "triangulation" in which they observe an individual's pattern moving to the connecting points in

TABLE 3-6A. CONNECTING POINTS.
(INNER TRIANGLE TYPES)

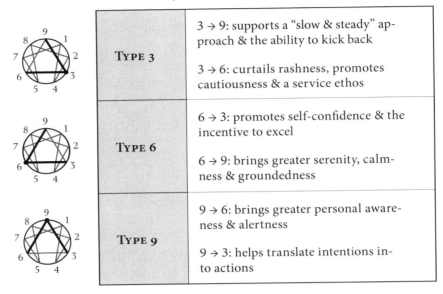

TYPE 3	3 → 9: supports a "slow & steady" approach & the ability to kick back 3 → 6: curtails rashness, promotes cautiousness & a service ethos
TYPE 6	6 → 3: promotes self-confidence & the incentive to excel 6 → 9: brings greater serenity, calmness & groundedness
TYPE 9	9 → 6: brings greater personal awareness & alertness 9 → 3: helps translate intentions into actions

order to pin down the type. Table 3-6a shows the connecting points for the inner triangle types (3-6-9); Table 3-6b shows the connecting points for the hexad types (1-4-2-8-5-7).

It may be of interest that the inner triangle types are often said to "slide" along the connecting points more easily than the hexad types, so they can potentially be harder to type than hexad types.

The Holarchic Enneagram

While the enneagram is a geometric system that can be used for diverse purposes, in this chapter we've focused on using it to describe the nature of personality types, their variants, their energy centers, and how the types are energetically related via the connecting points.

It's a lot to take in if you're new to the system (or if you're not used to seeing it described from a depathologized perspective). However, we will return to the types in future chapters, looking at them from many perspectives, e.g., in terms of

- how the nine enneagram types correspond to the nine stages of transformation as depicted on the process enneagram (Chapters 6–7)

- how the location of each type on the enneagram circle allows us to understand that type from a deeper perspective (Chapter 8)

- how each type tends to vary in the way it moves through the process of transformation (Chapter 9)

TABLE 3-6B. CONNECTING POINTS.
(HEXAD TYPES)

TYPE 1	1 → 4: allows judgment to be informed by deep conviction 1 → 7: brings spontaneity, enthusiasm & the ability to lighten up

TYPE 2	2 → 8: helps develop assertiveness & self-confidence 2 → 4: supports the deepening of emotions & a sense of genuineness

TYPE 4	4 → 2: provides the incentive to cooperate & connect with others 4 → 1: enhances self-discipline, self-reliance & the ability to behave appropriately

TYPE 5	5 → 7: brings a playful curiosity, ingenuity & the ability to see connections 5 → 8: enhances groundedness, assertiveness & the ability to act

TYPE 7	7 → 1: supports the development of precision & care 7 → 5: brings the ability to slow down, reflect & be still
TYPE 8	8 → 5: promotes greater sensitivity & a sense of interiority 8 → 2: supports the development of heartfulness & good will

- how the nine types (as *points of view*) can be mapped to Ken Wilber's eight AQAL perspectives (Chapter 10)
- how the nine types are associated with various lines of vertical development—and mapped onto Wilber's Spectrum model of development (Chapter 11)

Depathologizing the type descriptions is a necessary first step in exploring the enneagram from an integral perspective, because no integration is conceivable so long as we define the nine enneagram types in terms of emotional vices versus virtues, or cognitive fixations versus Holy Ideas—because who would seek to integrate such opposites? (Traditionally, vices are something to be eradicated, not integrated.) It is only when we start by defining the types in terms of their core energy that we can proceed to describe how that core energy looks when it is aligned versus misaligned.

Even then, we lack a way to describe how the type energy manifests at different levels of our being, i.e., its potential to receptively transcend our current locus of consciousness (opening to the wisdom of higher levels) or to take responsibility for more elemental aspects of our being (governing our instincts and other elemental processes).

This is where Koestler's holarchic model can provide a good jumping off point, allowing us to ask ourselves, e.g.: Which types are more naturally self-transcendent (receptive to Spirit)? Which types are more naturally self-assertive (protective of fragile or developing aspects of the self)? What

is the best way for each type to bring our upward- and downward-trending tendencies into balance? What strategies can we use to correct an imbalance?

It's not my intention to try to answer these questions here, only to ask them as a means of stimulating future thought. Fig 3-4 echoes Fig. 2-2 in Chapter 2, which depicts the self in the middle with self-transcendence in the upper circle and self-assertiveness in the lower circle. It also foreshadows the discussion on horizontal zones in Chapter 8, in which the enneagram is divided into three zones (Spirit-Ego-Soul), and the enneagram types are discussed in terms of how their zone position relates to their inner motivation and outer behavior.

Contemplating Koestler's holarchic scheme, we can envision each of the nine types looking transcendently upwards and assertively downwards, trying to attune to the higher and lower levels of its being.

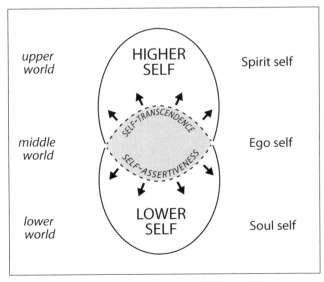

Fig. 3-4. Three levels of the self.

There is yet another way of working with the enneagram, and that is to envision each of the nine points of view as points or stages in a transformational process. This transformational or process enneagram is the enneagram originally taught by G. I. Gurdjieff, and is usually considered to be more basic or elemental than the personality enneagram that was developed by Oscar Ichazo several decades later.

Fig. 3-5 shows how the process enneagram works, how—starting at the top—we move clockwise around the enneagram circle. Each point represents a different transformational challenge we encounter as we progress. Although each circuit around the enneagram takes us through all nine stages of transformation, the actual degree of transformation experienced depends upon how well we meet the challenges posed at each stage. However, most of us learn at least a little something, which is why Point 9 at the end of the cycle is depicted as higher than Point 0 at the beginning.

As depicted in this figure, transformation is not a linear, ladder-climbing process but a cyclical macro-process involving many, many micro-processes, each of which can be depicted as a circuit around the enneagram circle. From a holarchic perspective, the process enneagram gives us a way to show not just how we resonate with higher and lower levels of our consciousness, but how we move up the spiral to higher levels of consciousness, all the while preserving our status as holons (i.e., our ability to simultaneously be receptive to higher levels and to assert our autonomy in relation to lower levels).

Notes

1. *In Search of the Miraculous* (1949/2001), p. 295.
2. Preface to *Enneagram Studies* (1983).
3. *The Commanding Self* (1994), p. 61.
4. Regarding the role of factors that play a role in determining temperament: although gender and other factors may play a role, our focus here is on the role of enneagram type because its influence on motivation is so great and yet remains unperceived by most people.
5. *Facets of Unity* (1998), p. 13.
6. For a full explication on the research supporting the position that type is innate, see my three-part article, "Type is With Us At Birth," originally published in the *Enneagram Monthly*, now available on my website. www.enneagramdimensions.net.
7. The three enneagram energy centers account for three of the four elements (fire, water, and air). The missing element—earth—is present in all the centers in the sense that they are all grounded on the earth through our embodied presence.
8. *Character and Neurosis* (1994), pp. 12–13.
9. Interestingly, from the perspective of Gurdjieff's process enneagram, the connecting points represent the means by which we mentally connect through thought or intention with other steps in a process (looking either backwards or forwards in a planning process); see the brief discussions in Chapters 6 and 7 or p. 42 in Blake's *The Intelligent Enneagram* (1996).

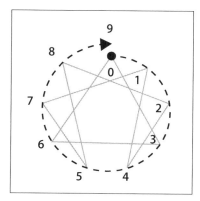

Fig. 3-5. The process enneagram.

4

IOS Basics

The evolutionary process is an awakening which arises from below and which is supported from above.
– A. G. E. Blake

"THERE IS NO SCIENCE without a metaphysical basis to it and without spiritual remedies at its disposal."

This is how Ken Wilber began the preface to his first book, *The Spectrum of Consciousness* (1977): with this quote from Frithjof Schuon. It was Wilber's aim at that point to introduce a system that could provide both: a comprehensive theory of human consciousness that stresses the importance of not only theory, but methodologies that facilitate the evolution of human consciousness. The eventual result was Wilber's Integral Operating System (IOS).

But at the beginning, there was no IOS. Instead, there was just an individual with the grand vision of synthesizing the wisdom of East and West in a form that supports transpersonal development.

Spectrum was a cutting-edge book for its time, so it's no surprise that it was well-received by both the transpersonal psychol-ogy community and the reading public. Its success gave Wilber the opportunity to keep developing his ideas and publishing books about them. By 2010, he had published over 25 books (as well as making a number of CDs), launched a website (www.kenwilber. com), and established a think tank Integral Institute in 1998 (www.integralinstitute. org). With such an extensive body of work, it is impossible in a short chapter to do his work justice in terms of a truly comprehensive exposition of his ideas (especially given his penchant for radically reframing his ideas every few years).[1] But fortunately, that's not really necessary. Although Wilber seems to have commented on countless (and I do mean countless!) philosophies, psychologies, and epistemological methodologies, there are a few major themes that have emerged in recent years that are especially useful for the purpose of describing the relationship between IOS and the enneagram. In this chapter, we'll look at some of the key ideas that are most central to Wilber's IOS; in Part III, we'll return to the ones that are particularly relevant for understanding the relationship between the IOS and the enneagram.

Discovering Wilber

I first became acquainted with Wilber's work from reading his spiritual memoir, *One Taste* (2000). Interspersed between his account of a recent trip to New York to find a publisher for his then-unpublished work, *The Marriage of Sense and Soul,* were reflections about his most seminal concepts: the pre/trans fallacy, the AQAL model as a basis for exploring human consciousness, and the idea that the evolution of consciousness involves multiple lines of development, not just one.

The approachability of *One Taste* made it the ideal entryway to Wilber's ideas. I was able to nibble around the edges of his work without feeling overwhelmed. The next two books I attempted were *The Marriage of Sense and Soul* (1998) and the ironically titled *A Brief History of Everything* (1996). At some point, I managed to get through *Grace and Grit* (1991), Wilber's moving account of the time spent caring for his ailing wife, Treya, who died after a five-year battle with cancer in 1989. As in *One Taste,* Wilber combined personal anecdotes with his integral philosophy.

I appreciated the mix of the spiritual and the personal in these works, which allowed me to see the person behind the philosophy and also to digest Wilber's ideas in small bites. (Beginning one's exploration of Wilber's ideas is a little like making homemade mayonnaise: everything depends upon add-

ing miniscule amounts of oil to the eggs in the early stages: if you try to go too fast, you soon wind up with a runny mess.)

It took awhile, but I finally reached the point where I felt prepared to plunge into the "heart of darkness": *Sex, Ecology, Spirituality* (*SES*; 1995/2000), an 851-page tome in which Wilber sets forth the most comprehensive vision of his work to date. Although this book contains a lot of ideas, the foundation that underlies the book is Arthur Koestler's theory of holons, which Wilber considerably expands by proposing 20 tenets that flow out of Koestler's holarchic approach (see Chapter 2). It was in *SES* that he first introduced his "All Levels, All Quadrants" (AQAL) model,[2] which proposes the existence of four main perspectives that shape our outlook on life—perspectives that can also be linked to three life domains (i.e., the Big Three value spheres of art, science, and ethics; see Chapter 4).

Although *SES* is not the easiest book to read, by the time I took it on, it wasn't too bad. I could follow the main ideas, although I was occasionally distracted by the polemical tone of the writing. (When trying to illustrate why his approach is superior to others, Wilber can sometimes skewer his opponents in a way that alternately evokes admiration and discomfort.)[3]

Key Concepts

Over the years, Wilber has explored many ideas from many perspectives. He is continually tweaking his approach to reflect shifts in his thinking. But certain concepts have become cornerstones of his approach, and those are the ones we'll look at here.

THE HOLARCHIC KOSMOS

Holarchy is probably the single biggest pillar in Wilber's pantheon of ideas, which is why I've already devoted an entire chapter to it (Chapter 2). As discussed there, *holarchy* is Arthur Koestler's approach to the idea that everything in existence plays two roles: that of a *part* and a *whole*. This assumes a multi-tiered (hierarchical) view of reality, one in which we function as (a) an autonomous whole composed of multiple parts and (b) a part of some larger whole, such as the Kosmos. The idea of a holarchic Kosmos became the foundation for *SES*,[4] which in turn became the foundation for Wilber's Integral Operating System.[5]

There are two things about the idea of holarchy that make it a particularly useful way to conceptualize reality. One is that it provides an alternative to what Wilber calls *flatland*: the view that physical (horizontal) reality is all that exists. This is the view of reductionist science, and it has come to be the view that predominates in modern industrial societies. Wilber devotes the entire second half of *SES* to explaining how this view came to predominate, thus precipitating "the collapse of the Kosmos:"[6] the collapse of the vertically-oriented paradigm that enabled us to conceive of life as existing on multiple levels, including non-material (spiritual) levels.

As Wilber puts it, "the vertical dimension of depth/height was ditched in favor of a horizontal expansion...instead of an infinite *above*, the West pitched its attention on an infinite *ahead*" (p. 420).[7] This created a popular culture where words like "progress" or "evolution" became exclusively associated with goals such as the creation of wealth, safety, and scientifically oriented values. The idea that there might be more to life than material reality was thus relegated to the realm of fantasy, unfounded belief, and wishful thinking.

As a serious spiritual practitioner who had direct experience of other levels of consciousness, Wilber objected to this flatland ideology, an ideology that offered no coherent account of either his own experiences or those of other reputable spiritual practitioners. The idea of holarchy provided a vertically oriented framework that could not only account for these experiences but could serve as a foundation for a new approach to inner work.

As discussed in Chapter 2, according to Koestler's original holon theory, self-transcendence is associated with a holon's "partness," (its ability to be receptive to higher-level holons) while self-assertiveness is associated with its wholeness (its ability to assume responsibility for lower-level holons). However, because of Wilber's desire to emphasize transformational work (and especially the transformation of the holon we call human consciousness), when he discusses holon theory, he focuses the bulk of his attention on the ability of a holon to change position in the holarchy, i.e., to move upwards (which he calls *self-transcendence*) or downward (which he calls *self-dissolution* or *self-immanence*).[8,9]

Wilber also adds a horizontal dimension to his theory of holarchy, observing on p. 49 of *SES* that "as a *whole*,...[the holon] remains itself; as a *part*, it must fit in." Here he is referring to the need of the human holon to remain an autonomous individual while at the same time retaining the ability to participate in the larger culture—and especially to find a balance between these two seemingly opposite roles, which are respectively termed *self-preservation* (agency) and *self-adaptation* (communion).[10]

PRE/TRANS FALLACY & RETRO-ROMANTICISM

When Ken Wilber first began studying human consciousness, he found that most transpersonal psychologists took the position that, at the moment human beings are born, we are in a state of spiritual union with the Divine—a union that is gradually lost as we develop the psychic structures that create our ego/personality or rational self. From this vantage point, human evolution is viewed as a process whereby we regain our lost union with Spirit. Because it is similar to the view of the 19th-century back-to-nature Romantics, Wilber later came to dub this view *retro-Romanticism* ("retro" because it is based on what he considers to be a retrogressive view of transformation).

In his first book, *The Spectrum of Consciousness*, Wilber tacitly accepted the retro-Romantic view. But when he attempted to use it as the basis for a theory of how human consciousness develops, it just didn't work. Wilber found himself confronted with a whole raft of logical inconsistencies that he just couldn't resolve.

Most notably, the Romantic approach offered no way to distinguish the non-rational consciousness of infancy from the non-rational consciousness of enlightenment. The only way to capture this distinction seemed to be by claiming that the infant is in a state of unconscious union while the enlightened person is a state of conscious union. But Wilber didn't like that idea, because the notion that

illumination/enlightenment can be unconscious didn't make sense. Neither did the idea that ego development causes us to lose our innate union with the Divine (because if we did, he reasoned, we would cease to exist).[11]

These discrepancies created major headaches for Wilber as a theorist. As he later commented, "Had I not the grounding of my manual job [as a dishwasher], and the steadiness of Zazen, I'm sure I would have busted a rivet here or there."[12]

But he didn't bust a rivet. Instead, he found a way to untie the Gordian knot. And in 1980, Wilber wrote an essay—"The Pre/Trans Fallacy"—for *Re-Vision* (a journal he cofounded) outlining his solution to the problem.[13] In this article, he posits a broad three-stage model of human evolution:

- **Stage 1** *(pre-personal)*: non-rational consciousness prior to the development of rationality or personality

- **Stage 2** *(personal)*: rational/egoic consciousness

- **Stage 3** *(transpersonal)*: non-rational consciousness that transcends but includes Stage 2 rationality

Wilber's revised model is cumulative, in that each stage forms the basis for the stages that follow. During the first stage, pre-personality, we do not possess much in the way of discernment although we are predisposed to develop the structures that will allow that discernment to gradually develop, allowing us to categorize, reason, and make meaningful value judgments: we are becoming a personality self. The differentiation embodied as personality paves the way for transpersonal development, for moving beyond the experience of ordinary life into subtle, ineffable realms that transcend the personal self. Fig. 4-1 compares the retro-Romantic model with Wilber's progressive model.

One central assumption of Wilber's revised approach is that *whatever our stage of development, we are always in a state of union with the Divine, whether or not we are consciously aware of it.* However, union is not the same thing as enlightenment: the former is a given while the latter presupposes some sort of developmental process.

A second of Wilber's assumptions is that *physical birth represents the lowest point of human development,* which necessarily means that all subsequent stages of development (both egoic and transegoic) are by definition progressive in nature. Thus, each step we take becomes the basis for the next step in

evolution—a view that sharply contrasts with the retro-Romantic idea that ego development is a regressive step that moves us away from Spirit.

A third assumption is that *as we progress through each level of development, each level we supersede needs to be integrated into the next* (i.e., so that the lessons learned, skills acquired, etc., on one level enrich our ability to operate at the next). This means that pre-personal development forms the basis for personality development, which in turn forms the basis for transpersonal development—an approach to transformation that Wilber calls "transcend-and-include."[14]

Wilber's approach avoids the trap of the pre/trans fallacy, which is the mistake of conflating pre-rational consciousness and

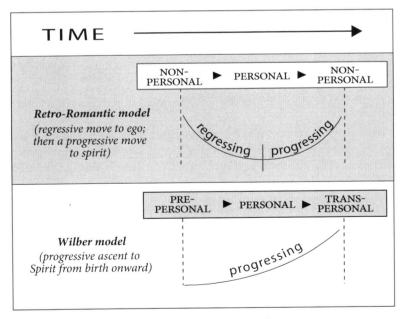

Fig. 4-1. Two models of transformation.

trans-rational consciousness, such that we view the purity and innocence of the new-born as essentially the same thing as the in-effable consciousness of a illumined master. Wilber argues that such a view—although widespread—is insupportable. He often cites Freud as someone who sees all non-rational behavior as pre-rational and Jung as someone who sees all non-rational behavior as trans-rational.[15]

While these arguments were impressive enough to gain Wilber permanent recog-nition as a formative thinker in the field of transpersonal psychology, they were also controversial because they put him at odds with the ideas of formative transpersonal thinkers such as Michael Washburn and Stanislav Grof.[16] This is one of the reasons that Wilber eventually abandoned the field of transpersonal psychology (although he also felt that it was overly focused on ideas and insufficiently grounded in spiritual practice, as discussed in the preface to the 3rd edition of *Eye to Eye*, 2001).[17] His new focus on integral theory and practice was de-signed to fulfill the vision he presented two decades earlier, in the essays written for the 1983 edition of *Eye to Eye*.

TRANSFORMATION VERSUS TRANSLATION

Given Wilber's focus on transformation, it's not surprising that he has made a point of distinguishing real change from the kind of change that is merely skin-deep. This was one of the first ideas I encountered in my explora-tions of Wilber's ideas, because it's discussed early in the first Wilber book I encountered, *One Taste* (2000). In a highly readable sec-tion (pp. 25–33), Wilber puts forth the idea

that, despite the blossoming of interest in spiritual transformation (especially in New Age circles), genuine transformation is rare, because it involves the difficult move from a given level of consciousness to a higher level of consciousness. Wilber explains the differ-ence thusly:

> With translation, the self is simply given a new way to think or feel about reality. The self is given a new belief—perhaps wholistic instead of atomistic, perhaps forgiveness instead of blame, perhaps relational instead of analytical. The self then learns to translate its world and its being in the terms of this new belief or new language or new paradigm, and this new and enchanting translation acts, at least temporarily, to alleviate or diminish the terror in the heart of the separate self.

> But with transformation, the very process of translation itself is challenged, witnessed, undermined, and eventually dismantled...with radical transformation, the self itself is inquired into, looked into, grabbed by the throat and literally throttled to death (p. 26).

Examples of translative change would be finding a new perspective on life, a better way to relate to others, or a more satisfying kind of work. Transformational change, however, would involve a much more radical reorien-tation of one's beliefs, especially about the nature of self. As Wilber has observed,

> authentic transformation is not a matter of belief but of the death of the believer; not a matter of translating the world but of transforming the world; not a matter of finding solace but of finding infinity on the other side of death. The self is not made content; *the self is made toast* (p. 27, *emphasis* mine).

Here Wilber speaks more favorably of transformation than translation. But this emphasis on transformation may be to convey as forcefully as possible the message that the two are very different. For a few paragraphs later, Wilber admits that both translation and transformation are necessary for our ongoing well-being. While translation may not be as deep or radical or shattering as transformation, he notes that it can nevertheless help people make sense of their lives, especially when they are still in the process of maturation (and thus need a sense of personal legitimacy to gain a foothold in life). But he goes on to say that "at some point in our maturation process, translation...simply ceases to console" (p. 27). For those who reach that point, only genuine transformation will suffice: because while translation may give us a sense of social legitimacy, only transformation confers genuine authenticity.[18]

So he concludes that "transformative spirituality, authentic spirituality, is therefore revolutionary. It does not legitimate the world, it breaks the world; it does not console the world, it shatters it. And it does not render the self content, it renders it undone" (p. 28).

Nevertheless, transformation potentially brings practitioners into direct relationship with something greater than they could ever even imagine on their own. Thus, a genuinely transformative experience engenders in them the desire to "shout from the heart" the truth that there is more to spirituality than translative religion allows. Wilber speaks of the moral obligation to witness the truth: "Speak out with compassion, or speak out with angry wisdom, or speak out with skillful means, but speak out you must" (p. 33).

STATES VERSUS STAGES

In addition to distinguishing transformation from translation, Wilber also distinguishes *states* of consciousness from *stages/structures* of consciousness. In Chapter 9 of *Eye to Eye* (1983), Wilber begins to describe what Visser calls a "ladder model" of consciousness in which

(1) someone climbs (2) the rungs of the ladder and (3) gains a new view from each rung. As the climber climbs the ladder, the view is constantly changing and widening. The climber represents the self or self-system in the individual, the rungs of the ladder represent the basic structures of consciousness, and the different views represent the transitional or replacement stages [new stages that completely supersede the old].[19]

Thus, it's obvious that Wilber has had a long-time interest in trying to describe the difference between those aspects of consciousness that are more or less permanent (those that constitute the core "self") and those which are dynamic (changing, evolving, developing). But at that point in time, Wilber was more focused on looking at the difference between the stable and dynamic aspects of the psyche than on variations in dynamism (i.e., the difference between *states of consciousness*—which are so dynamic as to be constantly shifting—and *stages of development*—which change over time, but not moment by moment).

Waking, REM sleep, and deep sleep are examples of *states of consciousness*; Piaget's model of cognitive development or Wilber's pre-rational–rational–transrational scale are examples of *lines of development*, vertical scales

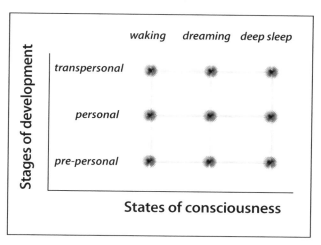

Fig. 4-2. States vs stages.

that are characterized by definite *stages* along the way. States are accessible to everybody and are transient in nature. However, stages tend to unfold in a definite (and unidirectional) sequence and are more stable in nature (Fig. 4-2).

What can get confusing is that in addition to normal states of consciousness, people can also experience states of *expanded awareness*, anything from ESP to near-death experiences to the highest of peak experiences (satori or enlightenment). While such experiences often seem to be somewhat more available to those involved in spiritual practices (meditation, prayer, breathing exercises, etc.), they can also occur completely out of the blue. This is why Wilber says they are available to anybody, noting in *The Integral Vision* (2007) that "you can be at virtually any level or stage of growth and have profound and authentic religious experiences, peak experiences, or altered states" (p. 139).

However, according to Wilber, how these states get *interpreted* depends on our stage of development on various lines (intellectual, ethical, emotional, and spiritual). A more developed individual will obviously interpret their experiences quite differently than a less developed individual. Considering the distinction between states and stages helps us to think more deeply about the nature of transformation and what it means to evolve.

Of course, the idea of distinguishing states and stages is not entirely new. In the Sufi tradition, teachers speak of the difference between states (*haal*) and stations (*maqam*).[20]

In Zen Buddhism, students are often admonished to avoid becoming interested in (much less attached to) fleeting states of exalted consciousness. In *A Path With Heart* (1993), Theravadan Buddhist teacher Jack Kornfeld points out that all states (however exalted) are transitory—which is why he is more interested in practices that help people gain ongoing insight into the nature of self (p. 143). And the "state versus stage" theme comes up many times in Marianna Caplan's *Halfway Up the Mountain* (1999), where a number of spiritual teachers interviewed by Caplan make the point that psychic powers or momentary openings have little to do with the spiritual journey.[21]

This idea that states are different from stages cannot be emphasized too highly, because we live in a culture that has traditionally offered very little in the way of support for direct spiritual experience. If anything, the opposite has been true: individuals interested in the mystical dimension of life have been discouraged from pursuing that interest—sometimes by force. As Caplan points out, "The reason that the West cannot offer a spiritual education is because it lacks a cultural matrix—a context within the culture itself that is created and sustained over time" (p. 18).

Thus, while we no longer burn people at the stake because of their desire to experience higher consciousness, neither do we offer much support for it. Between the flatland reductionism of science and a Western religious tradition that has been repeatedly stripped of its most transformative ideas and practices, it's hard for Westerners to find a path to higher consciousness without looking Eastward for spiritual inspiration.[22]

Wilber has challenged the hegemony of Western reductionism by asserting that it is not legitimate to critique inner experiences using primarily scientific criteria; such experiences must be evaluated using the methodologies appropriate to this kind of experience.[23] But the fact that we are still fighting the battle to prove that spiritual experiences are real (and not just artifacts of brain chemistry) explains why it can be so difficult for Westerners to develop any sort of subtle discernment when it comes to understanding what spiritual development really entails.

One last point on the nature of stages: Wilber often uses the word *structures* (or *structure-stages*) when discussing stages that create structural changes to emphasize that each level of development involves the actual restructuring of the psyche. This is why transformation is essentially a one-way process: because the new worldview we acquire at each new stage or sub-stage is based on the development of actual structures that do not easily disappear. And this is what makes

structure-stages so much more stable (and ultimately more influential) than states.[24]

MULTIPLE LINES OF DEVELOPMENT

A theme running through Wilber's work during the last two decades is that human evolution is not something unilinear but involves multiple lines of development, e.g., spiritual, cognitive, emotional, moral, etc. (Fig. 4-3). The idea that we evolve at different rates on different developmental lines means that at any given point in our evolution, we can be high on some lines, low on others, and in the middle on still others.

One of the things that makes us individuals is that no two people develop in exactly the same way. Mentally, we might like the idea of progressing evenly along a variety of lines so that our development doesn't get too lopsided. But since development is not a mechanical process (but is actually something rather mysterious), it's hard to come up with any sort of universal standard by which to judge the degree to which an individual's progress can be called "balanced."

Should a budding Mozart be allowed to pursue his musical passion at an early age, even if it means he may pay a lot less attention to other lines of development? To what extent should we push ourselves to develop both our weak and strong areas, not just our strong areas (and if so, to what degree)? These are the sorts of questions that arise when we start thinking about development along multiple lines.

Discussions of lines and levels pop up throughout Wilber's work. For example, in *Eye to Eye* (1983), Wilber discusses similarities among the levels used in three key lines of development (i.e., Maslow's, Loevinger's,

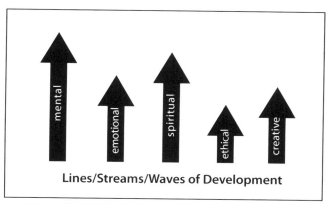

Fig. 4-3. Multiple lines of development.

and Kohlberg's). On pp. 214–215 in *SES*, he speaks of waves or streams of development, noting that they are relatively independent of one another. (Sometimes Wilber refers to the lines of development as *waves* or *streams* in order to get away from the idea that they are entirely linear in nature.) But his most extensive discussion of the developmental lines is in *Integral Psychology* (2000), where he not only discusses the nature of hierarchical development but lists over 100 lines of development (along with their levels) at the end of the book.

AQAL ="ALL QUADRANTS, ALL LEVELS" MODEL

By the early 1990s, Wilber had developed a theory of human evolution that posited multiple *levels* of reality (not just a flatland perspective), included multiple *lines* of development and multiple *stages* on each line. He had also developed a solid rationale for rejecting the notion that the development of ego/personality represents a move away from Spirit. However, at this point, he was still working with an essentially vertically-oriented model; there was little or no emphasis on the horizontal dimension of life.

But Wilber was beginning to realize that any truly comprehensive model of human consciousness would need to focus not only on vertical transformation but on horizontal perspective-taking. What he needed was a way to distinguish four kinds of perspectives we can take on the world: (a) individual versus collective and (b) objective versus subjective. To remedy this situation, Wilber developed his *AQAL model*, which represents his initial attempt to bring together the horizontal and vertical dimensions of his theory in a single, integrated entity.

Although AQAL obviously draws our attention to the fact that all the quadrant perspectives exist at all levels of development, from a practical point of view, AQAL is most often used for distinguishing four key horizontal outlooks:

- subjective-individual (personal = "I")
- subjective-collective (cultural = "we")
- objective-individual (scientific = "it")
- objective-collective (systems theory = "its")

Thus, AQAL provides us with a tool that facilitates our ability to see the world from four distinctively different perspectives, instead of just one (and especially instead of the one advanced by the champions of flatland empiricism). AQAL can also be used as the basis for the separate but related approach of conceptualizing the world in terms of three broad domains of life: Ethics, Science, and Art—domains which Wilber calls the "*Big Three*" *value spheres* (known historically to philosophers as The Good, The True, and The Beautiful).[25]

Fig. 4-4 shows how the three value spheres can be mapped onto the four AQAL perspectives:

- *Ethics* can be mapped onto the subjective-collective quadrant (because both focus on cultural standards and values).

- *Art* can be mapped onto the subjective-individual quadrant because poetically speaking, "beauty is in the eye of the beholder" (i.e., what appeals to us is a matter of personal preference).

- *Science* can be mapped onto both of the objective quadrants (the ones on the right in the AQAL model), because it focuses on what is objectively verifiable about both individual variables and systems.[26]

The "Big Three" approach gave Wilber a way to simplify AQAL (which came in particularly handy in *The Marriage of Sense and Soul*, a book intended for a less technically-oriented audience). It also gave him a way to bridge the gap between philosophy (which relied upon the categories alluded to by the "Big Three") and AQAL, so that he could justify AQAL as an extension of an already familiar way of categorizing the nature of human experience.

TYPES

The category of "type" is the most recent of Wilber's additions to his IOS. Like AQAL and the Big Three, it is useful as an approach for exploring consciousness in horizontal terms, i.e., by looking at how differences in temperament affect our values, habitual behavior, and individual preferences. In *Integral Spiritual-*

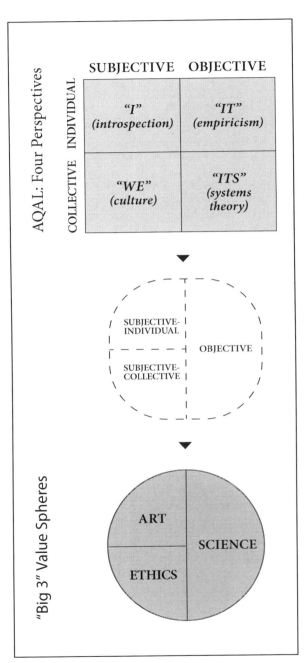

Fig. 4-4. Parallels between AQAL quadrants & Big Three value spheres.

ity (2006), Wilber defines types as "items that can be present at virtually any stage or state" (p. 11). This exceptionally generic definition is not terribly informative, because it tells us little about the precise nature of the type category (especially what distinguishes it from Wilber's AQAL quadrants). Perhaps the brief treatment of "type" is because "type" is a late addition to his theory, and so it has yet to be fully developed; perhaps it is because Wilber is less interested in individual differences than in other aspects of his theory, so he gives "type" a nod and then moves on. Whatever the reason, the examples given of the "type" category—gender, the 16 Myers-Briggs (MBTI) types, and the nine enneagram types—at least allow us to see that "type" must refer to meaningful variations that make people individuals: the kind of variations that tend to be innate, highly stable, and influential.[27]

Five elements of IOS

Although Wilber has at times loosely equated AQAL with his Integral Operating System (IOS),[28] he has increasingly attempted to formalize his model such that it provides a truly comprehensive framework for integral study. So although he has been talking about an integral system since the mid-1990s (after the introduction of AQAL in *SES*), the first time he presents this system in a highly formalized manner is in *Integral Spirituality* (2006), where he lists its five key elements:

- quadrants (perspectives)
- lines of development
- stages (or levels) of development
- states of consciousness
- types

He says that IOS "is the simplest model that can handle all of the truly essential items" (p. 26). He goes on to give examples of how it can be used to create more integral approaches in fields such as medicine, business, spirituality, or ecology. In his most recent book, *Integral Life Practice* (2010), he and his three co-authors provide concrete exercises (practices) designed to facilitate a more integrally-oriented approach to living.

Wilber's greatest strength seems to lie in his ability to collect, analyze, and synthesize information on human evolution in a way that is as systematic as it is compelling. His IOS is impressively comprehensive and his emphasis on integration comes at a time when the limitations of non-integral models are becoming increasingly apparent. What remains to be seen, however, is the extent to which Wilber's flair for structural and conceptual analysis will enable him (as well as his colleagues at Integral Institute) to further explore and delineate the process by which transformation actually takes place. This is where a knowledge of the enneagram can prove helpful, as we will see in Parts II and III.

Notes

1. Wilber has had five major phases in his work; for a synopsis, see Note 13 in Chapter 9.
2. Pronounced "ah-kwal."
3. Wilber discusses his polemical tone in the preface to the second edition of *SES*, where he explains that he took a deliberately provocative approach in *SES* in order to stir things up in the field of cultural studies, which he felt could benefit from a sharp analytical poke. Much of his writing since then has retained sufficient sharpness to make him a more controversial figure than he was prior to the 1990s.

However, it is not uncommon that as thinkers become clearer in their thinking (at least more settled in their position), they lose patience with addressing arguments coming from those whom they perceive to misunderstand their ideas. And indeed, Wilber has increasingly taken this position, especially in the last five or six years. See, most notably, Wilber's controversial "Wyatt Earp" posting in 2006 on his blog (www.kenwilber.com/blog/show/46; accessed 7-1-12.)

4. As Wilber succinctly puts it when referring to *SES*, "This is a book about holons" (p. 4).

5. See Chapters 1 and 2 of *SES* for a full exposition on the nature of holons, including Wilber's 20 tenets; see various online sources for a briefer discussion on the tenets (e.g., www.esalenctr.org/display/confpage.cfm?confid=10&pageid=113&pgtype=1; accessed 6-15-11.

6. This is the title of Wilber's Chapter 12 of *SES*.

7. This quote is slightly out of order, but nonetheless preserves the original meaning of the passage.

8. For the reasons discussed in Chapter 2, Wilber first called the downward movement of holons *self-dissolution*, later changing this to *self-immanence* (the depathologized version of downward movement). For a lengthier discussion of self-immanence, see Chapter 9.

9. As discussed in Chapter 2, I take Koestler's approach of talking about parts and wholes solely in terms of the vertical axis both because it (a) avoids certain theoretical complications and (b) focuses our attention on what makes holon theory so useful: its ability to help us bridge the gap between flatland and Spirit.

10. I would take the position that there need not be a trade-off between agency and communion—that in a balanced relationship, family, or culture, greater agency can actually produce greater communion and vice-versa; see the discussion in Chapter 12.

11. See Wilber's discussion in *The Eye of Spirit* (2001), p. 141.

12. *Ken Wilber: Thought as Passion* (2003), p. 68; see my Chapters 3 and 4 for a detailed breakdown of Wilber's move from his initial position on the nature of transformation to a completely different position that incorporates the insights of the pre/trans fallacy.

13. See *Eye to Eye* (1983) for a reprint of "The Pre/Trans Fallacy."

14. Wilber's transcend-and-include approach is an improvement over the traditional (and ascetic) ideal of transcending and excluding, in which we progress to the next level by cutting off any sort of connection with the previous level. Wilber notes that we transcend a level not by cutting it off but by ceasing to exclusively identify with its worldview; see www.enlightennext.org/magazine/j27/gurupandit.asp?page=1; accessed 4-15-12, for an illuminating discussion between Andrew Cohen and Wilber on this topic.

15. Regarding Wilber's characterization of Jungian psychology as retro-Romantic (falling victim to the belief that all non-rational states are spiritual) and Freudian psychology as its opposite (falling victim to the belief that all non-rational states are neurotic): Although this provides a quick and intuitive way to explain the pre/trans fallacy, it represents a view that I see as oversimplified, especially as regards the work of Jung, because Jung clearly drew a distinction between undifferentiated ("primitive") states and highly differentiated states. The real problem with Jung from Wilber's perspective may be that Jung discusses pre-rationality in a way that Wilber regards as romanticized, because it affirms the value of myths and legends (an approach to which Wilber does not particularly relate).

While I agree with Wilber about Freud, I do not see Jung as retro-Romantic since he never romanticizes primitivism *per se* (see Jung's comments on primitive psychology by accessing the index entry under "primitives, psychology of" in his spiritual autobiography, *Memories, Dreams, and Reflections* (1989).

What Jung does instead of embracing a Romantic view is to speak of how we have become alienated from our sense of "primordial oneness" as the result of "isolating the mind in its own sphere" (see Chapter 13 in *The Portable Jung*, 1971), a position clearly congruent with Wilber's "transcend-and-include" approach. Also, like Wilber, Jung is a staunch advocate of personality development, which he sees as essential for the fulfillment of our life's purpose (see Chapter 1). For more arguments on why Jung is not a retro-Romantic, see "Re-visioning Individuation: Bringing Jung into the Integral Fold, by Ray Harris : available at //www.integralworld.net/harris2.html; accessed 6-08-12.

16. For a critique of Grof and Washburn's work (on the basis that it incorporates a retro-Romantic

view of evolution), see Chapters 6 and 7 in *Eye to Eye* (2001).

17. See also Note 11 on pp. 50–51 of the new introduction to *A Sociable God* (1983/2005), which lists multiple online discussions by Wilber on what he terms the "demise" of transpersonal psychology.

18. The real target of Wilber's negative remarks on translation seems to be the kind of belief-based (i.e., pre-modern) religious traditions that lack the practices and philosophy designed to foster deeper transformations, although it can be hard to pin him down on this topic, since he does not want to be seen as targeting Christianity in a predominantly Christian culture; however, his remarks in Chapter 9 of *Integral Spirituality* (2006) leave little doubt as to his position on any philosophy, belief system, or religion that strongly favors translative beliefs over transformational practices.

19. *Ken Wilber: Thought as Passion*, p. 122.

20. Wikipedia distinguishes states from stations as follows: "A *maqam* is one's spiritual station or developmental level, as distinct from one's *haal*, or state of consciousness. This is seen as the outcome of one's effort to transform oneself, whereas the *haal* is a gift" (www:/en.wikipedia.org/wiki/Sufi philosophy). In *The Intelligent Enneagram* (1996), in referring to station, Blake says that "to be established means to be able to endure in the higher worlds" (p. 138). It is not easy to endure in the higher worlds because these worlds are far more interconnected than the physical world, and the higher frequency energy can be hard to bear.

21. See especially Chapters 5 and 6 in *Halfway Up the Mountain* (1999) for a discussion on spiritual states versus stages.

22. Esotericist Dion Fortune argues in *Sane Occultism & Practical Occultism in Everyday Life* (1987) that whereas we possess the cultural matrix necessary for esoteric work ("which comes down to us through the Qabalists and Alchemists," p. 101), the West is guarded and secretive about its methods, which is why Westerners—especially Theosophists—started looking to the East for spiritual wisdom. Fortune is somewhat exceptional in championing the western esotericism; her book, *The Mystical Qabalah*, 2000, is considered a classic.)

23. See Chapter 11 of *The Marriage of Sense and Soul* (1998) for a discussion of how valid methods of knowing (what Wilber calls *injunctions*) vary according to the area we are investigating.

24. This idea of distinguishing stages from structure-stages on the basis that stages involve no structural change may be more difficult than it seems, given current brain research, which suggests that virtually all neural activity involves the gradual tracing of pathways on the brain. From this point of view, each time we do something, we create some sort of structural change, however minor or temporary. So the real distinction seems to be between structures that are transient and those that are stable/habitual. See Norman's Doidge's *The Brain That Changes Itself* (2007) or *Sharon Begley's Train Your Mind, Change Your Brain* (2007) for more information on neuroplasticity, reprogramming the mind, and the effects of meditation on the brain.

25. I originally discussed the AQAL quadrant perspectives as *worldviews*, in accordance with common usage (where the term usually describes a difference in outlook or perspective; see, e.g., enneagram theorist A. G. E. Blake's use of "worldview" in the quote at the beginning of Chapter 11). But I later came to see that Wilber tends to use the term to describe differences in perspective that are more a function of vertical altitude (level) than a function of horizontal position. For a discussion of Wilber's approach to worldviews, see Chapter 4 of SES or pp. 109–110 in *A Theory of Everything* (2000). My warm thanks to Rev. Alia Zara Aurami-Sou for bringing this point to my attention.

26. It can be argued of course that objectivity has its limits, i.e., that what we think of as "objectively true" is not necessarily either more objective or more true—which is why Science has no inherent superiority over either Art or Ethics as an approach to knowing.

27. I will make the case in Chapter 10 that the similarities between Wilber's "type" category and his "quadrant" category may make these two categories combinable into a single category.

28. For one example of Wilber equating AQAL with IOS, see his discussion at http://wilber.shambhala.com/html/books/kosmos/excerptB/part3.cfm; accessed 6-10-12.

PART II
THE TRANSFORMATIONAL ENNEAGRAM

THE ENNEAGRAM IS A PROFOUND SYSTEM *with many dimensions. Although it is probably most easily understood as a tool for determining personality, its deceptively simple-looking geometry belies a complex system that can be used for many purposes. The enneagram has tremendous transformative potential, but this potential contracts or expands according to how we view the system—and how we view the role of human personality in inner work.*

The potential of the enneagram is limited to the extent that we envision its points of view (and the individuality they confer) from a retro-Romantic perspective: as personality fixations that hamper inner development (Chapter 5). Its potential expands when we are able to envision the enneagram from a broader perspective: as a system describing nine stages of transformation (Chapter 6) that can be linked to the nine enneagram personality types (Chapter 7). Adopting such a perspective allows us not only to see the link between personality and transformation, but to develop an Integrated "one enneagram" model (Chapter 8).

5

THE RETRO-ROMANTIC
ENNEAGRAM

Ego is not the extreme point of alienation and loss, but halfway back to the Source. The ego is a major increase in Essence, not a major loss of Essence.
— Ken Wilber, *The Eye of Spirit*, p. 374

The reason we are here as embodied beings on Earth is to develop the ego, as it...is this soul aspect... that is the source of our intentionality and our will forces, as well as our creativity.
— Hale Makua Kahuna, *The Bowl of Light*, p. 59

Our deepest fear is not that we are inadequate but that we are powerful beyond belief.
— Marianne Williamson

ABOUT A DECADE AGO, while living in London, I was invited by a friend to go to a talk by A. H. Almaas/Hameed Ali,[1] a spiritual teacher whom I knew to be affiliated with the enneagram. So I was interested to hear him talk, because he had just completed a new book, *The Inner Journey Home* (2004).

When my friend and I initially sat down in the auditorium, there was an empty seat next to me. Although the place got more and more packed, no one came to sit in that seat. At the last moment, a venerable-looking gentlemen with an aura of personal presence sat down. I couldn't help but wonder who he was.

Well, I never found out.

But during the Q&A, this gentleman raised his hand. Almaas called on him. After announcing that "I come from Ken Wilber," he went on to pose just one question: What did Almaas think of Wilber's 11-page commentary on Almaas' psycho-spiritual approach?

Almaas did not attempt an answer on the spot. He instead referred the questioner to his new book, in which he said he had thoroughly addressed Wilber's concerns. When I looked up the critique in Wilber's *The Eye of Spirit* (2001), I found that it concerned certain retro-Romantic ideas he had noticed in Almaas' Diamond Approach, ideas that Wilber saw as inconsistent with a progressive approach to human transformation.[2]

I found this critique to be an uncommonly brilliant piece of writing when it came to explaining the pre/trans fallacy and retro-Romanticism. I found Almaas' responses to be somewhat less convincing, for the reasons outlined below.

In Chapter 4, we took a brief look at retro-Romanticism. In this chapter, we'll take a deeper look at it, using Wilber's commentary as our guide. The focus is especially on the historically definitive role played by retro-Romanticism in the enneagram community: how it affects the way the types are viewed and the enneagram is taught. But first, we'll delve a little more deeply into the nature of retro-Romanticism and how it came to be so influential.

What is Retro-Romanticism?

Retro-Romanticism is Wilber's term for the belief that we start our lives in a state of idyllic oneness with Spirit, a oneness that is soon lost due to the development of differentiated structures variously referred to as ego, personality, or rationality. To the retro-Romantic, spiritual development is envisioned as the restoration of this original oneness, goodness or wholeness. Accordingly, differentiation comes to be equated with dissociation, not only psychologically but spiritually. And this is why Romantics tend to view the relationship between ego development and spiritual development as implicitly antagonistic.

The appeal of retro-Romanticism is probably captured most eloquently in Wordsworth's poem, *Ode: Intimations of Immortality*, especially the following passage:

But trailing clouds of glory do we come
From God, who is our home:
Heaven lies about us in our infancy!
Shades of the prison-house begin to close
Upon the growing Boy.

How can anyone fail to be moved by such a passage? It speaks to the very heart of the soul, to that part of us that grieves the loss of youth, of innocence, and of a time in life when we felt completely free. It also alludes to a spiritual realm (our "home") from which we are now cut off. So it captures the pathos of living in the "prison-house" of adulthood. And for what reason? We don't even know.

Although Wordsworth is able to articulate our alienation very well, he offers no remedy to heal our pain. As Meg Harris Williams puts it,

at one moment the child has its visionary eye; the next moment, or next year, this has gone; the child has left one abode and taken residence in another, and the most that can be hoped for is an occasional glimpse in periods of calm weather, to remind it of what was once its spiritual life.[3]

So we are left looking backwards at an ever-receding heaven, our only consolation being the memory of our true home.

Ken Wilber alludes to the same Wordsworth passage in *The Eye of Spirit* (2001), p. 368, where he observes that the "clouds of glory" we associate with infancy exist because the infant has just emerged from Spirit. Thus, the aura of holiness we see in the infant is genuine. It evokes a memory in us that serves to remind us that we are not merely human creatures but spiritual beings with a home not on this earth.[4]

However, unlike the Romantics, Wilber does not attach undue significance to the spiritual light that we see in the infant—not because it is not genuine but because it is a *reflected* light that has little or nothing to do with the infant itself or its structures of consciousness, which are not yet developed. And from Wilber's perspective, when it comes to transformation, it's the development of these *structures* that matter, not the reflected glory of the Divine.

Thus, Wilber is highly skeptical about the claim that infancy is a time of spiritual union:

> What is the neonate actually one with? Is the infantile self fully one with the world of poetry, or logic, or economics, or history, or mathematics, or morals and ethics? Of course not, for these have not yet emerged: the alleged "whole world" of the infantile self is a pitifully small slice of reality (p. 142).

Wilber's view is that the consciousness of the infant is actually more constricted than expanded, because this expansion cannot occur until the structures of consciousness become differentiated. In normal development, this differentiation proceeds in a manner that allows us to continually refine our thinking, feeling, and habits over time. He notes that while it is possible to develop in a way that leads to over-differentiation (and hence dissociation), *over-differentiation is the exception, not the rule.*

However, according to the retro-Romantic point of view, there is no such thing as normal differentiation; differentiation is by definition a form of alienation. Therefore, it only allows for one of two states: the *undifferentiated union* (fusion) of infancy or *over-differentiated alienation* (dissociation) of adulthood.

Wilber does not endorse this view. He says that we do not move directly from fusion to dissociation, observing that

> the differentiation of self is neither a fusion nor a dissociation, but the necessary process of differentiation-and-integration (transcendence-and-inclusion), which is the very process of growth itself. But once you are committed to seeing every differentiation as a dissociation, then development must be interpreted as a horrible dissociation...[such that] the oak becomes a violation of the acorn (p. 149).

Here Wilber powerfully articulates the core problem with the Romantic view: that it forces us to see any sort of development as intrinsically perverse. So while retro-Romantics may be well-meaning (and *Ode* may be a beautiful poem), retro-Romanticism is a less-than-adequate guide to living, because it leaves us no hope for ever finding fulfillment in life. While it speaks to our longing for union, it provides us with absolutely no way to translate that longing into anything productive: a philosophy, a practice, or some form of service. Instead, it mesmerizes us with its backward-looking vision of "Paradise Lost," so that we become paralyzed with malaise and unmotivated to change. It thus serves as the perfect justification for our unlived lives: for if life is nothing more than a prison, what's the use of banging on the prison walls?

And this constitutes the shadow side of Romanticism's appeal: its ability to provide people with a justification for ducking out of life's grittier challenges.

It's important to note, however, that not all Romantics embrace their ideals out of a desire for escape; many are simply trying to cope with the sadness they feel when confronted with a world that seems oblivious to what really matters in life. Tired of coping, they're just hoping for a little consolation to lessen the pain of a flatland existence. What can we say to such individuals? What would impel them to look forwards (not backwards) and to re-engage with life? What would motivate them—in Morris Berman's words—to seek some way to re-enchant the world?

That is the challenge that Wilber faces in putting forth a non-Romantic vision of evolution: one that depends upon our ability to move forwards towards our destiny, not backwards towards our memories.

Wilber's Critique of Almaas

Now that we've taken an up-close and personal look at retro-Romanticism, I can resume my story about attending the Almaas lecture and how it led me to investigate Almaas' reply to Wilber's critique.

It's useful to briefly explain Almaas' role in the enneagram community. He is an important figure who was one of Naranjo's SAT (Seekers After Truth) students in Berkeley,[5] so he learned the enneagram directly from Claudio Naranjo, who was in turn a student of Oscar Ichazo's. Almaas is the developer of the Diamond Approach and the Ridhwan School, a program of psycho-spiritual development which uses the enneagram as a major tool for self-understanding. He has also written one of the only theoretical books on the enneagram, *Facets of Unity: The Enneagram of Holy Ideas* (1998), and has many enneagram notables among his long-term students. It's for this reason that Wilber's remarks on the Diamond Approach are relevant: because they not only apply to the Diamond Approach

but to the enneagram teachings that served as the original foundation for that approach.

It is the Romantic philosophy embedded in the original enneagram teachings that is responsible for the negative descriptions of the nine types that we see in so many enneagram books. But I didn't realize the reason for this disparaging view of the types until I read Wilber's critique of the Diamond Approach. That is why it is worth relating here.

Briefly, this critique consists of a systematic analysis of Almaas' approach and how it has evolved between the publication of early works such as *Essence* (1986) to more recent works such as *The Pearl Beyond Price* (2000). Wilber's aim is to trace the apparent move from a retro-Romantic view to a non-Romantic view—a move that Wilber clearly applauds. At the same time, Wilber notices that Almaas does not seem fully committed to leaving behind his Romantic ideas. He obviously hopes that a discussion of the inconsistencies in *Pearl* will help Almaas to make a complete break with Romantic thought.

The gist of Wilber's argument is presented below; all page numbers cited (even those from Almaas' work) are from the critique in Wilber's *The Eye of Spirit* (2001).

In *Essence* (1986), Almaas takes the position that infants and small children are fully in touch with their essential nature. As ego develops, they gradually lose touch with each of the qualities of essence.[6] So in Almaas' words, "we can conclude that people are born with essence but end up without it later on" (p. 365).

Statements like these clearly place Almaas in the retro-Romantic camp. From this perspective, ego becomes (in Wilber's words) "the great enemy" of essence (p. 366). Here is how Almaas describes the process by which essence is displaced by ego:

> By the time of late childhood, essence is for the most part thoroughly buried and rendered only vaguely available. In its place are "holes"—the empty psychic spaces created by repression or loss of various aspects of essence...Individuals, *with virtually no exceptions*, arrive at adulthood as a bundle of holes and defense mechanisms dedicated to the avoidance of Being and essence (p. 366, *emphasis* mine).

Wilber notes approvingly that by the time Almaas writes *The Pearl Beyond Price* in 2000, he has mostly moved beyond the idea that ego displaces essence, to a position in which essence "primarily grows and develops rather...[than being] lost and restricted" (p. 367). Wilber goes on to note that it is Almaas' emphasis on developing essential qualities and working on very early traumas to the self that "allows Ali to make some truly important contributions to the techniques of spiritual transformation...by working with the very early traumas to the self."

However, on the same page, he observes that this new move towards developing essence (and away from denigrating ego) is not entirely consistent, noting that "Ali wobbles back and forth between...[his original position and his revised position] in some very self-contradictory ways" (p. 367).

For some reason, Almaas seems to have a hard time completely relinquishing the idea that the infant is fully God conscious or Self-realized. As a result, there are still statements in *Pearl* such as these: "When the Essential Self is present then, in a sense, the child is born; he is Self-realized. He is his true Self" (p. 369).

Because Almaas contrasts Being and ego in a way that sometimes rejects the Romantic view and sometimes not, Wilber seems to think that all he needs is a push in the right direction—which Wilber is happy to provide. So while Wilber's commentary is razor-sharp, it's also supportive. He bookends his remarks with many complimentary remarks about the Diamond Approach, which clearly intrigues him. It's because Wilber is so intrigued that he gives what he obviously considers to be constructive feedback.

Almaas' Reply to Wilber

Almaas was evidently concerned about Wilber's critique because in his next book, *The Inner Journey Home* (2004), he tries to muster a reply to Wilber's critique. However, when I read his reply (an entire appendix), what I saw was the same exact wobbling back and forth that Wilber had noted in his original critique of *The Pearl Without Price*. For example, here is how Almaas characterizes infancy in *Journey*:

> It would be difficult to think of the few-days-old infant as exhibiting selfish or destructive behavior (p. 151).

> When the infant's needs are satisfied, it will begin to act like an angel: peaceful, contented, and tender (p. 152).

> In infancy the soul has very little structure, [so] the human infant as a result can experience...essence...without restraint or fixed identification (p.151).

> [The infant's] dynamism is quite free and her forms are flexible (p. 153).

Compare this idyllic portrayal of infancy with descriptions of ego development, a process characterized by increasing "rigidity" and dissociation from essence:

> Ego development dissociates the soul from her essential ground (p. 166).

> [The developing infant] is prevented from recognizing her true nature… due to the duality arising from the development of ego structures (p. 537).

> The rigidity and fixated structures created through ego development can be seen as barriers to the function of autopoiesis [the maintenance of equilibrium] (p. 558).

Aren't these statements all just saying that ego displaces essence? They make it hard to avoid concluding that Almaas continues to embrace his Romantic roots.

At one point, when specifically trying to address the reasons that he and Wilber are in disagreement, Almaas wonders aloud whether it is because Wilber "does not have a place for the aspects of essence *as we understand them*, and this might be the central reason for his disagreement with our view of childhood experience" (p. 541, *emphasis* mine).

The "we" in this sentence may be the royal "we" of the writer, but it could also refer to his Ridhwan membership, all of whom are well-versed in enneagram theory. And in enneagram theory, the nine types represent the nine ego fixations that displace nine forms of essence (the Holy Ideas). So what Almaas seems to be hinting at here is that Wilber's unfamiliarity with enneagram theory is the reason he can't follow Almaas' line of reasoning.

If this is so, why doesn't Almaas simply explain the enneagram in sufficient detail that Wilber could better understand his line of reasoning? Perhaps he believes it would be hard to do, because no explanation would suffice without direct experience. But more likely, it's because he suspects that such an explanation would do little to alter Wilber's position—as it has done little to alter mine.

Facets of Unity

If we want further evidence that Almaas is still in the Romantic camp as of 1998, we have only to look to his only book written on the enneagram, *Facets of Unity* (1998). Whereas his position in other books might go back and forth, his position in *Facets* is unambiguously Romantic.

Throughout this book, Almaas speaks repeatedly of the idea that we lose contact with essence—and does so in no uncertain terms. He says that our experience is "obscured by ego structures" (p. 22), that "implicit in the ego…is a fundamental distrust of reality" (p. 44), and that each of the nine enneagram types obscures essence in a different way (that "all nine delusions make up the obscured… experience of egoic existence," p. 17).

Although he says we are born with our enneagram type—a claim that might make us think that type would have some sort of positive potential—he immediately goes on to say that inadequacies in our "early holding environment" lead inevitably to the loss of both contact with Being (essence) and our trust in life:

> The inadequacy of the early holding environment leads not only to the loss of

contact with Being...but also to the loss of *basic trust* (p. 14, *emphasis* his).

The idea that our early holding environment is bound to be inadequate is a bit strange, given that Donald Winnicott—the originator of the whole concept of our "holding environment"—never himself held such a belief. Winnicott was an optimistic therapist who stressed the value of play and creativity for developing the self; he is most famously known as the person who coined the term "good-enough mothering" to emphasize the idea that parents don't have to be perfect to raise healthy kids.[7]

When describing child development, Sandra Maitri tells a story similar to that of Almaas', although without citing Winnicott to support her thesis:

> Initially, we seem to be completely immersed in an ocean of Being, so to speak, in touch with our deepest nature but unaware that we are. Very gradually in the first few years of life, we begin to lose contact with this sense of connectedness with the entirety of True Nature that we seem to be born with. Little by little, we start to separate from that ocean of Beingness, or that sense of inner-connectedness, that sense of Oneness with everything.[8]

While Maitri manages to avoid the "holding environment" problem, she can't quite get around the logical contradiction involved in claiming that infants are in a state of "unaware awareness." In a more recent book, *The Enneagram of the Virtues and the Passions* (2005/2009), Maitri continues to focus on the idea that ego displaces essence/Being: "The understanding associated with the enneagram tells us that as we develop a

personality structure in early childhood, we gradually lose contact with Being" (p. 12).

The reason that such arguments can fly is that it is something people are used to hearing in a community in which retro-Romanticism is the norm. For although Almaas and Maitri are exceptional in putting their thoughts in published books and articles, the view of type as something that obscures essential being is taken mostly for granted; I have heard countless comments from different people (both teachers and students) that embody similar views.[9]

It is to his credit that Almaas (and following him, Maitri) is willing to go on record with his views, given the problems that crop up when we attempt to logically justify a Romantic view in writing. From his remarks in *Facets*, it's obvious that Almaas is trying very hard to stick to the teachings exactly as they were given to him—which is why he makes mention on p. 13 of the idea that the theory of the enneagram is "transmitted" (i.e., the product of spiritual transmission), thereby suggesting that they are unalterable. In taking this approach, Almaas is following the lead of Oscar Ichazo, who in his remarks in the Foreword, makes it clear that he is pleased that Almaas is rendering "an accurate transmission" of these teachings (p. *v*).

Thus, it seems that Almaas is in something of a bind when it comes to responding to Wilber's critiques in a way that would really address Wilber's concerns. If part of the "transmitted" wisdom of the enneagram is that the enneagram types represent obscurations of essence, who is Almaas (or anybody else) to challenge that notion? Even if he understands Wilber's logic—which he surely must—he cannot respond to it on its own terms.

Ego vs Essence

To get an idea of what Almaas is up against, let's take a look at what Oscar Ichazo and Claudio Naranjo (the foremost disseminator of Ichazo's teachings) have to say about ego and essence. As we saw in Chapter 2, Ichazo's original position on ego (stated in an 1973 interview with Sam Keen) was very clear:

> Every human being starts in pure essence. Then something happens: ego begins to develop...and man falls from essence into personality (*Interviews with Oscar Ichazo*, 1982, p. 9).

Ichazo goes on to comment further on the problems associated with ego, leading his interviewer to eventually sum up Ichazo's comments by remarking that "the fundamental problem of human existence, then, is the existence of ego," (p. 11)—an assertion that Ichazo does not dispute.

Oscar Ichazo's own remarks from this interview include the following:

> So long as we remain in ego we have wrong ideas about man and his place in the Cosmos (p. 12).

> We have no desire to strengthen the ego or make it happy (p. 15).

> When ego is broken,...essence quite naturally takes over (p. 20).

In this one interview, I counted over 30 negative comments about the ego and zero negative comments about essence. This combination of "bad ego" versus "ideal essence" leads to a very polarized view of human nature: a human being in ego is in a miserable condition while the same human being in essence is at one with himself and the universe.

Ichazo goes on to say that he has methods for helping people make this critical transition from ego to essence, although he doesn't say what those methods are. He does make some references to the nine enneagram fixations and passions, but doesn't reveal enough information to allow anybody to understand the details of the system. As far as the enneagram is concerned, Ichazo is firmly of the opinion that Arica offers the only correct approach for doing enneagram work.

Fifteen years later, Ichazo still hasn't changed his position on either the ego or the enneagram. In *Letters to the School* (1988), he refers to the lower ego as the "devil" (p. 78),[10] and severely criticizes Don Riso's efforts to differentiate the types by postulating nine levels of type development:

> If you make the lower diabolical ego comfortable and pamper it with caramel and sweetheart treatment, it will never in a million years start the process of breaking the pivotal fixation necessary to begin the process of serious awakening and growing up (pp. 83-84).

Eight years after that, in an *Enneagram Monthly* interview (Nov. 1996), Ichazo tells us that "the ego fixation has to be considered as a distortion and dysfunctional aspect of the instincts which cause them to produce vicious behavior" (p. 18).

Eleven years later, in Spring 2007, Ichazo finally seems to have softened his position on ego (although he still won't budge from his long-time position that Arica offers the only valid approach for enneagram work):

> Question: What is your vision of the future of the teaching of the Enneagram? And what is your opinion of the connections often made with

other humanist approaches which, lacking sufficient knowledge, attempt to find the means of overcoming the ego from within one's "typology"?

Ichazo: Quite simply, the ego doesn't need to be "overcome," but integrated, transformed and transcended as an everyday process of understanding, maturity and awareness. [However] without the clearly defined approach applied in the Arica Method, the ego becomes crystallized with no possibility of transcendence and freedom. Therefore, the future of the Teachings of the enneagram should be to provide an integral method for humankind to reach its highest potential for the benefit of all.[11]

Wow. It almost sounds here like Ichazo sees the ego (and the nine types) as something with positive potential—as something we should try to integrate rather than destroy. It's hard to believe, after so many years of condemning it in no uncertain terms. Ichazo's language now suggests a position that sounds compatible with Wilber's. (He even uses the word *integral* in his statement!)[12]

Claudio Naranjo, however, does not seem to have changed his anti-ego position, at least as of 2004. I saw this for myself at his International Enneagram Association (IEA) workshop given at the Washington, D.C., Conference, when he asked everyone present to chastise their ego for all the trouble it had caused them.[13] What an uproar there was—a ballroom full of people "emoting" so loudly that the groups in all the neighboring rooms complained.[14]

When I looked closely at Naranjo's books, more anti-ego material emerged; it's documented in Chapter 9 of *Archetypes of the Enneagram*. Although much of Naranjo's work

focuses on ego reduction from a psychological or psychiatric perspective, some of what he writes crosses over into a dimension which reminds us more of an Old Testament prophet:

Become aware of the ego, the illness or infection of sin that comes to us through generations—the visages of the accusing, fictitious Adversary—so as to be able to shield ourselves from its temptation" (*The Enneagram of Society*, p. 17).

This is a very negative view indeed—and one that closely echoes Ichazo's characterization of ego as "diabolical." Here ego is portrayed as an actively subverting force which tempts and deceives. As such, it recalls to mind a pre-modern era of fear and superstition, when accusations of witchcraft or heresy could destroy a person's life. These sentiments echo those expressed by Ichazo at the time when Naranjo received the teachings on the enneagram, around 1970. However, *The Enneagram of Society* was not published during the 1970s, but in 1995—and it was reprinted in 2004. The above-cited passage is from the Author's Preface, where it is included as one of the three main purposes of the book. Accordingly, we may conclude that Naranjo's negative views of the ego have remained steadfast throughout the years.

For better or worse, Naranjo is probably the single most influential individual within the enneagram community. He was the one who originally "leaked" the enneagram teachings to his students in the 1970s and 80s, who in turn leaked it to others. Every time the teachings were passed along, however, what remained was the central notion that ego obstructs essence—and that the nine types = nine kinds of obstruction.

Earlier, I said that Almaas and Maitri may have felt obliged to honor this idea, because they saw it as a core concept in enneagram teachings as imparted to them by Naranjo. However, we have now seen how (for Ichazo, anyway) this core idea that ego obscures essence has been recast in a much more positive light.

The fact that this is possible should tell us that it is not a core concept—that it is part of an interpretive framework that can change, depending upon cultural trends. But if this is to happen, we need to find an alternative way of answering an important question: *Why do so many of us feel cut off from our spiritual origins as adults? If ego does not cut off access to essence, what accounts for this sense of alienation?*

Relative vs Absolute Essence

Romanticism tells us that we feel cut off from our spiritual origins because we *are* cut off from them: that we have lost something we once had. In the enneagram teachings, we each lost the Holy Idea associated with our type—an Idea that was displaced by ego.[15]

This is a powerfully appealing argument, because it seems to reveal why infants have such a wonderful aura of spiritual innocence, while we (alas) do not!

But as pointed out earlier, even if babes *are* full of light, it's the reflected light of Spirit, not the light they are emitting themselves. Basking in the light of Spirit does not make them enlightened (just as sitting with a spiritual teacher does not make us enlightened, however blissful the experience). Transformation is about cultivating the ability to become a *source* of illumination, not just a recipient.

But to do this requires us to develop the structures of consciousness necessary for that purpose, starting with the structures of rational (ego) consciousness.

Admittedly, this process is not without its problems. And this is why it's easy to feel cut off from our essential nature—not because it goes away or is displaced by ego, but because of psychic splits and misalignments.

Wilber explains how this works by saying that while we can never lose touch with our essential nature as an absolute (our Ground of Being), we *can* lose touch with aspects of essence that develop at various stages. So he makes a distinction between two kinds of essence: *absolute* essence and *relative* essence. (He also calls the latter *essence-at-that-stage*).

He observes that, while essence in the absolute sense can never be lost, relative essence *can* be lost, repressed, denied, or distorted at any stage of development. When this happens, it can indeed result in psychic holes and feelings of dissociation.[16]

Here Wilber is treating essence both as (a) something innate and intrinsic to our being and (b) something that has the possibility of *being developed* during the course of our lifetime. So relative essence is something new, a new potential that can be birthed into life, if only we can discover how to bring it forth.

If our development is obstructed for some reason at a particular stage, this may interfere with the unfolding of relative essence at that stage—which can in turn, Wilber observes, result in the development of psychic "holes" and defenses.

However, what interests Wilber about these defenses is that they have the potential not only to block out primitive impulses (some of which may actually *need* to be blocked out, at least for a time), but to block out higher impulses, as well. As he observes, "A rigid boundary is a rigid boundary. A wall that keeps out *id* is a wall that can keep out God as well" (p. 371).

For this reason, he says, it's important to identify and heal psychic holes—which is one reason he applauds the Diamond Approach.

But Wilber is firm in his position that the loss of relative essence is due to *malformations* in the developing (ego) self, not the mere *existence* of an ego self. As he observes, the problems we encounter during the developmental process are often not a "no" but a case of "not yet." Ego brings differentiation, and differentiation paves the way for the emergence of higher states of consciousness.

While it's true that differentiation can be insufficient, distorted, or overdeveloped, there's another possibility: that it can develop in a relatively healthy fashion, so that we become differentiated and balanced, but not dissociated. But for diehard Romantics, it's hard to conceive of differentiation without dissociation. This is why, from their point of view,

> [ego] development must be viewed as primarily a dismal downhill slide, because every normal differentiation is going to be interpreted as a horrible dissociation, fragmentation, alienation (p. 149).

A Positive Alternative

Sigmund Freud is not usually regarded as someone who focused on the bright side of human nature. But even Freud saw the development of ego as something positive, because of its power to contain the instinctive impulses of a primitive *id*. Only during the 1960s did the focus shift to ego as the pos-

sible cause of our psychological incompleteness, mostly because ego was seen as something that blocked access to higher states of consciousness.[17]

What did not change at that time was the ongoing focus in clinical psychology on what is *wrong* with human psychology instead of what is *right*. Freud and his fellow psychoanalysts believed that focusing on the nature of pathology was the way to eliminate pathology. And this focus on pathology set the tone for most clinical work done during the 20th century.

As recently as 2009, when psychiatrist Daniel Siegel asked an audience of mostly mental health professionals how many of them had actually had coursework on mental *health* (as opposed to mental *illness*), very few hands went up. Siegel said that he asks this question all the time, always eliciting the same result. He wondered aloud how we are ever going to be able to help people become healthy if all we ever study is mental illness.

Psychologist Martin Seligman had begun wondering the same thing a few years before. Seligman was a social and clinical psychologist who became famed for his research on depression, research intended to yield up insights that Seligman could use to help his depressed patients obtain some measure of well-being. And by all objective standards, he did very well for himself: he became extremely successful as the most well-known researcher in his field; his work on learned helplessness even gained him a permanent spot in the history books.

There was only one problem. Despite all of his knowledge and his insights into the nature of depression—which he shared with his patients—all this insight didn't seem to translate into happier lives. As Seligman himself puts it, "I thought I would then get a happy patient. But I never did. [Instead] I got an *empty* patient."[18]

"There must be a better way," he thought, and set about finding it. And that's when his focus began to shift. Instead of concentrating on depression and depressed people, he started focusing on happiness and successful people. This was a huge shift for him, and it wasn't easy to make the transition. But he persisted in his efforts, eventually coming to see that eliminating depression and facilitating happiness are two entirely different things.

This shift led to a new kind of psychology—positive psychology—dedicated to helping people *flourish*, where flourishing is defined as having positive emotion, meaning, good work, and positive relationships.[19]

What if we were to apply those same lessons to the enneagram? What if we were to shift our focus from looking at "negatives" to looking a "positives"? What if we were to think of ways that our type helps us transform? This is not hard to do, once we're able to grasp Seligman's key point: that *eliminating a negative does not create a positive.*

The reason why eliminating depression doesn't create happiness is the same reason why eliminating personality doesn't create essence: because neither happiness nor essence are passive states, just waiting to be uncovered. Rather, they are dynamic potentials that must be developed. Like all attributes, the degree to which they are developed depends upon the degree of attention they receive—an idea often expressed by the idea that "energy follows attention," an expression often used in enneagram work. If energy follows attention, wouldn't it be better to put

more attention on the positive potentials of the nine types?

Although G. I. Gurdjieff spoke of personality and essence, he never saw personality as inhibiting the development of essence. He simply saw them as *two separate lines of development* (an approach Wilber would surely appreciate). Gurdjieff also observed that personality development is essential for inner work, maintaining instead that what matters is our ability to allow personality to become passive [receptive] so that essence can become active (presumably meaning that personality needs to become receptive to guidance). What really matters, then, is *our ability to develop an appropriate relationship between the two.*[20] (Gurdjieff also had very positive things to say about individuality, noting that those who have achieved the highest level of development "possess individuality in the highest degree").[21]

Gurdjieff theorist A. G. E. Blake takes a similar position, noting that "the lower self and higher self have to fuse," and more significantly, that *"the more common idea that the lower self has to be removed or neutralized misconstrues transformation."*[22]

Ken Wilber is even more pointed in his support for ego/personality development. In *One Taste* (2000), he points out that egolessness does not mean "the absence of a functional self (that's a psychotic, not a sage); it means that one is no longer exclusively identified with that self" (p. 276). He goes on to say that people tend to have an idealized picture of saints and sages as being devoid of personality:

> The typical person wants the spiritual sage to be 'less than a person', somehow devoid of all the messy, juicy, complex,

pulsating, desiring, urging forces that drive most human beings (p. 277).

But Wilber says that being "egoless" does not mean being *less* than personal, but actually being *more* than personal. It means we possess "all the normal personal qualities, *plus* some transpersonal ones." He observes that the great movers and shakers in the spiritual world

> were not small egos; they were in the very best sense of the term, big egos... the great yogis, saints, and sages accomplished so much precisely because they were not timid little toadies but great big egos, plugged into a radiant Kosmic course...Put bluntly, the ego is not an obstruction to Spirit but a radiant manifestation of Spirit (p. 277).

Balancing the Personality

As noted above, a "passive" personality is a personality that is receptive or attentive to higher guidance—that can (in Wilber's words) be plugged into "the radiant Kosmic course." Notice how similar this is to the holarchic idea of opening to the higher and caring for the lower. When this is how we approach life, we tend to come into balance as individuals, families, and communities.

A balanced personality is aligned with life. But for personality to become aligned, it must first develop. And this development must be genuinely encouraged (not merely tolerated). If we raise a child with mere tolerance, it does not develop properly.

If we give to personality our positive energy and attention, it does not become inflated, just confident. But this only works if we simultaneously develop both its expressive and receptive qualities. What we call ego inflation develops when we lack receptivity.

But a lack of receptivity is unfortunately quite common in modern culture, where so very few of us are taught how to pay attention to inner cues—to dreams, intuitions, gut feelings, inner voices, the sense of "knowing," synchronicities, near-death experiences, subtle impressions, and inner visions. Nor are we taught how to tell the difference between genuine intuitions and those rooted in fear, superstition, or delusion. Finally, we have few if any culturally acceptable spiritual practices that are specifically designed to enable personality to receive and integrate the potent energy from higher sources.

Between the secularization of modern culture and the long-time Church injunction against involvement in psychic phenomena (or cultivating methods of "direct knowing"), there's practically nothing in our culture to support the development of receptivity. If anything, the opposite is true: we're taught either to discount our inner experiences or to interpret them in a way that robs them of their power.

So the problem in a nutshell is not too much ego but *too little receptivity*, leading to imbalance—the kind of imbalance that makes us feel like "hungry ghosts." Retro-Romanticism is the philosophy associated with that hunger. It has come to cast such a long shadow over Western culture because it represents the futile cry of people raised without the least idea how to spiritually nourish themselves.

But this can change. And it *is* changing as we speak, because more and more individuals are discovering the lost secret of how to cooperate with life instead of competing with it. While competition is not necessarily a bad thing (as long as it is done in the right spirit), competing with life—especially in a grim, survival-of-the-fittest fashion—is a *lose-lose* proposition: we lose the ability to feel spiritually connected with the Kosmos and the Kosmos loses the opportunity to bring something into the world through each of us. Once we grasp the way that life really works, we can use that insight to turn things around, both individually and collectively.

In this chapter, the focus has been on using Wilber's pre/trans fallacy to demonstrate the disadvantages of retro-Romanticism as a guiding philosophy for enneagram work. I have used Wilber's critique of A. H. Almaas' approach to transformation as the focal point of our discussion, because it is so illuminating. However, it's important to note that despite my critique of Almaas' and Maitri's arguments, I greatly respect their efforts to put enneagram theory on a more solid theoretical footing. It is only because they made the effort to do so that any critique is possible. And it is only because of such efforts that fields are able to evolve.

But this still leaves us with the need to find some way to move beyond the ego-versus-essence way of thinking. Interestingly, the solution may be quite close to home. Because before Ichazo taught the personality enneagram, Gurdjieff taught the process enneagram—and the process enneagram is oriented towards transformation, not fixation. It thus depicts nine stages in transformation, stages that can be associated with the nine personality types, giving rise to the idea of *nine transformation types*.

In the next three chapters, I'll explain how to use the process enneagram to broaden our view of the personality enneagram types. Chapter 6 describes the process enneagram and the nine stages of transformation it depicts; Chapter 7 shows the parallels between these nine transformational stages and the nine personality types; and Chapter 8 presents an integrated ("one enneagram") model and explores some of the many ways that we can use such an Integral Enneagram model to explore the link between individuality and transformation.

Notes

1. A. H. Almaas is the pen name of Hameed Ali.

2. See Note 11, in Wilber's *The Eye of Spirit* (2001), pp. 365–377.

3. "The Chamber of Maiden Thought," Chapter 4, pp. 82-94, from *Wordsworth: The Visionary Gleam*, www.artlit.info/pdfs/Chamber-Wordsworth.pdf; accessed 11/20/11.

4. Focusing on the idea of lost innocence reminds me of a period when my Goddaughter Hanna began to grow out of toddlerhood and the conflicted feelings this produced in me. She had just turned two when her family came to live with me for two years. A delightfully spunky toddler, she was always on the go. She talked a blue streak and loved to watch airplanes, jumping up and down whenever they flew overhead. Her social skills weren't exactly stellar, though; she also had a disconcerting habit of biting other toddlers so she could snatch their toys!

Her parents were upset, of course; but she was not really malicious, she just knew that biting would make them drop the toy, and right away! We had to teach her that biting could produce less desirable results, as well, like a scolding followed by a timeout. But she didn't really understand much yet; she just wanted to explore the world and the interesting things in it. Neither did she understand our terror when she would take off running in a crowd (just for fun) or sneak away to play hide-and-seek in the clothing racks at Penney's.

While all these behaviors made her a handful, they were also hilarious, because she was so completely spontaneous and innocent of any intent to harm.

By the time she was three, she had begun to change. Now potty-trained and no longer biting, she became confident and then over-confident, to the point of megalomania. "I know everything!" she would proudly proclaim to anyone who would listen, very pleased with herself and her evolving ability to whine, wheedle, and manipulate the adults round her. As a four-year-old, she learned more: how to pose for the camera and say clever things, hoping for adult approval. She behaved for a year or two like one of the less endearing contestants in a child beauty pageant.

These changes were painful to witness. Where was the funny little toddler whose artlessness I so enjoyed? Alas, that toddler had vanished, never to return. Of course, I still loved and cherished my little friend, but I also grieved the loss of the baby she had been.

Meanwhile, she continued to grow, happily oblivious to my sense of loss. She was especially pleased with the "potty" jokes she told (although they were the kind that only another five-year-old would appreciate). But she eventually emerged from the potty joke stage, learning how to read, write, and ride a bike. Kind and protective, she looked out for other children, especially those bullied at school. She also became Mommy's helper and a responsible big sister to her little brother (even when she complained it was hard). Plus, she was fun to talk to; she said interesting things and asked thought-provoking questions. As I write, she is growing into a lovely young woman, both inside and outside.

I'm happy to report that I no longer miss the toddler I once knew. I still remember that time with fondness, but I no longer feel the pain of that loss. Now that period has became a source of entertaining stories, part of the family folklore. Both she and her brother both love to hear these stories about a time they can no longer remember but that the rest of us remember very well.

What I noticed with both of them is how eager they were even as babies to grow up. They enjoy the stories now that they are older, but when they were little, they did everything possible to be big: to move, to crawl, to walk. They didn't want to lie around communing with the Infinite; they wanted to be in the here and now, fully involved in life.

This experience made me wonder whether the "clouds of glory" we see in infants is something for them or whether it's more for the adults that are their caregivers. For it's we who appreciate the "clouds of glory," not the little ones. (It's like those stories my mom used to tell me about walking miles to school as a child; she wanted me to appreciate the much shorter walk I had to make. But I couldn't; I had never had her experiences so I couldn't use them to appreciate my easier situation. I had to have my own experiences.)

When I look back on my own childhood, my earliest memory is of being in the hospital steam room for tonsillitis—common among children in my day, when so many parents smoked. I was maybe a year old—old enough to have definite preferences but too young to verbally express them. The nurse said cheerily, "I'm going to bring in a little baby now." I clearly remember my dismay. I mean, who really wants a screaming baby around when you're sick? But what could I do? I couldn't say much and nobody would have listened, anyway.

I remember having that feeling a lot during early childhood—the feeling of having no control and wishing I did. Memories like this make me skeptical about whether infancy and early childhood is equivalent to a spiritual state from the infant's point of view.

5.   Naranjo's SAT group is named after the Seekers After Truth (SAT) group established by Gurdjieff during the early 20th century.

6.   Each quality of essence is said to correspond with one of the nine enneagram points, although Almaas seldom if ever mentions the enneagram directly in any book except *Facets of Unity* (1998).

7.   Winnicott did not view the annihilation of Being or the development of a false self as an inevitable part of early development. Winnicott instead focused most of his attention on the importance of early holding environment in promoting psychological well-being and on identifying the factors that characterized a healthy holding environment (such as "good-enough" mothering). See the discussion in Chapter 19 of Rodman's *Winnicott* (2003), the discussion on Winnicott's work in Chapter 2 of Sharf's *Theories of Psychotherapy & Counseling* (2000), or the discussion on Winnicott as http://mythosandlogos.com/Winnicott.html; accessed 11-28-12.

8.   *Enneagram Monthly* interview, June 2001, p. 19.

9.   Here are representative comments about ego and essence from several prominent enneagram teachers:

The child in essence is in a state of free-flowing energy and unbounded consciousness, a consciousness not constrained by ego and personality. In the course of childhood, the child becomes fixated in a certain way: it becomes crystallized, or stuck in a certain style of personality. – Don Riso

The ego is trying to imitate real qualities of Being, but it's not able to because it's an artificial construct…We have certain essential qualities, but they're blocked by our ego…The fixation, the whole personality really, is like a stuck part. – Russ Hudson

What replaces the essential connection with the environment connection is what spiritual tradition would call a false personality. – Helen Palmer

As I said in the main text, such comments are ubiquitous in the enneagram community; I include them here only to illustrate the degree to which these ideas are not just regarded as views or theories, but accepted facts.

10. The reference to a lower ego suggests the existence of a higher ego, but Ichazo makes no mention of it.

11. Address to the Enneagram Congress, Alsace, France (May 11-12, 2007).

12. It is likely that Ichazo's shift in perspective is due to the recognition that the "ego as enemy" position is no longer of interest to the vast majority of people in 21st century culture.

13. International Enneagram Association Conference, Washington, D.C. (August 2004).

14. Despite claims since the 1960s for the cathartic value of forcefully expressing negative emotions (common in approaches such as primal scream therapy and gestalt psychology), research shows that this approach does little to resolve emotional conflict; see, e.g., *Expressing Emotion: Myths, Realities, and Therapeutic Strategies* (1999), by Eileen Kennedy-Moore & Jeanne C. Watson.

15. As Almaas puts it in *Facets of Unity* (1998), "The delusion of separateness from the whole takes nine forms, representing the loss of the nine Holy Ideas" (p. 12).

16. For a discussion of the pathologies that can unfold during different stages of development, see either Chapter 4 in Wilber's *Transformations of Consciousness* (1986), pp. 107–126, or Chapter 8, "The Self and Its Pathologies," in *Integral Psychology* (2000), pp. 91–100. (See also the discussion in Chapter 11.)

17. As a young adult in the 1960s, I remember quite well how people discovered higher states through psychedelics and came to believe that wiping out ego was the key to accessing those states. For a discussion, see my article, "Deconstructing the Freudian Enneagram," available at my website; http://www.enneagramdimensions.net/articles/type_is_with_us_at_birth_part_II.pdf#start.

18. *Flourish* (2011), p. 54.

19. See Seligman's website for more information on positive psychology (http://www.authentichappiness.sas.upenn.edu/Default.aspx); see also the January 2000 issue of *American Psychologist* for background and research on positive psychology.

20. *In Search of the Miraculous* (1977/2001), p. 164.

21. Ibid., p. 310.

22. *The Intelligent Enneagram* (1996), p. 138, *emphasis* mine.

6

THE PROCESS ENNEAGRAM

The ideal meal contains the entire spectrum of qualities: it is at the right temperature; it has the right appearance; it has the right taste; it nourishes the body; it nourishes the feelings; it nourishes thought; it nourishes the community; it is a sacrament.
– A. G. E. Blake

WHAT IS A HUMAN LIFE? Where does it come from and what is it about? How can we chart a course in life that satisfies our need to feel happy not solely in the sense of satisfying our material and emotional wants, but happy in the sense of achieving what the Greeks called *eudaimonia* (where we meaningfully experience the presence of our "indwelling spirit")?

If we look to a purely biological model of evolution to answer such questions, we are going to run up against the limits of such a model very quickly, as noted in Chapter 1. There is simply no way within the parameters of scientific materialism to evaluate a human life from a qualitative perspective; this is one of Ken Wilber's objections to the hegemony of scientific materialism.

If we expand our horizons to embrace a view of evolution rooted in something beyond scientific materialism, we may be able to imagine an evolutionary path that is not a random process involving chance factors, but an intentional process arising out of the in-

nate desire to attune to the universal intelligence that animates the Kosmos.

This universal intelligence is the same intelligence that Gurdjieff considered a defining attribute of the enneagram—which is why he maintained that "all knowledge can be included in the enneagram."[1] If it seems strange to associate a geometric symbol with intelligence, it is only because modernity—for all its wonders—has lost touch with certain forms of symbolic wisdom known to the Pythagoreans and other esoteric schools. One of the lost secrets of these schools concerns the ability of geometric forms to "hold" specific forms of Divine knowledge, which is why certain forms are described as sacred.[2]

According to Gurdjieff, the enneagram is such a form—which is why he emphasized the importance not only of its teachings, but its actual geometry, as well.

Currently, the geometric form we call the "enneagram" is used for two seemingly unrelated purposes: (a) to identify nine points of view that can also be seen as personality types; and (b) to depict the nature of a transformational process that includes nine archetypal stages.

But if the geometry is identical, how can the two enneagram systems be entirely different? I had to conclude that they can't, that ultimately,

one geometry = one system

The only problem was finding the missing link that made two systems into one. And this was not so easy.

But I finally found that link upon reading a short section in Nathan Bernier's *The Enneagram: Symbol of All And Everything* (2003), pp. 325–337. This section begins with the question, "At what point do our endeavors fail?" The author proceeded to address that question in a way that explained the challenges encountered at each of the nine steps on the enneagram circle, where each step represented a stage through which we pass in transformational work. Many of these challenges sounded a lot like descriptions of type "fixations," despite the fact that Bernier's book is about the Gurdjieff (process) enneagram, not the personality enneagram. Thus, reading Bernier's analysis of the challenges made it possible to discern clear parallels between the process enneagram's nine stages of transformation and the personality enneagram's nine types and their respective motivations.

The more I juxtaposed the two systems, the more parallels emerged. However, what also emerged was the outlines of an approach for exploring the relationship between core motivation (as determined by our type) and our *dharma* or path in life (as determined by

the *position of our type within the transformational cycle*). This was a new and unexpected—but highly intriguing—development, because it had the potential to help people more fully understand the inner dynamics that drive the *dharma*. While it won't explain every last detail, it will explain how our core motivation determines the kind of challenges, attitudes, and lessons that are particularly relevant for someone of our type.

It can reveal why, for example, one person seems most "in sync" with life when engaged in humanitarian work while another seeks out tasks requiring great mechanical or intellectual precision. Or why some people are at their best in a chaotic or novel situation while others function optimally with more structure. Or why one person's spiritual path is another's spiritual dead-end.

These are critical issues to address, because while most people in theory believe that "everybody is different," in reality, individuals have a strong tendency to see their own point of view as more basic, worthwhile, valid, or objective than other points of view. Without realizing it, we tend to believe that the best way to solve problems is by converting others to the "correct" point of view. Thus, one of the biggest benefits of doing enneagram work is coming to realize that there is no one correct point of view—that people truly do have different perspectives, and that problem-solving is best accomplished by tackling it from multiple points of view, not just one.

But in my experience, this work is much enhanced when we (a) adopt a "type as potential" point of view and (b) begin to see how the type's position on the circle affects the role it plays in human evolution. I began to explore this dynamic in *Archetypes of the Enneagram* (see especially Chapters 4 and 7); I continue that exploration here.

In this chapter, we'll start by looking at Gurdjieff's enneagram as it is used to describe a transformational process, such as the transformation of food into a meal, by theorists such as J. G. Bennett, A. G. E. Blake, and Nathan Bernier. Then we'll look at how it can be used to describe another sort of transformation: the transformation of the characters in a dramatic story. We'll end with an imaginary trip around the enneagram where we look at the 18 personality wing types as roles we assume as we traverse the transformational arc, each of which naturally arises as the result of what directly precedes it.

A Geometry of Transformation

The process or transformational enneagram is the original enneagram taught by G. I. Gurdjieff in the early 20th century. As the name suggests, it focuses on ways in which something is changed (i.e., transformed) over time. Thus, the nine-pointed process enneagram breaks the transformational process into nine stages (Fig. 6-1). In *Enneagram Studies*, J. G. Bennett says that the enneagram is the "simplest and most natural way of looking at events and the way they occur" (p. 22). It can describe the life cycle of an organism, the creation of an invention, or the unfolding of a dramatic story. Whatever it describes, the process depicted on the enneagram is innately transformational or alchemical: it starts with raw or untransmuted substances and ends with a product that embodies those substances in a higher form.

The nature of transformational process is often described by using the example of cooking a meal in a restaurant. There are essentially three phases in the process: **Preparation**, **Execution**, and **Realization** (Fig. 6-2).[3] Below, we'll proceed through each phase as an exercise in seeing the process enneagram in action.

But a few observations are in order beforehand. First, as originally mentioned in Chapter 3 and shown in Fig. 3-5, the cycle depicted by the process enneagram is actually an upwardly-trending *spiral*—which is why the ending point of digestion is higher than the starting point of initiation in Fig. 6-2. This means that, according to process enneagram theory, transformation is not a zero sum game (i.e., it is not based on a retro-Romantic model) but is rather a cumulative process in which each stage through which we pass forms the foundation for the next stage of development

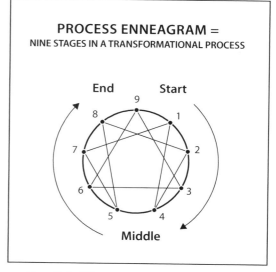

Fig. 6-1. The process enneagram.

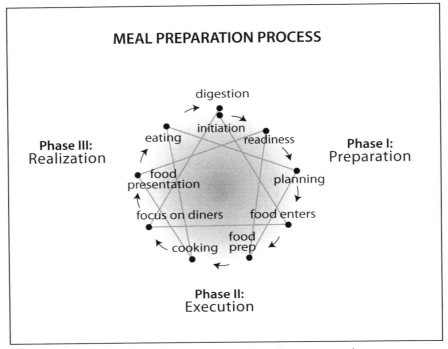

Fig. 6-2. Meal preparation as a tranformational process.

(an idea congruent with Wilber's "transcend-and-include" approach to transformation).

Second, in the step-by-step process descriptions below, there are references to the connecting points, so it is useful to understand the role played by the connecting points on the process enneagram.

On the personality enneagram, the connecting points depict relationships between different personality points of view. On the process enneagram, they symbolize two aspects of transformation: the *eternal* (as represented by the inner triangle Point 3-6-9) and the *ever-changing* (as represented by the hexad Points 1-4-2-8-5-7). If we think of the

physical part of a transformational process as following the path around the circle (traversing Points 0-1-2-3-4-5-6-7-8-9), the lines linking the inner triangle points (Points 3-6-9) define the parameters within which the process takes place; the lines linking the hexad points describe the flow of energy (intentions, thoughts, and emotions) backwards and forwards through *time*.

Although our main focus in this chapter and the next is on the material process of transformation (the movement around the outer circle), there is also some discussion of the influence of the connecting points on what unfolds at each stage.[4]

Three Major Phases

As mentioned above, the process of transforming food into a fully prepared meal consists of three major phases—preparation, execution, and realization—each of which is described below.

PHASE ONE (Preparation) starts at the top of the enneagram, with imagining what kind of meal(s) we as the chef might prepare, until our imaginings eventually impel us to start the actual planning of the meal-producing activities, which means moving from *Point 0/9* to Point 1, where we are beginning a new cycle. At *Point 1*, we have the kitchen, with its staff and equipment, ready to begin. We must start by thinking ahead, first deciding which equipment is needed for food preparation, which begins at Point 4. We must also have the imagination to generally envision the meal at Point 7. As we move into concrete planning *(Point 2)*, we have got to care enough about the meal to make it something special; we also have to begin to envision the meal-making process much more concretely, thinking especially about both preparation (Point 4) and the finished product as it will eventually be served to a customer (Point 8).

PHASE TWO (Execution) begins with the dramatic shift from mental preparation to the physical preparation of food. At *Point 3*, the food enters the process, thus kicking off this shift in perspective. *Point 4* represents the initial phase of food preparation, where the raw food is selected and prepared for cooking (transformation); this is the point at which mental planning begins to turn into a tangible reality. So there is a greater level of commitment from this point on. This is why, during the beginning of actual food preparation, it is important for us to mentally check back frequently (connecting with Points 1 and 2), to make sure that what is being done is really in accord with our original intentions. Connecting with Point 2 also means maintaining our ability to care about what we are doing.

At Point 4, we have got to make a more serious commitment to what we are doing; however, at this point, our plans are not set in stone. Our decisions are not irrevocable. So if a mistake is discovered, it can still be fixed. However, as the preparation proceeds, it becomes more and more difficult to change course. The transition from 4 to 5 represents the irrevocable decision to begin cooking the food, at which point permanent transformations begin to take place. By *Point 5*, the cooking is in full swing. Although there is still checking going on, it is now in anticipation of how the food will be presented (Point 7) and the dining experience itself (Point 8).

At *Point 6*, there is another dramatic shift, as the focus of activity switches from the kitchen to the dining room. Our role as chef is to step back and allow the server to take center stage, so that the food can be presented to the diners for their appraisal.

PHASE THREE (Realization) refers to the stage in which final preparations are made for the serving of the meal—and the stage at which the owner, chef, and staff are about to find out whether all their imaginings, plans, and preparations will meet the expectations of their customers, who are the ones that will actually evaluate the dining experience. *Point 7* represents the presentation of the food by the waiter, who must be aware of what meal was originally ordered (Point 1) and when to serve the meal, so that it is hot (Point 5). If the presentation is not appetizing, this can short-circuit the entire process (as in the case where the food is cold or the plate is sloppily arranged). If the diners find the presentation unsatisfactory, they may refuse the meal. Alternatively, diners who are especially pleased with the presentation may connect with Point 5 (wondering how the preparation was carried out) or Point 1 (praising its original conception).

But it's at **Point 8** where the ultimate evaluation occurs, because this is the place where the diners actually taste the food. At this point, the waiter usually asks whether "everything is all right," hoping for a positive response. If the food is well-received, the waiter breathes a sigh of relief; his cycle of service is complete. The diners, too, are satisfied: they have received what they desired: there is no need for re-cooking (Point 5) or choosing another entree (Point 2).[5]

The move to **Point 9** brings another shift in emphasis, because it is connected with the end of one cycle and the beginning of another. For the diners, it represents the hidden process whereby the food is digested and assimilated into the body. For the wait staff, it is where they clear the table and reset it for the next set of diners. For the kitchen staff, it's where they clean up the dirty dishes and (at the end of service) the entire kitchen, in preparation for the next day. For the chef, it's where she evaluates the success of the night's menu and thinks about what to serve the next day. For the owner, it's where she counts the day's receipts and evaluates the overall functioning of the restaurant on this particular day. Thus, symbolically, Point 9 is the point where the lessons of the previous cycle are as-

similated and become the experiences upon which we can draw in the future.

The Nature of Evolution

The example of making a meal is particularly appropriate as an analogy for the transformation of human consciousness, as J. G. Bennett makes quite clear on p. 10 of *Enneagram Studies*. Bennett says that we are involved in three different processes in life: having life experiences, developing an individual soul, and serving "some great [spiritual] purpose." Using the kitchen analogy, he likens our life experiences to the kitchen, our soul to the meal, and Spirit to the dining room (the setting for the "cosmic banquet"; Fig. 6-3).

Using this analogy, we can surmise that we evolve by having experiences in life, experiences that allow us to develop what Jung termed "personality": what I would term a *mature* or *developed* personality—or perhaps a personality with *character*, i.e., the kind of personality that can serve as a foundation for real spiritual work.

One of the most interesting things about this model is that it is based on a service-oriented approach to spirituality, where the purpose of spiritual development is to serve (i.e., to be a "meal" for) something greater than ourselves. When this happens, we become part of a greater whole. Such an approach, which is obviously holarchic, offers a way to explain how an entity at one level of the Kosmos (the level of the individual) energetically partakes of the energy of something at a higher level ("Spirit"): *by becoming receptive in such a way that the individual can be absorbed at some level into the greater/deeper/higher reality.*

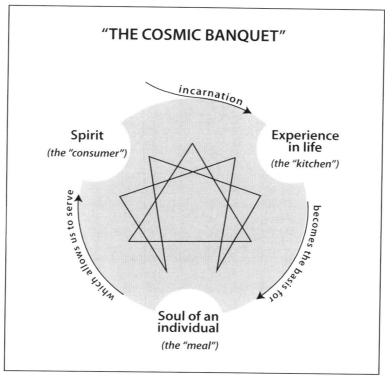

Fig. 6-3. Experience produces Soul
which becomes the food for Spirit.

However, in order to make that transition, we need a special stimulus that allows us to make the leap from one level (octave) to another—a stimulus referred to in the enneagram literature as a *shock*. The reason we need shocks to effect that transformational leap is that each level/octave is qualitatively distinct (just as, e.g., the world of emotions is different from the world of logic). So it takes extra energy to "pierce the veils" that separate the levels.[6]

There are three shock points on the enneagram, each of which is discussed below.

Enneagram Shock Points

Fig. 6-4 illustrates the three shocks points, which depict shifts that are not just a simple progression from one stage to the next, but a discontinuity followed by a major reorientation of emphasis. So there's a shift from one frame of reference to another, plus the introduction of new energy that has the potential to change the process in an innovative way.

The discontinuity introduces a feeling of uncertainty (a "hazard") into the mix. That uncertainty both creates dramatic tension

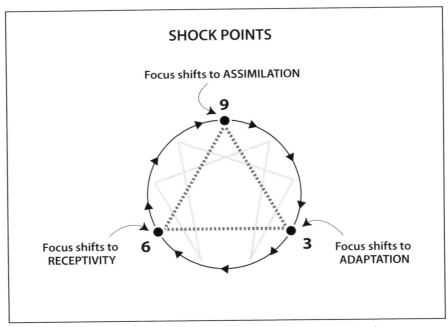

Fig. 6-4. Three shock points: where something new enters the process.

and the circumstances whereby transformation can take place.

In our kitchen example, at the ***first shock point*** (Point 3) food is introduced into the process. What could be shocking about that? Quite a lot—as any head chef knows very well. Suppose the food the cook planned to use is not available? Or it turns out to be of inferior quality? Or it does not arrive on schedule? These are just a few of the many things that can go awry once the actual food arrives—and which can cause the cook to retrace his steps, either to draw up new menus (Point 2) or to reconceptualize his whole approach (Point 1). Even if the food is just right, the shift from planning to execution means a major reorientation in focus, because it is the first time that the kitchen staff is actually

working with the materials in a way that requires ongoing engagement (= ADAPTATION).

At the ***second shock point*** (Point 6) the food has been cooked—but as it leaves the kitchen, it enters an entirely different domain: the domain of the dining room. So again, the reference point for the action shifts, but in even a more radical sense than before, because at Shock 1, only the activity changes (planning becomes execution). But at Shock 2, we see a shift in action (from making the meal to pleasing the audience = RECEPTIVITY), a shift in role players (from the chef to the waiters & diners), and a shift in power dynamics (because it is now the diners and not the chef that hold the power). At that point, what matters is the diners' response to the presentation of the meal (Point 7) and the diners' partaking of it (Point 8). If the meal has been properly prepared *from the perspective of the diner*, the realization of the goal is complete. If not, a new meal must be cooked (Point 5). Success at Point 8 depends in large part upon the degree to which the exercise of imagination at Point 2 (where we must anticipate the wishes of the diners) and understanding at Point 5 (of how to cook the meal in such a way that it can satisfy those wishes).[7]

The **_third shock point_** (Point 9) is extremely mysterious; very little is written about it, other than that it is a necessary part of the transformation process. One online writer confirms that to the extent that a teaching exists, it exists as an oral teaching with a very limited audience, but associates it with higher alchemical processes,[8] processes which I would associate with the integration of the

self into the greater Kosmos at a highly refined level (= ASSIMILATION). So the "cooking" that is associated with this shock point would be hard to translate into concrete terms.

Life as a Dramatic Story

So far, we've looked at transformation in terms of transforming food into a meal, an approach that is often used by Fourth Way (Gurdjieffian) teachers to introduce the system. Another way to understand the process enneagram is in terms of a dramatic story; Blake is fond of this approach, and has used it in Chapter 11 to describe two Arnold Schwarzenegger films, *The Terminator* and *Total Recall*.

I like this approach because it's similar to the story grammar approach used in cognitive psychology to describe how people make

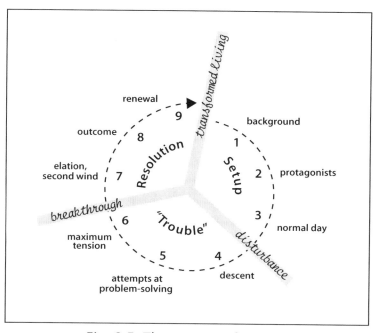

Fig. 6-5. Three parts of a story.

sense of the world: by telling (and living out) their personal stories. These stories have a characteristic structure that can be mapped onto the process enneagram.[9]

Using this story-oriented approach, we can once again divide the transformational process into three parts: Setup, "Trouble,"and Resolution; see Fig. 6-5.[10] Although we'll consider Point 1 the beginning, we could just as easily include the transition from Point 0 to Point 1 as part of the process, because that's the place where something new begins to stir, creating the impetus for some sort of dramatic progression.

SETUP (Points 1-2-3). During this part of a story, we as the readers of a story (or watchers of a film) are provided with the information necessary to understand the story: its genre, structure, and the culture in which the story takes place (**Point 1**). This part of the story is easy to overlook, because it's "just the background." But without it, we would have no way of relating to the story, no way to connect with the storyteller's intentions. In dramas involving moral, social, or political conflicts, understanding the standards that constitute the norm is critical for appreciating the conflicts which later arise.

At **Point 2**, we are introduced to the characters and their relationships with one another. This is important, because it allows us to empathize with them when the going gets tough. Alternatively, if the characters are not very likable, plausible, or interesting, it's the point where we might abandon the story to seek out another.

At **Point 3**, we see how the characters operate in ordinary life: what their habits are, how they get along with one another, and how they move through the day. We see which characters are pretty well-adjusted and which ones are not. We see areas of tension that are held in check by various coping mechanisms, both personal and social. There is usually a foreshadowing of what is to come when these coping mechanisms break down, due to either inner or outer events beyond the control of the protagonists. But at this point, nothing of real consequence has happened; the real action begins with a triggering event that challenges the protagonists' ability to develop new, more creative approaches to problem-solving.

Thus, the purpose of the introductory phase is both to introduce the characters and to establish a norm against which all subsequent activity can be measured. A successful introduction pulls us into another world and makes us interested in the events that are about to unfold there.

"TROUBLE" (Points 4-5-6). However we think of this phase—as the voyage into the unknown, the hero's journey, or the descent into the deep—it's the phase where the main protagonists encounter challenges that will test their resolution, ingenuity, and courage to an unprecedented degree. Calling it "trouble" (which is an intentionally vague term) emphasizes the unknown nature of the challenges involved and the anxiety felt by the main characters, as they find themselves catapulted out of their habitual routines and plunged into the unknown.

Point 4 is where the characters first really come to grips with the need to embrace the changes happening to them in a way that allows the story to unfold as it is meant to. It is called "descent" because it is where we can continue to engage with what is unfolding only by digging deeper into ourselves (i.e., to tap into inner resources not available to the persona self). Point 4 is where the characters *must* engage emotionally with what is about to unfold, so that it becomes a meaningful event in their lives—this is what gives them the impetus to continue. This emotional engagement often involves engaging with one's deeper (and darker) emotions, which is why it can put people into murky psychological territory, where they are in danger of being swamped by the untransmuted (shadow) elements within the psyche. So it's little wonder that the initial reaction is usually denial, followed by weak attempts at maintaining the status quo, which of course doesn't work. The only way forward is to face the problem on its own terms: to emotionally commit to do what is necessary to solve it. Once the characters realize this, the drama begins to unfold. And the characters begin to transform.

The passage from Point 4 to **Point 5** signifies that the characters have been able to work through enough of their inner baggage that they can bear the emotional burden of continued engagement with the problem. So at this point, they go into problem-solving mode in earnest, seeking out some path to resolution. Initially, their solutions are too rooted in habitual thinking to be very effective, and they tend to spectacularly fail. Other solutions are tried, but with unsatisfactory results.

But there is learning going on, nevertheless, as the characters come to understand all the things that *won't* work to solve the problem. At the same time, they are beginning to get more and more exhausted and discouraged; the pain they experience as a result brings out all their remaining negativity. But it can also bring out hidden reserves of strength and unseen qualities of nobility.

It's during this phase that we as third-party observers are particularly able to identify with the travails of the characters, as we remember the times when we were in similar situations. We hope they make it out (just as we hope to find a way out of our own problems).

As the story progresses, the characters often find some way of coping; however, this is not a real solution but a compromise of some sort. They resign themselves to the "new norm" and try to make a life on that basis.

So the move to **Point 6** represents a kind of re-emergence in life—a point in which the characters try to settle into the new norm and re-establish their routines. Things seem to be looking up. But appearances can be deceiving. Because the point of a dramatic story is to depict the transformation of its characters. And at this point, that transformation remains incomplete. As a result, at just about the point when it looks like things are settling down, there is a sudden turn of events that makes it clear that no real resolution is possible without complete transformation: without the hero facing what he fears most. In stories involving a hero and a villain, this is the moment when the two come face to face. The hero discovers that the villain is not vanquished; but happily, he seems less villainous and more accommodating than the hero believed him to be. But just as the hero is breathing a sigh of relief (as the villain is exiting the room), the villain casually turns around and remarks, "Oh, there is just one more small thing I need from you."

And of course, that small thing turns out to be something the hero cannot give without completely compromising himself. The moment he has dreaded is here: he has come face to face with his greatest fear and is completely filled with terror.

At this point, there's no going back to the status quo. The only way forwards is by taking a courageous leap into the unknown—by having the faith to do what he is most afraid to do, trusting that things will work out. So he takes the leap. And in that moment, he is transformed.

RESOLUTION (Points 7-8-9). The leap into the unknown brings a tremendous release of energy and an expansion of consciousness. The sense of elation is overwhelming. Everything in life seems new and interesting.

So at *Point 7*, the characters are filled with wonder; they want nothing more than just to enjoy this fascinating new world of light and joy. In a very real way, they are reborn. But like the newly born, they lack any real focus. So it can be very hard to get motivated at this point, especially where real work is concerned, because it reminds them too much of the constrictions they just escaped! The challenge at this point is to avoid declaring victory prematurely, in order to skate out on responsibility. Thus, in some ways, this is an even tougher challenge than fear because it is so seductive.

Assuming they pass up the temptation to remain as Peter Pans, as the characters approach *Point 8*, they begin to take into themselves the qualities that were previously associated with the world around them. They begin to inwardly embody the victory that is almost at hand.

They feel their own power and ability to take control. The question is, How do they comport themselves at this critical point?

Do they remain focused on the "big picture" or do they get over-confident and bigheaded (which could still cause them to fail at the 11th hour)?

Assuming they achieve their goals, are they gracious victors? Are they grateful for the help they received from others? Do they have a plan for using the momentum they've gained for some greater work?

If they can pass these tests, their arrival at *Point 8* is truly a cause for celebration. It's usually a public celebration intended to honor the victors, in recognition of the fact that the success of a small group (or even one person) elevates the entire community. It reminds the community that what is possible for one, is possible for all. The protagonists themselves understand that their role is not to take advantage of those who honor them but to in turn honor the potential in each individual and do what they can to encourage others to embark on their own journey of transformation. The final test, however, is to willingly step away from the spotlight—to resume their daily lives without constantly looking backwards to their "glory days."

It's at *Point 9* where the protagonists discover whether their transformations will have any lasting impact on their real lives. So while it's the least dramatic-looking (and most hidden) part of the story, it probably the part that actually matters the most in the end.

Having looked at the process of storytelling in a generic way, let's now look at how this process works in real life (or at least, on reality TV!) using the series *Out of the Wild* as an example. In this series, nine individuals are dropped in the wilderness somewhere and must find their way back to civilization—a process that takes an indefinite amount of time (that is, they are not told how long it might take, although in practice, it's about a month). There is no reward for sticking it out other than the satisfaction of making the journey; anyone who wants to opt out at any point can contact a helicopter that will whisk them back to civilization within a couple of hours. So the decision of whether or not to continue is completely up to them.

During the first couple of days, all the participants are determined and optimistic; on camera, they express the reasons why they have decided to challenge themselves in this way and say why they think they have the qualifications necessary to meet the challenges they will encounter (***Point 1***). They meet the other participants and begin to make friends, eager to bond with others on the journey (***Point 2***). They determine what equipment they will take with them, decide how to divide up the gear, and assume initial responsibilities for the welfare of the group (***Point 3***). They are on their way.

Initially, spirits are high. But it's not long before they plunge into the second phase of the journey ("trouble") as hunger, cold, rough terrain, and interpersonal friction begin to take its toll. At this point, the initial resolve of each participant is tested (***Point 4***); people begin to drop out for various reasons, some physical, some psychological. As conditions get tougher, superfluous concerns gradually drop away, one by one. Remaining participants learn to focus only on the things that really matter: food, shelter, physical self-care, and mutual support. They develop problem-solving techniques suitable for the conditions at hand (***Point 5***), gradu-

ally reaching a kind of equilibrium as they slowly adjust to the harsh conditions. However, as the journey wears on, even this new level of equilibrium is challenged as hunger, accidents, and disease continually threaten to tip the balance from bare equilibrium to unsustainability.

At the point of maximum difficulty (when virtually everybody is famished, exhausted, and in pain from various physical maladies), they are confronted with an obstacle that even this intrepid bunch finds hard to contemplate, much less overcome (***Point 6***). In the Alaska cycle (2009), it's the need to cross a pass with deep snow without proper equipment; in the South American cycle (2011), it's the need to portage a heavy raft around a waterfall and deep canyon. In both cases, even these well-seasoned participants initially balk at the news. The only thing that gets them through is their group loyalty and collective desire to support one another.[11]

In *Into the Wild*, the transition to Part III occurs when the group sights the first signs of civilization: the end of the journey appears to be at hand. But the group is still in a very remote area, so they have to maintain discipline and watch for more signs in order to find their way back (***Point 7***). On the two series I watched, both groups managed to avoid getting careless and figured out how to keep it together long enough to make the last moves necessary to find their way back to town, where they were delighted to be greeted by cheering friends and family (***Point 8***). Although this was the end of their journey as far as the series goes, in both cases, it was possible using the Internet to see how the participants fared after returning home (***Point 9***). Listening to their comments and those of their family and friends, it's pretty obvious that those who stuck it out continue to be transformed in a way that engenders continuing transformations in their everyday lives.

So in this respect, *Out of the Wild* represents a modern-day version of the hero's journey, where people test themselves by overcoming a series of increasingly grueling physical, mental, and emotional challenges. The enneagram can describe such a quest because it gives us a method for depicting the archetypal challenges involved at each point in such a journey.

Wings Around the Enneagram

There is one last way we can use the enneagram to describe a transformational cycle. And that is by using the descriptions of the personality enneagram's 18 wing types to describe 18 points in transformation. The following "wings around the enneagram" section is lifted from my first book, *The Positive Enneagram*.

*At the top of the enneagram, we find ourselves in a space of anticipatory expectation. At this point, we're just about to start a new project or cycle, but haven't quite done anything yet. We're simply being in the moment, content but alert. Slowly, something begins to stir. It's subtle, and it creates a slight but definite ripple of interest. We become the **Anticipator (9w1)**.*

*Energy begins to gather and move. It starts to swirl around without much form. This is a time of excitement, but also tension; we sense the need to develop a definite and precise matrix for imposing some sort of order. We are becoming the **Definer (1w9)**.*

*Imposing order on chaos is not an easy task; it requires discipline and concentration. It can also be nerve-wracking, because whatever we do at the start of a project will affect that project all the way through to completion. So it's a serious business. In order to minimize mistakes, we strive to find a way to judge whether we're really on track. So we seek to establish clear standards by which to separate truth from error. Once these standards are in place, we want to ensure they'll be taken seriously. We become the **Reformer (1w2)**.*

*Our efforts to this point have been based on an idealized abstraction. In order to take the next step, we need to involve others in order to humanize our ideals and also enlist support for them. As we do this, we begin to see how those ideals translate into plans with the power to help real people, especially those in need. We become the **Social Worker (2w1)**.*

*Part of the joy of helping others is knowing that we're not alone. We not only enjoy the companionship of others, we also see how other people can act as mirrors for our developing self-image. Each relationship mirrors back different aspects of ourselves, and this gives us an incentive to make more friends and contacts. We're now the **Socializer (2w3)**.*

*We soon realize how having a social network helps us accomplish our goals in life. But we now have so many friends and contacts that we're having a hard time keeping them straight; we have to organize our relationships. As our social proficiency and organizational skills grow, we increasingly find ourselves in positions of organizational responsibility. We're becoming the **Manager (3w2)**.*

Managing people is something we're good at, but we find that relationships can sometimes become messy and even interfere with getting things done. As we become increasingly intrigued by our work, we also become more aware of our-selves as individuals. We seek to develop the skills that enable us to shine as a **Professional (3w4)**.

Over time, we find that being a successful Professional, while rewarding, is not satisfying our deeper needs. Once we've achieved our goals, what next? We realize that we need more than ideals (Point 1), more than contacts (Point 2), or even more than outward success (Point 3). We need a sense of significance or meaning (Point 4). So we begin to engage in our work for its own sake, getting more and more knowledgeable as a **Specialist (4w3)**.

Despite our special skills, we feel increasingly dissatisfied with living on the surface of life. We want to delve deeper, to get to the bottom of who we actually are. We continue to hone our skills but to use them in the service of self-discovery, becoming ever more focused on ways to express our deepest selves. We are now the exquisitely skilled but highly sensitive **Artiste (4w5)**.

Finally, as we encounter the chaotic zone at the bottom of the enneagram, things reach a breaking point, and there's a dramatic collapse of the self as we have known it. The sense of "self-as-role" disappears, replaced by a new and curious-ly impersonal self that is less constrained by the need for social approval. We find ourselves with-out the need to adhere to social norms or even to maintain social appearances. We are now the **Iconoclast** (image-breaker) **(5w4)**.

However, we soon discover that it's exhaust-ing to go around breaking other peoples' images all the time. Also, they don't seem to like it very much. So for the sake of convenience, we allow our natural curiosity to lead us in a new direc-tion, into a space of pure thought and reflection. We find it extremely satisfying to become the **Thinker (5w6)**.

The more we think about things, the more we realize how complex life really is. This under-standing begins to make us a bit nervous. It also slows us down, giving us a tendency to hesitate before we act. Finally, it makes us feel our own aloneness and realize that we need companion-ship to avoid feeling alone and afraid. We seek ways to reestablish our social ties. How can we do this? Perhaps by volunteering to serve the needs of our family and community. We become the **Server (6w5)**.

Through serving, we get used to being around people without feeling uncomfortably intimate. It's easier to relax if we can play a well-defined so-cial role in the family or at work. Later, we begin to explore ways to step outside those roles. We're a little nervous about this but find that humor helps us relax in social situations. It makes other people laugh, too. We've become the **Wit (6w7)**.

The more social approval we get, the more confident we become. We start actually enjoying life, so much so that we tend to brush aside any-thing that might ruin the party. We don't, after all, want to go back to that place where we felt awkward or apprehensive. We amp up our enter-taining skills even more, becoming the life of the party—the **Comedian (7w6)**.

Of course, even humor has its limits. If we're going to continue to grow, we'll have to find new venues for expansion. It's an exciting time. New worlds are opening up for us; we're dazzled by all the things that life has to offer. Buoyed by con-fidence and the sense that life is an adventure, we become increasingly innovative and entrepre-neurial. We're now the **Adventurer (7w8)**.

We travel to the four corners of the world, gar-nering every possible experience we can. We find that we adapt easily to whatever environment we encounter. We collect interesting experiences the *way that some people collect stamps. But eventually, so many adventures takes its toll—we can't go on like this forever! We settle down enough to master "the art of the deal." We become the* **Power Broker (8w7).**

But we haven't quite reached the pinnacle of achievement. We realize that while we've mastered the ability to accomplish a lot of different things, it's much more interesting to focus on just One Big Thing. We turn our entire will in one direction to accomplish some great work that will stand the test of time. As we place the final brick in the edifice we have built, we know we have finally arrived: we are the **Powerhouse (8w9).**

We are now enormously powerful and influential. We've managed to climb out of the laboratory of ideas (Point 5), to apply those ideas to serve others (Point 6), to expand our horizons (Point 7), and to bring all our experiences together to manifest something of substance (Point 8). We've accomplished all of our goals and have nothing left to do.

Ironically, in bringing forth our great accomplishment, we no longer have the freedom we had at earlier stages of our journey. We are now so massively powerful that we literally can't move without affecting everything around us. We're obliged to simply stand still, to be the symbol that inspires others to follow their dreams. We've become the **Mountain (9w8).**

But even the highest mountain doesn't remain a mountain forever. Mountains wear down and dissolve into dust, until eventually there's nothing left. This is the end of the journey. It comes as a relief, because no matter how great the accomplishment, once it's done, it's done. There's nothing left to do, no place left to go. We can't ascend any further—at least not for the moment. All we can do is return whence we came: the primordial Sea (Point 9).

*In this timeless place we remain for a period, assimilating our experiences and recovering our sense of oneness with life. There are no borders or edges here; we bask in the primordial atmosphere of light and love. We experience a sense of fullness that seems to satisfy all our needs....until one day, when there's a stir. Something begins to arise—something new, something that beckons us onward. We become vaguely irritated. We begin to anticipate some sort of change (**9w1**), and the whole cycle begins once more.*

This story describes one cycle in a transformational process. It could be a long cycle or a short cycle; it could be deeply transformative or only moderately so; it could involve all aspects of our lives or just one particular area of life. Also, a lot depends on our temperament, what environmental conditions prevail, and the choices we make along the way. Each choice we make affects the entire cycle, and the power of those choices is greater than we might imagine.

We are now ready to look at the parallels between personality and process in a more direct fashion. That's the topic of Chapter 7.

Notes

1. Ouspensky's *In Search of the Miraculous*, p. 294.

2. The wisdom arising out of sacred geometry is not entirely lost, which is why we find mention of it in esoteric books as *The Secret Teachings of All Ages* (1977) by Manly Hall (see especially "The Life and Philosophy of Pythagoras," pp. *LVI–LXIII*) or books on sacred geometry (e.g., *How the World is Made: The Story of Creation According to Sacred Geometry*, by John Mitchell with Alan Brown, 2009). In *The Enneagram: Symbol of All and Everything* (2003), Nathan Bernier states flatly that "the harmony of the universe is based on the sacred mathematics underlying Creation" (p. 53). Wikipedia has an

entry on the significance of *mandalas* ("sacred energy circles") in Hindu and Buddhist scriptures; we know that Carl Jung created numerous mandalas, which he considered maps of the soul. Sufi teacher Irina Tweedie speaks of the healing power of *yantras* (the geometric equivalent of *mantras*); see www.seekeraftertruth.com/the-laughing-man-interviews-irina-tweedie/; accessed 6-11-11. And see the intriguing work of Dr. Hans Jenny on using wave generators to produce geometric patterns that demonstrate the link between sound vibrations and geometric forms (see Jenny's *Cymatics*, 1967/2001, or /www.cymatics.org/; accessed 6-15-2011 or www.cymatics.org/; accessed 6-15-2011).

3.   I'm using A. G. E. Blake's terminology for the three phases of a process; see Chapter 8 of *The Intelligent Enneagram* (1996) for a discussion.

4.   The significance of the two enneagram figures—hexad and inner triangle—is sufficiently abstruse and/or multi-layered that I can't begin to do it justice here. But the hexad signifies eternal movement while the triangle signifies eternal elements: the Trinity, unity in multiplicity, the presence of higher elements, the introduction of elements outside the process, and the unchanging aspect of life. For those favoring a holarchic perspective, the meaning of particular significance is "unity in multiplicity" (where Point 9 symbolizes unity and Points 3 and 6 represent multiplicity) because this focuses on the need for both wholes and parts in the creation. For a discussion, see Chapters 1 and 2 in *The Intelligent Enneagram* (1996) and pp. 148-149 in *The Enneagram: Symbol of All and Everything* (2003).

5.   For examples of owners and managers who fail to make this connection between Point 2 and 8—and who therefore have no clue as to why their customers do not like their products—see TV's Gordon Ramsey's *Kitchen Nightmares,* Robert Irving's *Restaurant: Impossible,* or Anthony Melchiorri's *Hotel Impossible.*

6.   See the discussion at https://sites.google.com/site/tanranreiki7/invisible-bookstore/in-search-of-the-miraculous-by-ouspensky; accessed 12-2-12.

7.   *The Intelligent Enneagram* (1996), p. 66.

8.   While the focus in spiritual work is generally on moving upwards (which is why, e.g., Wilber has adopted a transcend-and-include approach), information and energy obviously moves in both directions. Blake says that "one of Gurdjieff's crucial questions was how *higher influences reach into the lower worlds,*" p. 53 [*emphasis* his]; see Blake's discussion on pp. 87–90, along with its footnotes. We'll further explore this idea in Chapters 9 and 12, in the discussion on the nature of Divine love (Agape).

9.   For a technically oriented listing of resources on the topic of story grammar, see "Story Understanding Resources," compiled by Erik Mueller (http://xenia.media.mit.edu/~mueller/storyund/storyres.html). For a less technical and livelier introduction, see a ScienceBlog entry: "My Favorite Experiments: Bransford & Johnson," (http://scienceblogs.com/mixingmemory/2007/11/30/my-favorite-experiments-bransf/; accessed 11-5-12).

10.   The approach of dividing cycles into three main parts is particularly favored by those who work with the process enneagram (see, e.g., Chapter 11 in Blake's *Intelligent Enneagram,* 1996, or "Inventing Enneagrams: The 'Dramatic Story' and Two-Force Analysis," by Richard K. Moore, *Enneagram Monthly,* Aug. 1997). This approach is particularly useful for looking at the difficulties encountered as we approach the bottom of the enneagram, difficulties that tend to persist in some form until we reach Point 7; see the discussion on the nadir in Chapter 8.

11.   In the Alaska cycle of *Out of the Wild,* it turned out the participants didn't actually have to make an impossible ascent; just before the climb, there was a trail leading to a rail line; in the South American cycle, they *did* have to make the portage, which they found quite grueling. Interestingly, the four males still there were able to go on mainly due to the encouragement and quiet resolve of the only remaining female, who refused to call it quits. Soon after the portage, the ragged band encountered two natives in a motorized canoe who helped them with the final leg of their journey.

7

PERSONALITY & TRANSFORMATION

The unconscious can be integrated only if the ego holds its ground.
– Carl Jung

PERSONALITY IS A FASCINATING TOPIC. Most people are at least marginally interested in knowing what makes each personality different than all the others. That's why there are so many personality tests around, especially the kind designed to get us a job, a date, or just a better idea of who we are.

On the other hand, "personality" can be a rather confusing term, because it can be used in so many different ways. While most of us see the advantages of an appealing personality—one that helps us elicit political support, attract a partner, or impress a job interviewer—personality is something that can often seem to be as much of a liability as an asset (as when it makes us awkward or self-conscious).

Who has never been dissatisfied with his personality? Who has never wished to have more of some quality and to be rid of another? Who has never felt that there is something more to her that just her personality self—something deeper, higher, or more "real"?

These are common feelings, especially in modern culture, where personality can be so important to success—and yet can also seem like yet another thing to worry about in a world in which our attention is already pulled in a dozen different directions every day. So while we have tons of opportunities to excel as individuals, we may feel burdened by the need to put ourselves forward in a way that makes us feel as though we're moving *away* from who we really are instead of *towards* it.

The result of this conflict is a lot of mixed feelings around the idea of personality. Although we like the ability to make individual choices, we get tired of the need to function as solo operators all the time, especially when it requires us to spend more time cultivating our outer persona than our inner self.

Individuals drawn to spiritual work often feel this conflict most keenly—and are particularly prone to think of personality as more of a burden than a blessing. Also, many spiritual traditions portray the spiritual path as a choice between the self and God—and personality is clearly associated with the self.

Traditionally, it was the body that was associated with the self and its God-obscuring desires and appetites. But in modern times, the anti-body bias has become more of an anti-ego bias, where ego or personality has become associated with a non-spiritual (or even anti-spiritual) lifestyle, as discussed in Chapters 3 and 5.

Ego became especially unpopular in the 1960s, when a large contingent of naive young spiritual seekers (myself among them) came to see ego as the only thing that stood between us and spiritual illumination. This was an understandable mistake borne not only out of our youthful inexperience but our upbringing in a culture lacking in spiritual practices that facilitate the expansion of consciousness (e.g., meditation, special ways of breathing, mantras, hatha or bhakti yoga, tantra, etc.). In the absence of this understanding, it was all too easy to blame ego for our inability to remain in an expanded state of awareness.

In the ensuring decades, serious spiritual seekers have become much more aware of the true nature of spiritual work, which we now know involves more than simply dropping the ego. In fact, after guru scandals of the 1970s and 80s—in which people allowed themselves to be exploited sexually, financially, or psychologically (all in the name of ego surrender)—it became all too obvious that indiscriminate ego

dropping was more likely to lead to a loss of autonomy than an expansion in awareness.[1]

Although the 1960s have long since come and gone, the anti-ego sentiments of that era have retained a certain influence—and nowhere is this influence more evident than in the culture of the personality enneagram community, as discussed in earlier chapters.

However, as we have seen in Chapter 6, there is another enneagram community, the Fourth Way community associated with the teachings of G. I. Gurdjieff.[2] And as we have seen in Chapter 6, Gurdjieff and his followers—particularly J. G. Bennett—have employed the enneagram as a tool for exploring the nature of transformational processes. Thus, the goal in Chapter 7 is to link the two enneagrams together on a point-by-point basis, so we can begin to see why it makes sense to think of the nine points of view not as *fixation types* but as *transformation types*.

But before comparing personality and process, we need to take a closer look at the nature of personality.

Personality Defined

For our purposes here, I define personality as follows:

> *Personality is that aspect of the embodied self that develops as the result of our innate temperament, the influences of our environment, and the ongoing choices we make in life.*

Fig. 7-1 depicts these three aspects of personality. Our **temperament** is that inward essence that stamps us as a unique individual unlike any other. It's that "mysterious something" we are born with that is central to our core identity. Although it is reflected in our genes, it is more than our genetic heritage, because the latter only describes our temperament from a materialistic point of view. True temperament arises from a deeper source, that source which gives rise to all things material. Although science does not now (and will probably never) possess the means necessary to entirely explain how such a process works, it has already demonstrated that individuality is truly innate, that it exists from the very first day of life.[3]

Enneagram type relates to temperament by specifying the innermost or core motivation that informs our instincts, emotions, thoughts, and behavior. While it is not what makes us an individual (because there are only nine core types), it's what defines our *core values*—values that can be expressed in a multiplicity of ways.[4]

The **environment** includes both our immediate surroundings (family, friends, and teachers), outer cultural influences, and subtle inner influences (dreams, visions, and impressions). When I originally attended college during the 1960s, behaviorism still held sway on my campus (and most others), so most academic psychologists greatly overestimated the role played by conditioning in shaping our personality. While environmental factors do significantly affect our personality development, they are never the only factor that shapes who we become. Notice, by the way, that I mention here an environmental factor that is almost never mentioned under the heading of "environment": the effects of our *inner* environment.

Most of us think of environment as something "out there"—as something entirely external to the mind and body. But those of us who

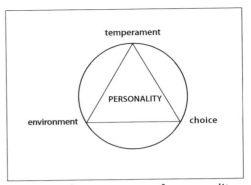

Fig. 7-1. Three aspects of personality.

don't see the two as synonymous can imagine environmental effects that are not "out there" (or at least are not "out there" in the sense of being relatively far removed). Some of the biggest events in my life have been linked to *dreams* and other inner experiences that—while they were not far removed—were still experienced as something external to the "me" with which I identify. Another example would be *near-death experiences*, which are shown even in scientific studies to be personality-changing in their effects, even though they (apparently) involve only the inner environment. Of course, many people would argue that these are in fact not just inner experiences, but are as real or more real than anything in the physical world. But we don't need to resolve this question to accept the possibility that environmental influences may be much more inward and subtle than we previously thought.

Choices are our responses, great and small, to whatever we encounter in each moment; they can be more passive (like reactions) or more pro-active (like initiatives). Choice is a powerful determinant of personality, because choice determines both how we develop the qualities with which we are born and how we habitually respond to our circumstances in life, strengthening certain tendencies and weakening others. Positive (healthy) choices have the potential to effect positive changes in our outlook and therefore our personality, changes that are often physiologically measurable.[5] This is why the new discipline of positive psychology focuses so much on helping people making more positive choices in life.

The truth is that learning how to make healthy choices in life is essential for the development of a well-balanced personality, because poor choices will trump innate ability and an ideal environment every time. This is actually very good news, because it means that we have the power to play a major role in determining the kind of person we will become. But it also means that we are tasked with the *responsibility* of making appropriate choices.

And this may be the real reason why the factor of choice is so often ignored: because to admit that choice makes a big difference in shaping our personality (and therefore our lives) means accepting responsibility for the less-than-optimal choices we make.

Another way to get off the hook when it comes to making better choices is to overemphasize the role of adversity (both natural and environmental) in determining what happens in life. Focusing on deficiencies in either our environment, personality, or both, allows us to feel less burdened by some of our less-than-brilliant choices. It's easier to view personality as something worthless than to develop it appropriately, which (as Jung points out) is not simply a challenge, but part of our true calling in life:

> True personality is always a
> vocation and puts its truth in it as in

God...Vocation acts like a law of God from which there is no escape.[6]

From this perspective, personality is not just a role we *play*, but the person we *are*. That is why I see the goal in enneagram work as the study and development of personality, so that it can serve as the vehicle for the fulfillment of *dharma*.

Thus, this approach to defining personality is designed to stress its essential *plasticity*, because this reminds us that personality is something to develop rather than something set in stone. While this is bad news for those who are uncomfortable with the idea of taking responsibility for their choices, it's good news for those who want that responsibility and therefore seek out the tools that support personality development.

Comparing Personality to Process

With this definition of personality in mind, we are ready to look at the specific relationship between the nine personality types and the nine points of transformation, using the descriptions delineated by Nathan Bernier in *The Enneagram: Symbol of All and Everything* (2003).

As we saw in Chapter 6, Bernier was interested in understanding why transformation sometimes fails. So he looked at the challenges that arise at the nine points and wrote a series of questions specific to each point, questions designed to help us pinpoint the nature of the challenge and the approach we need to take if we are to successfully negotiate it.

What I discovered when I read these questions was that they were highly evocative of type descriptions, in that the issues encountered at each step in transformation were strikingly similar to the issues commonly associated with the nine enneagram points of view. However, whereas the process enneagram points to challenges to be faced or issues to be resolved, the personality enneagram points to only one half of the equation: what happens when there is no successful resolution (at least, as it has traditionally been taught). Thus, instead of depicting nine types facing nine existential challenges, the personality enneagram depicts nine failed attempts to transform. Worse, this failure is seen as intrinsic to the types, in that it is part of their very structure.[7]

My intention was to take one step back, so that—instead of seeing each point of view as a failed attempt at transformation—I would use Bernier's questions to consider each point on the circle as a question in need of answering or a challenge in need of resolution. In that way, I could envision the nine types as nine opportunities to transform. This approach enabled me not only to back away from seeing the points of view as failed transformations but to gain insight into precisely the kinds of things that tend to go wrong for each point and to present that information in a format that is useful to individuals who wish to take advantage of the transformational opportunities afforded by their point of view.

Thus, my ongoing assumption is that each of the nine types is associated with a particular kind of transformational challenge which—once it is met—becomes a powerful asset for continuing development.

What Points Reveal About Types

In Chapter 5, using the example of a meal service, we saw that the challenges that we face at the beginning of a meal (e.g., organizing the kitchen) are different than those we face during preparation (where we must transform raw food into a cooked meal), which are in turn different from the challenge of presenting the meal to diners in an appetizing form. These three major phases can be broken into three sub-phases, which yields a total of nine transformational points or stages.

Now since each point requires a unique response, if we understand the nature of each point, we can begin to visualize the sort of person who would be particularly well-suited to respond appropriately to each type of transformational challenge. And as it turns out, these imagined prototypes look a lot like the nine enneagram personality types, such that, e.g., "Point 1 challenges" have requirements that are particularly befitting to a "Type 1 personality"; the same is true for the other eight points: Point 2 parallels Type 2, and so forth, around the enneagram circle.

If we focus on the ways in which transformation can go awry (such that we either fail to overcome the challenges at a particular point in development or do so in a way that is less than ideal), we can gain insight into the reasons that some transformational stages seem much more difficult than others for particular individuals. So in the case of a *Point 1* personality, for example, the One's one-pointedness, ability to set concrete goals, and follow through with principled action are obviously assets during the first stage of a new project. But the same tendencies may pose a challenge when the One encounters those stages of development which require the ability to be more sympathetic (*Point 2*), adaptable (*Point 3*), emotionally-committed (*Point 4*), dispassionate (*Point 5*), willing to fit in (*Point 6*), whimsical (*Point 7*), gritty (*Point 8*), and non-judgmental (*Point 9*).

(Please note that I picked these adjectives very carefully, because they all describe qualities associated with each point that Ones in particular would find challenging. If we were to go through the same exercise for each of the nine types, we would use different adjectives to describe the challenges for Type X at Point Y in the process. This is possible because each point is multi-faceted, which makes it possible for each type to experience the same point in a slightly different way.)[8]

The One who becomes aware of the affinity between Type 1 and Point 1 has additional information that can help her take advantage of her strengths and compensate for her weaknesses. It will also help her understand why she is naturally more attracted to certain kinds of people, activities, and situations than others. Of course, the same thing is true for all the types: the more we know about the personality enneagram, the process enneagram, and the link between the two, the more we know about the nature of transformation *as it applies to individuals with our particular temperament.*

Comparison of Points & Types

In the comparison that follows, I use Bernier's comments as guides to bridge the gap between the personality and process enneagrams. When Bernier discusses the challenges that arise at a given stage in his book, he uses the term "danger" to describe them; I have however substituted the term "hazard," adopting the terminology used by both Bennett and Blake for the same purpose. I prefer the term "hazard" because it is less melodramatic; it also makes it easier to think of these challenges as potentially surmountable (rather than as something to be feared and avoided).

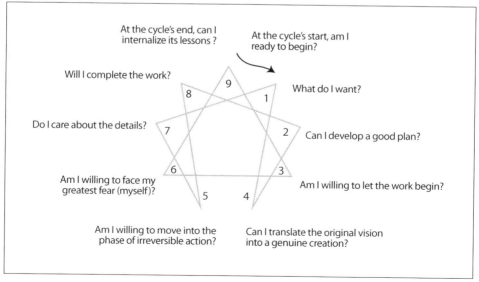

Fig. 7-2. Transformational challenges by stage.

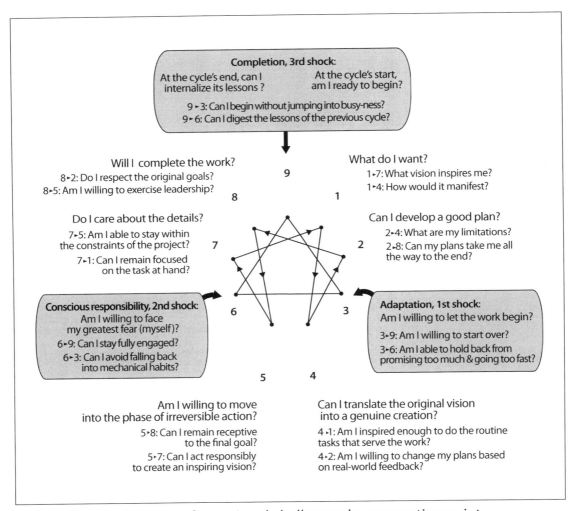

Completion, 3rd shock:
At the cycle's end, can I internalize its lessons ?   At the cycle's start, am I ready to begin?

9 ▸ 3: Can I begin without jumping into busy-ness?
9 ▸ 6: Can I digest the lessons of the previous cycle?

Will I complete the work?
8 ▸ 2: Do I respect the original goals?
8 ▸ 5: Am I willing to exercise leadership?

What do I want?
1 ▸ 7: What vision inspires me?
1 ▸ 4: How would it manifest?

Do I care about the details?
7 ▸ 5: Am I able to stay within the constraints of the project?
7 ▸ 1: Can I remain focused on the task at hand?

Can I develop a good plan?
2 ▸ 4: What are my limitations?
2 ▸ 8: Can my plans take me all the way to the end?

Conscious responsibility, 2nd shock:
Am I willing to face my greatest fear (myself)?
6 ▸ 9: Can I stay fully engaged?
6 ▸ 3: Can I avoid falling back into mechanical habits?

Adaptation, 1st shock:
Am I willing to let the work begin?
3 ▸ 9: Am I willing to start over?
3 ▸ 6: Am I able to hold back from promising too much & going too fast?

Am I willing to move into the phase of irreversible action?
5 ▸ 8: Can I remain receptive to the final goal?
5 ▸ 7: Can I act responsibly to create an inspiring vision?

Can I translate the original vision into a genuine creation?
4 ▸ 1: Am I inspired enough to do the routine tasks that serve the work?
4 ▸ 2: Am I willing to change my plans based on real-world feedback?

Fig. 7-3. Transformational challenges by connecting point.

Fig. 7-2 provides an overview of the questions that occur at each stage in the process; Fig. 7-3 highlights the effect of the shock points (see Chapter 5) and adds in the questions associated with each hexad connecting point.

Please note that these questions are simplified versions of Bernier's, because the latter are often sufficiently complicated to make it difficult to preserve them exactly as he wrote them. For the exact wording in the originals, see pp. 325-335 in *The Enneagram: All and Everything*. Also, Bernier includes connecting point questions only for the hexad points (1-4-2-8-5-7), not the inner triangle types (3-6-9). This is no doubt because (as mentioned at the beginning of Chapter 6), when it comes to the process enneagram, it is the connecting lines of the hexad that are particularly associated with dynamic processes (i.e., planning for the future and reflecting on the past). However, in the discussion below, I've taken the liberty of using my understanding of the personality enneagram connecting points to inform my development of appropriate "connecting point" questions for Points 3-6-9 on the process enneagram, based on the challenges commonly associated with those junctures.[9]

In the comparisons that follow, the boxed information shows Bernier's perspective on each point: what it's about, how it's affected by related considerations (the connecting points), and the special challenges that arise (the hazards). The discussion below each box presents my interpretation of Bernier's comments in light of my experience with the personality enneagram; this is followed by a comparison of the process enneagram point with the personality enneagram type.

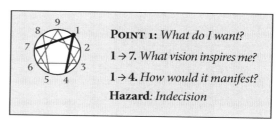

POINT 1: *What do I want?*
1 → 7. *What vision inspires me?*
1 → 4. *How would it manifest?*
Hazard: *Indecision*

At the first step in a new process or project, there are lots of possible ways to go, so the challenge is to decide on one and only one goal to pursue, trying to find inspiration (1 → 7) but also the means to deeply ground our vision in reality (1 → 4). So Point 1 is the place where we exercise both creative imagination and self-discipline, so that the two impulses balance one another. Another reason for self-discipline is so that we don't slip back into inertia (Point 9) or move prematurely into planning (Point 2). The hazard of indecision is associated with the possibility of failing to come to grips with the need to make a definite decision about how to move forward.

Point 1 and Type 1. Where Point 1 is about getting started, making goals, and determining standards, Type 1 is about taking the initiative, materializing ideals, and determining standards. So it's easy to see the parallels. Ones are often said to be prone to "black and white thinking." Understanding Point 1 in the process enneagram tells us why: because Point 1 is the place where it's necessary to move beyond vagueness or ambiguity (indecision). But moving from indecision to decision-making sometimes requires us to go to the opposite extreme, at least for a time (e.g., when we are young or in unfamiliar situations). One interesting thing about the discussion of Point 1 as a process is its emphasis on creativity (inspiration and imagination). Studying the personality enneagram, there is not much emphasis on Ones as creators (because there is so much focus on ideals, standards, and perfection), but perfection and creativity are often intertwined, because highly creative people are usually impeccable when it comes to their work; they adhere to strict standards and go to great lengths to perfect their vision.

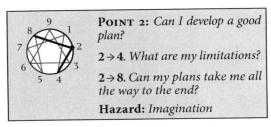

POINT 2: *Can I develop a good plan?*

2 → 4. *What are my limitations?*

2 → 8. *Can my plans take me all the way to the end?*

Hazard: *Imagination*

After moving forward from the indecisiveness of Point 0 to the perfected vision at Point 1, we are ready to buckle down and begin the work of planning to make our vision a reality. In the case of a transformational process, this may be the point at which we seek a specific teacher, practice, or philosophy that we think will further our progress. To make a good decision, we need to maintain a balance between the "big vision" (2 → 8) and the limits of what is realistically possible (2 → 4). If we allow our imagination to run away with us, we won't be able to make our vision a reality (to commit to our path or course) at Point 4 or to continue all the way to the end at Point 8. If we seize on the first thing we find, we may move prematurely to Point 3, without having really worked out the implications of our decision.

Point 2 and Type 2. On Bernier's version of the process enneagram, Stage 2 is planning; on the personality enneagram, Type 2 is variously called the People Person, the Giver, or the Helper. These are very different images! So how do we reconcile them? This was initially puzzling to me until I realized that they are actually more similar than I first thought. The difference lies not in the function, but in the *interpretation* of that function. At the beginning of a new project, a great deal of careful attention is initially required to set that project in motion—a function that Bernier calls *planning*. Similarly, when a baby is born, a mother devotes a great deal of time to care for and encourage the infant—a function that we call *nurturance*. They are actually identical functions, as seen through a masculine versus feminine filter! Generally speaking, the process enneagram utilizes an extremely masculine way of conceptualizing transformation (perhaps because Gurdjieff was an extremely "muscular" teacher—a probable Type 8).

The bottom line is this: that while we can view Point 2 as the phase where we begin working out a detailed plan of how we are going to proceed, we can alternatively view it as the place where we really start to emotionally invest in our transformational project or process—to care about it deeply enough to provide nurturance at a critical point in its development. Which way of thinking is best? It depends on whom you ask. But the divergence in these two perspectives raises interesting questions about potential differences in the masculine versus feminine paths to transformation. Interestingly, Bernier's Point 2 hazard (imagination) sounds like more of a feminine than masculine sort of problem, because it speaks to a scenario where we can become emotionally overinvested in what we are doing—the way that a doting mother can become too emotionally invested in planning her child's future.

POINT 3: *Am I willing to let the work begin?*

3 → 9. *Am I willing to start over again if necessary?*

3 → 6. *Am I able to hold back from promising too much and going too fast?*

Hazard: *Materialism; Procrastination*

It is at this point that we receive the first shock, in the form of some kind of input or energy from outside, e.g., where we receive the actual materials that must be transformed such as the food in a meal (or in the case of personal transformation, to begin to realize what the process really entails). This new energy or information makes the transformational process much more concrete. So it provides a "reality check" that shows us the necessity of adaptation to the realities of the situation, especially if what happens is not what we expected. So it requires, in Bernier's words, an "initial commitment" (p. 287). In trying to adapt, it is easy to either do too much (3 → 6 = overadaptation) or too little (3 → 9 = procrastination); the fear of the latter often creates the former. Bernier says it is at this point that time begins to matter and the material world begins to attract us—which is why spiritual or psychological materialism is something to watch out for here. A willingness to genuinely open to new input at Point

3 gives us time to make further changes and fully adapt to them, so that we avoiding moving prematurely to Point 4 (i.e., jumping in too deep too soon).

Point 3 and Type **3**. On the process enneagram, Point 3 is the first shock, a shock which comes because we discover the degree to which our initial impulses collide with everyday reality. That's why it's associated with the material world. It brings to mind the Zen teacher over-pouring the tea or stepping on his pupil's foot. Thus, on the personality enneagram, it's at Point 3 that we find individuals who are extremely practical and adaptable, especially when it comes to concrete work—even to the point of basing their entire self-image on their work. It's as though they are trying to balance the need to be open to input with the need to maintain a sense of security, and they seek to accomplish this by identifying with concrete goals having material manifestations.

POINT 4: *Can I translate the original vision into a genuine creation?*

4 → 1. *Am I inspired enough to do the routine tasks that serve the work?*

4 → 2. *Am I able to alter my plans based on real-world feedback?*

Hazard: *Detail & anonymity; Wishing to appear*

In a manufacturing process, the idea of translating a vision into a real product entails a deep commitment to the process. So at Point 4, we have to move beyond the surface to a deeper place of commitment, so that we are prepared to do whatever is necessary to make the work a success. In transformational work, this means allowing ourselves to be subjected to the process of "cooking" (alchemical transformation), in order that our inner work be accomplished. If we make the commitment to change, then the discipline necessary to complete all the tasks associated with that commitment is forthcoming (4 → 1)—and we are able to align our plans and intentions with our chosen path (4 → 2). If not, we need to delve a little deeper, until we know what we really want.

Bernier lists two dangers here: that of "[lack of] detail and anonymity" and "wishing to appear." The "lack of detail" problem relates to our unwillingness to do unpleasant or boring tasks (which indicates an absence of wholehearted commitment); the unwillingness to be anonymous has to do with the inability to allow the work (i.e., the transformational process) to take center stage, instead of us (because we still "wish to appear," i.e., to retain our self-image). Allowing self-image to take a back seat to the work is a critical requirement at this point, because only one can take priority after the crossing from Point 4 to 5. We can of course try to sidestep this requirement, moving prematurely to Point 5, but according to Bernier, such a move is particularly problematic: "The inopportune passage from 4 to 5 is harmful to the whole process. In this passage, transformation is irreversible, and the price to be paid for precipitation at this stage is high" (p. 329). So however strong the impulse to advance quickly, it is better to spend extra time at Point 4 working through self-image issues, rather than rushing into the phase of irreversible change—discovering too late that we have made a serious error in judgment.

Point 4 and Type 4. Point 4 comes shortly after we encounter the first shock, so it's the place where we get to take account of ourselves and sort out what is real versus false about the self; otherwise, we are in danger of making commitments that will permanently alter our lives without benefit of proper insight. This is why, on the personality enneagram, Fours are so deeply concerned with authenticity (sorting out outer appearances from inner reality). They instinctively realize the pitfalls of making a wrong decision at this point, which is why they are more serious than lighthearted. They do indeed tend to struggle with the desire of "wishing to appear" (to be appreciated and sought after) but at the same time realize on some level that what really matters is bringing something forth into the world that comes from a deeper place. This is why we find so many writers, artists, and dramatic actors at Point 4.

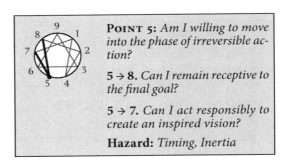

POINT 5: *Am I willing to move into the phase of irreversible action?*

5 → 8. *Can I remain receptive to the final goal?*

5 → 7. *Can I act responsibly to create an inspired vision?*

Hazard: *Timing, Inertia*

Point 5 is the first place we reach after crossing the chaotic area at the bottom of the enneagram—an area associated with the start of the "cooking" process (see the "nadir" discussion in Chapter 8). This crossing creates an awareness that big changes are beginning to happen, changes that are creating their own momentum as they go. This is why timing becomes such a critical issue: because this kind of momentum can create big problems if the timing is off. So we have to be prepared to act when the moment is right (not to hang back out of fear) but at the same time not to act prematurely, because at this point, our actions have irreversible consequences. So it is necessary at this point that we clearly know where we are headed (5 → 7) and our final goal (5 → 8). This is why Bernier strongly emphasizes the importance of having presence of mind at this point in the process: because we have to simultaneously understand the goal, the experience, the market, the client, and the further use of the work, so we can make informed decisions. Only through understanding do we get the confidence to feel fully prepared to act.

Point 5 and Type 5. Point 5 is a critical place in a transformational process, because it initiates the phase where every subsequent action taken represents a huge investment with real-world consequences. Thus, if Point 4 demands our emotional commitment to the process, Point 5 represents our mental commitment. Thus, Point 5 on the personality enneagram is the place where we find individuals who are preoccupied with knowledge-seeking and intellectual competence—individuals who want to understand every possible detail about what they are doing before beginning to initiate action. Given the nature of this transformational stage, this hesitancy is understandable: Fives are sensitive to the need to do research before acting. However, this innate fear of consequences can sometimes create timing problems (like fearful procrastination or ill-timed action that seems divorced from genuine emotional engagement). To move forward appropriately, Fives have to

figure out how to strike a balance not only between research and action, but between detachment and engagement.

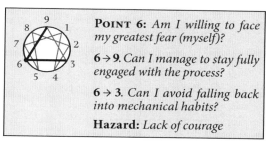

POINT 6: *Am I willing to face my greatest fear (myself)?*

6 → 9. *Can I manage to stay fully engaged with the process?*

6 → 3. *Can I avoid falling back into mechanical habits?*

Hazard: *Lack of courage*

Once we are willing to take responsibility for transformation, we move into the thick of the action, where we encounter the greatest obstacle imaginable: ourselves. Point 6 is the site of the second shock, where "we see ourselves as we really are." (No wonder it's a shock!) It is particularly here that Divine grace can enter, often in the form of negative feedback (or realizations) that are painful to face. But as Bernier notes, "negative shocks can be transformed into conscious shocks by intentional acceptance" (p. 330). In other words, if we accept what cannot be sidestepped and willingly adapt to it, it becomes the springboard to becoming conscious at a higher level (see Chapter 12). If we are unwilling to do so, we either stagnate (6 → 9) or fall back into mechanical habits (6 → 3). So this second shock is really a blessing in disguise.

Point 6 and Type 6. Of all the points on the enneagram, this is the one where the similarities between point and type are most apparent. The hazard here is *fear*—fear so potentially overwhelming that we would do almost anything to avoid it. But a lack of courage at this point would be most unfortunate, because we are at the place where "push comes to shove": where the only way to make it through is to summon up every bit of faith and willingness that we possess, so we can face even our worst nightmare, knowing that life always supports those who humbly ask for help to do what seems impossible. If Point 6 is where we face our fears, Type 6 is the individual for whom fear is the greatest challenge in life—hence, the tendency of Sixes to look for structures that can provide a steadying influence (family, church, the military)—structures that support the move from fearful paralysis to decisive action. Often, the greatest fear for this type is not so much physical as it is moral and spiritual: it has to do with listening to one's inner voice and heeding what is says, even when this means facing fears that seem insurmountable. The strong service ethos of this type can help them muster the fortitude to trust their intuitions and take the big leap into the unknown—that leap that will vanquish the fears that block their creative flow.

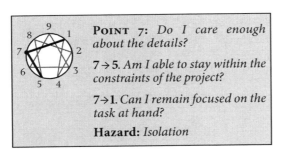

POINT 7: *Do I care enough about the details?*

7 → 5. Am I able to stay within the constraints of the project?

7 → 1. Can I remain focused on the task at hand?

Hazard: *Isolation*

At Point 7, we experience a tremendous sense of relief and exhilaration as the result of confronting our greatest fears and coming out the other side. Ironically, it is this exhilaration and sense of freedom that

can become the next obstacle on the path to completion, because it can be hard to focus on a transformational work-in-progress when life seems so joyful and we feel so free. What we really need to be doing at this point (to borrow a Sufi phrase) is "polishing the mirror of the heart"—to be joyfully perfecting our creation, whether this means a concrete creation (such as a meal or invention) or something intangible (such as our inner being). But to do so requires both inspiration (7 → 1) and focus (7 → 5), such that we accept the truth that "the devil is in the details": that we can't skate out on our ongoing obligations just because we're able to enjoy life. It is not hard to see why the tests at this point are subtle and easy to miss: because they involve staying focused in the midst of wonderfully attractive distractions. But should we become overly preoccupied with our personal fascinations, this preoccupation will eventually cut us off from both other people and the flow of life (which is why the hazard here is isolation).

Point 7 and Type 7. It is quite easy to see the parallels between Point 7 and Type 7, because the challenge in both cases is to live life freely while also gracefully coming to terms with life's limitations—as well as the need to use those limitations to transform raw talent into a truly refined form. This can be difficult for the restless Seven, who finds it hard to sacrifice his sense of freedom, no matter what the reward. As noted above, it is via that cultivation of inspiration (7 → 1) and focus (7 → 5) that Sevens can develop the self-refinement associated with the highest forms of artistic creation.[10]

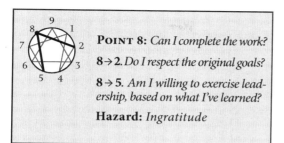

POINT 8: *Can I complete the work?*

8 → 2. *Do I respect the original goals?*

8 → 5. *Am I willing to exercise leadership, based on what I've learned?*

Hazard: *Ingratitude*

Point 8 represents the apex of the transformational journey, the place of mastery or completeness. However, it is also the place in which we have the opportunity to (in Wilber's words) "transcend and include" everything that has happened at each stage in the journey—and to do so in a fully embodied way. And it is, as Bernier notes, the place where the work of transformation is "presented, offered, and celebrated," often in a very public way. So the celebration is not just for the individual who completes the cycle but for all individuals seeking self-mastery. For to see someone achieve the goal reminds us that we too can do the same. The public celebration reinforces the link between the point of completion and all the points of becoming (so that we remember our roots). The hazard of ingratitude comes when we fall prey to the illusion that our current state of mastery is due entirely to our own will, talents, and efforts (when in fact nobody achieves such a goal without help from others). Thus, ingratitude is the product of willful forgetting—forgetting our debt to those who encouraged us from the beginning (8 → 2) and to those whose superior knowledge made our accomplishments possible (8 → 5).

Point 8 and Type 8. The processes described at Point 8 are quite similar to the qualities associated with Type 8. Strong, powerful, and naturally dominant, Eights are the type that are innately well-suited to embody all the qualities at each point on the enneagram. But they are also the type that has the most trouble balancing and containing their energy or acknowledging their appreciation for others. So the goal is always to develop their skills in a way designed to support people instead of dominate them. Well-balanced Eights realize that all mastery is ultimately self-mastery and have an highly developed sense of personal honor. They realize the importance of cultivating not only outer qualities such as leadership, but inner qualities, such as tenderness (8 → 2) and the ability to reflect deeply (8 → 5).

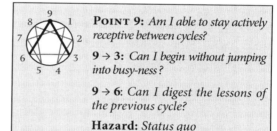

POINT 9: *Am I able to stay actively receptive between cycles?*

9 → 3: *Can I begin without jumping into busy-ness?*

9 → 6: *Can I digest the lessons of the previous cycle?*

Hazard: *Status quo*

On the process enneagram, Point 9 represents the period between cycles, so it's the time that we both digest the lessons of the last cycle and begin to prepare for the next cycle. However, in order to digest those lessons—so that they become deeply assimilated into our being—we have to become "actively receptive," even though we are not doing anything. So while this phase is about "being" (not doing), it's not about zoning out, going blank, or using busy-ness as an escape from active receptivity. So the challenge here is greater than it looks: How do we stay actively interested in life when there's "nothing to do"? Everyone can relate to this experience and the feelings of disorientation it can induce. The danger of "status quo" refers to the tendency to fall into unconscious routines that allow us to zone out, so we can avoid being present in the moment. But only when we are present can we genuinely assimilate the lessons learned during the last cycle (9 → 6) and properly prepare ourselves for the next cycle (9 → 3).

Point 9 and Type 9. While Point 9 is "between cycles," Type 9 is not "between types." Nines are just as much of a type as the other eight types. However, because of their position on the enneagram, they don't always *perceive themselves* to be a distinct type, but instead identify with all the types. They also identify with nature in an often mystical way and flow with time and space in a manner that makes it hard to be on time or to stay on track when it comes to projects. Ironically, the wonderful oneness they experience with life can make it hard to experience themselves as individuals—and to fully enter the cycle of transformation, instead of ruminating about the past (9 → 6) or staying busy with mindless activities (9 → 3). While they often benefit from outer reference points (like friends who support them to become more "themselves" or schedules that help them move through the day), in the end, it is their fertile imagination that eventually impels them to translate their dreams into a concrete reality.

Integrating the Enneagram

As we can see, juxtaposing the personality and process enneagrams reveals the striking parallels between the two. This is why we can plausibly speak of a one-to-one correspondence between Types 1–9 and Points 1–9.

While it can take a little while to get the hang of working from a "one-enneagram perspective," it allows us to use the enneagram not only to identify our type but to understand how its position in the transformational cycle determines the qualities commonly associated with the type, the challenges it finds most difficult, and the tools it must develop in order to move all the way around the enneagram circle.

Adopting such a perspective can help us find our path or *dharma* in life. While there is no magic formula for determining what career, lifestyle, path, or philosophy is best for a given individual, the enneagram provides a powerful tool for looking at the relationship between our inner nature (as revealed by our type) and the path most likely to bring about genuine transformation.

If we specifically look at spiritual paths, the one-enneagram or Integral Enneagram model proposed here gives us a clearer idea of why certain types have an affinity with certain paths. For example, we begin to see why

- ***Ones*** are attracted to inspirational but well-defined, highly-disciplined, or ascetic paths (they feel drawn to a higher calling)

- ***Twos*** are drawn to paths of love, devotion, and care-giving (they feel uplifted when nurturing those who respond to love)

- ***Threes*** cut their teeth on well-defined but demanding paths (they need the sensation of pushing through and over obstacles towards an aspirational goal)

- ***Fours*** follow depth-oriented paths in search of their true self (they cannot rest until they have plumbed the depths of their inner being)

- **Fives** are fascinated by intellectual, esoteric, complex, or shamanic truths (they are following the inner path of *gnosis*)

- **Sixes** appreciate paths that allow them to test their courage & serve the community (they draw strength & fortitude from contributing to the greater good)

- **Sevens** follow many paths and many masters (they are the spiritual explorers that envision new paths & ways to grow)

- **Eights** pursue paths of power & mastery (they embody their hard-won truths in the lives they lead)

- **Nines** gravitate towards imaginative, mystical, and nature-oriented paths (they enjoy following the natural rhythms of life)

The Integral Enneagram model also helps us understand why the transformational path that is exactly right for one person may be dead wrong for another. And this is very helpful, because without such insight, it's possible to spend years on paths that lead nowhere.

One last advantage of an Integral Enneagram model is that it has the intriguing property of bringing together time and space in a paradoxical but fascinating manner. What I mean is that the personality enneagram describes *spatial points of view* while the process enneagram describes *sequential points in time* (Fig. 7-4).

While it's clear that these points of space resonate with these points in time, what's *not* clear is what exactly this signifies. Contemplating this juxtaposition is like meditating on a Zen koan: you get the feeling that with enough meditation, you'd come to understand something truly profound about the nature of the time-space continuum. While I haven't exactly arrived at that understanding, I can still appre-

ciate the beauty of bringing each point on these two axes into relationship with one another.

I know of no other system that allows us to look at this juxtaposition. How can a single geometric figure delineate both dimensions? What does this tell us about the nature of the Kosmos? What does it tell us about the nature of the enneagram, human beings, or sacred geometry?

I don't have an answer for these questions—and thinking about them gives me a headache! But they lend credence to Gurdjieff's very strong claims about the significance of the enneagram, which he characterized as both the philosopher's stone and the fundamental hieroglyph of a universal language.[11] While those who now follow his teachings tend to look askance at the use of the enneagram for describing personality types, (viewing it as a trivialization of Gurdjieff's original vision),[12] we have to wonder whether they would be so averse to the personality enneagram if it were not used primarily for describing patterns of fixation.[13]

Actually, moving beyond the personality-as-fixation model is just the first step in broadening our horizons when it comes to the personality enneagram. Because despite its name, it isn't mainly about personality but about the nature of spatial reality, intentionality, perspective-taking, and unity in diversity. In the future, we can look forward to exploring the enneagram from angles we can only begin to imagine at this point.

But the focus in this chapter has been to demonstrate how the nine personality types/or points of view correspond to points on the process enneagram, so that we can better understand the relationship between them. The

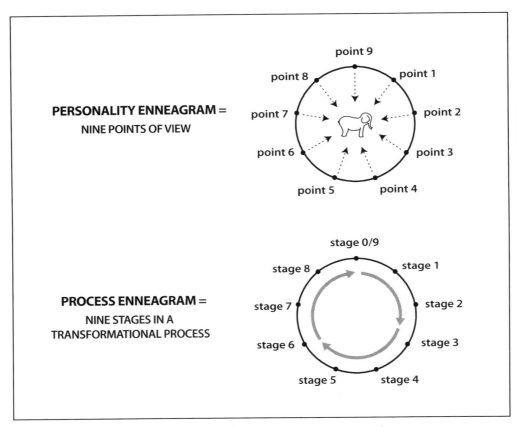

Fig. 7-4. Personality vs process perspective.

focus in the next is to build on this foundation to identify additional enneagram patterns that help us understand the relationship between individuality, transformation, and the fulfillment of *dharma*.

Notes

1. The desire to surrender the ego to some greater (seemingly transcendent) cause can overwhelm one's common sense in a big way—which was the lesson eventually learned by Arthur Koestler after his youthful infatuation with communism; see the discussion in Chapter 2 about the folly of allowing the drive towards self-transcendence to override the drive towards self-assertiveness.

2. The idea of a "Fourth Way" approach is based on the notion that most transformational paths focus on one of three things—body, mind, or emotion—but not on their integration. The Fourth Way approach, which is based on Gurdjieff's teachings, seeks to integrate all three and would thus qualify as an entirely integral approach to transformation.

3. See the work of Daniel N. Stern, e.g., *The Interpersonal World Of The Infant* (2000) and a veritable raft of researchers from the 1970s to the present; for a summary of early studies, see particularly *The Competent Infant* (1973).

4. By referring to the "core values" associated with the nine types, I am not suggesting that all individuals of a given type have identical beliefs, but simply that they share a similarity in outlook based on type-related ways of prioritizing what "really matters"—such that Ones tend to focus on standards, Twos on relationships, Threes on competency, Fours on authenticity, Fives on understanding, Sixes on safety, Sevens on variety, Eights on power dynamics, and Nines on harmony.

5. According to the Mayo Clinic, positive thinking is positively correlated with increased life span, lower rates of depression, greater resistance to the common cold, general psychological and physical well-being, reduced risk of death from cardiovascular disease, and better coping skills during hardships and times of stress (www.mayoclinic.com/health/positive-thinking/SR00009; accessed 10-18-12).

6. *The Development of Personality* (1954/1981), p. 175.

7. The glossary for the Diamond Approach (A. H. Almaas) describes the enneagram types in terms of "nine delusions" that "are principles inherent in all egoic structures," (http://glossary.ahalmaas.com/phrases/552). Enneagram Worldwide teacher Peter O'Hanrahan notes that "The [ego] defenses are part and parcel of our type structure," (www.enneagramwork.com/defense_systems.html). Rod Gozzard, relating his experience at a Riso-Hudson (Enneagram Institute) workshop on the psychic structures, reports that "the Superego is the machine that drives our behaviour and each type has a specific Superego message that must be satisfied," (www.internationalenneagram.org/artman2/uploads/1/IEA_Nine_Points_Jan-Feb10_1.pdf. All sites were accessed 11-5-12).

8. Here I would note that this way of looking at the unique interactions between *type* and *point* may address some of Wilber's concerns about seeing perspectives not simply in terms of the isolated percept of an individual perceiver, but in terms of the *interaction* between the perceiver and his or her environment; see his discussion in *Integral Spirituality* (2006), pp. 248–258.

9. The rationale for discussing connecting points for the three inner triangle types is that they are included in the transformational process and are thus subject to the same kinds of connecting point influences as the other six points.

10. The virtue for Type 7 is often said to be sobriety; however, sobriety is a very "heavy" concept, given the lightness-of-being associated with this type. While I've seen Sevens who are indeed sober, they seem to lack a certain spark, as well. I would thus propose *focus* as a substitute for sobriety, because it conveys the idea of cultivating sustained attention (which is important for Sevens) without imposing on them the need to be overly serious (which can be very deflating).

11. Ouspensky's *In Search of the Miraculous* (1949/2001), p. 294.

12. See the discussion in Bernier's *The Enneagram: Symbol of All and Everything* (2003), pp. 45–47.

13. As Blake has observed in *The Intelligent Enneagram* (1996) "the fixations are all 'negatives' [while] the worldviews I have described are all 'positive.' " (p. 286).

8

ENNEAGRAM ZONES OF TRANSFORMATION

Every place and position...has its own nature different from that of its neighbor.
– Al-Tirmirdi, *Stations of the Heart*

THE ENNEAGRAM IS FULL of patterns. These patterns are formed by the position of the nine enneagram points and the inner lines that connect them. The existence of these patterns is what makes the enneagram more than just a simple tool for categorizing personality types.

In Chapter 3, we took a look at some of the most well-known patterns employed for understanding the nature of the types on the personality enneagram. We saw how these patterns reveal the energetic nature of each type (according to its energy center, i.e., head, heart, or body/gut); its relationship to neighboring or "wing" types; its relationship to the types with which it connects through the inner lines (the connecting points); and how we can more specifically categorize each type according to its dominant subtype arena (self-preservation, sexual, or social).

But it's also possible to divide the enneagram into vertical and horizontal zones (based on their position on the circle) and to look at the effect of location on the nine en-

neagram points (Fig. 8-1). When we do, we discover additional patterns that can be used to understand the nature of *individuality* (using the personality enneagram), the nature of *transformation* (using the process enneagram), and the interaction between the two.

Exploring the patterns according to enneagram zone is the main purpose of Chapter 8.

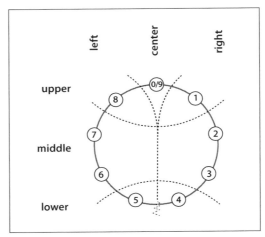

Fig. 8-1. Vertical and horizontal zones.

While the inclusion of both personality and process patterns makes the discussion complex, it also enables us to better see the parallels between these two enneagram approaches, thus helping to justify a "one-enneagram" or Integral Enneagram model. In addition, it lays the groundwork for adopting this model for integral work, an approach with a number of advantages that are discussed more fully in Chapter 9. (Briefly, its benefits include the ability to potentially resolve a long-term argument in both transpersonal and integral theory as to which matters more, immanent or transcendent spirituality. I will argue that the enneagram supports the idea that transformation involves both ascent and descent but that each is particularly important at different points in the transformational process.)

Chapter 8 is complex, so it's useful to have an advance preview of its organization:

1. **Personality Enneagram Patterns**
   (a) vertical zones (*feminine-masculine-androgynous*)
   (b) horizontal zones (*spirit-ego-soul*)

2. **Process Enneagram Patterns**
   (a) vertical zones (*descent-ascent-stillness*)
   (b) horizontal zones (*spirit-ego-soul*)

3. **Seven Zones of Influence**
   (how we can think of the enneagram circle as having seven combined areas of influence based on the discussions in previous sections)

4. **Significance of the Nadir**
   (a discussion of the critical role played by the enneagram nadir and its effects on both personality and transformation)

5. **An Integral Enneagram Model**
   (how what appears to be two separate enneagrams can be combined to create an integrated one-enneagram model)

Each of these sections lays the foundation for the section that follows. Although I've done my best to make the descriptions clear, because this material is not familiar to most readers, it's likely to pose a few challenges. So please be patient and allow for more than one reading.

Personality Enneagram Patterns

On the personality enneagram, we are looking at nine different temperament types and how they affect our self-image, relationships with others, and understanding of life. The types can be located in one of three vertical zones that are broken down based on polarity (feminine-masculine-androgynous) or three horizontal zones that are broken down based on three types or levels of consciousness (spirit-ego-soul). We'll start by looking at the vertical zones.

Vertical Zones on the Personality Enneagram

Although it is not part of formal enneagram theory, most people who work with the enneagram view the right side as more *feminine* and the left side as more *masculine*. The polarity of each half is very influential, because it strongly affects the outlook of the types in that half. However, Type 9 is right on the dividing line, so it occupies its own *androgynous* zone (Fig. 8-2):

- **Feminine**: subjective standards, intuition, evaluation based on feelings, relationships, nurturance, materialization, increasing complexity, focus on "I", creation of self-image, water, empathy, literature/fiction, art, diversity, elaboration

- **Masculine**: objective standards, cognition, evaluation based on thinking, object-orientation, systems, testing, abstraction, increasing unity, focus on "it", discovery of truth, air, clarity, non-fiction, science, unity, simplification

■ **Androgynous/Neutral:** non-judgmentalism, non-reactivity, non-evaluation, desire for meshing, impassivity, stillness, focus on "oneness," creation of harmony, integration, synthesis, inspiration, fairness, unifying of diversity, harmonization

When describing types in terms of their polarity, it's important to note that no type is purely masculine or feminine, just as no individual is purely masculine or feminine. That said, it's still possible to meaningfully categorize types according to polarity.

FEMININE TYPES: 1-2-3-4. *Ones* are feminine in a rather subtle and somewhat formal fashion: fussy, precise, and standards-oriented, they seek to describe the rules for civilized conduct and to ensure that they are followed. They also tend to have an artistic

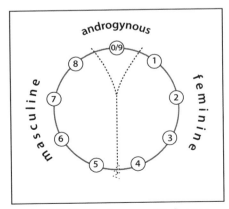

Fig. 8-2. Vertical zones of influence on the personality enneagram.

streak and to especially appreciate refined art and literature. *Twos* are probably the most archetypically feminine type on the enneagram, the one that all women in traditional societies are taught to emulate; here the focus is on feelings, romance, relationships, family, children, the home and providing nurturance in the form of childcare, nursing, and food preparation. *Threes* often seem less feminine in the obvious sense, because they are able to sublimate emotions into outer activity, such that they focus on advancement, team building, and generally adapting to the world around them. This focus on adaptation is a feminine trait, as is the Three's focus on the material world. *Fours* are extremely feminine in their inner orientation but are also extremely self-protective, so while they tend to be at least as emotional as Twos, they are often a lot less openly demonstrative. Their femininity shows up in their deep feelings, sense of emotional vulnerability, and sensitivity to aesthetics in dress and/or environment.

MASCULINE TYPES: 5-6-7-8. Among types on the other side of the enneagram, *Fives* are the most rationally oriented of all types, which makes them the most masculine type in the purely intellectual sense. Objective, detached, and reserved in manner, they tend to be very good at solving puzzles and problems of all kinds (especially those that have eluded others) because of their talent for noticing patterns and systematizing seemingly unrelated phenomena. Like Fives, *Sixes* like rational thinking (and thus are often found in scientific or technical fields), but they tend to be more concrete, more applied, and less systems-oriented. They sometimes have a counterphobic streak that attracts them to heroic pursuits (firefighting, rescue work, emergency medicine, police work, and the military—or to hobbies like skydiving or mountain climbing). *Sevens* are cooly mental types who particularly enjoy unusual ideas, innovative projects and utopian lifestyles; their restless energy attracts them to long-distance travel and adventure; it can make relationships more fleeting than sustained or (if long-term) based more on mental rapport than sentimental attachment. *Eights* are tough, practical, and action-oriented; they "think with their gut" and radiate the kind of tangible aura of charismatic authority and power that we associate with the masculine ideal.

ANDROGYNOUS TYPE: 9. As the only type that straddles the polarity line, *Nines* are not surprisingly the most impassive, accepting, and non-judgmental of all types; there is an aura of androgyneity about them that can seem somehow healing or soothing. It enables them to get along amicably with both sexes, and probably accounts for some of their well-known ability to create harmony out of discord.

Understanding the polarity of each type is helpful for interpreting their actions, because types on opposite sides of the circle may act in a similar way for quite different reasons. For example, a Four and a Five both tend to be private people, but a Four's need for privacy is associated with emotional sensitivity while a Five's need for privacy is associated with the need to avoid over-stimulation. Similarly, a Two and an Eight can both have a big focus on family, but for the Two, it's the emotional connection that matters most, while for the Eight, it's the ability to create an impregnable unit bound by blood ties.

HORIZONTAL ZONES ON THE PERSONALITY ENNEAGRAM

Just as the vertical zones of the enneagram differ in polarity, the horizontal zones differ in terms of their domain or level of consciousness. I introduced the idea of a three-level model of consciousness in Chapter 4 of *Archetypes of the Enneagram*, where I told the story of a spiritual facilitator who was trying to help his students connect with the higher self only to find that about a third of them were not successful. This teacher did not understand why until he encountered a Hawaiian *kahuna*, who said that it is not possible to properly connect with our higher self until we have connected with our *lower* self—with the primordial, child-like self that remains vital, organic, unconditioned, and receptive.[1]

Although some people connect with that child-like self intuitively, others lose that connection in the process of growing up. Without that connection, it is difficult to "break out" of ego consciousness in either direction (whether to engage in deep psyche work or to advance to higher stages of spiritual awareness).

So we have three kinds of consciousness available to us:

- spiritual or ethereal consciousness
- ego or ordinary consciousness
- soul or deep consciousness

These three kinds of consciousness are like the three parts of a tree: the branches, the trunk, and the roots. For the tree to grow properly, it needs to grow both up into the sky (spirit) and down into the earth (soul). And it needs a means to integrate the two, so they are in balance (ego). Here's an expanded summary of the three domains (Fig. 8-3):

■ **Spirit**: the sun, light, explosive expansion, containment & governance, ethics, fairness, discipline, exemplary action, leadership, responsibility, strength, the natural world, ethics & morals, justice, balance, harmony, embodying our spiritual potential*

■ **Ego**: the earth, everyday activity, work, play, practical applications, self-image, social & cultural roles, social networks, personal relationships, family ties, friendships, common sense, communication, civilization, entrepreneurship, innovation, society, embodying our cultural potential

■ **Soul**: the moon, mystery, darkness, inward orientation, imaginal world, shadow energy, chaos, originality, shamanism, deep psychology, upside-down perspectives, icon-breaking, alchemical transformation, annihilation, death & rebirth, embodying our hidden potential

As we can see, the domain of spirit is not just about expanded states of awareness, but about leadership, responsibility, and ethically based action in life. The domain of ego is not just about ordinary ("beta"-wave) states of consciousness, but about love, trust, cultural development, and community service. The domain of soul is not just about repressed material and shadow work, but about creativity, originality, and re-birth. Each domain has a different "feel" to it and a different purpose; all three play a necessary role in human life.

At the same time, the position of our type on the enneagram circle influences our relationship with the three domains, in that we tend to function best in the domain where our type is found and somewhat less well in the other two domains. As we can see from Fig. 8-3,

■ **Types 8-9-1** in the spirit zone = *spirit* types

■ **Types 2-3-6-7** in the ego zone = *ego* types

■ **Types 4-5** in the soul zone = *soul* types

Grouping types by domain provides us with more tools to understand the nature of each type, especially the energy dynamics to which it is particularly sensitive. The goal for all types is to achieve a reasonable balance between these three domains, because it is the lack of balance that creates the greatest barriers to growth.

Next, let's look at a breakdown of the types by the three domains.

SPIRIT TYPES (8-9-1). The types in this domain are oriented towards action in the outer or natural world. They have a natural affinity with the fiery world of creation or Spirit

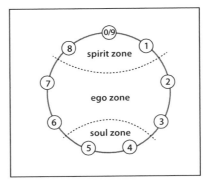

Fig. 8-3. Horizontal zones of influence on the personality enneagram.

---

*For purposes of discussing spirit zones and spirit types, I'm not capitalizing *spirit* (as I do when referring to Spirit in the transcendent sense) because I don't want to suggest that spirit types are more spiritual in the sense of being more evolved on the spiritual path; rather, they are spiritual in the sense of being powerfully animated by raw, fiery, active energy.

and an innate ability to anchor the energy of that world in this one, thus infusing matter with spiritual energy. For the same reason, they often function best in some sort of leadership, facilitative, or inspirational role—because they remind us of what is possible when we act in a way that embodies the laws that govern the Kosmos. *Type 1* seeks to articulate those principles in a top-down (spirit-oriented) fashion; *Type 8*, to embody them in a bottom-up (body-oriented) fashion; and *Type 9*, to reconcile the two.

Non-spirit types (especially those in modern, secularized cultures) can have a hard time grasping the nature of this realm because they don't feel it in their bodies (or in their "being") the way that spirit types do. However, soul types (Types 4 and 5) will tend to translate the energy of spirit (the transcendent psyche), by analogy, into the energy of soul (the deep psyche): *Type 4* uses it to find meaning in life and *Type 5*, to gain knowledge. So there can be a kind of resonance between spirit and soul domains.

For ego types, however, making sense of this domain may be tougher, especially for those on the right-hand side (Types 2 and 3) because they tend to be particularly focused on their activities in the material and social world. On the process enneagram, they are on the downward arc, getting more deeply involved in the material world. So *Type 2* is looking for someone to relate to and *Type 3* is looking for someone to please. Those on the left-hand side (Types 6 and 7) are moving towards the spirit zone, so they can be more attracted to it; also, as "air" types (see Chapter 3), they have a greater affinity with the fire associated with the spirit domain. *Type 6* can draw courage by connecting with the fiery energy of this domain; *Type 7* can use

the same energy to become less scattered and more contained.

EGO TYPES (2-3-6-7). The most sociable types on the enneagram are those in the middle zone: Types 2 and 3 on the right-hand side and Types 6 and 7 on the left. These are the types that seem particularly well-adapted to everyday activities, especially community-oriented activities. *Type 2* is drawn to hands-on helping, charitable giving, and convivial social events. *Type 3* is a friendly professional who focuses on goal-oriented activities such as team building, personnel management, and event organizing. *Type 6* seeks to create a social support system that provides personal and family security while facilitating community service. And *Type 7* is a natural networker who sees people as social resources and a source of innovative ideas.

Non-ego types can navigate in the ego realm, but they often lack a certain social comfortability when it comes to appropriately adapting to social situations; Eights and Ones can have overt problems with channelling their anger, for example (with *Type 8* tending to get impatient and *Type 1* tending to control anger by becoming overly rigid). *Type 9* adapts behaviorally by acting agreeable, hiding resentments by inwardly withdrawing into his own little world. Types 4 and 5 have trouble feeling deeply engaged, because what goes on can seem superficial and meaningless (*Type 4*) or energetically overwhelming (*Type 5*).

SOUL TYPES (4-5). The soul self is associated with the nadir of the enneagram, in the region around Points 4 and 5, an area that has been associated with both chaos and creativity, darkness and genius. In *The Intelligent Enneagram* (1996), A. G. E. Blake calls this an area of "turbulence, fire, and chaos" (p. 342); in *Enneagram Studies* (1983), J. G. Bennett associates it with "the point of maximum distress" (p. 55); Judith Searle associates it with the Abyss, the Void, the Dark Night of the Soul, and death.[2]

Thus, soul types tend to draw inspiration "from the depths," and thus spend more time alone, apart from others, because it is by delving into the roots of things that they achieve a sense of connectedness with life. *Type 4* seeks meaning and a sense of ongoing connectedness to the core self; *Type 5* seeks understanding and a sense of how the world works. We see the energy of the nadir reflected in the type characteristics of Types 4 and 5. Both Fours and Fives tend to experience a sense of aloneness, alienation, and inner intensity that separates them from others, especially those with wings that pull them towards the nadir (i.e., the 4w5 and 5w4).[3]

Non-soul types can find this realm intense, disorienting, or frightening, because of its association with the unconscious or shadow energy. *Type 9* is probably the least reactive to this energy because a Nine tends to be stimulated by intense emotions. Both Types 8 and 1 often react with resistance, trying to keep it at bay, because it can force them to acknowledge vulnerabilities that make them uncomfortable; *Type 8* screens it out energetically by denying it exists while *Type 1* is more likely to acknowledge its existence but deny its value (or worse, to identify it as something bad or wrong). Ego types (2-3-6-7) tend to react less strongly, although the energy of the nadir is perceived by *Type 3* as disquieting (because it's a portent of things to come) and by *Type 6* as threatening (because it might pull them "back into the abyss"). *Type 2* tends to be

more annoyed than threatened, because soul energy is not very sociable; and *Type 7* can find it fascinating—at least to a point. (Sevens eventually get fatigued by too much depth or intensity.)

So now we have two additional ways of characterizing the nine enneagram types: in terms of their vertical polarity and horizontal domain type. Let's see what happens when we look at the same dimensions on the process enneagram.

Process Enneagram Patterns

The process enneagram describes transformation cycles, both great and small. As we saw in Chapter 6, it can describe something as ordinary as the transformation of food during the making of a restaurant meal. But it can also describe the transformation of human consciousness over the course of a lifetime. When describing the latter, we can use the enneagram circle to depict the physical life cycle of a human being, where Point 0 = birth and Point 9 = death. What comes in between depends upon how we want to break down the life cycle. For our purposes here, we'll use the exact same approach that we did when breaking down the personality enneagram—looking at the vertical and horizontal zones—before talking about how each approach informs the other.

Vertical Zones on the Process Enneagram

On the personality enneagram, we looked at the circle by dividing it into three vertical zones in terms of their polarity, with the feminine on the right, the masculine on the left, and an androgynous in the center. On the process enneagram, we are looking at the same vertical zones in the context of time or a sequential process (rather than in the context of space or perspective-taking). From this process perspective, these zones are like stages through which we pass as we progress from *birth* to *death*. During the first half of life, we descent into the depths of life; during the second half, we ascend back to heaven (Fig. 8-4).

Although the shift at mid-life is a continuation of a progressive move around the circle, it is also a shift from descent to ascent. In Taoist philosophy, this shift is comparable to the end of a feminine (yin) cycle and the initiation of a masculine (yang) cycle. In esoteric philosophy, it is like the alternating of the Cosmic Tides, denoting the shift from the Cosmic Night to the Cosmic Day—a change in phase that "will always precipitate an evolutionary crisis," according to esotericist Dion Fortune.[4] According to Jung, when such a shift occurs, it "means the reversal of all the ideals and values that were cherished in the morning. The sun falls into contradiction with itself."[5]

Jung's image of the sun "falling into contradiction with itself" is apt. It helps us understand the radical nature of the shift from descent to ascent—and also why there is such a strong tendency at this point to violently reject formerly cherished values, often *en masse*: because they can appear to obstruct our new path of ascent. Many of us have the tendency not only to move too fast too soon (zealously burning our bridges as we go) but to see our former approach to life in a negative light—not simply as something outgrown but as something inherently bad (deluded, superficial, materialistic, egotistical, conditioned, self-limiting, etc.).

This is where it can be helpful to understand the nature of the life cycle: so that we realize that it is not necessary to pathologize the values of the previous cycle in order to move to the next stage of development but only to be open to change, so that outgrown patterns can gradually recede in the face of emerging values and priorities.

Whatever our life experiences, past or present, they are never without value, because they provide the raw substance necessary for ongoing development. Gurdjieff alludes to the same idea when he notes in *In Search of the Miraculous* that inner work depends upon the existence of "material [life experience] upon which work on oneself must be based" (p. 163). With that understanding, we're ready to take a closer look at each of the vertical zones.

DESCENDING/INVOLUTIONARY ARC (Points 1-2-3-4). During the first half of the life cycle, we're moving full tilt into the thick of life, learning basic skills, developing our talents, discovering our interests, and making creative adjustments to life's limitations. I think of this half of life as *involutionary* be-

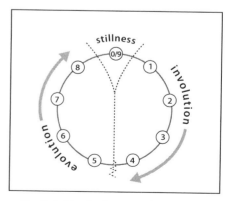

Fig. 8-4. Vertical zones of influence on the process enneagram.

cause it draws us into deeper and deeper involvement in life, in order that we can

- develop a well-defined and stable point of view (***Point 1***)
- learn how to love and be loved (***Point 2***)
- successfully adapt to cultural standards (***Point 3***)
- be true to ourselves and our personal standards (***Point 4***)

ASCENDING/EVOLUTIONARY ARC (Points 5-6-7-8). During the second half of life, we do not reverse direction, going back the way we came; we instead continue along the same transformational arc. This is an important point, because it means that the entire life cycle is progressive (transformational), whether it involves involution/descent or evolution/ascent. The degree of transformation experienced depends upon how we negotiate each step in the process—which means that every step affords opportunities for transformation.

During descent, the focus is on accumulating life experience, so that we can become an autonomous self. During ascent, the focus is on using that experience to expand our understanding in a way that serves life in the larger sense. From a holarchic perspective, if involution is about learning how to function as an autonomous whole, evolution is about learning how to function as part of something greater than ourselves:

- seeing the self and the self's experiences as part of a much larger context (***Point 5***)
- learning how to serve and support the larger social community (***Point 6***)
- collecting experiences that can connect the self with all that is beyond it (***Point 7***)

- understanding that personal power is subsidiary to Kosmic power (***Point 8***)

POINT OF STILLNESS/BEING/INTEGRATION (Point 0/9). Just as on the personality enneagram, Point 9 is the only point in the (narrow) middle zone. On the personality enneagram, Point 9 symbolizes neutrality or androgyneity; but on the movement-oriented process enneagram it signifies *stillness*: the point where we hover between heaven (disembodiment) and earth (embodiment). However, there is one big difference: on the process enneagram, this location signifies two very different points in the life process: birth (***Point 0***) and death (***Point 9***). The fact that these two points (0 and 9) overlap gives us a geometric hint that the life cycle is not really a closed circle but an open spiral.

Before looking at the horizontal zones on the process enneagram, I should note that associating the first half of life with involution and the second half with evolution is a clear departure from Wilber's model of the life cycle, which is purely evolutionary (ascent-oriented). So his approach could be called "*ascend-only*" while the approach associated with the process enneagram could be called "*descend-then-ascend*." We'll take a closer look at the difference in Chapter 9.

Briefly, Wilber's approach is designed to promote a progressive (rather than retro-Romantic) view of the life cycle, as described in Chapter 4. However, the process enneagram depicts a model that includes both involution and evolution[6] but is also clearly progressive, as we will see. The advantage of including involution as part of the transformational cycle is that it allows us to look at transformation in a new light, i.e., to focus less on the destination and more on the journey—on how willing we are at each point to

- notice what is unfolding in the moment (0)
- take principled action (1)
- emotionally support others (even when it means letting them alone) (2)
- take on difficult tasks in a balanced way (3)
- resist the social pressure to abandon our deepest intuitions (4)
- use our ideas in a way that is genuinely transformational (5)
- have the faith to stay the course (6)
- embrace the new without seeking escape from the old (7)
- lead by example (8)
- embrace all points of view, but mostly especially our own (9)

HORIZONTAL ZONES ON THE PROCESS ENNEAGRAM

Just as with the personality enneagram, we can meaningfully divide the process enneagram into three horizontal zones (Fig. 8-5). But on the process enneagram, they represent areas we traverse as we move from point to point on the circle. In the spirit zone (8-9-1), we are either at the beginning or end of the life cycle; in the ego zone (2-3-6-7), we are in the thick of life; and in the soul zone (4-5), we go within ourselves to find answers that cannot be found in outer life. Now let's take a look at each zone in turn.

SPIRIT ZONE (Points 8-9-1). At both the beginning and end of life, we are still primarily in the world of spirit. At the very beginning of life (*Point 0/9*), we come "trailing

clouds of glory," because of the reflected light of Spirit in the newly born. The fact that this light fades as we grow to maturity is not because we as individuals are becoming less spiritual, but because we are moving out of the spiritual *zone*. (The same thing happens when we leave the presence of a spiritual teacher: we feel uplifted in the teacher's presence but the feeling fades when we leave his presence.) At *Point 1*, we are moving from the spiritual zone towards the zone of ego—and as a result, there is a lingering receptivity to higher-level (spiritual) energies but relatively little life experience. So our spiritual impulses tend to become expressed in a form that is somewhat constrained by social convention (because we can then draw from the accumulated wisdom of past generations to structure those impulses). By the time we approach the spiritual zone again on the return arc, at *Point 8*, we have long ago lost our youthful idealism and may even be burdened with some degree of cynicism (which we may however think of as "realism") as the result of passing through so many difficulties while traversing the rest of the circle. However, we have gained a great deal of life experience,

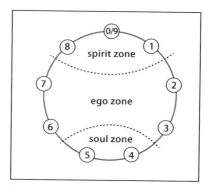

Fig. 8-5. Horizontal zones of influence on the process enneagram.

which potentially gives us the ability to tell the difference between real and false spirituality—and the understanding that the only real spirituality is the kind we can actually embody. As we approach *Point 9*, we move towards the zone of purely spiritual influence. But on the return arc, it's our life experiences, spiritual practices, and attitudes that play the biggest role in determining the nature of our experience: those who have come into true alignment with their inner nature tend to radiate an energy similar to the aura we see in small babies. But this time, the energy actually comes from within and is thus truly transpersonal in nature.

EGO ZONE (Points 2-3-6-7). Just as with the spirit zone, we pass through the ego zone twice during the life cycle: once during the first half of life (Points 2-3) and once during the second half (Points 6-7). Because this zone includes four points and occupies the largest space on the enneagram, it exercises a lot of influence. The first passage marks the entry into the world of relationships (*Point 2*) and skill acquisition (*Point 3*) and is thus associated with early- to mid-adulthood, when we are "coming into our own" in life. It is a productive but busy period where we develop a functional sense of self, the ability to think, and the skills required to move beyond youthful dependency. It is not a particularly reflective time, because we are busy establishing ourselves in the outer world: earning money, raising a family, promoting a career. The second time we find ourselves in this zone is during the second half of life, after we have passed through the unsettling soul zone, in which we find out just how uncertain life can be. Earlier, the focus was on

"me" (developing the sense of self); now the focus is on "we"—on the larger social fabric that holds civilization together. We look to it to provide us with a sense of situatedness in life. At *Point 6*, we are emerging from instability but feel afraid that we might somehow slip back into the previous zone. We assuage our fears by becoming involved in family and community and take comfort in the stability associated with social conventions. As we gain confidence, our horizons gradually widen. By *Point 7*, we are ready to venture forth into the wider world and to throw over conventions that have outlived their usefulness (although there is still a thread of anxiety present, such that we're prepared to retreat in the face of danger).

SOUL ZONE (Points 4-5). The zone of soul is on the bottom of the circle, and it is where we are pulled down out of our "normal" lives and into a space of soul-searching and solitude. At Point 3, we discover what can be achieved through hard work and determination; but as we move towards *Point 4*, we begin to become weary of work and in need of a change. But to find out what kind of change is needed, we have to stop pushing so hard and see what happens. And what usually happens is that those aspects of our persona that are not really part of our core self start to disintegrate. We begin to realize that much of what we've built to this point was built on an illusion: *the illusion that we are in full control of our destiny.* The only way to progress is to surrender that illusion and, with it, our self-constructed sense of order. The chaos we experience at this point is normal, because it represents the breakdown of everything that no longer serves us. The crossing of the nadir to **Point 5** represents the shift from seeing ourselves as the creator and controller of our own personal universe to seeing the self as part of a larger creation, a creation that is beyond the reach of our personal imagination. This realization is stunning; it forces us to contemplate the insignificance of the personal self in the face of the impersonality of life. And it creates within us an overwhelming desire to *know*: to understand how life really works. It is via the seeking of knowledge that we begin to develop a new foundation for living, an approach that eventually leads us back to the "surface" of life.

Seven Zones of Influence

Tables 8-1 and 8-2 summarize the zone information discussed in the previous pages, so that we can better see the relationship between personality zones (8-1) and life cycle/ transformational zones (8-2). If we compare each *type* description with its corresponding *stage* description, we can see that they bear an unmistakable resemblance to one another (similar to what we have seen in Chapter 7).

However, note in these tables how the type descriptions are more dynamic and subjective (because they describe personality types) while the stage descriptions are more detached and objective (because they describe the challenges faced at each point in a transformative process).

The next graphic, Fig. 8-6, shows what happens when we juxtapose the three horizontal zones (Spirit-Ego-Soul) with the vertical zones of the process enneagram (Ascent-Descent-Stillness). This approach potentially highlights how profoundly a difference in vertical direc-

tion (ascent or descent) can affect the process of transformation for types in each zone.

Types on the feminine right-hand side (0-1-2-3-4) are part of the descending (involutionary) arc; for them, transformation comes as the result of finding their personhood and coming to terms with the material world. Types on the masculine left-hand side (5-6-7-8-9) are part of the ascending (evolutionary) arc; for them, transformation often comes as the result of translating the energy of the material world into a more ethereal form.[7]

When we add in the three domains, we can generate seven zones of influence:

- **POINT 0/9: Stillness in Spirit**
  Harmonizing the opposites (descent & ascent)

- **POINT 1: Descent from Spirit**
  Grounding heaven on earth (voiced ideals)

- **POINTS 2 & 3: Descent through Ego**
  Participating in life to discover & develop the self through relationships & work

- **POINT 4: Descent into Soul**
  Finding the source of self (deep self)

- **POINT 5: Ascent from Soul**
  Finding the source of insight (deep truth)

- **POINTS 6 & 7: Ascent through Ego**
  Participating in life to discover where we fit in the larger scheme of things

- **POINT 8: Ascent to Spirit**
  Raising earth to heaven (embodied ideals)

This way of organizing the zones emphasizes them from a process-oriented perspective, enabling us to envision a transformational journey in which we start at the top of the enneagram in stillness, descend through the three involutionary zones towards the bottom of the circle, re-ascend through the three evo-

TABLE 8-1. PERSONALITY DESCRIPTIONS BY ZONE.

| | Masculine polarity
Focus on objectified self | Androgyneity
Focus on harmony | Feminine polarity
Focus on subjective self |
|---|---|---|---|
| **Spirit types** | Type 8: masterful leader who embodies his truth | Type 9: impassive harmonizer with a universal perspective | Type 1: impassioned articulator of pure ideals |
| **Ego types** | Type 7: futuristic planner with visionary ideas | | Type 2: warm supporter of family & friends |
| | Type 6: concrete analyst with a community focus | | Type 3: hard-working adapter who never gives up |
| **Soul types** | Type 5: detached & iconoclastic systemizer | | Type 4: committed seeker of authentic self |

TABLE 8-2. LIFE CYCLE DESCRIPTIONS BY ZONE.

| | Evolution: ascent to spirit
Focus on knowledge | Stillness
Focus on being | Involution: descent to matter
Focus on personal involvement |
|---|---|---|---|
| **Spiritual domain** | Point 8: understanding power & how to wield it | Point 0: imagination
Point 9: integration | Point 1: determining the standards that ensure ethical behavior |
| **Ego domain** | Point 7: understanding life systems & their interactions | | Point 2: seeing the self reflected in relationships with others |
| | Point 6: empirically testing reality & seeking mental development | | Point 3: gaining a sense of self through tangible achievement |
| **Soul domain** | Point 5: contemplating the objective nature of life | | Point 4: finding a way to know the core self |

lutionary zones, and eventually return to our point of origin, but at a slightly higher level (as depicted by Fig. 3-5 in Chapter 3).

But we can also look at the zones horizontally (primarily as spirit types, ego types, and soul types), which allows us to see how the position of each type on the transformational arc affects its personality characteristics, as discussed below.

SPIRIT TYPES by Transformational Arc. While all spirit types have a natural affinity with the spiritual world, *Type 9* is the most "purely" spiritual in the sense that spirit is so naturally a part of them that it's hard for them to see anything in life as bereft of it. So in this sense, they are the most innocent of all types. But they can become the most ignorant if they hold back from setting forth on the transformational journey because of a desire to remain in undifferentiated oneness. For them, transformation depends upon the ability to say yes

to the journey while still retaining their innocence ("inner sense"), so that what begins as unconscious union at the start can become the conscious integration of "the one and the many" at the end.

Types 1 and 8 are also within the spiritual zone, so they both have an affinity with the transcendent. But *Type 1* is *headed towards* the ego zone (the world of human affairs), so this type instinctively sees the value of building a civilization on earth that reflects the majesty of heaven. Therefore, whatever Ones do, it is with the expectation of introducing a new level of refinement into the world around them. The approach is top-down, in that it's based on an idealized and purified view of life.

While *Type 8* is also in the spiritual zone, it is part of the energy that is *emerging from* the ego zone. It is also located at the very end of the entire life cycle, so it has the benefit of implicitly understanding the rough-and-tumble na-

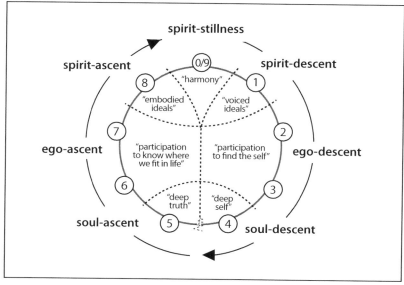

Fig. 8-6. Seven areas of influence.

ture of life experiences—which is why Eights possess such a highly pragmatic, earthy type of spirituality. Where Ones seek to somehow establish a spiritual ideal in a less-than-spiritual world, Eights fight to embody it within their own being. They instinctively know that what ultimately matters most is what we can exemplify in thought, word, and deed.

Ego Types by Transformational Arc. The concerns of all the types in the middle of the circle (Types 2 & 3 and Types 6 & 7) focus on daily life, especially the world of social interaction. However, Types 2 and 3 are on the descending arc, where the priority is on developing an independent sense of self and the skills that allow that self to maintain autonomy in the world. *Type 2* does this by cultivating relationships that help them to feel at home in the world; they also learn how to see themselves through the eyes of others. Because they are transitioning from Spirit to ego, Twos instinctively seek out the warmth and companionship that makes life on earth worth living. *Type 3* is in the same zone of ego descent; thus, Threes feel naturally at home in the world but in need of solidifying their position by skill building and tangible achievements. Like Twos, they still look to external sources for bolstering their sense of self; but their life experiences gradually help them to gain a sense of self that needs less external verification.

Types 6 and 7 are on the ascending side of the transformational arc. Like Twos and Threes, they are interested in social interaction. But that interest is tempered by the understanding that the world can be a hazardous place, an understanding gained during the passage through the nadir. Although this understanding actually represents a form of expanded awareness (in that it helps the self come into relationship with a much bigger reality), it also produces fear and awe. The fear isn't directly felt at Point 5 (because the awareness is too elemental); but by Point 6, it takes on much more substance, becoming solidified into a fear of environmental threats.

Thus, *Type 6* must find out how to open up to this awareness without feeling overwhelmed by fear. A Six typically uses a variety of tools to do this: supportive family structures and social networks (for social support), education in scientific and technical disciplines (for knowledge), the cultivation of hobbies that are a little scary but fun (for confidence-building), and a sense of humor (for releasing insecurity). The proper role of these support tools is to provide the Six with the stability and confidence necessary to look within, where she will find not only the source of her greatest fears but the inner strength to transmute them.

Fear that has been tranformed becomes awe—and is felt emotionally as joy and exuberance. A lot of energy is liberated in the transmutation process, which is why *Type 7* has such an amazing appetite for life experiences. Sevens use this appetite to seek out the experiences that allow them to connect with life in all its outer diversity, which is a way of connecting with themselves, in all of their inner diversity. To make the transition to Point 8, they need to start internalizing these experiences, thereby becoming more grounded and less scattered.

Soul Types by Transformational Arc. Both soul types, Four and Five, exist in a world that is set somewhat apart from ordinary life. It's a region associated not only with depth and complexity, but mystery, darkness, and unseen influences.

Type 4 is at the very bottom of the descending arc, at the point where we have developed a sense of self to the point where it cannot really be developed further. Anyone wanting to continue the transformational point, has to go within—to begin the process of working with unconscious processes. When we do so, we usually find that the energy is not very orderly. And this is why the area at the nadir seems so chaotic: because it is the place where the boundaries between the self and the not-self begin to dissolve, giving rise to a completely different (and reversed) perspective, as we move from one half of the circle to the other. *Type 5* has crossed over, but is in a peculiar place. The sense of alienation associated with this type comes not only from this reversal of perspective but from a concomitant reversal in direction: for the Five is the first type on the ascendent arc. Thus, this type is in some ways just like a new baby: at the beginning of both a new perspective (where the self becomes backgrounded) and a new direction (where the world becomes backgrounded). This is why this type is so open, curious, and in a very real sense, innocent. (It is also why they often get along well with small children.)

Significance of the Nadir

The nadir—the very bottom—of the circle is a highly significant point on the circle whose understanding helps us better understand why mid-life brings the arising of impulses which (if heeded) can help us shed unwanted conditioning and come into greater alignment with our true self—a process that Jung called *individuation*.

As discussed earlier, the nadir is where we make the switch in direction from involution

to evolution. On the enneagram, it is positioned exactly opposite Point 9, symbolically at the midpoint between birth and death.

The great esoteric teacher and Qabalist Dion Fortune takes the same view set forth here—that the soul descends during the first part of life deeper into the material world. In answer to the question, "What ought a man want?" she says that the answer depends upon our stage of development:

> The soul has to complete its human experience before it is ready for Divine Union. It must pass the nadir of the descent into matter before it can come on to the Path of Return...to try to escape from the Wheel [of Birth and Death] prematurely is to evade our training."[8]

However, this switch is not something that occurs overnight but as part of an ever-intensifying series of crises and resolutions, which—while inner in nature—can be accompanied by a significant shift in outer priorities. In *Dark Wood to White Rose* (1975), Helen Luke likens it to the beginnings of Dante's descent into the inferno:

> A man arrives there usually, but not by any means always, at the midpoint of life...it may come later; and often, especially nowadays, it comes much earlier—the moment when we awaken to know that we are lost—to realize, as Jung says, that we are not the master of the house (p. 9).

Given the nature of the situation—i.e., the destabilizing realization that "we are not the master of the house"—it's not surprising that traversing the nadir is not an overnight process. On the enneagram, the influence of the energy experienced at this point in life is best captured by depicting a zone of instability around the nadir extending in both directions and thus creating a three-zoned process involving descent/involution, instability, and ascent/evolution (Fig. 8-7).

The effects of the nadir begin to be felt about halfway between Points 3 and 4, which is why Threes with a Four wing tend to be more restless and introspective than Threes with a Two wing. Both Fours and Fives feel the effect of the nadir much more directly, although it is the types with wings towards the nadir (4w5 and 5w4) that are most affected.

This is what accounts for the need of these individuals for long periods of solitude: they are dealing with internal energies that are highly creative but also destabilizing. Between Points 5 and 6, the influence of the nadir begins to taper off, although one of the reasons Points 6 and 7 are "fear" types is because they contain within them the archetypal memory of the nadir, which they instinctively dread.

If this "three zone" idea sounds familiar, it is another way to account for the nature of dramatic stories, a topic discussed in Chapter 7. You will recall that it's the middle part—

the part that surrounds the nadir—which is defined by some sort of crisis, trouble, or descent into darkness. Juxtaposing the involution/evolution model and the three-part story model discussed in Chapter 6 (Fig. 8-8) allows us to better understand the inner dynamic underlying the crisis: to see that this crisis arises from the growing pressure to break out of personal conditioning and an overly-simplified view of life.

This is not a need that generally arises early in life (i.e., at Points 1–3), because during childhood and early adulthood, we are fully absorbed in the task of adapting to the values of our culture (Point 1), bonding with friends and family (Point 2), and developing the skills necessary to stand on our own two feet in the world (Point 3).

But once we've learned enough to make our way in the world, we begin to feel the restlessness that marks the transition from Point 3 to 4. Moving into Point 4 territory, we become more and more aware of impulses arising from some place deep within us, and these are what gives rise to "trouble," be-

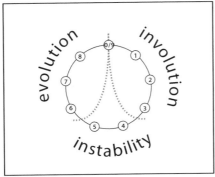

Fig. 8-7. Instability around the nadir.

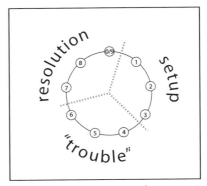

Fig. 8-8. Three parts of a story.

cause they tend to put us into conflict with the conditioned self (hence, the concern with authenticity at Point 4): the more we are able to put the two into alignment, the less harrowing the transition from Point 4 to 5.

Although the resolution of trouble begins at the nadir, there can be no complete resolution until Point 6, where we encounter our deepest fears. But the instability created by the nadir is what kick-starts the process of deep-level change.

As mentioned above, the nadir is the point where, in Jungian terms, we have the opportunity to *individuate* (as opposed to simply individualizing). It is where, in holarchic terms, we see that we are never just wholes (individuals) but also parts within some larger whole (the Kosmos). And in *dharmic* terms, it is where we begin to understand that life is not just about us.

So it's a momentous point in development that brings both new opportunities and risks. While it liberates us from the limited, person-centered view of the involutionary cycle, it throws us into a brave new (evolutionary) world where we feel utterly ignorant and in need of knowledge about life from a more impersonal point of view. The danger, of course, is that we'll throw the baby out with the bath water—that in the interests of embracing a more impersonal perspective, we'll violently reject all that is personal and subjective in life.

This is always the challenge when transitioning to a new stage: making the transition in a way that does not involve rejecting the old—at least not permanently. In the initial shift, the focus obviously has to be on adopting a new point of view which, by definition, is different than what came before. So it re-

quires our undivided attention. But focusing on the new is not the same as rejecting the old. However, it can sometimes accelerate the pace of change. But at what cost?

When effected in a non-integrative way, the crossing of the nadir results in a major split in consciousness, wherein the lessons learned during descent are rejected as inferior to ascent (or worse, as an actual impediment to it). This is how the masculine becomes divorced from the feminine, descent comes to be devalued, and transformation becomes associated solely with the process of ascent.

An Integral Enneagram Model

Our focus in this chapter has been on describing the enneagram zones of influence in a way that supports not only a more integral way of both working with the enneagram, but a more integral way of envisioning transformation. The model that emerges—a "one-enneagram" or Integral Enneagram model—provides many tools for exploring the relationship between individuality and transformation (Fig. 8-9).

This transformational model is entirely progressive (like Wilber's) but this model also includes both ascent and descent phases (like Jung's but unlike Wilber's, which currently only includes an ascent phase). Including descent as part of the transformational cycle has many advantages, as we will see in Chapter 9. It can also potentially bridge the gap between descent-oriented approaches (e.g., those of Abraham Maslow, Michael Washburn, Stan Grof, and Jorge Ferrer) and ascent-oriented approaches (e.g., those of Ken Wilber and Roberto Assagioli). [9]

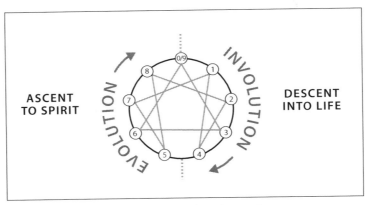

Fig. 8-9. The transformational cycle on the enneagram.

Summing Up Chapters 5–8

As we have seen in the four preceding chapters, the enneagram is much more than a system for identifying barriers to transformation: it's a system that points to our core motivation, relationships with others, and transformational potential. Accordingly, it is particularly effective as a tool for helping us discover our *dharma* in life.

My purpose in Part II has been to develop the foundation for a more integrally-oriented enneagram model—a model that moves beyond the limitations imposed by the current retro-Romantic paradigm (Chapter 5). But an integral enneagram depends not just on moving away from retro-Romanticism but on moving towards a model with the ability to reconcile different enneagram approaches.

In Chapters 6 and 7, we looked at how we can bring together two versions of the enneagram to create a one-enneagram model: Chapter 6 described the process enneagram (which breaks down any kind of transforma-tional process into nine steps or stages) and Chapter 7 described the parallels between the types on the personality and the points on the process enneagrams. Chapter 8 focused on the patterns that emerge when we divide the enneagram into different zones using an Integral Enneagram ("one-enneagram") model. And it introduced the idea that involutionary descent and evolutionary ascent are intrinsic features of such a model.

In Chapter 9—the first chapter in Part III—we'll take a closer look at this model and its potential for bringing the enneagram and Wilber's IOS into a more synergistic relationship.

ONE LAST NOTE: Once we understand that the numbers associated with the enneagram can refer not only to personality types but to points in a developmental process, this understanding may make some readers wonder whether the types having higher numbers (Eights or Nines) may be somehow more evolved than the types having a lower numbers (Ones or

Twos). But in truth, there is absolutely no relationship between our type number and our developmental level (although the type number *can* probably yield highly useful information about the core energy associated with the type/point).[10]

Notes

1.   The idea of conceptualizing human activity in terms of three worlds or domains (upper, middle, and lower) is well-known in both shamanic and esoteric circles. Mircea Eliade discusses the three worlds in Chapter 8 of *Shamanism: Archaic Techniques of Ecstasy* (1964/2004), noting that "the pre-eminent shamanic technique is the passage from one cosmic region to another—from earth to the sky or from earth to the underworld" (p. 259). In Chapter 9 of *The Body of Myth* (1994), J. Nigro Sansonese discusses the role of the three worlds in esoteric mythology. In Chapter 4 of *Bowl of Light* (2011)—Hank Wesselman's account of talks with Hale Makua Kahuna, a revered Hawaiian *kahuna*—the latter affirms the universality of the three worlds among indigenous cultures. And in *Shamanic Voices* (1979), Joan Halifax stresses the emphasis placed in shamanic work on obtaining a balance between the three worlds (pp. 18–21).

2.   "The Gap at the Bottom of the Enneagram," *Enneagram Monthly*, Sept. 1997 (www.judithsearle.com/articles/gap-at-the-bottom.html; accessed 10-19-12).

3.   I am aware of the intensity of the energy associated with the enneagram nadir from direct experience, because I'm a Four with a Five wing (4w5). And my former partner of many years is a Five. So when I originally read descriptions of Fours and Fives, they sounded quite familiar. Both my Five partner and I could be reclusive; but while I liked to lose myself in creative projects, he liked to read philosophy or closely study dance videos to learn new moves (we both liked partner dances, especially those involving unusual rhythms or obscure patterns). In large gatherings, he became a silent observer while I sought out

someone with whom to have a meaningful, one-to-one conversation. I've noticed similar patterns in many Fours and Fives. So from the beginning, I've associated the bottom of the enneagram with the inner world, inner work, mystery, descent, shadow work, unusual perspectives or activities, unconditioned insights, and the chaotic but elemental energies of the deep psyche.

4.   *The Cosmic Doctrine* (1949/1995), p. 120.

5.   "The Stages of Life," in *The Portable Jung*, ed. by Joseph Campbell (1971), p. 15.

6.   Regarding the role of involution and evolution in transformation: A. G. E. Blake says straight out that "we can see the circle of the enneagram in terms of descent and ascent" (*The Intelligent Enneagram*, 1996, p. 270).

7.   Here I've included Type 9 twice, alluding to its dual role in the process enneagram as the anticipator or dreamer of future action (where it is Type 0) and the synthesizer or integrator of accumulated experience (where it is Type 9).

8.   *Applied Magic* (1962/2000), p. 3.

9.   See Michael Daniels' discussion in Chapter 1 of *Shadow, Self, Spirit* (2005).

10.   The numbers assigned to each point on the enneagram come straight out of Gurdjieff's original enneagram teachings (see Chapter 14 of Ouspensky's *In Search of the Miraculous*, 1949/2001). These numerical assignments are unlikely to be arbitrary, since the enneagram is an esoteric, geo-metrically-oriented system—and in such systems, numbers and angles are inherently meaningful. However, our current culture does not recognize the deeper significance of sacred geometry, numerology, or gematria (the esoteric relationship between language and numbers). Thus, the significance of the type numbers remains an area for future study. However, when I began to look at the correspondences between the personality enneagram and the AQAL quadrants (see Chapter 10), I did notice several interesting patterns related to even- vs odd-numbered enneagram types; see the discussion in Notes 14 and 15 at the end of Chapter 10.

PART III
INTEGRATING IOS
& THE ENNEAGRAM

PART I INTRODUCED IOS AND THE ENNEAGRAM; *Part II brought together the personality and process enneagrams to create a "one enneagram" (Integral Enneagram) model. Part III juxtaposes the Integral Enneagram model and IOS to create a new synthesis that combines the best elements of both systems.*

Chapter 9 focuses on vertical transformation and how the process enneagram can inform Wilber's current transformational model. Chapter 10 focuses on horizontal perspective-taking, linking the personality enneagram to Wilber's AQAL perspectives, especially the eight hori-zones. Chapter 11 brings the vertical and horizontal axes together, mapping the personality and process enneagrams onto Wilber's nine-stage Spectrum model of development.

In Chapter 12, the focus shifts to a more feminine, embodied perspective on transformation, exploring the nature of "win-win" groups, the relationship between limitation and creativity, and the role of receptivity in spiritual ascent. Chapter 13 presents chapter summaries, point-by-point comparisons of IOS and the enneagram, and a discussion of dharma *and its role in weaving together the separate threads in our lives into a coherent whole.*

9
VERTICAL INTEGRATION:
GROWING UP & DOWN

We are happy when we are growing.
– William Butler Yeats

WHAT DOES IT MEAN TO GROW? What are the different ways we can grow—and what makes each of them distinct? When we think of growth, is it a "growing up" towards heaven or a "growing down" into our roots?

Is all growth transformational? If so, what is transformed? Is transformational growth something that unfolds naturally or something requiring extraordinary effort to sustain?

Does the process by which we transform matter? Or is it more important to reach a high level of consciousness as quickly as possible, whatever method we use? If we had to choose between an integral methodology vs reaching the goal faster, but non-integrally, which approach would be better?

Ken Wilber has taken a keen interest in questions such as these. At the end of *Integral Psychology* (2000), Wilber lists at least 100 different scales that can be used as signposts to human development, including Piaget's stages of cognitive development, Kohlberg's levels of moral judgment, Maslow's hierarchy of needs, and Fowler's stages of faith—scales that are widely accepted within the academic community. But because his focus is particularly on higher consciousness, Wilber also includes many scales not found in any psychology textbook: Sri Aurobindo's levels of Integral Yoga, Underhill's stages of mystical spirituality, Teresa of Avila's seven stages of spiritual life, Vedanta's five sheaths of the soul, Cowan and Beck's Spiral Dynamics, and Wilber's own Spectrum of consciousness model. These scales focus not only on the pre-personal and personal phases of development but on transpersonal phases, as well.

Wilber lists all the scales at the end of *Integral Psychology* in a way that enables readers to readily see the relationships between them. This impressive compilation represents the culmination of a project Wilber had been working on since the publication of his first book, *The Spectrum of Consciousness* (1977), where he says in the Preface to the first edition that his goal is to effect a synthesis of all the seemingly disparate approaches to the development of consciousness.

Whatever their differences, what all these scales share in common is their vertical orientation, such that higher levels on the scale describe a greater degree of development concerning some trait, ability, or state of consciousness. What they don't describe is the degree to which lower levels are included (integrated) as we go. So vertical scales are very good at measuring our highest level of achievement but less good at measuring our degree of integration.

A second problem with vertical scales is that the information they generate can sometimes be misused. One egregious example is the misuse of IQ tests in the 1920s to justify both the forced sterilization of supposedly low-IQ American citizens and the turning away of would-be immigrants also placed into that category, including Eastern European Jews—a policy with ultimately tragic consequences for those stranded in German-controlled countries during WWII.

A third problem concerns the development of unbalanced holarchies, the kind that exploit some holons for the unfair benefit of others. Wilber refers to these as domination holarchies and obviously does not support their development.

However, he acknowledges that the existence of such holarchies makes people want to reject the idea of hierarchies *per se*, but points out that this will not work. Because whatever our negative experiences with hierarchy/holarchy, the Kosmos is hierarchically organized, such that different things happen on different levels of reality. So it's impossible to get rid of the idea of hierarchy *per se*, because it's intrinsic to life. The better alternative is to contemplate the nature of healthy hierarchies so we can foster their development.

This was Koestler's goal when he formulated his theory of holons: to develop a model of organic systems that identifies their basic properties. In Koestler's holarchic approach, the emphasis is on the idea that living systems are vertically organized in a way that facilitates the cooperative interaction among the different levels of the hierarchy. As discussed in previous chapters, especially Chapter 2, each element in the hierarchy is a Janus-faced holon that is designed to be receptive to what is above and responsible for what is below. It is because of this Janus-faced characteristic of holons that energy can flow freely up and down all levels of the holarchy (Fig. 9-1).

One of the marks of a healthy holarchy is its ability not only to develop the system as a whole but the individual holons within the system, such that they experience transformation. The transformation of individual holons can also transform the holarchy of which they are a part. So there is a cooperative relationship between each holon and the system in which it participates.

In this chapter, our focus will be on the transformation of human consciousness—a process that (as we've seen) can be depicted by

Gurdjieff's process enneagram as the movement through nine steps/stages of development, each of which has a distinctively different character.

In Chapter 6, we looked at how these nine stages can be described both in terms of transformational processes and elements in a dramatic story. In Chapter 7, we explored ways the personality and process enneagrams can be linked. And in Chapter 8, we saw how this linking can give rise to a "one-enneagram" or Integral Enneagram model which allows us to deeply explore the relationship between individuality and transformation.

The Integral Enneagram model describes an initial descent into life, followed by a re-ascent to Spirit. So it can be characterized as a *descend-then-ascend* approach. As such, it differs from the transformational model currently utilized by Wilber, a model we could characterize as *ascend-only*, in that it's built on the assumption that all descent occurs *prior* to birth, making birth the low point of embodied consciousness.

The advantage of Wilber's ascend-only model is that it avoids the pre/trans problems that are associated with the transformational models in use when he formulated the pre/trans fallacy (problems explained in greater detail below). The disadvantage is that it leaves no significant role for descent in the transformational process. As a result,

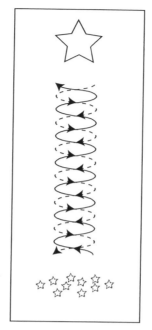

Fig. 9-1. The flow of energy up & down the holarchy.

it unavoidably privileges transcendence over immanence. My proposed Integral Enneagram model reincorporates descent into the transformational process, but in a way that does not create pre/trans problems, as we shall see.

In brief, here is how the discussion in this chapter will proceed. We'll begin where Wilber begins his discussion of transformation in *SES*: by looking at the two directions we can move when engaged in a transformational process (up or down) and the quality of each move (integrative or non-integrative). As we'll see, this gives rise to four potential transformational moves.

But before exploring these moves in detail, we'll take a look at the advantages of characterizing the first half of embodied life as a process of descent—and how this characterization necessitates the formulation of not four but eight transformational moves. This discussion is followed by an exploration of (a) the reasons why Wilber's current transformational model does not include a phase of embodied descent; (b) the advantages of adopting an enneagram-based model that *does* include a descent phase; and (c) the characteristics associated with this descent phase—in particular, its "include-and-transcend" (integration-oriented) focus.

At that point, there's a return to the topic of the transformational moves that occur during the descent and ascent phases (four moves per phase), followed by a comparison of three transformational models (retro-Romanticism, Wilber's "descend only" model, and my proposed Integral Enneagram model).

The chapter ends with a brief discussion of how our enneagram type affects the way we make the eight transformational moves and a longer discussion about the degree to which growth can be accelerated without sacrificing the ability to "integrate as we go."

Four Transformational Moves

As mentioned above, in any transformational process, we can move either *up* or *down* the hierarchy—and the move we make can be either *integrative* or *non-integrative*. This gives rise to four possible transformational moves (Table 9-1). The four moves depicted in Table 9-1 have been described in various passages in *Sex, Ecology, Spirituality (SES)* as part of a broader discussion about the nature of transformation. One of Wilber's aims in this book was to get across the idea that transformation takes place within the context of a holarchic model of the Kosmos, as discussed in Chapters 2 and 4.

You will recall from Chapter 2 that *SES* is the book where Wilber formally embraces the holon as linchpin for his integral approach—in order to demonstrate the inadequacy of purely horizontally oriented (e.g., web-of-life) philosophies that deny the need for hierarchies in life.[1] He tries very hard in *SES* to show that while hierarchy/holarchy is intrinsic to life, it doesn't have to be patriarchal, exploitative, or insensitive to human needs. So he is highly motivated to demonstrate that there is ample room in his new IOS for both upward (self-transcending) moves and downward (self-immanent) moves:

The first movement [of Spirit] is a *descent* of the One into the Many: ...Spirit *immanent* in the world. The other is a movement of return or *ascent* from the Many to the One :...Spirit *transcendent* in the world (*SES*, p. 330, *emphasis* his).

He goes on to make the point that, in Plato's work, "the two movements were given emphasis and equal importance," but that "when the unifying One is forgotten, the two movements fall apart into warring opposites...into ascetic and oppressive Ascenders... and shadow-hugging Descenders." While many people think of Plato as an Ascender, Wilber (citing Arthur Lovejoy's *Great Chain of Being*) portrays him in *SES* as a champion of both immanence and transcendence.[2]

Whatever Plato's approach, it's clear that Wilber endorses the idea that "the way up is the way down," i.e., that both immanence and transcendence matter. He associates *self-immanence* with Agape (the love of the higher reaching down to the lower) and *self-transcendence* with Eros (the love of the lower reaching up to the higher).[3] And so in individual development,

one *ascends* via Eros (or expanding to a higher and wider identity), and then *integrates* via Agape (or reaching down to embrace with care all lower holons), so that balanced development *transcends* but *includes*—it is negation and preservation, ascent and descent, Eros and Agape (p. 349, *emphasis* his).[4]

At this point, he also mentions that many wisdom traditions also emphasize the idea that as we ascend, Spirit descends to "pull us up," as it were, "inviting us to ascend." (Interestingly, Wilber does not talk about the opposite sort of invitation—the invitation to *descend*—perhaps because this is not something we see in the best-known wisdom traditions, most of which are more ascent- than descent-oriented.)

Next Wilber discusses what happens when we cannot integrate the opposites, and fall into one of two warring camps of Ascenders versus Descenders:

> To the Ascenders, "this world" is, in form and function, illusory at best, evil at worst—and the Descenders are the primary representatives of that evil. The Descenders [however] accuse the Ascenders of being repressive, puritanical, life-denying, sex-denying, earth-destroying, and body-ignoring (p. 356).

Whatever our camp, if we hate its opposite, then we are no longer acting out of the healthy desire for integration but out of the unhealthy desire to avoid that hated opposite. In that case, instead of ascending via self-transcendence (Eros), we ascend via *self-alienation* (Phobos). And instead of descending via self-immanence (Agape), we descend via *self-dissolution* (Thanatos). Unfortunately, when we ascend out of Phobos, we cut off access to lower levels, fearing they will impede or contaminate us. When we descend out of

Thanatos, we "fall" from the heights into the depths, regressing into oblivion.

In Table 9-1, you will notice that ascent is equated with forward movement while descent is equated with backward movement. This characterization gives rise to a model of evolutionary ascent, where forwards = up and backwards = down. Later we'll examine the related assumptions that (a) we evolve (transform) *only* via ascent and (b) forwards always = up. As we will see, while this idea holds true for the *second half of life*—when ascent is dominant—it does not hold true for the first half of life, when descent is dominant.

But I'm getting ahead of myself here. What matters at this point is understanding that transformation involves more than one kind of move—that it can be (a) up or down and (b) integrative or non-integrative.

Interestingly, although Wilber discusses each of these four transformational moves at various places in *SES*, he never discusses them all in one place. Nor does he ever devise a table like Table 9-1. Had he done so, he might have spotted a potential problem with his characterization of one of the moves: Agape (integra-

TABLE 9-1. FOUR POSSIBLE TRANSFORMATIONAL MOVES.

	INTEGRATIVE	NON-INTEGRATIVE
FORWARDS (ASCENT)	*EROS* (self-transcendence)	*PHOBOS* (self-alienation)
BACKWARDS (DESCENT)	*AGAPE* (self-immanence)	*THANATOS* (self-dissolution)

tive descent), a problem we will now look at in greater detail.

The first inkling that something is amiss shows up in a discrepancy in Wilber's discussion of Agape/self-immanence in *SES*. Although he discusses Agape in the context of Ascenders versus Descenders (see, e.g., the discussion in *SES's* Chapter 9 and in the Notes, pp. 759–760), it is nowhere to be found in his discussion of the capacity of holons to descend; there *he focuses only on descent from a nonintegrative perspective* (in terms of Thanatos, not Agape). As a result, he characterizes the descent of a holon as self-dissolution on p. 52.

When this characterization was called to his attention by a colleague, Fred Kofman, he said *mea culpa*, and characterized the omission as inadvertent in a subsequent Shambhala interview. But he went on to say in that interview that he often continues to describe the downward drive as self-dissolution, "simply because that is so much easier to understand in an introductory statement. But my actual position should now be clear, thanks to Fred."[5]

Hmmm....if the correct version of integrative descent is actually "self-immanence," why the wish to hang onto the incorrect version (self-dissolution)? And why is it characterized as much easier to understand?

Questions like these nagged at me when I read this material; it made be feel that there must be something missing in Wilber's account. Knowing of Wilber's transcend-and-include ethos, I couldn't help but puzzle at his reluctance to associate descent with self-immanence. From his writings, it's quite evident that he has done a lot of thinking about such issues, because he is able to iden-

tify the pathologies that arise at each level of development in the absence of integrative ascent—pathologies that can persist even at very advanced stages of spiritual development (see Chapter 11; see also Wilber's Chapter 8 in *Transformations of Consciousness*, 1986).

I always saw this insight concerning nonintegrative ascent as one of Wilber's most brilliant pieces of work, because it cuts straight through the illusion that once we get past the ego-based stage of development, we're more or less home-free. Wilber offers a convincing case that this is *definitely* not so—that *any* stage of development can be either healthy or pathological. Nevertheless, he seems to associate integration primarily with our ability to enfold earlier stages while continuing to ascend rather than with temporarily descending to earlier stages in the service of transformation. Similarly, when speaking of earlier stages in development (especially pre-rational stages or cultures), he almost invariably emphasizes their "down" side over their "up" side.

The more I examined this tendency, the more I realized that it affects his transformational model in some pretty significant ways, including the way he conceives of the four transformational moves discussed above. Thus, before further discussing these moves (and especially how they can be expanded from four to eight moves), it's necessary to set up the context for the discussion by first taking a closer look at Wilber's views on both descent and pre-rationality.

Wilber's Take on Descent

Wilber's views on involution, descent, and pre-rationality (i.e., "downwardness") go back a long ways, back as far as his very first book, *The Spectrum of Consciousness* (1977), which contains the following dramatic quote near its start:

> The Above has been denied, the Below has been ignored—and we are asked to remain—in the middle—paralyzed."[6]

What Wilber wants to emphasize here is that most of us in modern culture are stuck in flatland and need a way to get out. But notice the difference between his treatment of "up" and "down": while he clearly seeks to affirm the Above (which has been denied), he seeks only to *acknowledge* the Below, not necessarily to affirm it.

Later in *Spectrum*, when discussing what he would later come to call pre-rational structures of consciousness, Wilber associates them with Freud's model of subconsciousness, which posits the existence of the *id*, a chaotic mass of seething impulses that subvert our ability to function appropriately in life. He does not associate pre-rationality (à la Jung) with the *prima materia* necessary for alchemical transformation. When discussing Jung's archetypes in *Spectrum*, Wilber associates them exclusively with higher structures of consciousness, even though Jung himself views them as primordial (a belief which later allows Wilber to reject Jung by saying he falls prey to the pre/trans fallacy; see Note 15 in my Chapter 4). Interestingly, Wilber never renounces Freud to the extent that he renounces Jung (despite the fact that Freud's approach clearly has pre/trans problems, in that it denies the reality of higher states, reducing them to nothing more than "oceanic fusion"; see p. 103 in *One Taste*, 2000). Why the differ-

ence? Because Freud viewed pre-rationality as something pretty dark and disturbing, which is the same view that Wilber seems to have held when writing *Spectrum*.

By the time Wilber writes *The Atman Project* (1980), he has formulated the pre/trans fallacy and taken the position that all descent occurs prior to birth. While it might be plausible to speak of the descent (involution) from Spirit to matter simply as a move of the soul into planes of increasing density and limitation, he instead notes that "at each stage of involution, the soul construct[ed] a substitute self and a substitute world...but the substitutes eventually failed at each stage, and the self—terrified of its own dissolution—did not accept the death of its substitutes but merely contracted and then passed out in terror" (p. 200). So this characterization of involution has little to do with healthy self-immanence.

In *Up With Eden* (1981), although he speaks of the downward movement during involution as *lila* (Divine play)—making it sound like something delightful—when it comes to the specifics, Wilber describes involution as a "successive increasing of alienation, separation, dismemberment, and fragmentation" (p. 317). In the same book, he entitles the section on pre-rational culture "New Realizations, New Horrors" (p. 120), discussing at length the blood rituals and sacrifices thought to be associated with Great Mother cultures, making little if any effort to focus on their positive contributions. This gives the impression that such feminine-oriented, pre-rational cultures have little of worth to offer.

Fourteen years later, in *SES*, Wilber is still focusing on the down side of pre-rationality, this time by making references to the negative effects of mythic-level Christianity on modern Western culture (see, e.g., pp. 360–365). He continues this theme in *The Marriage of Sense and Soul* (1998), where he refers to "the brutal oppression often effected by premodern religion" (p. 44).

And in *Integral Spirituality* (2006), after observing that "50%–70% of the world's population is at the ethnocentric or lower level of development," Wilber makes the startling conclusion that "Nazis rule" in Chapter 9—hardly the kind of thinking we'd expect of someone with a transcend-and-include ethos. This is *not* to say that Wilber does not sincerely endorse the idea of transcend-and-include—but it does suggest that he may find it hard to square his philosophy with his personal distaste for pre-rational culture.

The ambivalence about pre-rationality also shows up in Wilber's tendency to classify anything remotely numinous, interesting, or resonant with truth as post-rational rather than pre-rational, e.g., archetypes and the collective unconscious (see Chapter 10 in *The Spectrum of Consciousness*) and shamanic states (see pp. 56–58 in *Up With Eden*).

And since Wilber likes to stress the parallels between individual and cultural development, the criticism he heaps on pre-modern cultures and religions becomes by extension a critique of pre-rational psychic structures within the individual.[7]

But perhaps nowhere is Wilber's lack of enthusiasm for downwardness more evident than in a story from his own life that he tells in *Grace and Grit* (1991), his book about the life and death from cancer of his beloved wife Treya. When describing his anguish about his wife Treya's imminent death and refusal to come to terms with it, he tells the story of

the day he wandered into a little German pub (they were in Germany for her treatment), totally distraught and just looking for a beer and a little distraction.

The pub was full of old men dancing in a line who beckoned him to join them. He somehow let himself be dragged into the line, and found himself alternately laughing and crying. "For fifteen minutes, I seemed to lose all control over my emotions...I stayed in that pub for two hours. I never wanted to leave. Somehow, in that short period, it all seemed to come to a head, to rise up and wash through my system, to be exposed and to be accepted."

But when Wilber recounts this painful but poignant experience of inner healing, he says wistfully that he'd really like to claim that this breakthrough came from "some powerful meditation session with blazing white light," but that it actually happened "in a little pub with a bunch of kindly old men whose names I do not know and whose language I did not speak" (p. 307).

Wilber's moving story clearly documents an experience of integrative descent; however, the experiencer seems disconcerted that his deliverance was brought about by *descent* rather than ascent. He seems to have missed the key point of the experience: that it is *because of descent* (not in spite of it) that many transformational breakthroughs occur. By wishing it were otherwise, he effectively deprives descent of its transformational significance.

Such examples are easy to come by because of Wilber's ongoing ambivalence about descent: although he seems bound by the logic of holon theory to say that both ascent and descent can be positive (and bound by his own impeccable logic to incorporate a "transcend-and-include" ethos into his work), the nature of his comments suggests that he has not fully come to terms with the virtues of descent.

My intention in citing these examples is not to bash Wilber but to point out areas in need of further development in his integral theory. Given these examples, it's not hard to see why those in the Descendant camp may be skeptical about Wilber's ability to be as appreciative of embodied spirituality as they are.[8]

They may have a point there.

In the following section, we'll take a brief look at why it can be hard not only for Wilber, but for anyone raised in American culture, to see descent in a genuinely positive light.

Up is Good, Down is Bad

The idea that transcendent ascent is the goal of spiritual life is not exactly new. It's been the ideal of ascetics of every stripe for many centuries, if not millennia. What *is* new is the idea that this kind of self-denial may have significant psychological disadvantages. This is why modern seekers tend to see Wilber's transcend-and-include model as a big improvement over the old "transcend-and-deny" approach.

However, it's one thing to speak of integrative ascent and quite another to embrace the kind of experiences that actually promote it. This is because "integrative" experiences are frequently those that are preceded by *dis*-integration, i.e., a temporary descent to a previous level of functioning. While such reversals may be a natural part of life—and may be much admired when told from the perspective of eventual success—they are not experiences that people seek out. In truth, most people are terrified of reversals. This fear of reversals is extremely widespread—not just in spiritual work but in life. We ordinary mortals do not find it easy to contemplate losses in life. We are afraid that if we fall too far, we may never rise again.

This a huge and mostly unacknowledged cultural taboo. It's so deeply entrenched in our culture that it's actually hard-wired into the English language. In their fascinating book, *Metaphors We Live By* (1980), George Lakoff and Mark Johnson analyzed commonly used metaphors to see what they tell us about our cultural beliefs about "up" and "down." They ended up making the following observations:

> *Happy is up; sad is down.*
>
> *Conscious is up; unconscious is down.*
>
> *Life is up; death is down.*
>
> *Control is up; dependency is down.*
>
> *More is up; less is down.*
>
> *High status is up; low status is down.*
>
> *Rational is up; emotional is down.*

They concluded that we live in a culture where "up is good and down is bad" (p. 16)—a finding that probably comes as little surprise to most of us. I would also add that "forward is up and backward is down"—an idea that turns out to be relevant for transformational work, because we tend to see the two as synonymous. Forwardness is associated with spirituality, truth, and light; backwardness is associated with ignorance, confusion, and darkness.

This is why Ascenders still outnumber Descenders by a goodly margin, despite the fact that we now speak a little less harshly of descent than in the past. Certainly within the enneagram community, the idea that "up is good and down is bad" is alive and well. It is clearly reflected, e.g., in Claudio Naranjo's characterization of lower versus higher energy centers (where the lower centers are depicted as inferior in every way).[9]

The same idea shows up in more detail in the Riso-Hudson's Levels of Health model—a model originally developed by Don Riso during the 1980s to characterize the nine types in terms of nine descending levels, each of which is said to be less healthy than the previous level.[10,11] While this nine-category breakdown is certainly useful, especially in clinical work, the variable under discussion ("degree of psychological balance") is actually categorical rather than hierarchical. We know it's categorical because it can be measured using factor analytical clustering techniques—which has been done by psychological researchers who use the "Five Factor" or "Big Five" Personality Model, the only personality test to have gained full acceptance within the field of academic psychology.

The Big Five generates five clusters of characteristics (openness, conscientiousness, extraversion, agreeableness, and neuroticism), the last of which is basically the same measure that Riso and Hudson seek to capture with their Levels of Health model (although the latter has the advantage of describing the degrees of pathology for each of the nine enneagram types).

However, what is described from the Riso-Hudson perspective as a level on a vertical scale is more accurately described as a categorical variable that can be present at virtually any level of development. This idea that pathology can be present at any level is also discussed by Wilber in Chapter 4 of *Transformations of Consciousness* (1986); see also Chapter 11. However, in a culture in which "higher is better," it's not surprising that psychological health has become something viewed along a vertical continuum.

In addition to the idea that "up is good and down is bad," there are a couple of other factors that have probably influenced Wilber's ongoing diffidence when it comes to descent: (a) his pre/trans work and (b) his naturally intellectual bent.

The Pre/Trans Fallacy

When Wilber wrote his first two books, *The Spectrum of Consciousness* (1977) and its less technical counterpart, *No Boundary* (1979/1981), the model he used for describing human transformation was 100% retro-Romantic. As noted in Chapters 4 and 5, this model is based on the premise that we are born into a state of pure being or essence but repress it during ego development. Thus, each step "forward" into life is envisioned as a struggle between awareness and repression.

At this point in his work, Wilber characterizes the process by which we repress awareness as *evolution* and the process of regaining wholeness as *involution*. Notice the strangeness in this terminology; its usage is counterintuitive, since we usually associate evolution with some kind of growth, not the repression of growth. So in both books, he lists the stages through which we proceed (which he visually depicts as a gradual *descent* from persona to ego to total organism to unity consciousness). See Chapter 1 of *No Boundary*.

He determined that the next logical step would be to break down this developmental process in greater detail—to explain how it works at each stage of the life cycle. But when he tried to do this, it just didn't work.[12] It took him three whole years to figure out why.

At the root of the problem was the assumption that non-rational states are basically equivalent—that pre-rational states are much the same as transrational states—an idea Wilber characterized as the *pre/trans fallacy*. Wilber got around this problem by envisioning three main stages of development—pre-rationality, rationality, and transrationality—that are cumulative in nature.

When characterizing his work years later, Wilber spoke of this move he made from retro-Romanticism to formulating the pre/trans fallacy as the transition from "Wilber-1" to "Wilber-2." Frank Visser articulates this move by observing that "in Wilber-1, the individual *descends* from the personal to the transpersonal; in Wilber-2 the individual *ascends* from the pre-personal, via that personal, to the transpersonal" p. 75, (*emphasis* mine).[13] Visser also notes that, in Wilber-2, individuals who do not continue to progress towards transpersonal awareness tend to regress towards an earlier stage of development: "By regressing, we become aware of the subconscious; by progressing, we become aware of the superconscious." Visser also notes that at this point, Wilber alters the way he uses the terms "involution" and "evolution."[14,15]

This revision is such that it's actually a complete reversal of his earlier position. In Wilber's third book, *The Atman Project* (1980), he adopted a view diametrically opposed to his earlier view. So in that book he flatly states that "the mystic *seeks* progressive evolution. He trains for it"(p. 183, *emphasis* his).[16]

Thus, from Wilber-2 onward, the initial involutionary move down the plane into physical incarnation is characterized as *occurring entirely prior to birth*. After birth, any form of involutionary (downward) movement is by definition regressive. As a result, Wilber's new approach relies on a model of

transformation which focuses almost entirely upon evolutionary ascent.

Although Wilber concedes that regression can have a legitimate role to play in inner healing—a role he refers to in Chapter 17 of *Atman* as "regression in the service of the ego"—his use of the term "regression" implies a move that interferes with (or at least delays) our transformational journey, rather than a move that potentially enriches it.

But at the point when he set forth this model (1980), Wilber had just broken with retro-Romanticism; he had just published his breakthrough article on the pre/trans fallacy.[17] So his backgrounding of descent makes perfect sense—as does his idea of depicting birth as occurring at the lowest point on the developmental arc. By making birth the beginning of the upward path, he completely avoids pre/trans problems, creating a model that is entirely progressive (and much more positive) in focus (Fig. 9-2).

So Wilber's initial rejection of involution was useful for emphasizing his new focus on progression. However, a model that emphasizes progression will tend to de-emphasize paths that appear to be less progressive, i.e., those that are more process-oriented, mean-

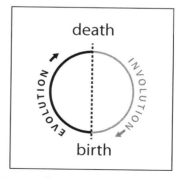

Fig. 9-2. Wilber-2 ascend-only model.

dering, indirect, or up-and-down in nature. Even when regressive moves are technically acceptable, they remain a departure from the norm—and something that we hope to avoid.

A Mental Point of View

In addition to the anti-down bias of the culture and Wilber's long-standing crusade against retro-Romanticism, there is one additional factor that almost certainly contributes to his lukewarm enthusiasm for descent: his basic outlook on life or point of view, which seems extremely intellectual, categorical, and logical in nature.

Despite his efforts to be fair and impartial, Wilber just doesn't seem to like emotional, ambiguous, or paradoxical situations very much, as evidenced not only by his comments about his transformational experience in the German pub, but by his ongoing focus on the development of a system that relies very heavily upon categorical distinctions. While he can be extraordinarily passionate when discussing ideas in which he is invested, his passion tends to be more intellectual than personal, which is why it has such a masculine, forceful quality. Compare this to the unbidden upwelling of inner feeling or resonance that is more feminine and subtle in nature.

His discussions of shadow work also reflect this same intellectual orientation, in that he is more interested in delineating procedures for dispensing with psychological conflicts in an expeditious fashion than on exploring the shadow dynamics for the sake of discovering the hidden depths of the psyche.[18] Unlike Jung, Wilber has never shown any particular interest in the creative or transformational potential of the shadow—at least not that I can discern. In addition, he does not seem particu-

larly focused on body-based or nature-oriented approaches to transformation, e.g., nature mysticism, shamanic journeying, organic growth, body-based yogas and healing methods, regression-oriented healing approaches, karma (service-oriented) yoga, natural or cyclical processes, individual differences, synchronicity, devotional practices, depth psychology, paths of emotional differentiation, the transformational potential of a descent into the deep, embodied spirituality, artistic absorption, and attuning to inner impressions. But this is hardly surprising, given his analytical perspective on transformation.

While it is considered presumptuous in enneagram work to state an individual's enneagram point of view, two things are certain: that all individuals have a point of view and that this point of view gives us a highly stable and focused perspective in life. As a result, each of us cannot help but be much more attuned to the perspective associated with our enneagram type than that of other types. And in Wilber's case, it's hard to avoid concluding that his perspective must arise somewhere in the head triad (Types 5-6-7), because these are the most intellectually oriented points of view on the enneagram.

Head types are also more likely to see upwardness in a positive light, because they associate it with both mental clarity and spiritual illumination—and both of these with truth. By the same token, they tend to associate downwardness with material encumbrance, messy emotions, and confused thinking—because this is how they experience it.

On the process enneagram, these types are just pulling away and moving upwards from the enneagram's nadir—which gives them the sense that moving upwards is going with the natural flow of life while moving *downwards* is going against the flow. And this may indeed be true for these particular types, because of their position on the enneagram circle. It may be even more true for *male* head types, because the masculine polarity is always more oriented towards Spirit than matter.[19]

Just before going to press, I was able to confirm that not only is Wilber a mental type but that he is a self-identified Type 5.[20] If so, it's no surprise that Wilber's strength as a theorist lies in his ability to think clearly and comprehensively.

Knowing Wilber's enneagram type helps us understand why he's like a modern-day Aristotle in his ability to weave together diverse idea threads into a philosophical framework that is as broad in scope as it is precise in specification. We can understand how he has been able to construct the comprehensive yet detailed IOS that has attracted so much attention over the last four decades. But we can also see why he may be on less solid ground when exploring those dimensions of transformation which are strongly associated with either a feminine approach or the physical earth: because while IOS can technically accommodate them (because of its comprehensiveness), it cannot easily foreground them. It's for this reason that it can still benefit from input from diverse approaches, including the enneagram.

In this section, we've looked at three factors that likely played a role in the development of a model of transformation that favors ascent over descent: (a) the culture's strong anti-"down" bias; (b) the need to develop a model that does not violate the pre/trans fallacy; and (c) Wilber's mental focus of attention, which is naturally inclined towards ascent.

Despite these influences, Ken Wilber has nevertheless devised a framework for integrally oriented transformational work with the kind of open architecture that allows for ongoing revision and refinement.

Wilber is fond of characterizing many unsolved problems not as a "no" but as a "not yet." This is the way I regard Wilber's ascend-only model. It is a good model for describing the progressive nature of transformational work and emphasizing the idea that each stage in development becomes a foundation for the following stage. However, it currently lacks a way to describe the self-immanent journey we make during the first half of life—a journey that is more like a descent into the material world than an ascent to Spirit.

The model introduced in Chapter 8 and discussed more fully below solves this problem—transforming a "not yet" into a "yes"—by using the process enneagram to re-incorporate descent back into the transformational process. The next section describes how this works.

A Figure-8 Flow

When we map transformation onto the process enneagram, we can describe such diverse processes as the transformation of light into energy via photosynthesis, the transformation of an idea into an invention, or the transformation of consciousness during the human life cycle.

But the process depicted by the process enneagram only shows the flow of energy during the incarnate part of the transformation process. To depict the entire transformational process requires us to show how the process is mirrored in Spirit, which creates a figure-8 model where energy spirals back and forth between Spirit and matter (Fig. 9-3).

Here's a detailed breakdown of the process. During **Phase 1**, energy descends from Spirit into matter but retains some of its spiritual qualities because of its proximity to Spirit. During **Phase 2**, energy *continues to descend*, but since it is now in the realm of matter, it increasingly takes on the qualities of the material world: we develop a sense of self-identity, the ability to make decisions, and the skills to navigate in the world. During **Phase 3**, the energy ascends back to Spirit: our priorities change such that our personal endeavors begin to matter less than finding a purpose beyond the self. Even without any special effort to evolve, we have hopefully learned enough through our life experiences to make some sort of advance such that, by the end of life, we have arrived not just "back where we started" but at a somewhat higher level of consciousness. During **Phase 4**, the lessons learned during life are assimilated in some way into Spirit, however we envision it, thereby expanding and enhancing the Kosmos. The cycle is complete.

Now what is interesting here is that birth occurs at the mid-point of involutionary descent—at the nexus between Spirit and matter. This accounts for why infants "come trailing clouds of glory": because they have so recently been in the realm of Spirit and are now half-descended through the downward flowing figure-8.

The involutionary descent that occurs during the first half of embodied life (Phase 2 in Fig. 9-3) is part of a cycle that moves us "away" from Spirit but for a purpose that is *entirely spiritual*—i.e., for re-creation, testing, growth, or service. So it is not a mistake or problem from a spiritual perspective and should in no way be viewed as spiritually inferior to Phase 3, although it is admittedly a move into greater limitation. But the fact that

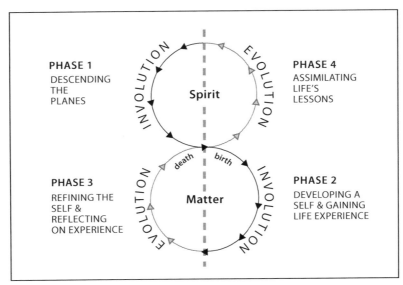

Fig. 9-3. Four phases of the figure-8 life cycle.

involution brings limitation does not mean it is bad; it just means it is challenging! (See Chapter 12 for a discussion on how limitation can foster creativity.)

With regard to self-development, involutionary descent is more associated with psychological development while evolutionary ascent is more associated with spiritual development, although there can be no rigid separation between the two, because they are complementary processes: without psychological stability, little spiritual development is possible; but without spiritual unfoldment, psychological development has no purpose. So both are obviously an integral part of the tranformational cycle.

And what is the term best suited to describe involutionary descent? It is *self-immanence*: that phase of development during which we become fully incarnate in the world of physicality.

But Table 9-1 has no place to describe this kind of self-immanence, because it is based on a model that only focuses on evolutionary ascent. To make a place for self-immanence, it is necessary to re-introduce involutionary descent back into our model of transformation. And this can be most easily done using the process enneagram, which has *always* included self-immanent descent as part of any transformational cycle, including the human life cycle.

As A. G. E. Blake notes in *The Intelligent Enneagram* (1996), "we can see the circle of the enneagram in *terms of both descent and ascent*" (p. 270, *emphasis* mine). Blake brings his point home by including an enneagram on p. 313 that depicts a descent of "increasing complexity" followed by a re-ascent of "increasing unity." Similarly, in *The Enneagram: All and*

Everything (2003), Nathan Bernier includes countless examples depicting the right side of the enneagram as a process of descent and the left side as a process of ascent.[21] Thus, when I make the claim that involution is part of the embodied life cycle, I am not pulling that inference out of thin air. It is an established part of process enneagram theory.

This idea has definite implications for integral theory, one of which is that Agape is not a particularly good symbol to associate with self-immanence, especially self-immanence in the context of transformation. Because as Wilber notes, Agape is the "reaching down to embrace with care all lower holons" (*SES*, p. 349). While this is a poetic description, (appropriately evoking the image of God, angels, or enlightened beings rendering assistance to us mortals in life), it is not a particularly good image to associate with the experience of a human being who descends into the world of limitation for purposes of self-transformation. Because while human beings may experience such a journey in many ways, they seldom descend in a manner that affords them the luxury of a transcendental stance. Even highly evolved souls tend to find themselves enmeshed in all sorts of difficulties—the kind that sorely try their ability to maintain a loving attitude.

It's for this reason that I have regretfully retired Agape as an image to symbolize self-immanence and replaced it with *Gaia*, the Greek Goddess of the Earth. Gaia captures the visceral, embodied, deeply engaged and ongoing nature of the soul's descent into matter. (However, Agape *does* have a role to play in transformation; see Chapter 12.)

In addition to changing the symbol, I have used it to describe the now-included involutionary half of the transformational process

(Fig. 9-4). So we now have a model with two main phases—Involutionary Descent and Evolutionary Ascent. Assuming we are progressing in an optimal fashion, we are mainly moving downwards during the first half of the cycle (into the thick of life) and upwards during the second half of the cycle (in the direction of Spirit):

- During *involution*, down = forwards and up = backwards.
- During *evolution*, up = forwards and down = backwards.

This may seem strange to spiritual seekers who tend to equate "up" with goodness. But as we can see, if we move upwards when we need to be moving downwards (or vice-versa), we can find ourselves out of sync with the natural rhythms of life. However, there are times when we need to be moving in the non-dominant direction. If we try to move forwards when we need to be moving backwards, our forward movement is non-integrative because it goes against the need of the moment. Thus,

an integrative move (whether up or down, forwards or backwards) is by defnition a move that is attuned with the need of the moment.

Table 9-2 summarizes our progress to this point. Having two major phases (descent and ascent), we now have four transformational moves for each. Integrative descent, which is now part of the descent phase, is no longer symbolized by Agape but Gaia. However, we still have four more "missing" moves to fill in.

But before proceeding to that step, we'll linger a bit to discuss the implications of adding an involutionary descent phase. If we liken the life cycle to the hero's journey, the *retro-Romantic model* would depict that journey as futile from the start (because it takes us away from our true home). Our return involves the retracing of our steps (going back the way we came—along with the realization that we never should have left in the first place!). This is clearly a regressive approach.

Wilber's *ascend-only model* would revise this vision, such that the journey is seen as

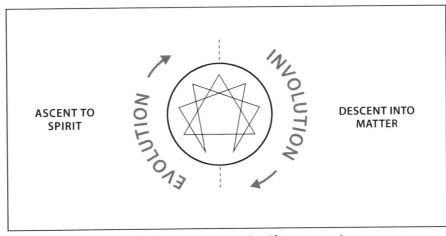

Fig. 9-4. Self-immanence and self-transcendence.

TABLE 9-2. MISSING TRANSFORMATIONAL MOVES.

ASCENT PHASE

	INTEGRATIVE	NON-INTEGRATIVE
FORWARDS (ASCENT)	*EROS* (self-transcendence)	*PHOBOS* (self-alienation)
BACKWARDS (DESCENT)	**?**	*THANATOS* (self-dissolution)

DESCENT PHASE

	INTEGRATIVE	NON-INTEGRATIVE
FORWARDS (DESCENT)	*GAIA* (self-immanence)	**?**
BACKWARDS (ASCENT)	**?**	**?**

valid (rather than some sort of mistake or fall from grace). But it would treat the entire journey as a return; the "going forth" phase is seen as something that happens prior to birth (and is therefore not an accessible part of the transformational process).

The *descend-then-ascend* model proposed in this chapter adopts Wilber's progressive approach but includes involutionary descent as part of the transformational journey. Because it depicts the journey as a circular spiral, the going forth and coming back is part of the same process, which is why it's depicted as the progression along a *transformational arc*, a progression which leads to greater wholeness—or more properly, "greater holonness"—at journey's end (Fig. 9-5).

The first implication of this model is that both involution and evolution play an important role in transformation. The second is that what we learn during involutionary descent sets the stage for what we learn during evolutionary ascent. The third is that it's possible to devise a model that includes descent that is still progressive (not regressive) in nature.

We'll talk more about these implications below. But first I want to focus briefly on involutionary descent and how it emphasizes the importance of not just Wilber's *transcend-and-include* approach but an approach I call *include-and-transcend*.

Include and Transcend

"Transcend and include" has become a unifying idea for people who embrace Wilber's

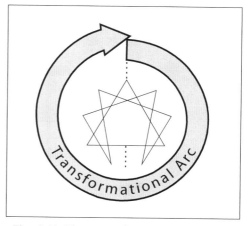

Fig. 9-5. The transformational cycle.

IOS. The image of moving through a transformational process, including as we go, is a very satisfying way of conceptualizing transformational growth. However, once we add back involutionary descent to our transformational model, we need a way to describe that phase of the process, which is a little different. While both involution and evolution involve transcendence and inclusion, I would make the claim that inclusion (integration) is more important during involution while transcendence is more important during evolution. This is because integration helps us engage more deeply with life. And without such engagement, there is nothing to transcend.

I recently read about the story of Wayne Knoll, an inspired young man who felt called to serve God many years ago. He enrolled in an all-male high school designed to prepare him for the priesthood, went to seminary, and took his priestly vows upon completion. He never dated or did much in the way of other teen activities. Although the next two and a half decades as an instructor at a Jesuit university were fruitful, as the years passed, he increasingly felt that something was missing in life. That "something" turned out to be a partner.

After years of trying to deny his yearning, he finally left the priesthood, ultimately marrying late in life. But it was a gut-wrenching decision to leave, because he had to break his vows after decades of being a priest. Knoll's story shows us the consequences of unintentional spiritual bypassing, in which the passionate idealism of youth catapulted him past the very experiences that he needed to feel fulfilled in life.[22]

Others have related similar stories: in search of Something Big (whether spiritual, material, or relational), they inadvertently overlooked opportunities for fulfillment that were right in front of them—simply because they were so focused on some end result that they never learned how to appreciate the joys of everyday living. Compare Knoll's experience with that of Tenzin Palmo, who spent her teen years dating and having other experiences typical for a young person her age. Although she chose to be a Buddhist nun early in life, she was able to make that choice based on genuine self-insight, because she had already had such rich life experiences that she was ready to embrace her spiritual vocation.

Fig. 9-6 describes the two-phased descend-then-ascend model; Table 9-3 summarizes the differences in emphasis between the *include-then-transcend* (descent) phase and the *transcend-and-include* (ascent) phase; Table 9-4 provides additional ways to compare them. Differences between the two are summarized below.

Include-and-transcend is a primarily feminine approach to transformation in which inclusion (psychological integration) is particularly emphasized and transformation is seen more as a by-product of inner balance than the result of accelerated spiritual practices. This path of transformation tends to be organic, spontaneous, meandering, and unstructured in nature. It is particularly associated with embodied life and everyday activities. At the same time, it tends to have an aura of mystery and unpredictability, because those who follow such a path are less invested in future planning than in being open to whatever is arising in the moment. Thus, the focus is on attuning to both our inner senses and the outer world, so we can bring the two into dynamic alignment—and can attract the experiences that tend to transform us. From this perspective, transformation is experienced less as a form of "rising above" and more as a form of "going within." The emphasis on responsiveness, feeling, healing, sensitivity, indirectness, surrender, and the cycles of nature is what makes it a deeply embodied and feminine approach to inner work.

Transcend-and-include is a primarily masculine approach to transformation, in which spiritual transcendence is emphasized, with inclusion playing a significant but secondary role in the process. The primary focus is on a direct progression forwards along the transformational arc. While integration is recognized as necessary for balanced development, it plays a supporting role to a path that is essentially goal-directed, one-pointed, and vertically-oriented. There is an emphasis on transcendence for its own sake and the utilization of practices designed to accelerate that process. In healthy transcendence, there is usually an emphasis on responsibility and service that acts as a check on the natural

impulse to seek higher states simply because they confer greater freedom, power, or bliss: to the extent that an individual bent on ascent realizes the responsibility that ascent entails, problems such as spiritual materialism or spiritual bypassing are avoided. The individual can ascend gracefully towards his goal, in a way that supports the development of self-dominion.

As we have seen from the foregoing discussion, include-and-transcend tends to be more associated with the first half of life while transcend-and-include tends to be more associated with the second. At the same time, different individuals are more naturally drawn to one approach than the other. Women especially tend to favor more integrative, intuitive paths, whatever their phase in life.

Table 9-4 lists attributes of both approaches in a way that does not emphasize their link with a particular phase in life. It's useful to remember that we are always in a dynamic interaction

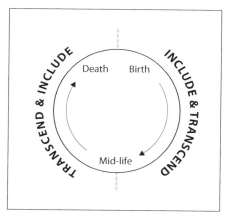

Fig. 9-6. Descend-then-ascend model.

TABLE 9-3. TWO COMPLEMENTARY PHASES OF DEVELOPMENT.

Approach	Transcend & Include (♂)	Include & Transcend (♀)
Primary Focus	Getting established at higher levels	Becoming psychologically integrated (open to the "now" moment)
Secondary focus	Integration of outgrown levels to support healthy ascent	Healthy ascent as the natural outcome of integration

TABLE 9-4. DESCEND-THEN-ASCEND PHASES.

Transcend-and-include	Include-and-transcend
more masculine	more feminine
ascent-oriented	descent-oriented
more direct	more meandering
more planned	more surprising
more practice-oriented	more intuition-oriented
effort is emphasized	acceptance is emphasized
more heavenly/idealistic	more earthy/practical
more single-pointed	more diffuse/multi-focused
more goal-oriented	more process-oriented
transcendence is the goal	transcendence is a by-product
will is key	willingness is key
more traditional	less traditional
more levels-oriented	less levels-oriented
achieving mastery	attracting Grace
more orderly	more spontaneous
scaling the peaks	healing the earth
mastery	mystery
attainment	attunement
clarity sought	ambiguity tolerated
categorical	metaphorical
more clear/obvious	more veiled/subtle
more formal	less formal
chain of command	shared responsibility
path of justice	path of mercy
responsibility	responsiveness

with life such that our focus is constantly shifting, as we move back and forth on the following continuum:

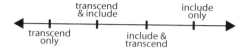

However, associating include-and-transcend particularly with the first half of life allows us to see the advantages of re-including descent in any integrally oriented transformational model: because it is during the descent phase that we acquire the psychological foundation necessary for effective transformational work.

Eight Moves on the Transformational Arc

To summarize where we are at this point: we have seen how the theory associated with the process enneagram allows us to re-include involutionary descent as part of the embodied life cycle. We have also looked at the qualities that tend to be associated with descent, in preparation for discussing the transformational moves associated with involutionary descent.

Thus, we are finally in a position to talk about all eight transformational moves on the enneagram. You will recall that Table 9-2, which posits eight transformational moves, only lists half of them: three moves associated with evolutionary ascent and one associated with involutionary descent. If we're going to fill in the rest of the blanks, it's probably easiest to start by focusing on evolutionary ascent, because we're only missing one move there: *integrative descent.*

In our earlier discussion, I already made the leap of re-locating self-immanence to the right-hand (descent-oriented) side of the cir-

cle, because it's perfect for describing healthy descent during the first half of life, when descent moves us forwards along the transformational arc.

But how shall we describe the kind of descent that occurs during the *second* half of life, when a move downwards represents a move *against* the upward progression back to Spirit? We already have a term for describing unhealthy (non-integrative) descent: Thanatos (self-dissolution). What is its integrative counterpart?

It is *Psyche*, the Goddess of Death and Rebirth—at least, this is my proposed choice, on the basis that Psyche symbolizes a descent made for a necessary purpose: dying to the self in order to prepare for a higher form of spiritual union. Not only is Psyche a symbol of integrative descent; she is the Divine consort of Eros, who is already associated with integrative ascent. So we have an apt pairing here: Eros symbolizes the desire to ascend without leaving love behind while Psyche symbolizes the willingness to descend into the depths, if necessary, to test the genuineness of that love.

So we now have a complete 2x2 matrix describing evolutionary ascent. If we now turn our attention to involutionary descent (the process occurring during the first half of life), we have only one box filled in at this point, the one describing integrative descent (i.e., self-immanence or Gaia).

If self-immanence is the healthy version of descent, what is its less healthy counterpart? It seemed to me that it must be self-forgetting or *Lethe*—a descent into life in which we mostly forget our Divine origins and thus tend to become over-identified with our flatland self. Unfortunately, this kind of forgetting is very common in modern life—which is yet another reason for making a special effort to re-dignify the role of self-immanence in transformation.

We are now left with two moves to account for: the integrative and non-integrative reversals that occur during involutionary descent. During involution, the dominant movement is "downward" into life. Thus, the reversals that occur at this time reflect the inability to engage (or at least to engage productively). So they are mainly psychological in nature.

Integrative reversals happen when we allow things to unravel in a way that brings about inner healing. It is thus paired with *Chiron*, the wounded healer, because those who heal themselves tend to develop the ability to help others heal.

Those who resist the need to heal are compelled to simulate wholeness by employing various psychological and social tactics designed to cover over their weak spots. As a result, they tend to spend a lot of their time and energy focusing on themselves—which is why I associate this move with self-absorption and *Narcissus*, the youth who spent all of his time gazing at his own reflection.

So now that we have a complete summary of the eight moves (see Table 9-5 and Fig. 9-7), we can look at them within the context of the transformation life cycle.

First half of Life: descent

Integrative Moves. During the first half of life, moving forwards is about committing to the process of embodiment in a way that allows us to fully descend into the midst of physical life. This is most easily done when we feel sufficiently in touch with our spiritual origins that we are able to make this descent into limita-

tion with courage, confidence, and a sense of adventure—to become fully incarnate in life (= *self-immanence or Gaia*). Because life is not perfect, even the most well-integrated among us sometimes experience setbacks as part of the process of growing up and adjusting to life in the planes of limitation; moving backwards is legitimately done in order to "fill in" inner splits and gaps that would otherwise hamper our continued ability to grow. So integral reversal is usually associated with psychological work done to strengthen our inner stability and sense of self (= *self-healing or Chiron*).[23]

Non-integrative Moves. During descent, many of us lose touch with our Divine origins, especially when the cultural consensus tells us inner or spiritual experience is not real (= *self-forgetting or Lethe*). When this happens, we have no sense of groundedness in Spirit, which in turn robs us of confidence and makes us prone to hang back, in an increasingly regressive and self-centered refusal to grow up (= *self-absorption or Narcissus*).

Second half of Life: ascent

Integrative Moves. During the second half of life, moving forwards is about reflecting on our life experiences, assessing our present situation, and moving beyond mere self-fulfillment (= *self-transcendence or Eros*). It's also about finding out who we really are, which may necessitate a descent into the psychic depths in order to sort out the real from the unreal. So moving in reverse is legitimately done mostly in the service of deep-level inner work. While it may have psychological overtones, it is not done primarily to create greater psychological stability but to separate the core self from its self-image, so that only the former remains.

TABLE 9-5. THE EIGHT TRANSFORMATIONAL MOVES.

TRANSFORMATIONAL MOVES
DURING ASCENT

	INTEGRATIVE	NON-INTEGRATIVE
FORWARDS (ASCENT)	*EROS* (self-transcendence)	*PHOBOS* (self-alienation)
BACKWARDS (DESCENT)	*AGAPE* (self-immanence) *PSYCHE* (self-rebirth)	*THANATOS* (self-dissolution)

TRANSFORMATIONAL MOVES
DURING DESCENT

	INTEGRATIVE	NON-INTEGRATIVE
FORWARDS (DESCENT)	*GAIA* (self-immanence)	*LETHE* (self-forgetting)
BACKWARDS (ASCENT)	*CHIRON* (self-healing)	*NARCISSUS* (self-absorption)

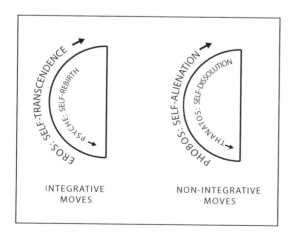

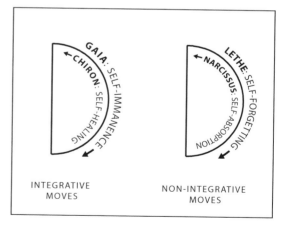

Fig. 9-7. The eight transformational moves.

This can be a tortuous (Dark Night of the Soul) process; so it is not essential nor even desirable for everyone. When undertaken at the wrong time or for the wrong reasons, it can create the kind of inner chaos from which it is difficult to recover. But when approached at the right time and for the right reasons, the ultimate result is not psychic distintegration but inner renewal (= *self-rebirth* or ***Psyche***).

(Can you see why I find Psyche a better symbol for describing this process than Agape? Psyche is not only the consort of Eros, but is associated with the most extreme form of sacrificial descent—whereas Agape evokes neither the image of descent into the deep nor sacrificial death.)

Non-integrative Moves. If we have not worked out most of our psychological kinks during descent, once we cross over the nadir, we find it hard to deal with the spiritual challenges of re-ascent, because we remain fragmented, and this fragmentation tends to amplify our fears. If our ascent becomes too fearful, it can turn into an attempt to escape from psychological conflict, leading to over-detachment and/or asceticism (= *self-alienation* or ***Phobos***). This is a high-risk ascent strategy, because the lack of emotional balance is likely to derail us at some point (just as soon as we stop strongly clamping down those errant emotions and bodily impulses!). At that point, what happens is what psychologists politely call "decompensation": the Fall, which is often associated with Point 6 (where we encounter our greatest fears) or Point 8 (where, on the brink of success, we find ourselves disintegrating, because we can no longer adequately control the powerful forces within us). At that dramatic moment, all our defenses suddenly give way and we literally fall to bits, back down to the bottom of the circle, the place of maximum chaos and confusion (= *self-dissolution* or ***Thanatos***). Gestalt psychologist Claudio Naranjo describes such an experience of the Fall in Chapter 12 of Marianna Caplan's *Halfway Up the Mountain* (1999), describing how he spiritually ascended too high too soon, until he precipitously fell to a much lower level of consciousness.

Comparing Three Models

Now that we have described key aspects of the Integral Enneagram model and its eight moves, we can look at it in relationship to the two models described in Chapter 4: the retro-Romantic model and Wilber's progressive but *ascend-only* model.

In the ***retro-Romantic model***, the life cycle is more or less divided in half: during the first half, we move away from Spirit (a move that is regressive in terms of spiritual development) while during the second half, we move back towards Spirit (a move that is progressive in terms of spiritual development). This model can thus be visually portrayed as a half-circular movement in which we cycle down in life (involution) and cycle back to Spirit (evolution). However, there is only a half-arc because the cycling down is not seen as progressive, but regressive; therefore, the only direction is back the way we came. So involution is a regressive fall away from Spirit; evolution is the *retracing of our steps* back to Spirit (Fig. 9-8).

Because this model makes no provision for whatever we might happen to learn during life, it makes life a zero sum game that has no intrinsic meaning (because it implicitly portrays the journey away from Spirit as a mistake to be reversed rather than a path to be followed).

Wilber's ***ascend-only model*** is designed to specifically reject the idea that life is a zero sum game. He instead adopts the position that the embodied life cycle is a progressive move in the direction of Spirit. So although we start out in a relatively undifferentiated (pre-personal) stage, we move into a more differentiated (personal/rational/egoic) stage, and from there—if possible—into a transpersonal stage that transcends and includes all previous stages of development. In this model, there is no dramatic turnabout in direction during mid-life but rather a continued movement through life upwards through the planes of consciousness, as we see in Fig. 9-9 (which depicts essentially the same model as Fig. 9-2, placed here for the sake of convenience). Both depict a simplified version of Wilber's chart on p. 319 in *Up From Eden* (1981). The horizontal lines in the middle represent the planes of consciousness; the involutionary cycle occurs *prior to birth*, which is why it's grayed-out.[24]

The ***Integral Enneagram model*** posits four phases of transformation, two during embodiment and two outside of embodiment (Figs. 9-3 & 9-10a). Just as with Wilber's model, in Fig. 9-10a, the disembodied part of the cycle is grayed-out—allowing us to focus primarily on the bottom half of the figure-8 (Fig. 9-10b), which is essentially the enneagram.

This model is based on the premise that birth/death is at the nexus of the figure-8 (Point 0/9), where birth = Point 0 and death = Point 9). Hence, at birth, we are at the midpoint of a descent into physicality. During the first half of embodied life, we continue that descent until we reach mid-life, whereupon there is a dramatic reversal of direction (as in the Romantic but not the Wilber model). But while we reverse direction at mid-life, we continue along the same transformational arc, such that *we never retrace our steps* but rather build upon what has come before. So the Integral Enneagram transformational model is, like Wilber's, entirely progressive.

The figure-8 in Fig. 9-10a is deliberately asymmetrical in order to suggest that the Point 0 where birth occurs is actually slightly *lower*

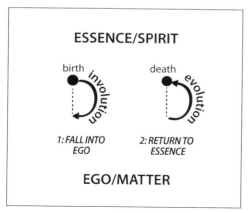

Fig. 9-8. Model of retro-Romantic return.

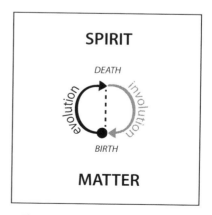

Fig. 9-9. Wilber-2 model (Wilber's answer to retro-Romanticism).

than Point 9 at which death occurs. Why? Because moving from Point 0/9 to Point 9 clockwise around the circle is assumed to be *an educational experience* that transforms us in many ways. The first time we find ourselves at the nexus of the figure-8, we are inexperienced; the second time, we are ripe with experience—and able to translate that experience into something of eternal value. Thus, Point 0 (physical birth) is slightly lower than Point 9 (physical death).

If we conceive of transformation not just as a single life cycle, but as a process that takes place over and over again in life (in ways small and great), we can envision each traversing of the circle as adding to our understanding. Even failures contribute to that understanding (although they are obviously less appealing than successes!). After experiencing many cycles around the circle—each involving a unique set of challenges—the lessons learned

each time begin to add up. If we are receptive, there comes a point where it is possible to make the leap to another major level of consciousness. Precisely how this happens and how long it takes is not easy to ascertain (see the discussion at the chapter's end).

A critical characteristic of the figure-8 version of the Integral Enneagram model is its depiction of birth as something that happens midway in descent. Why does this positioning matter? Because it means that we each have the chance to play an active and co-creative role in determining how that descent unfolds. This presupposes that we are not just passive objects manipulated by genes or conditioning, but actors in our own lives whose intentions and subsequent actions shape what happens during this process of descent into the heart of life. This understanding greatly dignifies the descent process, such that it becomes possible to understand that "self-immanence" really means *tak-*

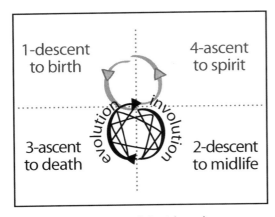

a. Figure-8 model with 4 phases

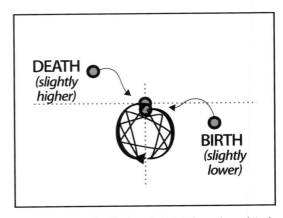

b. Bottom half: death is higher than birth

Fig. 9-10. Progressive figure-8 flow.

ing dominion over that which is ours to have and to hold on the physical plane of life. It is this taking of dominion which enables us to become so fully involved in life—and with our life's purpose—that when we eventually turn our attention upwards, we do not ascend empty-handed, but carry with us all that we love and cherish about life, all that we have put into our hearts.

The other two transformational models do not really touch upon descent from this perspective. In Wilber's model, descent occurs prior to birth, so it offers no way to describe self-immanence in terms of an opportunity to uplift life by our participation within it. In the retro-Romantic model, the opportunity exists in theory but is inevitably spoiled by factors over which we are said to have no control: ego development and social conditioning. It is only the Integral Enneagram model that allows us to see descent as playing a positive and progressive role in transformation.

Fig. 9-11 summarizes the three models for easy comparison. Please note that whenever I characterize a phase as progressive, I am referring to its *potential*; since we all have free will, we can exercise it to either progress or regress, as we like. What is interesting, however, is that even regressive choices often have a mysterious way of eventually facilitating progressive moves; e.g., regressive choices like criminality or drug addiction can sometimes become springboards to transformation—if only we can figure out a way to turn them around, using our experience of failure to transform us in some way.

Sometimes people have to fail many times before learning vital lessons. Focusing on those failures makes them harder to overcome

whereas focusing on eventual success brings opportunities for overcoming. In the end, the greatest barrier is our unwillingness to experience that which will transform us. Nonetheless, eventual progress is the rule and unmitigated regression, the very rare exception.

Below is a summary of the advantages of the Rhodes figure-8/Integral Enneagram model:

- *First*, it includes both descent and ascent phases without violating the pre/trans fallacy by placing both on a single transformational arc.

- *Second*, it allows us to foreground the role of self-immanence in the transformational cycle.

- *Third*, it accounts for the "trailing clouds of glory" phenomenon associated with the newly born.

- *Fourth*, it's congruent with modern research on neonates, which has consistently shown that they exhibit individuality at birth.

- *Fifth*, it shows why Gaia (not Agape) best captures the nature of self-immanence.

- *Sixth*, it enables us to differentiate descent from reversal and ascent from progression.

- *Seventh*, it has more explanatory power (yielding eight transformational moves instead of four).

We could also add that employing the enneagram to develop an enhanced transformational model illustrates the value of enneagram work for anyone interested in exploring integral theory from an innovative and deeply sourced perspective.

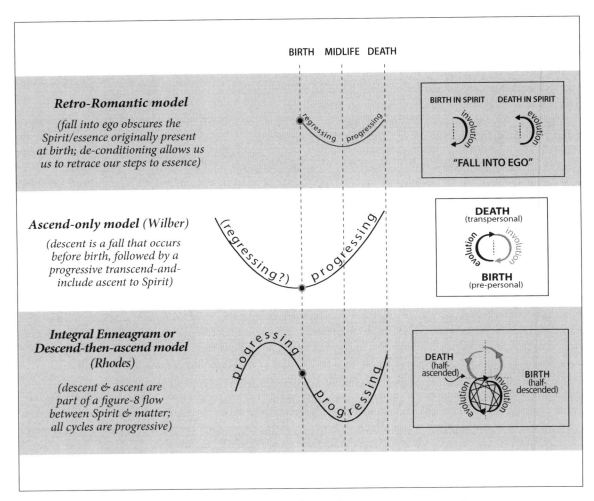

Fig. 9-11. Three models of transformation compared.

How the Types Traverse the Arc

Now that we've looked at the eight transformational moves and the model upon which they are based, we can take a brief look at how differences in type affect each of these moves (Tables 9-6a & 9-6b). The look is necessarily brief because it would take many pages to explore the eight moves by type in detail. Another complicating factor concerns the fact that—despite type-related similarities—there is also a great deal of variety *within* each type such that no two individuals (even of the same type) walk the same transformational path. So it's tricky to talk about type-related similarities without overgeneralizing, especially when it comes to variations in process.

Nevertheless, there are several interesting things to notice in these tables. The first concerns the difference between involution and evolution. Using these examples, it's very easy to see how, during the first part of life (involutionary descent), the focus is on the development of selfhood in a very concrete, practical, and essentially *psychological* sense while during the second half of life (evolutionary ascent), the focus is on growing beyond the self in some way, which is why it's *spiritual* rather than psychological in character.[25]

The second concerns the relationship between the life cycle and holarchy—how the moves during the first half of life focus on the development of *wholeness* (self-assertiveness) while those we make during the second half focus on the development of *partness* (i.e., spiritual receptivity). According to holon theory (Chapter 2), both are necessary for a balanced approach to living.

The third concerns the cumulative nature of the entire process, in that the experiences we have during descent in the first half of life set the stage for those we have during ascent in the second half of life, such that "the rich get richer and the poor get poorer." That is, those who start off with an integrative descent (or who are later able to go back and pick up the "missed stitches") tend to reach the nadir with the kind of inner poise that facilitates spiritual ascent during the second half. Those with a rocky descent (and who are for some reason unable to reverse direction in order to regain their sense of inner wholeness) tend to find the process of re-ascent more rugged and the outcome less certain.

The descriptions in these tables also make it obvious that psychological reversals tend to be less traumatic (and dramatic) than spiritual reversals, in part because spiritual reversals usually involve both psychological and spiritual factors (since the process is cumulative). The less integrative the path, the farther we tend to fall if we experience a sudden psychological or spiritual decompensation. This is why it's almost always a better idea to get into the habit of working with reversals *early* in life (when habits are less entrenched and options for change are more numerous). The farther we move into the life cycle, the more limited are our "degrees of freedom" and the more challenging it is to change our habitual responses.

At the same time, some of the most inspiring stories come from those whose early experiences were anything but integrative but who nevertheless managed to pull their lives together in the end. But to the extent we can understand the relationship between our inner nature and the nature of transformation, we can avoid the problems that arise simply because we lack the insight to make a better choice.[26]

TABLE 9-6A. MOVES DURING *ASCENT* BY ENNEAGRAM TYPE.

	INTEGRATIVE	NON-INTEGRATIVE
FORWARDS (ASCENT)	1 - refining & raising up one's energy in a noble effort to dignify the Divine ethos	1 - rigidly, zealously & ascetically pursuing a steeply vertical path to the Divine
	2 - using self-love to love & raise up humanity	2 - cultivating spiritual pride/hubris/manipulation
	3 - moving beyond material success, worldly concerns & the need for outer recognition	3 - substituting false growth for real growth; spiritual materialism & ambition
	4 - translating the desire for personal authenticity into a desire to authentically experience the Divine	4 - trying to ascend without ego surrender (taking heaven by storm); dark practices creating imbalance
	5 - seeking deep wisdom & ultimate truths without becoming a spiritual "know-it-all"	5 - substituting intellectualism for unattachment; confusing truth with ideas about truth; mad scientism
	6 - cultivating the grounded faith & true devotion necessary to serve a higher cause	6 - settling for a conventional and narrowly defined approach to higher wisdom
	7 - following our inner vision; developing creative adaptations of traditional paths	7 - settling for spiritual dilettantism/adventurism/sampling/grandiose schemes/New Age-ism
	8 - cultivating mastery and the ability to personally embody/unify/impart it	8 - seeking spiritual power, authority, and ability to teach without sufficient foundation
	9 - embracing the natural world, seeking world harmony/cultivating spiritual maturity & realism	9 - overidealizing the spiritual path, unconscious merging, or blindly following a spiritual leader
BACKWARDS (DESCENT)	1 - surrendering spiritual perfectionism & the need to focus on extreme purification	1 - the refusal to bend causing a break; possible Jekyll & Hyde move or spiritual blindness & paralysis
	2 - opening to access deeper aspects of own being in the service of humanity	2 - the persistence of pride/lack of personal surrender causing an utter loss of intimacy with the Divine
	3 - recognizing spiritual materialist tendencies, admitting failures, letting go of false self-images in order to seek the genuine path	3 - long-term self-delusion about the true nature of self giving way to numbness & complete paralysis by the looming prospect of failure
	4 - surrendering when surrender is called for & opening to the need for deep healing work	4 - the refusal to heal or surrender to the work leading to nihilism, self-hatred & the desire for self-annihilation
	5 - allowing certainty to be supplanted by deep curiosity, giving rise to deeper & more intimate inner work (inner child work, shamanism, etc.)	5 - the refusal to surrender mental certainty/control leading to alienation, dark fantasy, desire for revenge upon "enemies" & inability to be circumspect
	6 - summoning up the courage to face one's deepest fears rather than wallpapering them over; refusing to give in to fear, however daunting	6 - the persistent refusal to face one's fears leading to sudden decompensation & release of deeply repressed psychic material that can overwhelm the ego
	7 - slowing down to cultivate stillness/patience/responsibility/gratitude; adhering to the limitations of a spiritual tradition	7 - the persistent flight from spiritual responsibility/*dharma* leading to extreme flights of fancy, sexual/drug-related debauchery, escapism & hedonism
	8 - letting go of the drive to dominate, admitting vulnerabilities, relinquishing leadership position when called for, learning to lead by following	8 - the utterly refusal to bend the knee, the abuse of power (especially spiritual power), and the wreaking of social havoc leading to an absolute fall from Grace
	9 - allowing anger, resentment, & anxiety to surface in a way that unblocks the ability to truly grow up/accept responsibility/individuate	9 - the consistent refusal to wake up, grow up & accept responsibility for inner development leading to deep resentment/flatness of affect/turning to stone

TABLE 9-6B. MOVES DURING *DESCENT* BY ENNEAGRAM TYPE.

	INTEGRATIVE	NON-INTEGRATIVE
FORWARDS (DESCENT)	1 - translating transcendent ideals into a noble ethos for daily living	1 - the need to maintain standards leading to black and white judgments about what is Bad vs Good
	2 - self-love & self-nurturance giving rise to healthy bonding, especially with intimates	2 - emotional neediness driving us to develop co-dependent relationships
	3 - plunging with exuberance into the marketplace of life, where we cultivate skills & individuality	3 - the need for success & recognition driving us to be overly competitive and self-centered
	4 - being true to the inner self without losing the ability to function in the outer world	4 - the need to be authentic leading to the rejection of any form of outer accommodation or compromise
	5 - developing the capacity for deep thinking while maintaining the ability to connect with others	5 - a concentration on ideas & inner life creating barriers to intimacy and outer involvement
	6 - developing faith in people and trust in life, so we can live in friendship & community	6 - the inability to trust causing the preoccupation with finding protection in a dangerous world
	7 - learning to live joyfully & spontaneously (but responsibly) in the moment	7 - the need to live free & unencumbered bringing many experiences but the inability to commit long-term
	8 - developing self-control/temperance/the ability to exercise dominion without becoming overly controlling & protective of one's domain	8 - the need for outer control & dominance predominating over the ability to exercise self-control/inner dominion
	9 - cultivating the ability to reconcile the desire for harmony with the need to be an individual	9 - the need for peace-at-any-price making it necessary to suppress anger, which creates deep-seated frustration
BACKWARDS (ASCENT)	1 - letting go of self-judgment & the justification for intolerance and scapegoating	1 - remaining increasingly stuck in black-and-white thinking and condemnation of the Bad
	2 - allowing ourselves to self-nurture & to stop manipulating others via guilt & blame	2 - falling into patterns of emotional regression, immaturity & manipulation
	3 - focusing less on achievement & more on self-knowing, relationships & spontaneity	3 - focusing only on achievement & success, whatever the cost to self, friends & family
	4 - exploring ways to become more receptive and less reactive without sacrificing authenticity	4 - allowing the need for independence/individuality to cut us off from everything else in life
	5 - investigating methods for participating in life while maintaining appropriate psychic boundaries	5 - building elaborate inner & outer barriers designed to prevent psychic intrusion at all costs
	6 - having the courage to open up & reach out to life despite our reservations and/or shyness	6 - narrowing our focus in order to feel safe & secure and to guard against unpredictable outcomes
	7 - slowing down & paying attention in ways that help curb impulsivity & the desire for escape	7 - speeding up & seeking out escapist activities to drain off excess mental energy & anxiety
	8 - cultivating self-control, inner discipline & inner calm in order to channel anger & develop leadership abilities	8 - becoming increasingly defensive, angry & closed to constructive feedback in order to avoid inner work
	9 - refusing to be only a follower who has no opinions; taking time for ourselves & our needs	9 - allowing ourselves to be swallowed up in the "crowd," unable to make decisions, follow through, or stand on our own two feet

How Fast Can We Grow?

One last question to consider when looking at transformational processes from an integral perspective is the relationship between the speed of transformation and the degree to which it's truly integral (i.e., the degree to which we're integrating our lessons as we go).

In the enneagram community, although there is a considerable amount of interest in transformation, there is not so much emphasis on transforming quickly—although there was at the beginning, in that many of those who were originally drawn to Ichazo's 1970 Arica retreat were attracted by the rumor that he was a Sufi teacher who knew the Shattari method of Sudden Enlightenment. In the ensuing decades, while the interest in spiritual development has remained strong, there has been more focus in the personality enneagram community on self-understanding and interactions among the types than reaching a particular level of spiritual development.

However, in the Integral community, there has always been a strong interest in levels of development and how to progress up those levels, no doubt because this is so emphasized in Wilber's writings. Many of those attracted to integral work are therefore interested in the vertical dimension of spiritual work. In recent years, accelerated development has been a hot topic, especially since Ken Wilber began the ongoing "Guru and the Pandit" series of talks with spiritual teacher Andrew Cohen. Many of these conversations focused on how it's possible to move large numbers of people up to a higher level of consciousness in order to bring about a more enlightened world culture.

In *Integral Spirituality* (2006), Wilber speaks of the idea of a "spiritual conveyor belt" to move greater numbers of people into higher levels faster by eliciting the support of spiritual leaders of ethnocentric [read *pre-rational*] religious groups, such that their followers are able to see their traditional beliefs from a higher level of awareness (and thus to become more open and less rigid in their approach). Thus, it's not surprising that at Integral events, whatever the topic, there's always an underlying focus on making the leap from first- to second-tier consciousness.

The idea for a radical leap comes from Clare Graves—the individual who inspired Beck and Cowan's Spiral Dynamics—who wrote an article for *Futurist* in 1974, "Human Nature Prepares for a Momentous Leap.[27] The "momentous leap" refers to the leap in consciousness from *subsistence*-based living to *being*-based living. From that time to the present, there has been a lot of talk in New Age, transpersonal, and Integral circles about global shifts, unprecedented openings, and cycles of accelerated change.

In a 2003 interview, "The Momentous Leap From First Tier To Second Tier Consciousness," Ken Wilber expresses his interest in facilitating such a leap and his belief that it's something that can happen in a relatively short amount of time. He would like his evolving IOS to play a role in that process, such that people can ride the wave of change instead of being inundated by it. And he is optimistic enough to think that ILP (Integral Life Practice) techniques (particularly meditation) can greatly accelerate this process, such that people can arrive at the Centaur/Vision-logic level of consciousness in just a few years. (See also his comment on p. 548 on *SES*, in which he says that "the great quest for postmodernity...is for the bodymind integration of the Centaur in worldcentric Vision-logic, and there are signs everywhere that this is in fact occurring.")

However, this claim remains controversial, despite recent evidence showing positive effects for meditation, even among short-time meditators.[28] The problem is that the transformation of consciousness involves a change in the actual *structures* of consciousness. And such structures do not develop overnight.

But just how quickly *can* they develop? Wilber believes that it can happen in just a few years. On p. 263 of *One Taste*, he says that "meditation speeds up evolution"; in CD 4 of his *Kosmic Consciousness* interview (6:38), he says that meditation, "accelerates movement" through vertical stages of development. And on p. 139 of *A Theory of Everything* (2001), Wilber says that research shows that in a group where only 2% of the members were at second tier consciousness, after four years of meditation, that figure went up to 38%.

This result sounds impressive. Unfortunately, it is not well-documented. Wilber doesn't give any specifics about the research—who did it, how it was done, or whether it was replicated. Instead, he refers us to Chapter 10 in *The Eye of Spirit* (2001), where he reveals the researcher and partially describes the results of an unnamed study in an endnote. (He does reveal the principal investigator—transcendental meditator and researcher Charles Alexander—to assess the effects of TM on the ability of subjects to advance on Loevinger's scale of ego development.) But Wilber's description of the work—while glowing—lacks the kind of detail that would enable us to evaluate the results for ourselves. Instead, we have to take Wilber's word for it that we would interpret the results the same way he did—leading critics such as Jim Andrews to dispute Wilber's claim that meditation has been empirically shown to accelerate development.[29]

From a scientific point of view, it is not a trivial task to determine the effect of meditation on an individual's rate of development, in part because development can be measured in so many different ways (and the fact that people disagree about which way is best). It is much easier to document the effects of meditation on variables that are easily quantified (e.g., heart rate, blood pressure, or mortality rates).

Traditionally, spiritual seekers have been told that it takes most people many years (even decades or a lifetime) of practice to make a serious "transformational dent" in their level of consciousness; sometimes, the estimate is more like *multiple lifetimes*. Esotericist Dion Fortune says that it takes at least three lifetimes of steady effort even to be initiated into an esoteric order.[30] Buddhist teachings clearly tell us that enlightenment is reached over multiple lifetimes. And as for Hinduism, "Hindus know that all souls reincarnate, take one body and then another, evolving through experience over long periods of time."[31] Even if we think in terms of just one lifetime, evolution takes time: Sufi mystic Irina Tweedie once remarked to Andrew Cohen that after 30 years of practice, she was just beginning to understand what her teacher was trying to tell her.[32]

Just think of how long it can take for even "non-spiritual" transformations to take place, the kind that happen not as the result of spiritual practice but the result of dealing with physical and/or psychological traumas such as a stroke.[33] How much longer does it take to bring about permanent changes in our higher (spiritual) vehicles?

We might also wonder whether too much emphasis on a speedy ascent could promote the kind of spiritual materialism, bypassing, and narcissism that can become a barrier to inner work. Or whether it could prevent us from realizing that it's possible to do worthwhile spiritual work at any level of development.

Esotericist Elizabeth Haich reminds us that "the truly spiritual states are very easy: one is simply *here now*" (*emphasis* hers). She also notes the value of creative work that we can enter into "heart and soul" for spiritual development, observing that "the work is the essential thing, for we develop with it."[34] When we focus on the work, we do not focus so much on the self—especially where the self is positioned on some scale of development, spiritual or otherwise.

The process enneagram also focuses our attention on the work by linking personal transformation to concrete transformational activities such as making a meal, creating an invention, or building a house, thus reminding us that transformation occurs through the vehicle of our involvement in creative activities. It also reminds us that *everything that happens, happens in cycles*—which means that harmonious development depends upon our ability to stay in sync with the natural cycles of life. Thus, while it helps us to focus on the realization of a goal, it alerts us to the interaction between where we are headed with where we are right now. This makes it easier to understand how the future naturally unfolds out of the present moment. It also makes it easier to look at the relationship between cycles of different lengths (minutes, hours, days, weeks, years, centuries, and longer), thereby facilitating the kind of thinking that is grounded in a Kosmic view of change, rather than the human view, which tends to see things in terms of what happens in a few months or years.

Such a Kosmic view can be hard to acquire, especially in cultures where we think in terms

of finishing our spiritual work in a single incarnation rather than over multiple incarnations. Whether one literally believes in reincarnation or not, meditating upon the possibility of reincarnation helps us reflect on the patterns that supersede the span of our short lives.[35]

Because modern life is fast and people are impatient for results, it's easy to focus so much on accelerating our spiritual development that we adopt a frame of mind that actually inhibits this kind of acceleration. As mentioned above, a lot of people were originally attracted to Ichazo's work because they thought he could give them instant enlightenment. But how many of those so eager for overnight enlightenment actually achieved it (even in the long run)? To make genuine progress, the desire for results has to be matched by the willingness to put up with the process by which it is achieved—whatever this means and however long it takes.

There are always a few mysterious souls who seem to have been born with an unusual spiritual bent, and who advance very rapidly once they begin to practice. But for every such individual there are countless others whose progression is much more gradual (and often, full of ups and downs). The spiritual literature often hints that such spiritually gifted individuals are not starting from scratch but are merely reprising previously learned lessons. Ordinary practitioners trying to push the envelope in hopes of emulating the accelerated progress of such individuals more often end up with a "spiritual emergency" than a spiritual emergence.

If we really do live at a time of momentous shifts, then we may be fortunate enough to benefit by them, since a rising tide raises all ships. If so, then we would want to prepare for such shifts by getting as grounded and integrated as possible, since such shifts can be pretty disorienting. If fortune favors the well-prepared, then focusing on the present moment, creative work, and integration can support our transformational process as it unfolds both in the moment and over the millenia.

In this chapter, the focus has been primarily on vertical transformation: what it means, what it entails, and how it varies according to enneagram type. But in an integral approach, the vertical dimension is only half of the landscape. We also have the horizontal dimension to consider, a dimension which Wilber traditionally depicted as something akin to a subset of vertical ascent (see "Transformation versus Translation" in Chapter 4).

However, in personality enneagram work, the horizontal axis is primary, not secondary, because the focus is on understanding our own point of view and reconciling it with other points of view. Those who work with the enneagram know just how transformational that kind of approach can be.

So in Chapter 10, we'll use the foundation provided by the personality enneagram to look at the nature of perspective-taking and the critical role that it plays in transformation—but only after describing some very interesting parallels between the enneagram personality types and Wilber's AQAL quadrants, the Big Three value spheres, and eight hori-zones.

Notes

1. See Chapter 1 in *SES* for a discussion on the shortcomings of web-of-life approaches.

2. For a discussion of Wilber's outlook on Plato's view on transformation, see *SES* (1995/2000), pp. 331–336.

3. The use of Agape works well to explain a phenomenon such as Divine grace but less well

for characterizing self-immanent descent; see the discussion in Chapter 12.

4. In *Integral Psychology* (2000), Wilber reiterates the importance of integration in a transformational process: "To say that evolution proceeds by differentiation and integration is to say that it proceeds by transcendence and inclusion. Each stage includes its predecessors, then adds its own defining and emergent qualities: it transcends and includes" (p. 151).

5. http://wilber.shambhala.com/html/interviews/interview1220_2.cfm/; accessed 10-1-12.

6. *The Spectrum of Consciousness* (1977), p. 11.

7. When discussing the way that consciousness is organized, people in the enneagram community tend to speak of *psychic structures* while Wilber prefers to speak of *structures of consciousness*. For our purposes here, they can be considered synonymous.

8. For a critique of Wilber's position on embodied spirituality, see (a) many of the essays in *Ken Wilber in Dialogue* (1998), especially Peggy Wright's; (b) Michael Daniels' discussion of immanence versus transcendence in Chapters 1–3 and Chapter 10 of *Shadow, Self, Spirit* (2005); and (c) Jorge Ferrer's 2011 article, "Participation, Metaphysics, and Enlightenment: Reflections on Ken Wilber's Recent Work," available at http://www.ciis.edu/Documents/reflections%20on%20kw%20recent%20work.pdf; accessed 1-15-13.

9. See p. 8 in Claudio Naranjo's *Character and Neurosis* (1994) for a chart depicting "higher" versus "lower" aspects of the self.

10. See Chapter 4 in Riso and Hudson's *Understanding the Enneagram* (2000) for a more detailed discussion of the Levels of Health model.

11. Although the Riso-Hudson Levels of Health model is not truly hierarchical, there is another Riso-Hudson approach—the Strata model—that *does* fit the requirements for a true hierarchical scale, in that it measures the depth of insight acquired as we progress in our spiritual journey. The Strata model is compared with other develomental models in Table C-2, Appendix C, at the end of this book; it is discussed at greater length in my article, "Personality, Process, and Levels of Development," available on my website, www.enneagramdimensions.net.

But at this point, the Strata model not as well-developed or widely promoted as the Levels of Health model, which is one reason that it has not been adopted as a general model of transformation within the personality enneagram community as a whole. However, Chris Cowan and Don Beck's Spiral Dynamics (SD) system—an approach which looks at human development in terms of the evolution of cultural values along a vertical spiral—has elicited more general interest in recent years.

Fabien and Patricia Chabreuil were early SD enthusiasts who explored the relationship between SD levels and enneagram types in a 2005 interview with the *Enneagram Monthly* (available at http://www. integratedsociopsychology.net/sd-enneagram.html; accessed 4-28-13). The International Enneagram Association (IEA) subsequently invited Don Beck, one of the co-developers of Spiral Dynamics, to be the keynote speaker at the 2006 IEA conference in Chicago. In 2010, Deborah Ooten and Beth O'Hara published "Levels of Consciousness," in the *Enneagram Journal*, which discusses the authors' efforts to map each of the nine enneagram types onto each of the Spiral Dynamics levels (available from the Conscious Living Center at www.goconscious.com/home/levels_of_consciousness.html; accessed 4-3-13). And in 2012, Peter McNab discussed the relationship between the enneagram types and Spiral Dynamics levels more deeply in his article, "Towards an Integral Enneagram," in the *Enneagram Journal*.

Thus, a common interest in SD may serve as an initial bridge between the enneagram and Integral communities, because SD has become very much a part of Integral culture—probably because Wilber found it intriguing and started incorporating it into his writings around the turn of the 21st century (see especially Chapter 1 in *A Theory of Everything*, 2001).

In the long run, however, it may make more sense to look less at how all nine types progress along a single line of development (like SD) and more at how each type progresses differentially on a variety of lines (i.e., to examine how differences in type give rise to differences in preferred lines of development); for a discussion, see Chapter 11.

12. For an insightful discussion of Wilber's efforts to resolve pre/trans problems, see Chapters 2–3 of Frank Visser's *Ken Wilber: Thought as Passion* (2003); see also Note 11, in Wilber's *The Eye of Spirit* (2001), pp. 365–377.

13. Wilber has so far had five phases in his work. In *Wilber-1* (early 1970s–1979), he embraced a retro-Romantic model of transformation, a model which

he subsequently rejected in 1980 in favor a purely progressive (non-Romantic) model (*Wilber-2*). *Wilber-3* (mid-1980s) introduced the idea that there are multiple lines of development broken into different stages; each stage of development can be characterized as either normal or abnormal in character (see Chapter 11). *Wilber-4* (1995 – mid-2000s) introduced a holarchic framework and AQAL; it is a shift away from transpersonal psychology to a more integrally oriented approach. *Wilber-5* (mid-2000s–present) represents a shift towards "integral post-metaphysics," i.e., a post-modern and experientially oriented approach to transformational work. For a brief summary, see www.integralworld.net/phases. html; accessed 12-1-12; for a more detailed account, see Paul Helfrich's "Ken Wilber's AQAL Metatheory: An Overview" (2007), at www.paulhelfrich.com/library/Helfrich_P_AQAL_Overview.pdf; accessed 12-1-12. See also Visser's *Ken Wilber: Thought as Passion* (2003); the index has an excellent breakdown under "Wilber's five phases" or Reynolds' *Where's Wilber At?* (2006); see "phases" in the index.

14. See Visser's Note 6, p. 292.

15. I am citing Visser because he offers a particularly clear retrospective summary of the move from Wilber-1 to Wilber-2; however, readers interested in Wilber's own discussion of this shift can consult his essay, "The Pre/Trans Fallacy," Chapter 7 in *Eye to Eye* (1983/1996).

16. In *The Atman Project* (1980), Wilber includes an extensive discussion of his revised (Wilber-2) position on involution and evolution.

17. "The Pre/Trans Fallacy," *ReVision*, 1980.

18. Wilber's "3-2-1" technique for shadow work is designed to change the way we relate to disowned feelings (where we move from *thinking* of them in the third person to *dialoguing* with them in the second person to *owning* them in the first person). While the technique itself seems quite useful (see *Integral Spirituality*, 2006, Chapter 7 for a discussion), it has not so far been presented in the context of a comprehensive and thoughtful theory of human motivation. Nor has it thus far proposed a role for descent (regressive or otherwise), which seems like a topic that cannot be overlooked in the context of shadow work.

19. The nature of transformation is often discussed from a highly analytical perspective, an approach with many advantages. However, one of the disad-

vantages is that it becomes difficult for those with a predominantly feminine perspective to participate in the discussion, because the very nature of a feminine perspective is empathic, spontaneous, and experiential.

The feminine is the voice of intuition, not reason—the voice that whispers, not shouts. As a result, females who wish to put forth an alternative vision often do not know where to begin. If we adopt a masculine approach, we betray our feminine roots. If we adopt a feminine approach, we risk being viewed as intellectual lightweights. It's a no-win situation.

I have consciously tried to balance masculine analysis with feminine storytelling—which is why I try to make points using both an intellectual and experiential approach.

20. In Peter McNab's, "Towards an Integral Enneagram," in the *Enneagram Journal,* he characterizes Wilber as a "self-confessed Five" (p. 83); Peter indicated that he got this answer from Wilber, in response to his query about Wilber's way of working.

21. For examples of enneagrams that depict a right-hand descent followed by a left-hand ascent, see, e.g., the enneagrams on pp. 382, 384, and 386 in Bernier's *The Enneagram: Symbol of All and Everything* (2003).

22. From *The Priest and the Medium* (2009), by Suzanne R. Giesemann.

23. I am indebted to Charmaine Sungy for her suggestion of Chiron as the most appropriate symbol for therapeutic work done during the first half of life.

24. Wilber's focus is on identifying major stages of development; however, within each major stage are many minor stages (sub-stages and sub-sub-stages), such that progression is a gradual process—until we reach that critical point when we are ready for a radical leap to a new and qualitatively different level of understanding. But it's the repeated cycling through the minor stages that's the bread and butter of self-development, because it's during these repetitive but important cycles that we build up the habit patterns which support our ongoing development—and which prepare us for those rare leaps in consciousness that are more revolutionary than evolutionary.

25. The second half of life is spiritual even for individuals who are not very spiritually-minded in the sense that it's during the latter half of life that we have to come to terms with the unavoidable fact that physical life is ending. Those who cannot conceive of looking self-transcendently *upwards* at this point tend to look self-translatingly *outwards*—on finding some way to provide an ongoing legacy to their family or culture.

26. Although it is obviously better to transform over the course of a lifetime (rather than putting if off to the end of life), Sufi teacher Llewellyn Vaughn-Lee once remarked that during the last two years of life, there is a special period of spiritual grace during which we can reverse (or at least mitigate) negative circumstances in our lives. This idea should encourage those who have a hard time believing that it's never too late to change.

27. Graves' article on the forecasted leap to second-tier consciousness is available at www.claregraves.com; accessed 10-7-12.

28. See "meditation" in Wikipedia for numerous empirical studies citing positive effects for both long- and short-term meditation.

29. In "Ken Wilber on Meditation: A Baffling Babbling of Unending Nonsense," (available at www.integralworld.com; accessed 6-14-13), Jim Andrews presents a critical but well-documented argument challenging Wilber's claims that meditation has been scientifically shown to dramatically increase the rate at which we traverse developmental stages.

As a scientist, I see Andrews' point. Good science relies on the ability of scientists to exercise caution when citing the implications of a study's findings. And Wilber's claims that science has validated the idea that meditation quickens transformation are more enthusiastic than cautious.

30. *Esoteric Orders and Their Work & The Training & Work of an Initiate* (1987), p. 77.

31. For more on Hinduism and reincarnation, see e.g., the discussion at the website of the Himalayan Academy (www.himalayanacademy.com/resources/pamphlets/KarmaReincarnation.html; accessed 7-25-12).

32. "A Sufi Should Never Give a Bad Example (1991), *What Is Enlightenment?* magazine, 1-1, p. 9.

33. Regarding the difficulty of even physical self-transformation in just a few years: We can look at the experience of Jill Bolte Taylor, who lost most of her left-brain function after a devastating stroke; it took her eight full years to fully regain her faculties

(see her book, *My Stroke of Insight*, 2009). Ram Dass was similarly subjected to a devastating stroke and has had to work for years just to regain partial functioning, a process documented in the film *Fierce Grace* (2001). Debbie Ford, author of *The Darker Side of Light Chasers* (1999), who has been fighting cancer for 11 years, said in a 2013 interview with Oprah that transformation "is not an overnight process. People in our society are always looking for the 'quick fix'. But it's not a quick fix. It's [about] long-term transformation. You can learn about the shadow in your mind, but it's useless. You must learn through the integration of your mind and heart."

34. All quotations are from the end of Chapter 13 of Haich's *Sexual Energy and Yoga* (1982).

35. Reincarnation is a controversial topic for writers in Western culture because they cannot assume that their readers will accept the idea that we live more than once (although a recent Gallup poll reported that about 20% of Americans now believe in reincarnation).

Despite many claims that Christianity originally embraced reincarnation, it was dropped from the official canon sometime prior to the sixth century A.D. and became anathematic after that point (for an account on the history of this controversy, see, e.g., http://cryskernan.tripod.com/christian_reincarnation.htm; accessed 7-15-12). However, mystical Judaism does not necessarily reject it (see the recent discussion by Rabbi Adam Jacobs in the Huffington Post (http://www.huffingtonpost.com/rabbi-adam-jacobs/reincarnation-in-judaism_b_811379.html; accessed 3-23-13). The same is true of Sufism (see, e.g., Hazrat Inayat Khan's remarks at http://www.hazrat-inayat-khan.org/php/views.php?h1=2&h2=8; accessed 4-28-13). Wikipedia also documents the existence of minority branches within the Abrahamic religions (Judaism, Christianity, and Islam) that embrace reincarnation.

In Western esoteric, mystical, or hermetic circles, reincarnation tends to be accepted, probably because esoteric practitioners understand just how long it can take to become solidly established in higher stations of consciousness. This is why so many of them speak of the transformational journey not just in terms of years, but lifetimes. This is not to discourage people seeking higher

consciousness, but to help them understand the necessity for thorough preparation and patience.

Manly P. Hall, author of *The Secret Teachings of All Ages,* says that reincarnation has played a role in the teachings of Pythagoras, the Druids, the Eleusinian Mysteries, and many Native American tribes (see the index for citations; Los Angeles, The Philosophical Research Society, 1977). The anonymous "three initiates" who wrote *The Kybalion* have observed that "Hermeticists regard the chain of lives as continuous" (Chapter 11; e-book edition). Plato is often said to have embraced the idea of reincarnation, as well (see, e.g., www.john-uebersax.com/plato/plato4.htm; accessed 7-20-12).

In *Sane Occultism & Practical Occultism in Daily Life* (1987), Dion Fortune speaks of "the great fundamental doctrine of reincarnation...the oscillation of the soul between the seen and the unseen" (p. 15). In *Sexual Energy and Yoga* (1982), Elizabeth Haich observes that the "supreme goal" [of enlightenment] is achieved only by those who bring with them from previous existences a nervous system with the stamina needed to endure...the ever-mounting tension [of the path]" (p. 29). Esoteric teachers Madame Blavatsky and Alice Bailey also embraced the doctrine of reincarnation.

Traditionally, Ken Wilber has been reluctant to comment on reincarnation, because "once you take sides in this issue, you alienate...half of the audience" (http://wilber.shambhala.com/html/books/kosmos/excerptG/part3.cfm/; accessed 7-15-12). However, his comments certainly suggest that he embraces its reality.

The disadvantage of sidestepping the issue of reincarnation is that, in its absence, it can become difficult to account for so many things in life, e.g., the incredible variance in individual development, such that some people seem very much like "babes" even as adults while others are precocious to an extraordinary degree, possessing in early childhood advanced talents or wisdom far beyond their years. When proposing a cyclical theory of transformation—a theory based on the idea that we grow by gradually accumulating the wisdom gained as the result of diverse life experiences—it makes a great deal of sense to think of growth as occurring over multiple lifetimes, each of which involves distinctively different circumstances.

10

HORIZONTAL INTEGRATION:
AQAL & ITS VARIANTS

We want to find ourselves at home in the Kosmos. We want to touch the truth in each of the quadrants. We begin to do so by noticing that each speaks to us with a different voice.

– Ken Wilber

AS WE SAW IN THE LAST CHAPTER, Ken Wilber is extremely interested in hierarchies—interested enough to collect at least a hundred examples in *Integral Psychology* (2000). Out of this project emerged the insight that all of them seemed to be in one of four major classes:

> Some of the hierarchies are referring to *individuals*, some to *collectives*; some are about *exterior* realities, some are about *interior* ones, but they all fit together seamlessly (p. *xiv, emphasis* mine).

This observation became the basis for AQAL, Wilber's "all quadrant, all levels" approach that became the foundation for his Integral Operating System (IOS). It is based on the idea that there are four major perspectives we can adopt, regardless of our level of consciousness (Table 10-1).[1]

AQAL represents Wilber's first big foray into the horizontal dimension of life. Before

he presented it in 1995, he had been focusing mainly on the vertical dimension, somewhat discounting the horizontal (at least in the context of transformational growth). However, as his thinking continued to develop, he became increasingly interested in the interaction between the two, and began to expand his theory to include the horizontal axis.

In this chapter, we'll explore the horizontal axis and what Wilber has to say about it, focusing particularly on AQAL's four perspectives and its derivatives (the eight zones of arising and Big Three value spheres). The goal is not only to talk about the nature of these perspectives/zones/value spheres, but how they are related to the points of view delineated by the enneagram. As we will see, the correspondences between AQAL perspectives and enneagram points of view are so striking that it's hard to believe they were independently conceived.

TABLE 10-1. AQAL MODEL.

	Interior/Subjective	Exterior/Objective
Singular/ Individual	"I" (subjective)	"It" (objective)
Plural/ Collective	"We" (intersubjective)	"Its" (interobjective)

So this is an exciting chapter for anyone interested in linking the two systems because it reveals just how similarly they portray differences in outlook. However, the enneagram does have one significant advantage when it comes to describing different points of view: it can also describe not only points of view but the *relationship* between them. In this chapter, we'll explore how this works and what it signifies.

Two Converging Lenses

AQAL presents us with four lenses through which to view the world. As touched upon in Chapter 4, the left-hand column focuses on our subjective impressions—our internally-oriented states of awareness (upper-left or UL) and culturally-oriented perspectives (lower-left or LL). The right-hand column focuses on more objectively-oriented perspectives—those generated by systematic analysis of isolated behavioral variables (upper-right or UR) or the analysis of systems and their interactions (lower-right or LR). Each of these AQAL perspectives reveals four potential contexts in which transformation can take place. Tables 10-2 and 10-3 provide examples of how each perspective shapes the method-

ologies by which we determine what we "really know" (Table 10-2) and the values we particularly esteem (Table 10-3).[2]

Wilber introduces the AQAL perspectives in *SES*, but the discussion there is pretty theoretical. Where AQAL really comes to life is in *A Brief History of Everything*, where Wilber uses a lively Q&A format to answer questions from a hypothetical questioner. There, he observes that if we want our interpretations of life experiences to be as full and complete as possible, we would seek to see them through the lens of all four quadrants, not just one quadrant,[3] noting that all these quadrants are interpretive (subjective) in nature, which means that "all meaning is context-bound."[4] On the next page, when discussing spiritual experiences, he suggests that it's possible to develop the ability to see things from a perspective that encompasses all four quadrants, "an interpretation from the context of the Kosmos in all its dimensions":

> **KW**: Since Spirit-in-action manifests as all four quadrants, then an adequate interpretation of a spiritual experience ought to take all four quadrants into account. It's not just that we have different levels—matter, body, mind, soul, and spirit—but that each of these manifests

TABLE 10-2. "HOW WE KNOW" ACCORDING TO AQAL PERSPECTIVE.

	Interior/Subjective	Exterior/Objective
Singular/Individual	Intuition/personal conviction Dreams/visions/"grokking" Meditation/journeying Psychological depth work Contemplation & reflection	Skepticism Objective inquiry Rationalism Behaviorism/positivism Empiricism
Plural/Collective	Mutual resonance Group solidarity/consensus Participatory action Family & cultural traditions Hermeneutics	Sociology Systems theory Chaos & complexity theory Cybernetics Economics

TABLE 10-3. KEY VALUES ACCORDING TO AQAL PERSPECTIVE.*

	Interior/Subjective	Exterior/Objective
Singular/Individual	Truthfulness Sincerity Depth Authenticity Commitment	Truth Objectivity Accuracy Detachment Differentiation
Plural/Collective	Justice, Mercy Humanitarian action Integration/communion "We" space Mutual support	Systemic focus/integrity Linked multiplicity Diversity of viewpoints Dynamic flow/interactions Homeostasis/energetic balance

*The descriptions are a combination of those originally devised by Wilber and those added based on my interpretation of each quadrant.

in four facets—intentional, behavioral, cultural, and social.

Q: So a balanced or integral view would include all of that.

KW: Yes, I think so. A truly integral view would be "all level, all-quadrant."[5]

Wilber's reply here seems hesitant. Why is this? I suspect it's because he finds it hard to realistically imagine someone adopting four disparate views at the same time. To me, this hesitancy makes sense, because as a cognitive scientist, I'm well aware of the limitations of attention in ordinary consciousness—limitations that seem hard-wired in the system by virtue of our physical make-up. What repeated research has shown is that (a) the amount of information that we can receive at any point in time is extremely limited (the amount is around 4-7 bits for most of us) and (b) each of us has perceptual filters that determine which bits of information get in. Stated very broadly, most of the information that we take in is information which fits our concept of who we are and what the world is about.[6]

Similarly, in Wilber's discussions of AQAL, he says that most of us tend to prefer one or two quadrants and ignore the rest.[7] So one of the primary goals of Integral Life Practice (ILP) is to consciously cultivate the ability to take more perspectives and to "notice that every perspective is both true and partial," so that we are less defensive of our own point of view and more open to new ways of seeing things.[8]

This approach is also a staple in enneagram work, where it is common to see enneagram type panels interviewed in front of an audience in order to illustrate the different perspectives of the nine types.

As we have seen, the personality enneagram can describe the nine enneagram points either from a personal or impersonal point of view (i.e., as either types of people or abstract perspectives). But the AQAL quadrants as currently formulated describe their perspectives from only an *impersonal* point of view. However, one of the great lessons of enneagram work is that anything that can be described impersonally can also be described *personally* (from a more subjective, embodied point of view)—which means that the AQAL perspectives can also be personified, if only we can discover how to do this.

Linking AQAL with the enneagram gives us one way to translate disembodied perspectives into embodied points of view (i.e., types). As a result, mapping the quadrants to the enneagram also allows us to apply what is known about the enneagram types to AQAL. Thus, such a mapping can (a) enhance our perspective-taking ability, (b) help us discern the relationships between the AQAL perspectives, and (c) better understand the limits of enhanced perspective-taking (to realize that however integral our point of view, we will always retain a dominant point of view that acts as a "master filter" for our percepts, cognitions, and decisions).

It is critical to know our limits, both so that we can learn how to intelligently work within them and also so we can gradually expand them. But we cannot expand what we do not understand. If we try to do so—to adopt an integral (four-quadrant) point of view without understanding what this actually entails—it's all too easy to do so superficially while remaining firmly but unconsciously stuck in our own point of view. When this happens, we may be capable of saying all the right things and making all the right moves, but our words and actions lack conviction. This is the path of spiritual correctness, which leads nowhere fast.

Familiarity with both AQAL and the enneagram helps us avoid problems like this by giving us a truly informed approach to perspective-taking. Using AQAL theory, we can ponder ways to expand our ability to take multiple perspectives (something not as emphasized in enneagram work). Conversely, using the enneagram, we can consider the role of our dominant perspective (how it helps or hinders the taking of particular points of view). Thus, simultaneously working with the enneagram and AQAL can provide a richer, more multidimensional approach to perspective-taking.[9,10]

Four Quadrants = Four Types

So just how do we map the enneagram to the quadrants, and vice-versa? We'll start our discussion by mapping four of the enneagra points of view (4, 5, 2, and 7) to the four quadrants. For purposes of this discussion, the intention is to describe the link between the four quadrant perspectives and the dominant point of view associated with each enneagram point of view:

- **UL quadrant: "I" (Singular/Subjective).** The focus here is deeply interior and oriented toward personal interiority, sincerity, subjective conviction, and originality of expression—a view compatible with **Point 4** on the enneagram. Fours tends to

be deeply reflective, emotionally sensitive individuals who are drawn to plumb the depths for meaning and to translate what they find into intensely personal forms of expression.

- **UR quadrant: "It" Singular/Objective).** The focus here is on rationality, depth of inquiry, empirically-oriented investigation, and originality of thought—a view compatible with that of **Point 5** on the enneagram. Fives take great pains to separate elements into their constituent parts, thoroughly examine them, and reassemble them according to some objectively-oriented system or framework.[11]

- **LL quadrant: "We" (Plural/Subjective).** The focus here is on seeing things from an intersubjective perspective, where individuals with shared personal/family/cultural values form relationships based on those values and solidify their sense of self based on their interactions with others—a description compatible with **Point 2** on the enneagram. Twos are the type whose social interactions play a central role in determining their emotional well-being, social identity, and sense of purpose in life.[12]

- **LR quadrant: "Its" (Plural/Objective).** The focus here is on seeing things from an interobjective point of view, one in which the focus is on systems and how they interact—a description compatible with **Point 7** on the enneagram. Sevens are fascinated by dynamic interactions, networking, systems theory, and connecting the dots to create cooperative communities.

Table 10-4 maps these four types onto the four AQAL quadrants; Fig. 10-1 maps the AQAL quadrants onto the enneagram. However, as presently arranged, AQAL generates

TABLE 10-4.
FOUR ENNEAGRAM TYPES = FOUR AQAL PERSPECTIVES.

	Interior/Subjective	Exterior/Objective
Singular/ Individual	**TYPE 4** individuality, personality, introspection, meditation, deep feeling, self-reflection, originality, dreams, hopes, core intentions/motivations	**TYPE 5** objectivity, rationality, skepticism, detachment, scientific method, logical inquiry, philosophy, pure intellect
Plural/ Collective	**TYPE 2** personal relationships, caring, sharing, communication, communion, culture, humanitarian ideas, social causes, inclusivity	**TYPE 7** systems thinking, egalitarian focus, linking, connecting, networking, planning & projecting, Internet cloud

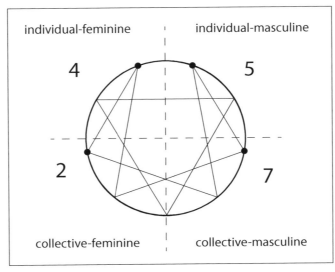

Fig. 10-1. The enneagram on AQAL.

an enneagram that is upside-down and re-versed. To translate AQAL onto the enneagram as we know it, we have to flip and reverse both axes. This should not be a problem in that the AQAL rows and columns are not arranged in any special way (see Fig. 10-2).

In Fig. 10-1, the Objective column on AQAL is now labeled "masculine" while the Subjective column is now labeled "feminine"; this is in keeping with the labels used in Chapter 8 to describe the energies associated with each side of the enneagram circle. These labels also remind us that masculine energy tends to be exterior, outward, and objectively-oriented while feminine energy tends to be interior, inward, and subjectively-oriented.[13,14]

If we focus on the rows, the Individual row on AQAL would be associated on the enneagram with the de-contextualized perspective of the self; the Collective row on AQAL would be associated on the enneagram with the contextualized perspective of the self. We'll explore what these patterns signify in the discussion below.

Eight Hori-zones = 8 + 1 Enneagram Types

In *Integral Spirituality* (2006), Ken Wilber introduces a number of refinements to his integral theory of consciousness, including the expansion of his AQAL model from four perspectives into eight horizontal zones ("hori-zones")—also characterized as eight "primordial perspectives"—which he describes as

eight fundamental dimensions/ perspectives of an individual holon...

eight fundamental ways that anything can be viewed (p. 254).

He further explains that

each of these zones is not just a perspective, but an action, an injunction, a concrete set of actions in a real world sense. Each injunction *brings forth* or discloses the phenomena that are apprehended through the various perspectives (p. 34, *emphasis* his).

In this second passage, Wilber is trying to stress the active, dynamic nature of the hori-zones—the fact that they are not just static lenses through which we view the world but dynamic shapers of consciousness.

Upon reading these descriptions in 2006, I immediately wondered whether the eight hori-zones could be mapped onto the nine enneagram types, since Wilber's definition of the hori-zones is also a perfect definition of the nine enneagram types/points of view. It is interesting that Wilber attempts to provide a rational explanation as to *why* there are eight fundamental points of view (see below), which enneagram theory does not (at least, not to my knowledge). All Wilber's quadrant approach lacks is the ninth point of view. But this is an easily fixed problem, as we will see, since one of the enneagram points of view (Point 9) represents a synthesis of the other eight.

However, before looking closely at the relationship between the points of view and the hori-zones, it's first necessary to see how Wilber divides his quadrants to come up with eight zones. You will recall that the quadrants are generated by categorizing the perspectives on the basis of whether they are (a) individual or collective or (b) objective or subjective. To generate eight zones, he adds another dimension: inner or outer. This gives us three dimensions per zone:

(a) individual or collective

(b) objective or subjective

(c) outer or inner

Unfortunately, dimensions *b* and *c* sound pretty similar. And they in fact *are* similar in that both relate to the polarity of our perspective, i.e., whether it's masculine or feminine. Actually, dimension *a* can also be categorized by polarity, where individuality = masculine and collectivity = feminine. Thus, it's useful to make distinctions for two of the three dimensions based on something other than polarity:

- individual vs collective = *breadth of focus*
- objective vs subjective = ♂ vs ♀ *polarity*
- outer vs inner = *degree of intimacy* (an inside-out vs outside-in point of view)

But for me, the easiest way to distinguish them is to map the hori-zones onto the enneagram, generating eight of the nine points of view. Then we can study the hori-zones using the many sources that inform us about the nature of the nine enneagram types.

Here is how this mapping works:

- **Taking the "we" (cultural) perspective**, we can either view this "we" as something to analyze from the outside (Point 1) or something in which we participate (Point 2).

- **Taking the "I" (personal) perspective**, we can view the "I" from the outside looking in (Point 3) or the inside looking out (Point 4).

- **Taking the "it" (scientific) perspective**, we can view life as an object (an "it") that remains totally outside of us (Point 5) or as something penetrating (intrusively) inwards (Point 6).

- **Taking the "its" (systems) perspective**, the system as something in which we participate (Point 7) or as something we encompass and unify (Point 8).

As mentioned above, the ninth point of view—Point 9—represents the androgynous synthesis of the other eight. On the process enneagram, it is often referred to as Point 0 when describing the beginning of a new cycle and Point 9 when describing the end of the old cycle. In the previous chapter, Point 9 was described as the nexus point on the figure-8, the place where Spirit and matter meet (Fig. 9-3). Thus, in Table 10-5, I've placed Point 9 in the center of AQAL, directly touching the other eight points.

Now that we have categorized the nine types as hori-zones, we can depict the hori-zones on the enneagram by flipping the axes of the AQAL matrix, which yields Fig. 10-2. This puts us in a position to see whether the zones and the points of view are really a good match.

It turns out that they are a very good match, good enough to strongly support the idea that the enneagram and Wilber's hori-zones are describing the same underlying construct—the first from a *geometric* point of view and the second from an *analytical* point of view. (Notice the symmetry here, the way that the order of the hori-zones corresponds to the order of the enneagram types.)[15]

The next section provides a more detailed breakdown on the correspondences between the hori-zones and points of view.

TABLE 10-5.
ENNEAGRAM POINTS OF VIEW & HORI-ZONES.

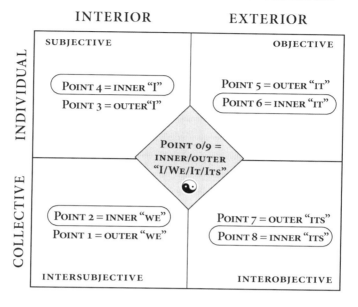

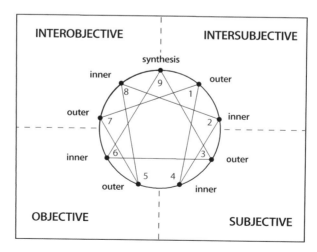

Fig. 10-2. AQAL hori-zones on the enneagram.

Comparing Hori-zones & Types

Each quadrant contains two enneagram points of view, one corresponding to the outside-in (outer) perspective and the other corresponding to the inside-out (inner) perspective.

Intersubjective quadrant. At *Point 1* (outer "we" focus), we seek out criteria by which to live, to order our world, and to guide our actions. So the focus here is on culture, ethics, religion, and law—those broad-based concerns that relate to life in the public world. *Ones* see themselves as arbiters of cultural values and, as such, stand slightly apart from their environment, in order to properly identify, set forth, and uphold the values they see as correct.

Once we have gained an initial foothold in the world, our attention shifts from delineating the broad parameters of that world to seeking ways to connect with those around us, a move that occurs at *Point 2* (inner "we" focus). Whatever the nature of these bonds—whether intimate, friendship, or social—they are very personal and involve the kind of hands-on emotional engagement that we would associate with a highly interiorized perspective. So *Twos* seek out emotionally rewarding occupations, deeply intimate relationships, and the feeling of being needed by those they love.

Although both Ones and Twos look beyond the self, Ones want to order the cultural world while Twos want to relate to its inhabitants.

Subjective quadrant. At *Point 3* (outer "I" focus), we learn how to cultivate the ability to operate as a social persona that can adapt and survive, so self-image genuinely matters. So *Threes* have the ability to exteriorize the self in a way that allows them to perform in emo-tionally-wrenching situations which would defeat individuals with a less objectified sense of self. However, because Threes find it easier to relate to their "persona self" than their interior self, they are the ones who—when told to "Be yourself"—have a hard time knowing how to proceed. Their challenge is therefore to pierce the persona to get to the interior self.

At *Point 4* (inner "I" focus), it's the other way around: *Fours* are so completely interiorized that they can have a hard time getting outside of themselves—which is why they can at times feel "stuck in the depths" and frustrated by the inability to express their inner impulses in outer life. Autobiographical creative expression brings them out of themselves and into the world, fulfilling their need to make a meaningful contribution while retaining their personal authenticity.

Both Threes and Fours are focused on the self, but Threes are more naturally attracted to the development of practical skills and the cultivation of a functional outer persona while Fours are more preoccupied with their inner experience and finding a way to express it in outer life.

Objective quadrant. The move from Point 4 to *Point 5* (outer "it" focus) involves two dramatic shifts: the move from an "I" to an "It" focus and from an inner to an outer focus. In a nutshell, we move from an extreme subjectivity to extreme objectivity. Thus, it's not surprising that Point 5 objectifies both the self and the world, such that they become objects to be analyzed and/or manipulated. As a result, locating a personal, partial self can be quite a challenge. (Relating to others is even more challenging.) But this extreme objectivity can also give *Fives* an unusual sharpness of mind and the ability to break things down into their constituent parts and then reassemble them into new configurations.

At *Point 6* (inner "it" focus), there is a mix of exteriority and interiority, such that **Sixes** feel conflicted about whether it's better to objectively analyze their world or to trust their emergent intuitions—which they typically regard with considerable suspicion, because intuition is hard to mesh with objectivity. Thus, their "inner voice" can seem intrusive until they learn how to reconcile their subjective impressions with their need to exercise mental control.

Although both Fives and Sixes are highly mental and respect rational thinking, Fives are more emotionally detached and iconoclastic while Sixes have a more inward psychic or emotional streak that can disturb their tranquility but potentially brings enhanced inner attunement.

Interobjective quadrant. At *Point 7* (outer "its" focus), we move back to a cooler, more detached space. But it's also a much expanded space because of its collective focus—so expanded that **Sevens** seek to locate the self by seeking its corollaries in the outer world. This is why they are naturally drawn to travel, adventure, and meeting people from diverse cultures. Although Sevens often seem friendly like Twos, their relationships tend to have a more cerebral, impersonal character, as though they are viewing the people they meet as potential nodes to be added to an ever-expanding mental network. The more nodes they add, the more expanded their sense of self.

At *Point 8* (inner "its" focus), the Seven's world of external multiplicity becomes interiorized, such that the Kosmos is now within, not without. This creates tremendous energy but also powerful internal pressures, thereby compelling **Eights** to develop a very strong, unifying psychic structure that is capable of containing and channelling this high-octane energy. Even so, Eights usually find containment an ongoing challenge, which is why they can be prone to temper problems. Even those who have mastered (literally "tempered") their inner energies still project an unusual intensity of being that is hard for others to ignore.

While Sevens travel both literally and metaphorically from place to place (or from person to person), having different outer experiences, Eights magnetically attract the experiences and people they seek, which they energetically "take into" themselves.

Integration of all quadrants. So we have now accounted for all but one enneagram point of view—*Point 9*—which as indicated above, is uniquely situated on the enneagram circle. **Nines** are traditionally considered the "root" type for all the others; they thus represent each type in its undeveloped form. They also represent the final synthesis of all nine types. But this synthesis can only manifest in a particular Nine to the extent that he is willing to develop his particular and individual qualities, so that he can reconcile his integrative tendency (which gives him the ability to reconcile the individual and the collective, the interior and exterior, and the inner and the outer) with the human need to become a real person, not just a blank persona.

Wilber sees the hori-zones as so important to AQAL that he says in *Integral Spirituality* (2006) that they are actually the primary topic of the book (p. 40). But they have yet to make a major impact within the Integral community, probably because Wilber's hori-zone descriptions are so abstruse. (For reasons unclear to me, in addition to his very abstract descriptions of the hori-zones, Wilber introduces a mathematical calculus into these discussions—a calculus that is guaranteed to scare away a lot of readers.)

Thus, it's no surprise that the hori-zones are noticeably absent in the books written after *Integral Spirituality* (2006), such as *The Integral Vision* (2007) and *Integral Life Practice* (2008), both of which are intended for a non-technical audience.

Given their potential, it's a shame that the hori-zones have remained a topic for discussion primarily among those with a talent for arcane math or philosophy. Because the hori-zones are a very interesting and useful construct—if only we could make them more accessible to the ordinary person. The purpose of the foregoing discussion was to do just that: by linking them to the nine enneagram points of view.

3 Spheres = 3 Energy Centers

Now that we've looked at AQAL's quadrants and eight hori-zones, we're ready to look at a close cousin: Wilber's Big Three value spheres. When Wilber was formulating his original AQAL model, he realized that it could be seen from another angle. By collapsing the "it" and "its" quadrants into one category, Wilber now had three domains instead of four: a group he dubbed The Big Three value spheres. Wilber sees them as three domains of human experience, referring to several historical models:

- Plato's The Good, The Beautiful & The True
- Habermas' three validity claims: justness, sincerity & truth/truthfulnes
- The Three jewels of Buddhism: the Sangha, the Buddha & the *Dharma*
- Karl Popper's three worlds: cultural, subjective, & objective

As we can see, The Good refers to the realm of morals, ethics, and proper social conduct; The Beautiful refers to art, aesthet-

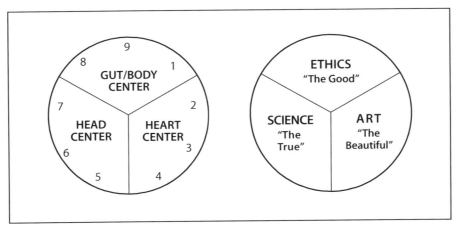

Fig. 10-3. Enneagram energy centers & Wilber's value spheres.

ics, and personal subjectivity; and The True refers to philosophy, science, and other ways of apprehending truth.

Fig. 10-3 shows an overview of the three value spheres as compared to the three enneagram energy centers and how the two can be mapped onto one another. Tables 10-6 and 10-7 provide a point-by-point comparison. It's not hard to see the striking similarities between the two:

- Key attributes associated with the Body/Gut Center include *right action, ethics, fairness, self-control, self-discipline, and honor* ("The Good").

- Key attributes associated with the Heart Center include *feeling, beauty, imagery, impressions, empathy, femininity, the arts, ecstasy, and expressivity* ("The Beautiful").

- Key attributes associated with the Head Center include *contemplation, truth, science, logic, understanding, philosophy, and learning* ("The True").

So the correspondence between the Big Three value spheres and the enneagram's three energy centers is not just approximate, but exact. We are talking about precisely the same distinctions. This means that the observations made by Wilber regarding the Big Three can be usefully applied in enneagram work and vice-versa.

The enneagram's three energy centers describe the nature of our inner energies (mental, emotional, and instinctual); the Big Three value spheres depict the way those energies are expressed in the outer world (within the domains of Science, Art, and Ethics). When we compare these two approaches, the parallels are impossible to miss (Table 10-6).

From an Integral point of view, studying the enneagram energy centers allows us to see the inner roots of our outer behavior; from an enneagrammatic perspective, studying the Big Three allows us to see how our inner energies can be positively expressed in the outer world. More significantly, it allows us to conceptualize the centers in a way that has nothing to do with ego defenses or cognitive distortions. (This may sound like a minor point to someone unfamiliar with the enneagram, but it is impactful in a field where the energy centers are virtually never associated with cultural refinement.)[16]

Until now, we've been looking at the powerful correspondences between AQAL and the enneagram points of view. So the question arises: Are the AQAL perspectives and enneagram points of view basically the same thing? I think the answer must be yes: despite differences in framework, languaging, and cultural outlook, the underlying constructs are identical. I have been exploring the parallels between the perspectives/horizones and enneagram points of view since 2006; and the more I study, the more correspondences I find.

If these correspondences really exist, this has three significant implications for the current formulation of Wilber's IOS:

- The first concerns the *nature of the horizones*, which—given their extreme similarity to enneagram types—can actually be considered synonymous with enneagram types.

- The second concerns the *number of elements* in Wilber's IOS, which I would propose reducing from five to four, based on the idea that the two horizontal

TABLE 10-6. BIG 3 VALUE SPHERES.

	ETHICS	ART	SCIENCE
ELEMENTAL ENERGY	fire	water	air
ENERGETIC NATURE	grounding	creating	drying
DOMINANT MODALITY	sensing	feeling	thinking
ASPIRATION	integrity	authenticity	truth
PRACTICAL GOAL	upholding standards	personal expression	objective understanding
DOMAIN	natural world	social world	mental world
REFERENCE POINT	moral perspective	subjective perspective	objective perspective
POLARITY	neutral	yin/feminine	yang/masculine
MODE OF EXPRESSION	being	appreciating	knowing
EVOLUTIONARY ROLE	originating	involving	evolving
SOURCE OF INSPIRATION	eternal values	personal values	objective values
EMOTIONAL TONE	hot	warm	cold
ACADEMIC FOCUS	law/theology	arts/humanities	science/logic
PLANE OF EXISTENCE	physical/spiritual*	emotional	mental

*The Ethics value sphere is both physical and spiritual in the sense that it focuses on the anchoring of eternal (spiritual) values on the physical plane.

TABLE 10-7. ENNEAGRAM ENERGY CENTER ATTRIBUTES.

	BODY/GUT CENTER	HEART CENTER	HEAD CENTER
ELEMENTAL ENERGY	fire	water	air
ENERGETIC NATURE	grounding	creating	drying
DOMINANT MODALITY	sensing	feeling	thinking
ASPIRATION	integrity	authenticity	truth
PRACTICAL GOAL	upholding standards	personal expression	objective understanding
DOMAIN	natural world	social world	mental world
REFERENCE POINT	moral perspective	subjective perspective	objective perspective
POLARITY	neutral	yin/feminine	yang/masculine
MODE OF EXPRESSION	being	appreciating	knowing
EVOLUTIONARY ROLE	originating	involving	evolving
SOURCE OF INSPIRATION	eternal values	personal values	objective values
EMOTIONAL TONE	hot	warm	cool
ACADEMIC FOCUS	law/theology	arts/humanities	science/logic
PLANE OF EXISTENCE	physical/spiritual*	emotional	mental
PATH TO INNER SELF	right action	self-discovery	understanding
SPIRITUAL QUALITY	presence	devotion	contemplation
SOUL DESIRE	oneness	ecstasy	awe

*The Body/Gut center is located at the place between heaven and earth; see Chapter 9.

elements—"AQAL quadrant/hori-zone" and "type"—belong in essentially the same category.

- The third concerns the *significance of horizontal perspectives* (which appear to be much more than mere translations of vertical structures).

We'll look at each of these implications in turn below.

Implications for the Hori-zones

As discussed above, mapping the hori-zones onto the enneagram makes them much more accessible to our understanding, because they can then be thought of not just as abstract perspectives, but as personifications (i.e., personality types). But there is an additional advantage to mapping the hori-zones onto the points of view: that this mapping can help us discover which perspective is most *dominant* (i.e., which one corresponds to our enneagram type). Enneagram theory is rooted in the idea that our dominant point of view exercises an enormous influence on our lives, both inner and outer. So to the extent that we can pin down our dominant point of view, we can pin down the core motivation around which everything else revolves.

Seeing our dominant hori-zone as a dominant personality type helps us recognize the profound influence that this dominant perspective has on how we habitually perceive the world. Because while the ultimate goal may be to expand our horizons—so that we are not forever stuck in one narrow perspective—we have to begin by recognizing our native point of origin. Only then can we move beyond it.

From the perspective of integral work, this understanding can help people avoid getting caught up in idealistic assumptions about what is possible regarding our potential to become aperspectival observers. The truth is that we will never become either completely *aperspectival* or *fully perspectival* in our outlook. We will always have a point of view—and this point of view will always be *partial* (and hence *subjective*). In holarchic terms, this is the same thing as saying that we will always be a *holon*—that we will never jettison our "partness" to become solely a "whole."

Once we come to terms with this idea of having a dominant hori-zone, we can use it to gradually broaden our perspective (see the discussion in Chapter 11).

Implications for IOS

You will recall from Chapter 4 that in Wilber's five-element system, "types" are that element defined by Wilber as "items that can be present at virtually any stage or state." I mentioned at that point that this definition is exceptionally generic, in that it tells us little or nothing about the nature of these "items"—perhaps because Wilber was unwilling to accord them the status of full-fledged psychic structures. Whatever the reason, the type category includes any sort of individual differences that are stable over time, e.g., gender, enneagram type, and MBTI type; these are all examples given by Wilber of types.

Other examples in the "type" category might include characteristics such as conflict resolution style (Thomas Kilman), locus of control (Julian Rotter), personality as measured by the Big Five personality scale (Costa & McCrae), introversion/extroversion (Hans Eysenck), decision-making styles (Myron Zuckerman), enneagram subtypes (self-preservation, sexual, or social orientations), and enneagram wings.

These are only a few of the possibilities we can dream up when it comes to focusing on individual differences that can be expressed as a "type."

But if AQAL quadrants and their variants, the hori-zones, and Big Three value spheres can be mapped onto the enneagram—which they clearly can—then technically speaking, the quadrants must also be included in the "type" category. If that sounds funny, it's because Wilber talks about AQAL perspectives in such an abstract way that it's hard to envision them as personality types, as mentioned above. But with a little imagination, it's not all that hard to move along the following continuum:

hori-zone > perspective > point of view > type

A perspective is a perspective, whether described impersonally (as an AQAL hori-zone) or personally (as an enneagram type). In the enneagram community, the terms *type* and *point of view* are regarded as synonyms; which one we use depends entirely upon context. When we want to stress personality characteristics, we speak of *types*; when we want to stress the perspectives, we speak of *points of view*.

However, in the Integral community, people are used to separating types and perspectives—which is why Wilber has five IOS elements, not four. But if the only difference between *type* and *AQAL perspective* is contextual, why not combine them into a single category?

In the literature of scientific psychology, this category already has a name, the one I used above: *individual differences*. All the variables listed in the above examples describe individual differences among people. AQAL and hori-zone perspectives also qualify for that category. So I propose subsuming *AQAL quadrant perspectives* and *type* under the

heading of individual differences, generating a version of IOS as follows:

- **lines of development**
- **levels/stages of development**
- **states of consciousness**
- **individual differences**
  (AQAL perspectives = enneagram types)

The only problem with this proposal is that AQAL perspectives are now such an iconic part of Wilber's approach that I doubt he would want to get rid of it (or subsume it under a new category name). But how to work with this information is not my main purpose here; the aim is just to point out what I have observed and let Wilber and his colleagues at Integral Institute ponder how to respond.

But even if no changes are made to IOS in terms of consolidating two categories into one, I would hope that pointing out the link between the two will at least foster a deeper understanding of what it means to have a dominant point of view—and how such a point of view can be influential enough to become a living, breathing personality type.

Implications for Horizontal Structure

There is a third important implication that flows out of our discussion on the parallels between AQAL perspectives and the enneagram points of view. And that is the idea that *horizontal entities such as the AQAL perspectives and enneagram points of view have structural correlates that are just as stable and therefore significant as vertical structures of consciousness.*

If the idea that horizontal points of view are structural in nature seems counterintuitive from an IOS perspective, it's not counterintuitive from an enneagram perspective. The idea that the nine types are structural entities is so well-accepted in the personality enneagram community that the two most well-known teacher training programs—Enneagram Institute and Enneagram Worldwide—incorporate that idea into their core teachings. Enneagram Institute even has a special workshop devoted to exploring the type structures.

And if the types/points of view are structural in nature, then *so are the IOS/AQAL perspectives*. This means that we have both horizontal and vertical psychic structures, not just vertical structures. We'll discuss this idea further in Chapter 11, but for now, we can begin with the question, "Why do the two communities differ so much in their assumptions about horizontal structures?"

The single biggest reason is that Wilber has long put forth the idea that *psychic structures are primarily a function of our level of consciousness*—which means that they have to be essentially vertical in nature. As a result, Wilber tends to see vertical work as the primary focus in transformation; horizontal work may also be necessary, but it is done for the sake of vertical ascent, not for its own sake. This is why horizontal processes are seen as a subset (translation) of vertical structures.

However, in enneagram work, horizontal processes are the primary focus. And this is precisely what makes enneagram work so valuable: its ability to depict the dynamic interactions between diverse points of view (both in terms of internal forces and externalized relationships).

The resulting insights are very powerful. But to understand the potential of such an approach, it's essential to invest enough time and energy in enneagram work to grasp its

import; simply learning the type attributes is not enough. It is only with deep and hands-on engagement in the work that the enneagram comes to life—and that people experience life-altering changes in beliefs, habits, and relationships.

We might of course ask the question: If horizontal structures are so real and important, why have they gone unnoticed by those engaged in integral work?

It's for the same reason identified by Wilber regarding the invisibility of *vertical* structures. The problem, he says, with identifying structural elements of consciousness is that we can't directly perceive them. He cites Graves and Cowan's Spiral Dynamics as an example: "You can sit on your meditation mat for decades, and you will NEVER see anything resembling Spiral Dynamics" (*Integral Spirituality*, 2006, p. 38, *emphasis* his).

The exact same observation can be made about horizontal structures, e.g., enneagram types or AQAL structures: while they may be profoundly influential in shaping our view of the world, *they are part of the framework that does the observing*. And as such, they tend to be invisible to the observer. It is not until somebody points them out that they become noticeable. Just ask anyone who recently became aware of his or her enneagram type—it's a pretty eye-opening piece of information!

Nevertheless, until the existence of the nine types was pointed out by Oscar Ichazo in 1970, nobody noticed their existence. Claudio Naranjo started using them in his psychiatric practice but without revealing this new tool to his patients. He said they were amazed at his uncanny ability to understand them—which is why he finally couldn't resist disseminating the teachings to his SAT group (despite an earlier pledge of secrecy to Ichazo): he felt the information was too valuable to keep to himself. Of course, some of his students felt the same way Naranjo did, which is how the teachings gradually leaked out, obtaining public recognition.

Based upon the foregoing discussion, it is possible to envision an IOS model that includes (a) eight hori-zones that are seen as equivalent to the nine enneagram points of view, one of which is dominant for each individual; (b) four main elements (lines, levels, states, and individual differences); and (c) vertical and horizontal structures of consciousness. While these proposed changes may be controversial, they are certain to provide ample food for thought.

In Chapter 9, we looked at the vertical dimension of transformation; in Chapter 10, we looked at the horizontal dimension. In Chapter 11, we'll explore the interplay between the vertical and horizontal dimensions—and between IOS and the enneagram.

ONE LAST NOTE: An apology to those Wilber fans who habitually use Wilber's hori-zone numbers for talking about each zone. I can't adopt the same numbering system because the enneagram has a different system (and moreover, a system in which the numbers have some sort of esoteric significance and thus cannot be altered; see Note 10 in Chapter 8). To make things easier, in Table 10-8, I've juxtaposed the type numbers with Wilber's zone numbers (as delineated in Wilber's table on p. 39 of *Integral Spirituality*). Inside the circles are the inside-out perspectives and outside the circles are the outside-in perspectives.

TABLE 10-8. WILBER'S ZONE NUMBERS TRANSLATED INTO ENNEAGRAM TYPES.

	Interior/Subjective	Exterior/Objective
Singular/Individual	Type 4 = ZONE 1 Type 3 = ZONE 2	Type 5 = ZONE 6 Type 6 = ZONE 5
Plural/Collective	Type 2 = ZONE 3 Type 1 = ZONE 4	Type 7 = ZONE 8 Type 8 = ZONE 7

Notes

1. Technically speaking, AQAL represents the *combination* of vertical and horizontal dimensions (that's why it's "all levels.") However, from a practical point of view, the AQAL quadrants/horizones are used primarily to discuss differences in horizontal outlook/perspective. Wilber does not really need the "all levels" part in his AQAL matrix, because his theory already includes two others elements (lines and levels of development) to describe the vertical dimension of consciousness. Thus, the inclusion of levels seems a bit redundant. But at the time that Wilber unveiled AQAL in *SES* (1995/2000), he had not yet put together a formal model like the one in *Integral Spirituality* (2006) that lists each element in IOS (including levels of development). Thus, he may have wished to include levels when devising AQAL in order to remind his readers that all horizontal perspectives can occur at any level of development.

2. Wilber uses two different approaches for labeling AQAL rows and columns, depending on what he wants to emphasize. To take a more personal perspective, we can speak of Individual vs Collective for the rows and Subjective vs Objective for the columns; from a more impersonal perspective, we can speak of Singular vs Plural for the rows and Interior vs Exterior for the columns. For the sake of completeness, I use both.

3. *A Brief History of Everything* (1996), p. 91.

4. Ibid., p. 93.

5. Ibid., p. 94.

6. This is not to say that our cognitive filter/framework cannot accommodate new ideas, simply that it cannot allow in so much new information at a time that this information would "swamp" its ability to maintain a stable perspective. How much we can handle at a time depends to a large degree on our inner balance. A well-balanced individual with a flexible framework is able to allow in more information (and better able to assimilate that information) than an unbalanced individual with a fragmented or overly-rigid framework, for whom new information would be destabilizing.

7. *Integral Life Practice* (2008), p. 37.

8. Ibid., p. 68.

9. Context can also obviously play a role in which AQAL perspective we adopt. In spiritual contexts, the emphasis has traditionally been on the UL (personal/subjective) quadrant, in contrast to modern culture, which favors the UR (scientific) quadrant.

While there has been a lot of attention during the last few decades on the LR (systems theory) quadrant, Wilber tends to focus on its drawbacks in both *SES* (1995/2000), and *Integral Spirituality* (2006), mostly because he thinks that systems theory has been perceived as a way to bridge the gap between science and spirituality, a view he does not embrace (see the discussion, e.g., on pp. 113–114 of *SES*). Wilber has become more interested in the LL quadrant (the "we" space), with its emphasis on social responsibility and shared values, because of its potential to help people evolve beyond the narrow confines of monological science and spirituality (see the discussion on pp. 175–178 of *Integral Spirituality*).

10. One might wonder at this point: Which system (AQAL or the enneagram) is better? The answer is: It depends—because context is everything. For certain purposes, Wilber's IOS is particularly useful (e.g., looking at lines of development, comparing different interpretations of the Kosmos, understanding the pre/trans fallacy) while for others, the enneagram may be particularly useful (e.g., when we're looking at points of view from a personal or interactive standpoint). Also, individuals of some personality types (e.g., the more rationally-oriented ones, such as Types 5, 6, and 7) may be more attracted to Wilber's system while individuals who are feeling- or body-oriented may be more attracted to the enneagram. The point is not so much which is better but which is better *for a particular purpose*. See Chapter 13 for a point-by-point comparison of both systems.

11. The perspective I take for our discussions in this chapter is based on an epistemological view of the quadrants, i.e., as *perspectives*, *points of view*, or *perceptual filters* that we use to take in information from the world. A potential source of confusion in our discussion arises from Wilber's labeling of the UR quadrant as "behavioral"—something he has done from the beginning (see the AQAL frontispiece in *SES*, 1995/2000). Judging from his initial discussion in *SES* (see p. 128), Wilber's original intention was to associate the UR quadrant with *behaviorism*, a form of empirical inquiry focusing only on exterior observation. But by labeling the UR quadrant "behavioral," he

opened the door for misunderstandings (i.e., for his readers to see behavior as the characteristic that distinguishes the UR quadrant from the other three quadrants).

Thus, it is necessary to stress that (a) there is a huge difference between physical behavior and a behavioral *perspective*; and (b) *any of the four quadrants can focus on behavior*—as seen through the filter of personal intuition (UL), cultural beliefs (LL), empirical assessment (UR), or a systems theoretical perspective (LR).

12. When discussing the LL quadrant, although Wilber focuses on collectives in the more global sense, the "we" perspective can refer to any subjectively-oriented unit consisting of more than one individual. So it can include perspectives shaped by intimate relationships, friendships, or families (not just large groups).

13. I almost wrote here that masculine energy tends to be objective (rather than objectively-*oriented*). This is a fine but important distinction, because having an objective orientation does not mean an individual is actually more objective in his or her understanding. All AQAL perspectives are equally subjective in that they are all partial outlooks.

14. It is interesting that the enneagram types most associated with femininity/interiority are even-numbered (2 and 4) while the types most associated with masculinity/exteriority are odd-numbered (5 and 7). This is not a coincidence; in esoteric number theory, femininity is associated with even numbers and masculinity with odd numbers (for a discussion, see, e.g., www.freemasons-freemasonry.com/esoteric-masonry-tetragrammaton.html; accessed 11-9-12).

Recent research also indicates that this is actually how people psychologically perceive them (see www.livescience.com/15859-odd-numbers-male-female.html; accessed 11-9-12).

So when we translate the eight hori-zones into enneagram types , the same pattern repeats itself, with even-numbered types (0-2-4-6-8) having a greater degree of interiority and odd-numbered types (1-3-5-7-9) having a greater degree of exteriority, thus giving credence to the numerological principle that even = feminine and odd = masculine.

15. Parallel to the idea that odd numbers are masculine and even numbers are feminine (see Note 14) is the idea that the enneagram types which are mapped onto the original AQAL quadrants (2, 4, 5 and 7) are the ones most "naturally" at home in the four quadrants, in that 2 & 4 (on the left-hand or subjective side of AQAL) are more "purely" subjective in orientation while 5 and 7 (situated on the right-hand or objective side) are more "purely" objective.

The other four types are "mixed": 1 and 3 are objective types in the subjective column and 6 and 8 are subjective types in the objective column. This means that it may be harder to reconcile these internal differences. Alternatively, it could mean that they are more diverse and hence, better balanced in certain respects.

(I never would have noticed this pattern had I not mapped the types onto the hori-zones. So here's one example of how mapping one system to another can identify new areas for exploration.)

16. For discussions focusing on types as personality distortions, see, e.g., Chapter 1 in Maitri's *The Spiritual Dimension of the Enneagram* (2000) and *The Enneagram of Passions and Virtues* (2005), Chapter 7 in Riso and Hudson's *Understanding the Enneagram* (2000), or Chapter 2 in Hurley and Dobson's *My Best Self: Using the Enneagram to Free the Soul* (1993).

11

INTEGRATING THE
VERTICAL & HORIZONTAL

The fixations are "negatives." The worldviews I have described are all "positive." Putting the two sets of terms side by side is mutually illuminating.

— A. G. E. Blake

ONE OF MY FAVORITE FILMS is *Pleasantville*, where two modern teens, David and Jennifer (wonderfully played by Toby McQuire and Reese Witherspoon) are magically transported back to a 1950s sitcom, where they reluctantly adopt the personas of "Bud" and "Mary Sue," joining a cast of characters stuck in two-dimensional, black-and-white TV roles. Everyone in Pleasantville represents a stereotype: the dutiful wife, her predictable partner, the goofy but lovable kids, and the guy who runs the soda shop where all the teens meet after school. Pleasantville is a really nice place to live, the quintessence of 1950s suburbia: a clean, well-ordered, and friendly place that has zero crime, accidents, or fires. There's only one problem: nothing new ever happens there.

But this doesn't bother the Pleasantville residents because they're used to it. They don't realize their lives are so narrowly circumscribed. They only begin to wake up after the new arrivals start asking awkward questions—questions like "What's outside of Pleasantville?" This innocuous-sounding query—initially addressed by a bored and cynical Jennifer to her geography teacher—opens the door to a veritable Pandora's box of new ideas. She keeps not only asking questions but initiating the Pleasantville teens into the mysteries of dating and romance—not to mention sex. And from there on, a chain of events ensues that ensures that Pleasantville will never be the same again. And neither will David and Jennifer.

One of the film's messages is that transformation is so intrinsic to life that not even a static place like Pleasantville is immune to change. Although the residents initially seem slotted into predictable routines, it doesn't take much provocation to get them interested in something new (especially the teens). Their eagerness allows them to open to a larger reality, both within and without.

Pleasantville has another important message: that transformation looks different for every individual. So although the desire to change is critical, no real change is possible until we discover what kind of change is right for each of us as an individual.

In *Pleasantville*, we know there's been a significant breakthrough when a black-and-white character suddenly changes to color. But the experiences that create this transformation are unique to each person. For some people, transformation is about becoming independent while for others, it's about becoming interdependent. Some people fall in love while others find the courage to walk away from sterile relationships. In the case of the visitors from the future, unassertive David finds his inner warrior (when he defends his adoptive Mom from bullies) while bubbly Jennifer finds her inner scholar (when she discovers that she likes studying better than promiscuous sex). But whatever the means of transformation, only those who discover their true nature find themselves transformed from black-and-white into glorious color!

Thus, *Pleasantville* reveals the innate link between horizontal development (our ability to understand our uniqueness as individuals) and vertical development (our ability to move beyond our current level of consciousness). The reverse is also true: that vertical development supports an enhanced understanding of our uniqueness by allowing us to see ourselves from a different level of our being.

And that is what this chapter is about: exploring the relationship between the vertical and horizontal dimensions, something we have already done with the enneagram in Chapter 8. In the current chapter, we add Wilber's IOS into the mix—playfully juxtaposing IOS and the enneagram in ways that allow us to see the advantages of integrating both the two systems and the two dimensions.

But before plunging into that discussion, we first need to take a closer look at how the vertical and horizontal dimensions are currently conceptualized in IOS. So we are picking up the thread of a discussion begun in Chapter 10, where I made the point that the psyche must have both horizontal and vertical structures of consciousness, not just vertical structures.

However, this idea runs counter to Wilber's "transformation versus translation" approach discussed in Chapter 4—an approach based on the idea that vertical transformation is more primary than horizontal translation. Below we'll take a closer look at this assumption, with the aim of suggesting that it may be time to move from a vertically-oriented model to a model in which vertical and horizontal development are considered to be complementary and equal partners in transformation.

Transformation vs Translation: a Second Look

As we saw in Chapter 4, Wilber distinguishes two kinds of change: *transformation* (which he characterizes as vertical) and *translation* (which he characterizes as horizontal). Transformation is defined as the move to another level of consciousness while translation is defined as a move within our currently established level of consciousness. According to Wilber, transformation is accompanied by structural changes in consciousness while translation is not. This way of conceptualizing the psyche (as having only vertical structures) and transformation (as involving only vertical shifts) gives the vertical axis a clear edge over the horizontal axis.

This edge shows up repeatedly in Wilber's writings. For example, on p. 47 of *The Atman Project* (1980), Wilber likens vertical transformation to moving up to a new floor in a building while he likens horizontal translation to moving the furniture around within a given floor. Such an observation suggests that translation is nothing more than a superficial kind of change.

In *Eye to Eye* (1983), he says that "the process of *translation*, by its very nature, tends to screen out all perceptions and experiences that do not conform to the basic limiting principles of the translation itself" (p. 110, *emphasis* his). What he is getting at here is that translation is actually a kind of psychological defense mechanism—he actually uses that phrase—but that it is nevertheless "normal, necessary, and healthy." But the way he talks about it doesn't make it sound very healthy. Next, he gives us an extensive discussion on all the problems associated with mistranslation, which he defines as the active repressing or suppressing of "aspects of...[the] deep structure."

When discussing the nature of holons in *SES* (1995/2000), Wilber observes—regarding translation—that a holon "*translates* the world according to the terms of its code or regime" whereas in transformation, "a *whole new world* of available stimuli becomes accessible" (p. 67, *emphasis* his). Here again, translation sounds like something that shuts us down while transformation is something that opens us up.

Elsewhere in *SES*, Wilber speaks of flatland as reflecting the triumph of translation over transformation in modern culture: "There is no longer a deeper or higher happiness, only a wider happiness" (p. 439).

In *One Taste* (2000), Wilber associates translation with conventional religious practice, which he sees as something more designed to render people content than aflame with the desire for inner change. After making a number of negative remarks about translation and positive remarks about transformation, he says that "although I have obviously been favoring transformation and belittling translation... both of these functions are incredibly important" (p. 27). However, he immediately goes on to once again belittle translation, characterizing it as something that is "given" to people which enables them to "translate their world, to make sense of it, to give meaning to it, and to defend themselves against the terror and the torture never lurking far beneath the surface of the happy self."

It's hard to reconcile the idea of translation as an "incredibly important" function with the idea of it as a temporary hedge against psychic terror.

A few pages later, Wilber comes out as an advocate for translation, on the basis that we need to find

> more *benign and helpful modes of translation...before we can effectively offer authentic transformations* (*One Taste*, 2000, p. 30, *emphasis* his).

Although transformation is still what really matters, Wilber is at least recognizing here that translation is something more than just a psychological defense—that it has a genuine role to play in the transformative process. Hence, he goes on to say that he's in agreement with the idea of introducing non-dual systems through the use of "lesser" practices (including translative practices, such as those developed by both Chogyam Trungpa Rinpoche and Adi Da, noting that although many of these practices are "simply translative," they may have the potential to prepare people for "the obviousness of what is" (p. 31).

He ends the discussion by observing that

> an integral approach to spirituality combines the best of horizontal and vertical, translative and transformative, legitimate and authentic [practices] (p. 32).

I couldn't agree more.

But a truly integral approach to spirituality must recognize the *intrinsic equality of both dimensions*—horizontal and vertical—and this is something that Wilber finds hard to do. While he intellectually understands the value of horizontal work—especially after 1995—he just doesn't seem to like it all that much. This is why he finds it so much easier to notice its distortions than its benefits.

As a result, he's prone to conflate constructive horizontal work (which integrates the psyche and expands our perspective-taking ability) with obstructive horizontal work (which blocks genuine development, both vertical and horizontal). The truth is that—just as there is a healthy and unhealthy version of each vertical level (discussed later in this chapter)—there is a healthy and unhealthy version of each horizontal perspective (whether we refer to AQAL perspectives or enneagram points of view). Moreover, as discussed in Chapter 10, the horizontal dimension is just as structural as the vertical dimension, which is why it's possible to describe the nine enneagram types in terms of distinctive differences in psychic structure.

Wilber's continued ambivalence about the horizontal dimension shows up as recently as 2006, in his last theoretical work, *Integral Spirituality*, where he distinguishes two categories of enlightenment, one of which (vertical or "structure-stage" enlightenment) is said to be superior to the other (horizontal or "state-based" enlightenment"). Briefly, what Wilber is trying to do here is to introduce an important distinction between those who are enlightened in a way that confers deep wisdom versus those who are enlightened in a way that seems incomplete (because they remain startlingly unenlightened in other areas of life). But the way he does it is to once again associate the horizontal plane with an inferior brand of spirituality. And for no real conceptual reason, since there's nothing intrinsically "horizontal" about "state-based" enlightenment.

From my standpoint, the term "horizontal" should clearly be reserved for talking about aspects of integral theory that are genuinely horizontal, e.g., perspective-taking, zones of arising/hori-zones, value spheres, enneagram points of view, enneagram energy centers, and the relationship between the individual and the community. Thus, it's my hope that in future works, Wilber will find an alternative way to discuss these two different approaches to enlightenment. (My suggestion would be to view what he calls "state-based" enlightenment as illumination on the spiritual line and "structure/stage" enlightenment as illumination along multiple lines which are linked in a way that allows the practitioner to have a more integral "view from the top.")[1]

In the 1970s and 80s, the transformation-versus-translation idea served the useful purpose of distinguishing inner work done to reach a higher stage of awareness from inner work designed to promote our ability to accept a flatland existence. So it's no wonder that Wilber saw translation as a potential dead-end.

But now that many more people are aware of higher levels and searching for the means by which to reach them, overemphasizing the vertical dimension can potentially make people see horizontal development as something superficial, inferior, and even self-delusional. And this is a real problem, because without horizontal work, we have no way to "transcend and include," because inclusion involves integration, and integration involves some pretty nitty-gritty horizontal work (as anyone who's worked extensively with the personality enneagram can attest).

So I can't help but wonder whether the "transformation vs translation" idea—while historically useful—is now at the point where it has outlived its usefulness. For as Wilber's system continues to expand horizontally—focusing on the "we" space and the cultivation of ways to facilitate a more harmonious world culture—the idea of making horizontal growth inferior to vertical growth seems increasingly counterproductive.

From this point onwards, might it not be better to think of the vertical and horizontal dimensions in terms of how we can best coordinate their functions, in order to accomplish productive inner work? *Productive* work would be that which promotes our inner and outer alignment with life, on whatever dimension it occurs.

By taking such a balance-oriented approach, we can emphasize the cooperative nature of the horizontal and vertical dimensions—dimensions that truly have much in common. This is why we can map them onto one another, as we have already done with the personality and process enneagrams—and as we will soon do with Wilber's AQAL quadrants (converting them to four sequential phases in life) later in this chapter.

But we'll begin our exploration by looking at the relationship between the horizontal perspective-taking associated with the nine points on the personality enneagram and the vertical lines of development particularly emphasized in IOS.[2]

Expanding in Two Directions

According to personality enneagram theory, we have one dominant point of view—a view that strongly shapes our perceptions of the world. Early in life, this view is pretty one-pointed—which makes it hard for us to imagine life in somebody else's shoes. But as we develop, our one-pointed view can potentially expand, especially if we seek out that kind of expansion.

A tool like the enneagram can accelerate the expansion process by giving us a tool for identifying our dominant point of view and how it's connected to other points of view, which kickstarts the process of befriending either little-known or previously disowned parts of ourselves—a process of horizontal integration. It is closely related to the vertical process of development, because we can only develop what we have first claimed as part of our "me-ness."

However, the idea that we identify our point of view in order to develop its potential is not a traditional goal in enneagram work, which has been more about identifying the type in order to free ourselves of its negative influence (see Chapter 5). So this is where a mental shift to IOS-style thinking is extraordinarily helpful, because it is such a developmentally-oriented system. It also has an extremely well-developed body of theory supporting the validity of personality development—not to mention an extensive compilation of well-known lines of development (as discussed at the start of Chapter 9). When we map these IOS lines onto the personality enneagram, we have the foundation for an approach in which personality (or more properly, individuality) is recast as a resource to be developed—and the enneagram is recast as a tool that can further that development.

Using this approach, we start by envisioning each enneagram point of view as the *point of origin* for a particular line of vertical development (Fig. 11-1). The nature of the line is closely related to the nature of its origin point. So we could say that the two co-arise and that they are mutually attractive. It is because of this natural attraction that our best-developed line is likely to be one most closely associated with our dominant point of view.

Fig. 11-2 depicts the differential development of an individual on the nine lines. In this example, the individual depicted is probably a Seven, because the line arising out of Point 7 is the best-developed, followed by the lines arising out of its wing points (Six and Eight) and connecting points (Five and One).

The figure itself is akin to what Wilber refers to as an *integral psychograph*, a graph depicting our position on diverse lines of development (see pp. 83–84 in Wilber et al.'s *Integral Life Practice,* 2008, for psychograph ex-

amples). However, because this psychograph is organized by enneagram point of view, it can yield additional information as to (a) the special role of the dominant line and (b) its relationship to all the other lines.

Fig. 11-3 adds descriptors to the lines, which—as we can see—are not just single lines but families or clusters of *related* lines, all of which express some aspect of the core energy associated with each point (see Chapter 3).

Mapping the lines of development onto the enneagram has three key advantages:

- *First,* it reveals the interplay between the enneagram's horizontal points of view and Wilber's vertical lines of development (showing how identifying our point of view can help us determine promising lines of development and, conversely, how identifying lines of development can help us determine our point of view).

- *Second,* it reminds us that no scale is more objective and complete than any other (by associating each one with an enneagram point of view, all of which are subjective and therefore partial).

- *Third,* by emphasizing the partial nature of both each line of development and the point of view out of which it arises, it highlights the value of developmental diversity for both individuals and cultures.

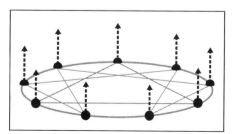

Fig. 11-1. Potential lines of development by enneagram point.

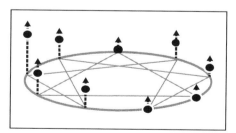

Fig. 11-2. Different rates of growth by enneagram point.

While this last idea of developmental diversity (i.e., developing along multiple lines) has always been emphasized in IOS theory,[3] translating theory into practice can be a challenge, especially when we're trying to develop abilities in ourselves that are not particularly compatible with our dominant point of view (see the discussion in the next section—see also Appendix D for a discussion of the lines of development depicted in Figure 11-3).

Developmental diversity can also be affected (and perhaps limited) by cultural values. For just as individuals have a dominant enneagram point of view, so do cultures (especially long-established cultures). Thus, it's common in enneagram circles to speak of the enneagram type of a culture.

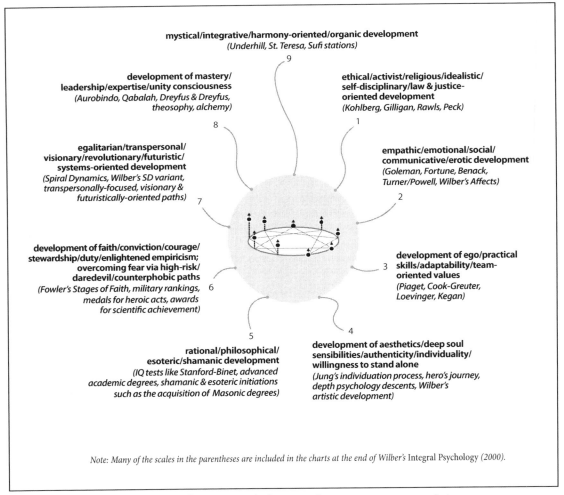

mystical/integrative/harmony-oriented/organic development
(Underhill, St. Teresa, Sufi stations)
9

development of mastery/
leadership/expertise/unity consciousness
(Aurobindo, Qabalah, Dreyfus & Dreyfus,
theosophy, alchemy)
8

ethical/activist/religious/idealistic/
self-disciplinary/law & justice-
oriented development
(Kohlberg, Gilligan, Rawls, Peck)
1

egalitarian/transpersonal/
visionary/revolutionary/futuristic/
systems-oriented development
(Spiral Dynamics, Wilber's SD variant,
transpersonally-focused, visionary &
futuristically-oriented paths)
7

empathic/emotional/social/
communicative/erotic development
(Goleman, Fortune, Benack,
Turner/Powell, Wilber's Affects)
2

development of faith/conviction/courage/
stewardship/duty/enlightened empiricism;
overcoming fear via high-risk/
daredevil/counterphobic paths
(Fowler's Stages of Faith, military rankings,
medals for heroic acts, awards
for scientific achievement)
6

development of ego/practical
skills/adaptability/team-
oriented values
(Piaget, Cook-Greuter,
Loevinger, Kegan)
3

rational/philosophical/
esoteric/shamanic development
(IQ tests like Stanford-Binet, advanced
academic degrees, shamanic & esoteric initiations
such as the acquisition of Masonic degrees)
5

development of aesthetics/deep soul
sensibilities/authenticity/individuality/
willingness to stand alone
(Jung's individuation process, hero's journey,
depth psychology descents, Wilber's
artistic development)
4

Note: Many of the scales in the parentheses are included in the charts at the end of Wilber's Integral Psychology (2000).

Fig. 11-3. Developmental clusters by enneagram point.

For example, most people familiar with the enneagram consider American culture to be pretty Three-ish (because of its emphasis on material achievement, efficiency, and busy-ness). But it started out more as a One-ish culture (at least in the northeast, where the Puritans landed). The culture shifted as the nature of its immigrants shifted (from people seeking religious freedom to those seeking social and economic freedom).[4]

Individuals whose enneagram type is compatible with their "culture type" usually feel more at home in their environment than those whose type is less compatible. Nevertheless, in a healthy culture, there is sufficient tolerance for minority points of view that developmental diversity is still possible.[5]

A Type 2 Example

Now we'll take a look at a concrete, step-by-step example of using the enneagram to expand our horizons vertically and horizontally. We'll start by imagining an individual who has identified himself as a Two—someone with a friendly, helpful, and emotionally responsive personality type.[6] He hopes the enneagram can help him make more informed decisions in life. If he's young, he may be seeking insights to help with romantic relationships or how to parent young children.

If he's older, he may be dealing with "empty nest" syndrome or other concerns involving the loss of love or valued relationships with others. Whatever his age and situation, his attention is probably drawn to love, relationships, feelings, and giving.

Like anyone first approaching the enneagram, this Two can begin the process of expanding his *horizontal perspective* (Fig. 11-4) by first identifying his type—and in particular, its gifts and its challenges—because this is how he can become grounded in a way that establishes the foundation for future work. As a Two, his gifts include loads of empathy and a deep desire to connect with others; the challenges involve the tendency to become emotionally overbearing or to over-give. So initially, a lot of his inner work involves learning to love while still setting boundaries.

After initially exploring his dominant point of view, this Two could broaden his perspective by learning more about the outlook of the other eight points. Watching enneagram type panels (panels composed of individuals of each type) is especially helpful for that purpose, because this allows him to see how he is both the same and different from people with other points of view.

Often, a Two will find it easiest to relate to types with similar perspectives, e.g., his wing

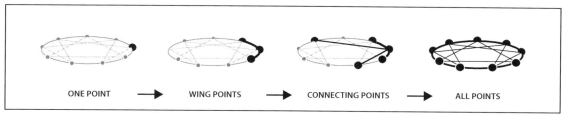

Fig. 11-4. Example of horizontal growth (Type 2).

points (1 and 3), especially the wing point that is most dominant. The Two who can access his "inner One" can expand his perspective in a way that allows him to combine caring with a sense of inner restraint. The Two who can access his "inner Three" can expand his perspective in a way that allows him to socialize without getting overly sentimental. If he leans into both of his wing points, he begins to move from a one-pointed to a three-pointed perspective.

The Two can also expand his perspective by opening to his connecting points (4 and 8). Connecting with his inner Four helps him tap into his emotional depths while connecting with his inner Eight helps him realize his leadership potential. He can then move from a three-pointed- to a five-pointed perspective.

As his experience with the enneagram deepens, the Two can keep expanding his horizons to include the perspectives of other, less directly connected points of view: the three mental types (Five, Six, and Seven) and the only body type with which he lacks a direct connection: Point/Type 9. It can be harder for the Two to imagine the world from these points of view, because they are considerably more dispas-

sionate in outlook. Nevertheless, they still represent aspects of his inner psyche, aspects with the potential to enrich his inner life, if he is sufficiently motivated to integrate them.[7,8]

At the same time that the Two is expanding his horizontal perspective-taking with the enneagram, he can open doors to *vertical development* by using IOS to identify the vertical paths associated with each enneagram point of view, following more or less the same sequence as above, i.e., moving from identifying (a) his dominant line to (b) the lines associated with the wings and connecting points to (c) all other lines (Fig. 11-5).

Thus, he is likely to realize that the lines to which he feels most attracted involve the development of the kinds of roles, skills, and modes of awareness that enable him to fulfill himself as a Two, i.e., to come into relationship with others, especially in the role of nurturer, supporter, lover, or empathic listener. He will likely be additionally attracted to lines of development that indirectly support the development of relationships, such as those associated with his wing points and connecting points: the lines that enable him to develop *ethical boundaries* (Point 1), *hands-on skills* (Point 3),

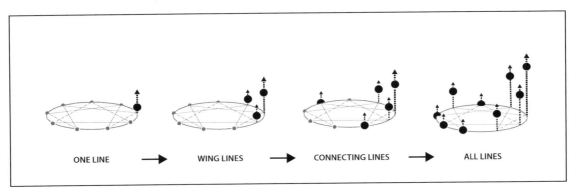

ONE LINE → WING LINES → CONNECTING LINES → ALL LINES

Fig. 11-5. Example of vertical growth (Type 2).

emotional authenticity (Point 4), and *leader-ship* (Point 8). These lines help him balance the desire for intimacy with the need to avoid co-dependency. With the foundation he gets from these five lines of development, he may then opt to seek development on the more chal-lenging lines for someone of this type—those involving *logical discernment* (Point 5), *careful observation* (Point 6), *mental invention* (Point 7), and *impartial receptivity* (Point 9). While these latter paths are particularly challenging for the empathic Two, they may also be the most transformative (because they address shadow aspects of the psyche that may seem opposed to his primary line of development).

While this example focuses on Type 2, the same basic approach can be used to work with all the types. The aim has been to demonstrate how an IOS-informed approach to enneagram work can fruitfully combine horizontal inte-gration with vertical development.

However, this is not the only way we can bring the vertical and horizontal together. There are additional ways to playfully jux-tapose IOS and the enneagram—and in so doing, to more deeply explore the comple-mentary relationship between these two di-mensions.[9] The remainder of the chapter in-troduces some other ways to do so.

However, in the next few sections, instead of using the personality enneagram as a refer-ence point, we'll use the process enneagram. We will then proceed to map three IOS con-structs onto it: two horizontal IOS constructs (the AQAL quadrants and the Big Three value spheres) and one vertical IOS construct (Wil-ber's three fulcrums of development). Then we'll turn the tables, using Wilber's nine-stage Spectrum model of development as the reference point—and we'll map the process and personality enneagrams onto it.

While these juxtapositions introduce a level of complexity that can be a little daunt-ing for those new to either system, it can open new doors for those familiar with both sys-tems. But if the material becomes more trou-ble than it's worth, you won't miss anything vital by skipping ahead to Chapter 12.

AQAL on the Process Enneagram

In Chapter 10, we looked at the parallels be-tween AQAL perspectives and personality enneagram points of view. Because we were only concerned with the horizontal perspec-tives at that point, we did not look at AQAL perspectives on the process enneagram. But there's no reason why we can't, because as we've already seen in Part II, it's possible to link the personality and process enneagrams. And if we can (a) link the two enneagrams and (b) further link AQAL perspectives with personality points of view, then we can (c) link AQAL perspectives with phases on the process enneagram.

When we do, the result is a completely new way of viewing the AQAL quadrants—as four phases we pass through during the life cycle (Table 11-1):

1. **Intersubjective phase** (*involution-collec-tive*): birth to early adulthood

2. **Subjective phase** (*involution-individual*): early adulthood to mid-life

3. **Objective phase** (*evolution-individual*): mid-life to retirement

4. **Interobjective phase** (*evolution-collec-tive*): retirement to end of life

While thinking of the four AQAL quad-rants as four AQAL phases in the life cycle

TABLE 11-1. AQAL QUADRANTS AS PHASES OF LIFE.

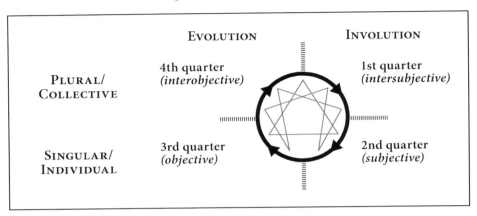

may take a little getting used to, this conversion can give us a new perspective on the underlying similarities between the vertical and horizontal axes.

The discussion below lays out how it works to view the quadrants as quarterly phases. We'll see why, e.g., the first and last phases in life are more oriented towards collectivity while the middle two are more oriented towards individuality. Also, since we are talking about a developmental process, we'll see how we can think of these four quarters as cumulative in their effects, such that what happens in the first phase affects the second, how the first and second affect the third, etc.

Table 11-1 shows all four AQAL phases in enneagrammatic order (see Chapter 10 for an explanation of how we flip Wilber's axes to come up with this arrangement).

We can see how, during the **first quarter** of life (intersubjective phase), we are subjectively immersed learning the lessons of life from the *collective's* point of view. This is because, al-

though we possess the seeds of individuality from the very moment of birth, that individuality is not yet developed. So the only standards we really have to go on are the standards of those who are around us, especially early caregivers and other family members. When we go off to school, we encounter the values of the larger collective, to which we must adapt. So at this point in the life cycle, we adopt those values for both personal and social survival.

During the **second quarter** (subjective phase), assuming normal development, our *individuality* begins to emerge, at first tentatively and later, in a much more noticeable way. Initially, we develop a social persona which enables us to function in life while we are gradually discovering who we are apart from our collective identity. So during this phase, we are moving from a relatively undifferentiated state to a social persona to a semiautonomous personality self with differentiated feelings and the ability to make independent decisions, a process that typically takes place during early- to mid-adulthood.

But in addition to developing a sense of ourselves as individuals with our own feelings, we also need to develop our sense of self in a cognitive and metacognitive fashion (objective quadrant), such that we know what we think and have a rational means of justifying our position. This is what develops during the ***third quarter*** (objective phase) of life, when we finally have enough life experience to develop a more dispassionate, objective type of awareness. However, during the time we are developing that kind of awareness, we often find ourselves either separated from the collective or interacting in a somewhat stereotyped fashion because we cannot complete the process of individuation without some distance. This is the kind of period many of us experience during mid-life or somewhat after.

By the time we reach the ***fourth quarter*** of life (interobjective phase), if we have developed our differentiated feelings and mental processes, we tend to find ourselves drawn back towards the *collective*, but this time not in an unconscious fashion but in a conscious fashion that allows us to use our individual abilities to serve something larger than ourselves, such that we can be "*in the world but not of the world.*" Also, the collective into which we are drawn is not just the culture of a family or nation but the collective in a much more expanded sense, the collective as embodied in the idea of the Kosmos or All That Is. If all has gone well, we remain interested in life and able to pass along wisdom to the younger generation but without becoming overly attached to outcomes.

In summary, this approach can be used to conceptualize how each of us

- starts off as a mostly undifferentiated self that is part of a larger collective (Quarter 1)

- becomes identified as a separate but differentiated self possessing a subjective sense of identity (Quarter 2)

- begins to see this individualized self from a more objective, dispassionate perspective (Quarter 3)

- achieves the ability to retains our individuality while at the same time participating in the larger collective (Quarter 4)

While Table 11-1 translates the four AQAL quadrants into four phases of the life cycle, we could use the same approach to translate the eight hori-zones into eight phases of life (with the outer zones preceding the inner ones; see Fig. 10-2).

Big Three Value Spheres on the Process Enneagram

Since Wilber's Big Three value spheres are closely related to his AQAL quadrants (see Chapters 3 and 10), they can also be fruitfully mapped onto the process enneagram.

When we juxtapose the value spheres onto the process enneagram (Fig. 11-6), the first thing we notice is that the beginning of the enneagram cycle is at Point 9 (the top of the enneagram)—which is right in the middle of the "Ethics" value sphere. This means that the life cycle is "book-ended" by Ethics, such that Ethics is of particular concern at the beginning and end of life, with Art taking predominance during early to mid-life and Science taking predominance during mid-life to retirement. We'll explore what this means below.

Ethics at the start of life. At the beginning of life, we have a instinctually-conferred will

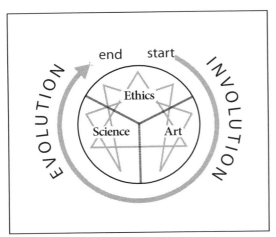

Fig. 11-6. Big Three value spheres on
the process enneagram.

to live but little self-control of any kind: physical, emotional, or mental. So at the beginning, ethics is about making value judgments about the world and what it is like. We determine whether the world is basically good or bad—whether it is an open, loving place where basic needs are met or a terrifying unpredictable place where survival is a constant challenge. Obviously, these value judgments set the tone for all that follows.

Early on, much of what is good is conditioned by environmental factors, because we are so helpless and dependent. However, our temperament and choice also play a definitive role. And the further we move along the arc of the life cycle, the more these three factors—environment, temperament, and choice—interact to determine our ethical orientation in life (see Chapter 7).

Art. Most people tend to think of art in terms of artistic talent. However, the realm of art is much broader than that. Beauty is, as they say, in the eye of the beholder; so the realm of art is the world of subjectivity, the domain in which we actually create a sense of self out of the raw energy of our being (including our type) using our experiences in life to understand who we are and what we might become.

In the realm of art, we often begin by noticing the most obvious (outer) characteristics of an artistic work, especially the degree to which it affects us subjectively. Later, we become aware of subtler nuances that we did not initially notice. We begin to see the art more as something that exists for its own sake, regardless of our subjective response to it.

Such is the case with self unfoldment: we start by looking for subjective approval from others; we see ourselves as a function of the way people respond to us. Later, we see ourselves in terms of the image we're able to project out into the world. Finally, we come to realize that the self we are creating is more than just someone who can please others or succeed in the world—that there is a deeper, more authentic self with a tremendous range of exquisitely nuanced emotions.

The cultivation of such a self does not, however, take place in a vacuum but is rooted in the ethical habits cultivated during the first-quarter (Ethics) phase, because these are the habits we use to develop the kind of relationships and abilities that create a sense of self that can competently function in life. In the absence of an ethical foundation, it is difficult to cultivate a self that can function in life (much less to arrive at the point where we can develop our subtler emotions or re-create ourselves in unique new forms).

Science. Just as we tend to think of art in terms of talent, we tend to think of science in terms of academic inquiry, i.e., as the rational or scientific method. But science is not just about rational analysis and empirical testing, but (in Idries Shah's words) "knowing how to know." It presupposes having a certain amount of experience in life—experience that serves as the foundation for objective inquiry.

It is the need for life experience that makes it impossible to begin the scientific phase at the beginning of life. We have to wait until we have a rich set of data (i.e., many diverse life experiences) that can serve as "grist for the mill." We also have to have the mental capacity to reflect on those experiences in a way that allows us to productively analyze them. Only then is science really possible.

A healthy entrance into the scientific phase presupposes the ethical foundation necessary to discipline our thinking and the artistic foundation necessary to love deeply (not just conventionally) and think imaginatively (not just mechanically). If the ethical foundation is lacking, then intellect can become unhinged from moral responsibility (leading to "mad scientist" syndrome). If the artistic foundation is lacking, intellect can become exceeding dry, linear, and hyper-analytical, such that "the more we study, the less we know." So to move through the scientific phase in an integrated way, it's necessary to cultivate objectivity in a way that allows it to mesh with both our ethical foundations and sensitivity to the artistic side of life.

Ethics at the end of life. As we approach the end of life, we are in the paradoxical situation of having accumulated a lot of life experience but being increasingly unable to fully express ourselves because of limitations in the physical vehicle. So the chief challenge is how to deal with limitation—and to do so in a way that integrates our elemental values, artistic sensibilities, and scientific understanding.

This phase is ethical in that it tests our ability to retain our core values in the face of physical infirmity, emotional loss, and intellectual decline. In this phase, our courage and "grace under fire" are tested, especially our willingness to remain conscious as we contemplate the end of life in a physical body. However, we will tend to have fewer difficulties to the extent that we have developed (a) good habits early in life (an ethical lifestyle), (b) highly differentiated emotions and a sense of self ("art"), and (c) the ability to exercise our mental faculties ("science")—because all of these abilities serve as the platform for moving to a higher level of awareness, a platform that enables us to see the movement of Spirit in matter.

So can you see how mapping the value spheres onto the process enneagram provides us with yet a different way of conceptualizing the transformational life cycle? Next we'll look at mapping Wilber's three major fulcrums of development onto the process enneagram.

Wilber's Major Fulcrums on the Process Enneagram

So far, we've been mapping horizontal IOS quadrants and value spheres (which traditionally describe horizontal categories) onto the process enneagram (which describes vertical stages of development). We can also map Wilber's stage-oriented fulcrums of development onto the stage-oriented process enneagram. So here the conceptual leap is not so great, because we are mapping a method of depicting three stages in vertical developmental sequence (Wilber's three major fulcrums) onto another system which also depicts stages of development (the process enneagram).

Here's a brief description of each fulcrum:

- **Pre-personal**: Individual consciousness, though present, is not well-differentiated; we are part of everything and everything is part of us.

- **Personal**: Individual consciousness becomes differentiated to varying degrees; the more differentiated we become, the greater the shift from collective to personal values.

- **Transpersonal**: Highly differentiated consciousness creates the foundation for identifying with something beyond the personal, both horizontally and vertically.

Fig. 11-7 depicts the correspondences between the two ways of mapping a developmental sequence. When we divide the process enneagram using Wilber's three-fulcrum model, we can see how each stage in the process enneagram belongs with one of the three IOS fulcrums: how Points 0–3 are associated with the Pre-personal fulcrum, Points 4–6 are associated with the Personal fulcrum; and Points 7–9 are associated with the Transpersonal fulcrum. The implications of these juxtapositions are discussed below.

During the **pre-personal phase**, despite our nascent individuality, our consciousness is diffuse and permeable, open to the influences of our environment, especially our immediate environment (***Point 0/9***). What especially matters at this point is developing clearly defined psychic structures that can serve as the basis for a cohesive sense of self. As we move from birth to early childhood, that sense of self is further developed as we enter the social culture and internalize familial and cultural standards (***Point 1***) and develop an emergent social self by seeing ourselves mirrored in the eyes of others, especially intimate caregivers (***Point 2***).

During the **personal phase**, we gain greater independence and the ability to inhabit a social persona (***Point 3***), which paves the way for gaining the kind of individuality that does not depend upon social approval (***Point 4***), culminating in a sense of self that is more identified with pure thought than social identity (***Point 5***).

During the **transpersonal phase**, we move towards a sense of consciousness that transcends the idea of an independent self but without losing the self-consciousness developed thus far (therefore "transcending and including" all the previous stages). At ***Point 6***, an emergent transpersonal awareness creates both feelings of trepidation and a sense of stewardship, as we try to come into right relationship with life (in this expanded sense) without losing ourselves in the process. So this is a particularly stressful challenge. Upon reaching ***Point 7***, we have worked through these difficulties to the extent that we are more pulled by the desire for expansion than the need to feel safe, although we are still trying to balance the sense of self (what is "in here") with the world around us (what is "out there"). It is only once we approach ***Point 8*** that the "in here" and "out there" begin to merge, enabling us to embody both simultaneously. Ironically, just about the point where this becomes possible, the end of life looms, necessitating a shift from embodiment to synthesis, so that we can translate the fruits of our labor into a form that transcends physical death (***Point 9***).[10]

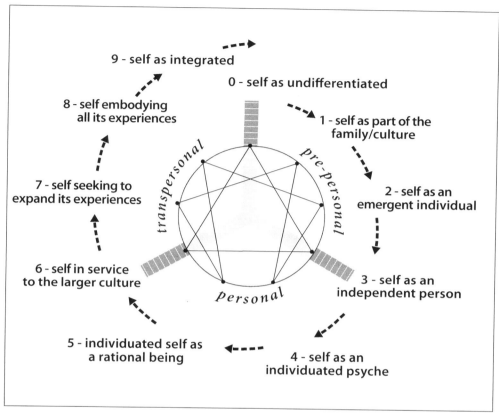

Fig. 11-7. The process enneagram divided by Wilber's fulcrums.

So to this point, we have mapped three of Wilber's IOS elements onto the process enneagram. Now we'll do the reverse, mapping the personality and process enneagrams onto Wilber's Spectrum model.

Wilber's Spectrum of Development

In *Transformations of Consciousness* (1986), Wilber outlines a Spectrum model of spiritual development that provides detailed descriptions of nine fulcrums or levels of conscious-

ness. He describes the nine levels (Chapter 4), discusses the potential pathologies associated with each level (Chapter 5), and potential treatments according to level (Chapter 6).

From this description, we can see that one of Wilber's fundamental assumptions is that *any level can be either normal or pathological*, from the lowest to the highest. We can also see that pathology is *level-dependent*, i.e., that each level is associated with a different kind of pathology. And this is why Wilber found it necessary to include an entire chapter on potential treatments: because if the pathologies differ for each level, so do the treatments.

There are two significant implications here for anyone who works with the enneagram. The first is that our level of development on Wilber's Spectrum model is not equivalent to our level as defined on Riso-Hudson's Levels of Health model, for the reasons described in Chapter 9 (see the "Up is Good, Down is Bad" section). The second and related implication is that, according to Wilber, not all pathologies we encounter during spiritual development are the result of ego defenses (because two-thirds of them are not at the ego level of development). This implication is significant for those who work with the enneagram, because of the traditional assumption in the enneagram community that ego is the principal barrier to spiritual development. However, if pathologies exist that are not ego-driven, then ego is not the only (or perhaps even the principal) barrier to higher consciousness.

Below are descriptions of each level, its potential pathologies, and typical treatments, along with a description of the enneagram process stages and personality types that correspond with each level. Each perspective has something unique to offer to our understanding of transformation:

- **Wilber's Spectrum model** provides the meta-framework to contextualize the transformational process.

- **The process enneagram** depicts the cyclical movement of energy *between* micro- and macro-levels.

- **The personality enneagram** depicts the interactive movement of energy *within* each level.

Fig. 11-8 visually depicts these differences; Table 11-2 (at the chapter's end) summarizes the factors emphasized by each approach by level. For each level, there is a summary of the remarks of both Ken Wilber and Frank Visser (who includes a detailed analysis of the levels in his book, *Ken Wilber: Thought as Passion*, 2003). This is followed by my *italicized* comments on the significance of their observations from the perspective of both the process and personality enneagrams. See Appendix C for a discussion on how three more models— Jane Loevinger's nine-level model, Suzanne Cook-Greuter's refinement of that model, and Riso-Hudson Strata model can be juxtaposed with those shown in Table 11-2.

THREE FULCRUMS OF DEVELOPMENT

Wilber has broken down stages of development in many ways. His simplest scheme is by three major levels—pre-personal, personal, and transpersonal—each of which has three sub-levels, resulting in nine levels total.

As we will see, the first four or five levels of development are similar to those described by Piaget and take us to the level of mature adult thinking and even metacognition (thinking about thinking). The last three levels as described by Wilber are clearly transpersonal. While the pathologies and therapies described for the lower levels are similar to what we would expect, given the current level of psychological understanding, the pathologies and therapies for higher level maladies are less familiar. So we will accordingly spend more time on them. (Please note: the terms *level*, *point*, and *stage* can all be used to describe a particular point in the developmental process.)

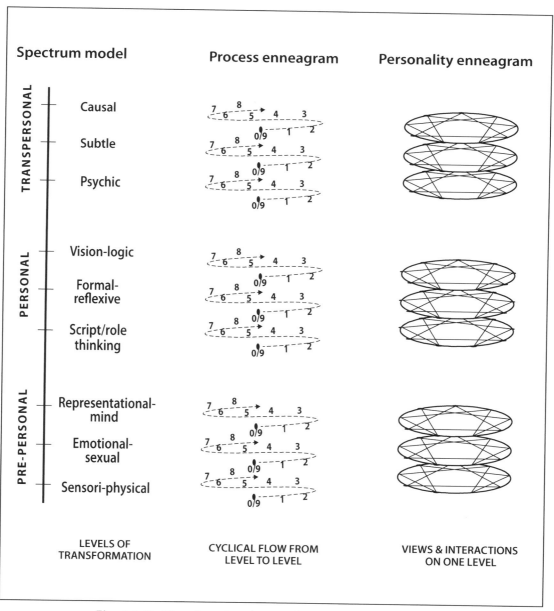

Fig. 11-8. Nine levels, nine cycles, nine perspectives.

PRE-PERSONAL FULCRUM

The pre-personal phase corresponds to that part of the human life cycle prior to the emergence of a clearly delineated sense of self and the ability to reason and exercise judgment. Please note that, as regards the three enneagram types that fall within this phase (Types 1-3), this does not mean that these types are less mature or developed than other types, only that they are particularly sensitive to the energy available on this level: binary evaluation (Type 1), emotional bonding (Type 2), and sensate operations (Type 3).

Level 1: Sensori-physical. This is the realm of matter, the senses, and perception; it is the most primal level of development and occurs during the earliest part of life. Although Wilber's discussion of this level is extremely brief, he does observe that its pathologies involve the inability to separate the self from "other." Visser is more specific, talking about the use of sedation for dealing with pathology at so early a phase of development. (It occurs to me there is little to say about adults at this level of development, because it is extremely rare.)

Point 0 to Point 1 on the process enneagram. *At the beginning of a new cycle, we need a basic way of relating to ourselves and our surroundings, a basic sense that life makes sense: that it is good, not bad. So the impulse is to move toward the good and away from the bad, and it is this impulse that provides a basic (instinctive) orienting response—a response that forms the foundation for later judgments.*

Type 1 on the personality enneagram. *Ones are known as "black and white" thinkers, but perhaps it would be more accurate to call them would-be positive thinkers whose desire to* move towards the light requires them to identify and thus avoid its opposite. So a two-category approach will also make sense to a One, because it is their natural "modus operandi." But discriminating Ones will gradually learn how to determine "good" from "bad" using increasingly refined and complex criteria for determining goodness, and in so doing, avoid substituting rigidity for discernment.

Level 2: Emotional-sexual. This is the self at the level of the sexual impulses and emotions. Wilber sees this as the level of the simple "image" mind that requires positive mirroring for healthy development and sees narcissism/grandiosity as the pathology that can take hold at this level. Visser comments that this is a period of emotional development, that it requires structure, and that providing such structure will be a key element in any therapeutic approach.

Point 1 to Point 2 on the process enneagram. *Once there is the sense that life is good, it is possible to take the risk of interacting emotionally with others, especially those closest to us (often our mothers). But the interactions need to be supportive without fostering emotional dependency, so that the developing child can become empathetic without becoming overwhelmed by negative emotions due to feelings of insecurity.*

Type 2 on the personality enneagram. *Twos are the most overtly emotional type on the enneagram. Hence, they are sensitive to their emotional environment and are particularly in need of emotional support and mirroring, especially early in life. But they also need to learn how to mirror themselves so that they can engage in intimate relationships without becoming over-dependent on the approval of others.*

Level 3: Representational-mind. According to Wilber, the representational mind describes a self that is beginning to work with symbols and concepts. So from his perspective, it is a step up from the image orientation of the previous level. As the self becomes more complex (now possessing instinct, emotion, and rudimentary mental operations), so do its pathologies; this is the level of ordinary neurosis, where instinct can conflict with emotions, emotions with mind, or instinct with mind. Whereas the lowest two levels are more instinctive, this level represents the emergence of more conscious mentation. However, there is still a certain automaticity operating here, although we are on the cusp of higher-level mentation. Visser says that it's on this level that repression really becomes possible—which is why therapy for neurosis often consists of helping people uncover repressed material.

***Point 2 to Point 3 on the process enneagram**. The focus here is on acquiring life skills so that the helplessness at Point 1 which is replaced by dependency at Point 2, can finally be (if not quite left behind) at least temporarily set aside in the interest of establishing a foothold in life. The temptation to suppress instinct and emotion is strong because of the dawning realization that competency is critical for living and must therefore take priority over inner (emotional or instinctual) needs. The focus is on tangible striving and results.*

***Type 3 on the personality enneagram**. Threes are known for their ability to adapt to environmental circumstances in a way that allows them to develop practical skills that rely on the ability to think concretely. However, they can have a harder time with deep feelings or taking time for intimacy, because they are so focused on the practical, achievement-oriented side of life. It is only after they have achieved a certain level of competence, material security, and social recognition that Threes are ready to turn their attention to the more subtle, intimate, or playful aspects of living.*

PERSONAL FULCRUM

Wilber observes that those who focus on psychopathology often don't go beyond Level 3 in their discussion, in part because the prepersonal pathologies are the most debilitating (at least for ordinary people living an ordinary life). However, he makes the point that simply getting beyond Level 3 in no way guarantees a pathology-free passage up the levels, because of the increasingly subtle challenges that arise as we ascend.

Level 4: Script/role thinking. At this level, we are moving to a higher level of mental functioning and deeper reflectivity, which allows us to become aware of both the social roles we play and to understand the role of another. Wilber notes that the conflicts that arise at this point concern the desire to fit in, to belong, and to understand the subtle rules by which things work. This new awareness also brings with it the possibility of consciously manipulating others. Visser notes that this is the point where the self can start to feel quite insecure about itself and how to behave in different social situations and says that script analysis can help by providing tools for becoming more aware of the nature of the roles we play, which can help us become more self-aware.

Point 3 to Point 4 on the process enneagram. Our expanding self-awareness allows us to become more attuned to another's point of view, which gives rise to a deeper sense of empathy. But it also allows us to realize for the first time that the roles we adopt are not the same as the people we are. Realizing that there is a "role me," we realize there must be a "real me"—and that the two are not the same. While this discrepancy is unsettling, it also opens the way for cultivating a deeper sense of self.

Type 4 on the personality enneagram. Fours tend to be aware (sometimes painfully so) of the conditioned nature of the self with which they currently identify, which gives rise to self-consciousness and the desire to move beyond the "role me" to the "real me." The challenge is to bridge this gap in a way that allows them to accept the need to retain a social persona (and to accept the rules of social behavior) while at the same time not allowing social conventions to prevent them from accessing and expressing the deeper self that lies within.

Level 5: Formal-reflexive mind. Wilber observes that it's at this point that we can begin to "think about thinking." This kind of metacognition allows for hypothetico-deductive and propositional reasoning, but the plethora of possibilities introduces new levels of complication. Here we confront philosophical problems that are hard to ignore and the need to allow the self to actually emerge as an entirely independent entity. Visser says that there are so many possibilities that arise that it can be difficult to make a pragmatic choice. Both Wilber and Visser recommend introspection for sorting out the chaff from the wheat; Wilber

additionally makes the point that to be silent at this point is to be absent (worthless), so expressing one's thoughts can bring greater balance. Thus, Wilber sees the value of Socratic dialoguing at this point.

Point 4 to Point 5 on the process enneagram. This is the mid-stage of the existential crisis beginning at Point 4 and the crossover point on the bottom of the enneagram, known as a region of chaos and confusion. It signifies the move from a self-centered perspective to an "other-centered" perspective, simply because the "otherness" of life can no longer be denied. The multiplicity of things and ideas in the world can seem overwhelming, creating the need to get a grip on reality by developing some sort of rationally-based framework.

Type 5 on the personality enneagram. Here we see the individual who has a sense of expansive thinking and the ability to reflect deeply on life with a fair degree of detachment. However, the ability to break down things into separate categories can result in over-compartmentalization, not just intellectually but socially, because everything in life can become an object in need of classification.

Level 6: Vision-logic (Centauric awareness). A new, more panoramic kind of logic begins to emerge, a kind of higher-level synthetic or integral awareness that transcends ordinary logic. This is the level that Wilber strives to put forth as a goal, because it represents the point at which we are on the cusp of a new kind of awareness—poised to make the transition from personal to transpersonal consciousness. However, for that same reason, existential concerns come to a head, creating a whole raft of concerns: existential depression, inauthenticity, isolation, aborted self-actualization, and existential anxiety. These problems are ironically the product of self-expansion (based on the awareness of a self that is beginning to grasp the vastness of life and potentially recoiling from that vastness by retreating into overly-conventionalized views and routines). Wilber speaks to the need at this point for seeking out a more humanistic, expansive perspective that can accommodate our newly-emergent Centauric awareness. Visser says that our ability to keep opening at this point depends upon knowing there is a valid reason to do so; in order to proceed, we need to know, "What difference does it make?"

Point 5 to Point 6 on the process enneagram. This is the move from an extreme emphasis on compartmentalization and systematization to a higher-order synthesis of ideas that begins to take into account the larger (transpersonal) context. But in order for that synthesis to occur, we have to be able to open to those transpersonal stirrings in a way that allows us to mentally assimilate them, so we don't feel overwhelmed by too much too soon. So this is a point of inherent instability but also a jumping off point for inner expansion.

Type 6 on the personality enneagram. Type 6 is the type most associated with issues involving fear, faith, and courage. The foregoing discussion reveals the reasons why: because the Six sits at the point on the circle where there is an incipient leap to a new expanded level of consciousness. As a result, both old and new fears come rushing to the surface of consciousness, creating anxiety and seeking resolution—which is why Sixes can particularly benefit from structure, support, and stability in their lives.

TRANSPERSONAL FULCRUM

The move from personal to transpersonal levels takes most of us into unfamiliar territory, which is why Wilber describes the challenges we face in a considerable amount of detail: because they are not the sorts of problems with which we are likely to be familiar. The discussion below will therefore be more detailed than the discussion of pre-personal and personal levels.

Level 7: Psychic level. This is the point, Wilber says, where the kind of abilities associated with the "third eye" begin to emerge: transcendental, transpersonal, or contemplative forms of awareness, also kundalini awakenings. These developments can bring about profound openings, but also the potential for inflation, disorientation, transient psychosis, imbalance due to faulty practice, dark night of the soul, "split-life" goals (spiritual vs earth-oriented problems), pranic disorders, inability of body to handle higher-level energies.[11]

Wilber identifies three general ways that an individual can experience psychic level openings that are likely to create imbalance: spontaneous (i.e., by accident), in a psychotic-like fashion, or as a beginning spiritual practitioner. In the case of spontaneous openings, the person can either "ride it out" (with or without the help of a professional therapist) or can choose to deliberately engage with the process "by taking up a contemplative discipline" (p. 139). Psychosis-like episodes may respond well to deep (probably Jungian) therapy because it aims to build the kind of psychic structures that translate psychosis-inducing material into a more assimilable form. Beginning spiritual practitioners are susceptible to a kind of inflation or disorientation that requires structure-building and/or insight into the nature of the delusion experienced.

The *Dark Night of the Soul experience*, Wilber notes, can bring about profound despair that is often best addressed by reading about the experiences of others who have encountered the same painful experience in their path or via petitionary prayer. *Split-life goals* are the result of living in a culture where spiritual values and cultural values start to diverge so much that the individual feels psychologically pulled apart. Wilber recommends trying to integrate spiritual and cultural life as much as possible rather than seeking an ascetic approach (presumably because it then becomes difficult to re-integrate at a later point in time.

When depression or anxiety arises at this stage, it is often best, Wilber says, to break off or lighten up on practice rather than intensifying practice, because this will likely result in psychic splitting.

Pranic disorders are those which have a somatic element based on psychological causes; Wilber's focus is on various bodily-oriented yogas designed to address body issues and possibly acupuncture.

Yogic illness (physical illness): Wilber recommends prevention when possible via purification of the body and/or treatment by restricting the intake of caffeine, sugar, drugs, etc.

Visser's general comment is that imbalances at this level tend to occur because the body and the soul are not sufficiently integrated; so the way to greater balance is through practices, therapies, etc., designed to promote integration.

Point 6 to Point 7 on the process enneagram. This move is like a transformative leap to a new, expanded level of consciousness where we "arrive" in a world that is of a whole different order than anything we have previously encountered—a world that can inspire awe but also make us feel scattered or disoriented. This move is often associated with grace, with the kind of reaching down from above which "transports" us as individuals beyond our own self-conceived borders. Focusing instead on activities designed to enhance groundedness can be helpful for restoring equilibrium and a sense of normalcy.

Type 7 on the personality enneagram. Sevens are in an airy, expansive space and have the intuitive ability to connect the dots in life but can also find it hard to locate and maintain the kind of stable reference points that will keep them from "flying off into space." They can benefit from some sort of central theme that keeps them on track but still allows them the freedom to move and change.

Level 8: Subtle level. It's at this point that an awareness of the "archetypal forms, of subtle sounds, and audible illuminations" begins to emerge. These phenomena can be very impressive and powerful, but they are based on forms and are thus not part of the highest level of (formless) awareness. The problems that can arise include the failure to let go of more limited forms of identity, subtle illusions, and the false sense of realization.

About the failure to let go of more limited forms of identity (*integration failure*), Wilber notes that he is not aware of any solution other than to seek some means to relax the contraction (especially via insight), which will otherwise result in being overwhelmed by the powerful energies received at this level.

Regarding the *subtle illusions* we can experience (especially that of believing ourselves to be at a higher level than we actually are), he says that many traditions include ways to check our actual level of development, so that we can avoid getting caught up in illusion.

Pseudo-realization seems to be Wilber's (albeit puzzling) way of referring to the extreme pain of being caught between the desire to continue onward and the desire not to; I believe he refers to what happens when energies become so intense that the individual feels as though he cannot go either forward or back (like a woman in childbirth at the moment of crowning). The only real option, he observes, is to continue one's practice.

Point 7 to Point 8 on the process enneagram. *The transition from Point 7 to 8 is the movement from the gathering together of all the separate bits of the self from an external vantage point to the unification of all those bits into a coherent whole that is experienced as something internal, not external. Because we are still within the realm of form (although it is a very high level of form), we can mistake the forms we perceive—including our own form— as the ultimate reality, which it is not. It is not until what has been unified merges into the greater whole that the cycle is complete.*

Type 8 on the personality enneagram. *This type represents the highest embodiment of Spirit in form and as such is subject to intense internal pressures that make the achievement of a calm and steady approach to living quite a challenge. It is not that Eights are better or more advanced than other types but that they are subject to powerful internal forces*

that require them to develop self-discipline, restraint, and mastery. The Eight who elects to take on this challenge finds that he has access to a tremendous pool of energy with which to work. So the energy at Point 8 is a double-edged sword that demands complete commitment.

Level 9: Causal level. This is the level in which we are immersed in the unmanifest, where form is transcended and we make the final disidentification from the limited sense of self. Challenges revolve around the need to differentiate/*detach oneself* from all previous levels of self-understanding while at the same time to understand that these levels are perfect expressions of "unobstructed Wisdom" (p. 144), rather than defilements (violations) of that Wisdom. Wilber's comments allude to the pull of the "inner teacher" on the student, so as to eliminate any final source of separation; perhaps the simplest way to characterize this process is as the final surrender to the Infinite, such that even the subtlest of "I/Thou" differences disappear. At the same time, there is the need to acknowledge the creation as being entirely as it should be, not as something "less than" the Infinite that gives it life. It is the need to simultaneously surrender the creation while at the same time realizing its inherent goodness that makes this final transition such a challenge.

Point 8 to Point 9 on the process enneagram. *This transition is one of the most mysterious on the enneagram, involving the move from Allness into Nothingness in a way that affirms the essential sameness of the two (which is why it represents the highest form of integration/synthesis). The individual who has completely internalized the Kosmos* *paradoxically becomes just a particle within the vastness of that Kosmos. This is the ultimate synthesis of the One and the Many.*

Type 9 on the personality enneagram. *Type 9 is the one most identified with inner being and creative potential, as well as synthesis, harmony, and receptivity. But it's also the type most identified with lack of motivation and indecision, because the innate awareness that "we are all the same" makes it hard to see the benefits of particularity. This is why it's especially important for Nines to get involved in life in a way that allows them to gain a real sense of who they are: so that they can function both an individuals (autonomous wholes) and members of the larger Kosmic order (self-transcending parts).*

IMPLICATIONS

Table 11-2 summarizes Wilber's lines of development, along with their corollaries on the process and personality enneagrams. They are arranged with the lowest level on the bottom and the highest on the top. As the table shows—reflecting the discussion—Wilber's levels, the process enneagram's stages, and the personality enneagram's perspectives can be meaningfully juxtaposed. What this suggests is that *Wilber's Spectrum model and the Integral Enneagram model describe very similar if not identical stages of development.*

Thus, the seeming differences between the two approaches are not all that substantive, especially if theorists on the enneagram side are willing to let go of a purely retro-Romantic approach to enneagram work. An understanding of Wilber's Spectrum model facilitates this process by providing a "third force" (i.e., a reconciling paradigm) that can

integrate the way we view the personality and process enneagrams, such that—instead of seeing the personality enneagram as describing obstructions to transformation and the process enneagram as describing the unfolding of transformation—we begin to see both enneagrams as describing the same thing: nine challenges that can function as either opportunities or obstacles, depending on our ability to successfully negotiate them. One of Wilber's main goals is of course to provide the kind of insights that will allow us to work more intelligently with the obstacles in our path, so that instead of getting increasingly frustrated and discouraged by the challenges we encounter, we're able to find new ways to turn lemons into lemonade.

Integrating IOS & the Enneagram

In Chapter 8, we looked at correspondences between the vertically-oriented process enneagram and horizontally-oriented personality enneagram to create an Integral Enneagram model. In Chapter 11, we've done something similar but more complex: looking at correspondences between the Integral Enneagram model and Wilber's IOS (both of which have vertical and horizontal elements).

Initially, we mapped key elements of Wilber's IOS—the four AQAL quadrants, the Big Three value spheres and Wilber's three major fulcrums—onto the process enneagram. Then we mapped the enneagram (both personality and process versions) onto Wilber's Spectrum model of development. In this way, we were able to look at the process of transformation from two very different perspectives.

By mapping IOS onto the process enneagram, we could examine specific aspects of Wilber's system within the context of a

TABLE 11-2. PARALLELS BETWEEN LEVELS, PROCESS & PERSONALITY.

		Wilber's Stages/Levels	Process Enneagram Stages	Personality Enneagram Challenges
Transpersonal	9	Causal level	Final synthesis	Presence & integration
	8	Subtle level	Unified awareness	Mastery & leadership
	7	Psychic level	Expanded awareness	Freedom within limits
Personal	6	Vision-logic	Fear & intuition	Transmuting fear into faith
	5	Formal-reflexive mind	Cognition	Understanding
	4	Script/role thinking	Self-identity	"Role me vs real me"
Pre-personal	3	Representational-mind	Competency	Concrete adaptation
	2	Emotional-sexual	Connecting	Bonding & self-mirroring
	1	Sensori-physical	Orientation	Dual category definition

micro-oriented process enneagram—a system that is designed to provide an up-close-and-personal view of transformation (one which we can use to look at what is happening right now and figure out where it belongs on the transformational circle).

By mapping the enneagram onto IOS, we could examine specific aspects of the enneagram within the context of a *macro-oriented* framework designed to provide a way to think about the nature of the Kosmos, especially its overall organization. This interest in comprehensiveness is reflected by book titles like *A Theory of Everything* and *A Brief History of Everything*. By contrast, the process enneagram provides more of a "theory of anything," in that it delineates the process by which anything transforms.

By looking at each system from the perspective of the other—something we've been doing in Chapters 9 and 10, as well—we not only see the parallels between the systems but get new perspectives on transformation, perspectives that may help us reconcile ideas or positions that at first appear irreconcilable.

In Chapter 11, we've explored transformation from a pretty analytical and linear perspective—in short, from a masculine point of view. In Chapter 12, we'll shift gears to look at transformation a more feminine, embodied perspective: the perspective of integral living.

Notes

1. Horizontal enlightenment as discussed by Wilber has little if anything to do with the idea of expanding our outlook to be more inclusive, such that our enlightenment would reflect a greater development of horizontal structures. It's my impression that Wilber simply needed a way to visually depict the difference between structure-stage enlightenment (which entails oneness with all

stage-structures and states) from "state enlightenment" (which entails oneness with all states but not all structure-stages). So he developed with Allan Combs a matrix (the Wilber-Combs Lattice) which places states on the horizontal axis and structure-stages on the vertical axis—which is how one kind of development comes to be called "vertical" while another is "horizontal." (See Fig. 4-2 in Chapter 4 for a simplified version of this matrix.)

Using this approach allows Wilber to conclude that vertical enlightenment is superior to horizontal enlightenment. But it also unavoidably denigrates the horizontal.

The likely problem with state-based enlightenment is not that it is *too horizontal* but that it is *not horizontal enough*! That is, it is the kind of enlightenment which is so narrowly focused on spiritual ascent that it remains uninformed by other lines of development. That's why I would suggest that—instead of speaking in terms of vertical versus horizontal enlightenment—we would instead speak in terms of *integral* versus *non-integral* enlightenment. Those seeking a more integral path would pursue not just one but multiple lines of development (which would take longer but yield a richer, more integrated form of illumination).

2. Although the enneagram is a truly profound system, it can be hard to convey its multidimensionality to an Integral audience, because there's a historical tendency in the Integral community to think of the enneagram solely as a system for describing discrete personality types, not embodied perspectives. This is not true of an enneagram audience, who generally find it easy to see such parallels—because they are used to thinking of the enneagram as describing both outer personality types and internal points of view.

3. For a discussion on multiple lines of development, see pp. 81–86 in Wilber et al.'s *Integral Life Practice* (2008).

4. Unlike the enneagram type of an individual, which does not change, the enneagram type of a culture *can* change over time, as its inhabitants change. It is in any event a looser concept (but still useful from a practical point of view, especially for understanding conflicts between individual and cultural values).

5. If we look at Western culture, we see that it has historically emphasized lines of development designed to promote morality (Point 1), a sense of duty (Point 6), and a regard for authority (Point

8). These are no longer valued as they were in the past (although public regard for paths of sacrificial duty has dramatically increased since 9/11).

Lines of development that are particularly introverted or feminine (e.g., empathic development at Point 2, mystical development at Point 9, or depth-oriented psychological or creative development at Point 4) have tended to be marginalized in the past (particularly when pursued by males). And despite much modern rhetoric upholding the worth of feminine values, they continue to be marginalized more than most females would like.

In contrast, in modern culture, lines of development associated with logic/computer skills (Point 5) and science (Point 6) are highly valued; so are those that promote practical skills and image development (Point 3). Point 7 lines of development—which are associated with freedom, innovation, and global connectivity—are particularly popular right now in American culture, with its focus on youthfulness, fun, and global information exchange.

These cultural values obviously have an impact on individuals whose types are respectively associated with popular vs unpopular lines of development. But if we understand the dynamics involved, we have a better idea of how to resolve the problems caused by conflicts between the two.

6. People sometimes worry that they have incorrectly typed themselves. Mis-typing is pretty common, especially for individuals new to the enneagram. But even experienced teachers can mis-type themselves. One well-known teacher said he thought for five years he was Type 1 before realizing he was actually Type 3. He wasn't so much trying to avoid being a Three as to embrace the values of a One, because his teacher was a One, and he really admired him. Although he finally realized that Type 3 was a much better match, he said he learned a lot through the experience of mis-typing himself.

7. I suspect that it is unrealistic to expect most people (even very high-functioning people) to integrate all nine points of view. And perhaps it is not really necessary from a *dharmic* perspective, in that we do not need to be all things to all people in order to fulfill our purpose in life. But we *do* need to be integrated enough to avoid the problems that come from a view that is so narrowly-constricted that it makes a real dent in our ability to stay balanced or get along with other people.

8. Although the enneagram wing points and connecting points offer natural points of expansion, those who work a lot with the enneagram usually notice more and more ways to link the types over time, based on noticing new ways to geometrically link the points. The more we know about the system, the more ways we can identify to move from a single-faceted perspective to a multi-faceted perspective.

9. There are two justifications for considering the vertical and horizontal dimensions as complementary equals. The first is based on the fact that it is so easy to demonstrate direct correspondences between the personality enneagram (which is a horizontal system) and process enneagram (which is a vertical system). The second is based on the information in Section 1-1 of Dion Fortune's *The Cosmic Doctrine* (1949/1995), which explains that it is the nature of a Cosmos to consist of two spinning rings of force that are at right angles to one another, both of which are contained by a third ring (the Ring-Pass-Not). According to this esoteric source, both the rings within the Ring-Pass-Not are necessary for the existence of a Cosmos; if either of them ceased to exist, the Cosmos would cease to exist. So while they have different properties (because they are at right angles), they are both equally basic to the Cosmos.

10. When we link the process enneagram to Wilber's three fulcrums, the divisions between each fulcrum are marked on the enneagram by the shock points discussed in Chapter 6 (which occur at Points 3, 6, and 9). These shock points, you will recall, are places of discontinuity, where we must make a jump to get to the next major phase (octave) of development; they are also places where "something new" can enter the cycle. This "something new" is an energy that changes our orientation, such that we relate to life in a fundamentally different way. This is why Points 3, 6, and 9 have a somewhat transitional or receptive quality about them: because they are the points where we receive the energy that will help us to productively engage with the next phase of development.

11. Some of Wilber's Level 7 pathologies would probably be more closely associated by process enneagram theorists with Point 6, which, as noted by Bernier, is "the portal at which we see ourselves as we really are. Occultist schools call this 'the Threshold', and say that here we face the terror of the threshold: ourselves" (*The Enneagram: Symbol of All and Everything*, 2003, p. 330).

12

INTEGRAL LIVING

When I look at people who have had any kind of trauma, I ask, "What have they gained?"
– Jill Bolte Taylor

Everybody wants to save the world; nobody wants to help Mom do the dishes.
– P. J. O'Rourke

IN THE LATE 1970S, two visionary thinkers, Marshall Landman and Brian Livingston, founded Cascadian Regional Library (CAREL) to draw together community-minded networkers from all over the Pacific Northwest. Their first major undertaking was to organize the Equinox Gathering, a spring conference of about 400 community organizers in Sandy, Oregon:

> Discussion centered on how living in the Northwest helped shape the lifestyles of ecologically minded people, and it went on to considerations of how local problems and projects could be approached on a regional basis. The conference ended with a resolution to make the Equinox Gathering an annual event. CAREL was set up to coordinate future meetings, open local offices to serve as information centers, and begin publication of a regional magazine.[1]

While this is an accurate summary of what happened at the Gathering, it doesn't quite capture the atmosphere of the event. I was at that first Gathering, attending with my housemate, Sue Pritchard. We were living in nearby Gladstone, Oregon, and we had been looking for something interesting to do during Spring break. When Sue saw a poster for the Equinox Gathering at the local food co-op, she showed it to me. Although we didn't know what it was or anybody who was attending, something about the flyer looked appealing. So we decided to go.

The four-day event took place in a rustic conference center in the woods, with a circular main hall and lots of little cabins for sleeping and meeting in groups. In order to keep costs down (and also facilitate a spirit of community), every participant was asked to do a two-hour stint as a volunteer sometime during the conference, either making food, doing cleanup, or performing other necessary tasks to keep the conference afloat. The food was all vegetarian and prepared from scratch; most of it was also locally grown. (Marshall was a big fan of local self-reliance.)

Costing only $25, the conference attracted over 400 individuals, most of them grassroots organizers of some sort, interested in alternative energy, energy-efficient technologies, innovative educational approaches, organic food and farming, alternative communities, and then-emerging spiritual approaches. Although there was an incredible diversity of views represented, most participants were united by a common desire to live in a world based on bottom-up, community involvement—one in which individuals felt free to share ideas, support one another, and come together in the spirit of community.

The conference was very open-ended. Although there was one large gathering a day, much of the time was spent in small groups focusing on topics of interest to participants; although some were set up by the organizers, participants were encouraged to form their groups and post them on the bulletin board. In order to avoid the problem of overlapping groups, people were asked to take notes at each session, type them up on IBM Selectric typewriters, and run them off on the clunky but reliable Xerox machine the organizers lugged all the way from Eugene. (This was back in the days when *all* the copiers were Xerox copiers!) This meant that within an hour of any given session, you could pick up notes from any other session—something unheard of in the pre-computer era.

When the whole group came together, we began our sessions by chanting the OM, do-

ing Sufi dances, or singing spiritual songs, like "Listen, Listen, Listen, To My Heart's Song," one of the most beautiful songs I've ever sung. Gosh, what an experience. It may sound a little trite or dated now, but it wasn't at all in the 1970s. These simple practices brought us together in a heartfelt way.

The group discussions were dynamic yet respectful. The atmosphere was inclusive but not cloyingly so; this was not a politically correct sort of crowd but a bunch of highly creative people with extremely diverse opinions. And yet it all worked, and worked very well.

What made the Equinox Gathering so successful? Three things come to mind. First, there was the *venue*, which was a wooded site with log cabins and a rustic but warm hall for meeting. This was not a city conference in a big hotel; it was more like a retreat where we could be alone in nature or come together in communion.

Second, there were the *participants*, who—though independent and creative—were truly imbued with the spirit of cooperation. Their independence allowed them to come together without losing their own sense of self.

Third, there was the *leadership*, which was inspirational. Marshall was a charismatic but totally unselfish community leader who knew how to lead by example. He was the most adept facilitator I ever saw, always listening carefully to what was said, summarizing it succinctly, and often adding some small observation that managed to tie together everybody's ideas into a coherent whole. Brian was a brilliant and innovative thinker who had a knack for coming up with ways to solve unsolvable problems; he was probably the one who designed the ingenious note-taking system. (Years later, he went on to become a well-known Windows guru.) These two individuals worked in total harmony with one another; their unusual bond created the hidden glue that held the entire event together.

Sue and I were so inspired by our experience at the first Equinox Gathering that we volunteered to become the Portland contacts for CAREL. Later, I moved to Eugene and worked at the main office for a year and a half, organizing conferences and writing blurbs for *Cascade*, CAREL's networking journal (another innovative way to get people connected in the pre-Internet era).

Although the group only lasted a few years—the "alternative community" was never a great source of financial support!—I never forgot my experience there. Organizing CAREL conferences gave me a taste of what it was like to participate in a community in which *both individuality and communion mattered*—and in which both the vertical (spiritual) and horizontal (political) axes came together to form a matrix that fostered both inner attunement and outer cooperation.

And this is what integral living is all about: the ability to become self-immanent in a way that benefits both the individual and the group to which he or she belongs. We discussed self-immanence in Chapter 9, because healthy self-immanence is one of the eight transformational moves that are possible during the life cycle. I made the point at that time that self-immanence is not the same thing as Agape, although they both involve the descent of Spirit. However, with self-immanence, Spirit descends into the world through the incarnation of the human soul in physical form; with Agape, Spirit descends in the form of Divine love—the kind of love that symbolizes the covenant between the Divine and the creation—which is why it is often associated with prayer and surrender.

However, there is a genuine role for Agape in transformational work, a role we'll explore later in this chapter. For now it suffices to say that self-immanence describes our ability to become deeply involved in embodied life while Agape describes our ability to open to that which transcends it, thus drawing down Divine grace. Both are involved in the figure-8 flow between Spirit and matter.

The problem with deep involvement in embodied life is that it can bring us into conflict with others, especially those whose values differ from ours. So it's tricky to maintain the kind of balance that allows us to care deeply about our activities as individuals while simultaneously creating a sense of community. The only way it's possible to maintain such a balance is when individuals are as committed to inner work as to participating in community, so that they possess the inner resources that make social cooperation possible.

In the absence of such resources, individuals tend to look to the group to provide them with the support they need to feel loved and valued. But when they do, they create groups that are more co-dependent than cooperative. CAREL avoided this problem by organizing events designed to encourage individual initiative just as much as group cooperation.

Facilitating Cooperation Among People

Cooperation was a major theme at CAREL. One day, shortly after the first Equinox Gathering, those of us now involved with the group sat down to decide what we were trying to do, to develop a unifying vision around which we could organize our efforts.

By that time, there were about eight or nine of us involved, scattered around the Northwest. After a whole day's worth of discussion, what we came up with was this: *facilitating cooperation among people.*

"*Facilitating*" tells us that this is a friendly rather than coercive process, that it is up to the facilitators to attract the interest of possible participants. So the facilitators have to grow in a way that allows them to attract participants; and since they are facilitators (not bosses, generals, or gang leaders), they have to "lead from behind," allowing participants to come to the fore as much as possible. And this was a distinguishing feature of CAREL events, which were always about helping the participants to find common ground and move in a direction that gave expression to the will of the group.

"*Cooperation*" lies at the heart of what we did: to create an environment in which cooperation tended to spontaneously emerge. But it also relied upon the willingness of participants to cooperate, which is why we so carefully targeted our audience: because we needed to attract the kind of early innovators that were ready to cooperate. Most of the time, this worked very well. Only once—during the Northwest Natural Food Conference—did participants find cooperation more difficult, mainly because the diversity was so great that it was hard to find common ground. We had attracted both sole proprietors of small whole foods stores (this was well before Whole Foods came along) and people involved in both food co-ops and the wholesale distribution of natural food to those co-ops. The latter group included several very big collectives with a hard-core commitment to "leveling the hierarchy." The collectives saw the sole proprietors as threats to their collectivist ideals, and there was not a lot we could do to change their minds. But this was an exception to the rule; most of the time, the desire for communion trumped such political differences.

And the phrase "*among people*" draws our attention to the universality of the process: that cooperation is not for any special group but for anyone who wants to participate. It's an entirely grassroots process that tends to level the playing field, rather than privileging special interests. It draws our attention to the importance of mutual respect, because without that respect, no cooperation is possible.

And respect for the individual was also a hallmark of CAREL events, which was why we were able to attract such a diverse group of participants and to create the kind of events that people really enjoyed. Although CAREL was only around for a few brief years, for years afterwards, I had people come up to me thanking us for those conferences and speaking fondly of their experiences there.

Immanence in Action

Working at CAREL was a great experience that I'll never forget. But I was fortunate enough to have a few other experiences showing me that it is really possible to live in a way that brings Spirit right into everyday life. One of them was through my six year involvement with SGI-USA, the U. S. Branch of Soka Gakkai International, a Japanese-based lay Buddhist organization based on the teachings of the Lotus Sutra.

The main spiritual practice consists of individual chanting and morning and evening prayers. There was also a strong social component, focused on our shared goal of promoting world peace; however, the group was otherwise quite diverse in terms of values, politics, interests, etc. This is one of the things that attracted me initially: that there were few if any formal precepts (other than doing the practice every day).

The commitment to individual practice promoted vertical integration; the shared commitment to world peace promoted horizontal communion. Also, when we chanted together as a group in a true spirit of unity, amazing things happened—things that forever changed my view of what life could be like if people came together in harmony.

Part of the group culture included large conferences of up to 10,000 participants where we would chant together for world peace. In 1974, the conference took place in San Diego. Because of the numbers of people involved (at least 5,000), the group rented the entire SeaWorld complex for an evening, so that the only people at SeaWorld present were members of SGI.

The atmosphere was utterly magical; I can't begin to convey what it was like. Sea World is in a very beautiful location to begin with, but there was a beauty present that evening that was absolutely surreal. It was like a little slice of heaven on earth. Although I had this experience 40 years ago, I've never forgotten it. It made me want to have such experiences all the time, and to create a world where a magical atmosphere is the rule rather than the exception.[2]

A third example of immanence in action was my experience during high school as a Girl Scout volunteer at Vacation Camp for the Blind (VCB). VCB put on weekend retreats for the blind who lived mostly in New York City; coming to VCB was a chance to get out of the city and commune with others who understood their needs and perspectives. I don't know what it's like today, but when I was involved, it was run by two remarkable individuals, Fran and Harry Minkoff. I remember their names because Fran used to write songs for the famous folk group, The Weavers; one of them, *Come Away Melinda* was a hit, recorded by both Judy Collins and Harry Belafonte. I sang the song on my guitar, so when I found out Fran was the author, I was thrilled.

My first time at VCB, I was introduced to the work by being given my initial tour of the grounds blindfolded, so I would know the place from a blind person's perspective. (It also taught me how a blind person likes to be guided—not by being pushed around but by being allowed to take the arm of a sighted escort.)

I forget the name of the guy who was the trainer but boy, was he tough! He made us "new hires" really sit up and take notice, immediately letting it be known that whatever our assigned chores—whether making beds, preparing food, or cleaning up—the campers came first. That's what we were all there for: to give them a great experience. He also taught us that they deserved our respect and support, but not our pity.

Bottom line, he made damn sure that we gave these clients our very best; many of them were elderly and somewhat infirm, having tragically lost their sight to diabetes. He was determined to make us part of the team that made the world of those campers just a little brighter.

But it wasn't only the campers who had a memorable experience; it was everybody involved with the place. As Girl Scouts, we were there to do the scut work, but we did so much more. Fran and Harry loved and respected humankind in a way that we seldom see; they lived their transpersonal ideals in real life. And they especially loved creating community. So that's just what they did.

They were very spontaneous and liked to do things on the fly, often enlisting the talents of anybody present, including campers. One man was a pianist; even blind, he still played beautifully. There were gifted singers, too, who appreciated the chance to perform.

When they found out I played guitar, they encouraged me to do sing-alongs, a popular activity at the time (and it was the 1960s, so everybody was singing *500 Miles* and *Michael Row the Boat Ashore*). I was not at all confident in front of a group, but I felt so encouraged that I got up the courage to bumble my way along, despite my shyness. The campers were so happy to sing together; it was gratifying to see them smile. The Minkoffs always closed the weekends with a dance—the old-fashioned kind, where the partners actually get to embrace. And the last song played was always that lovely waltz, *Good Night, Irene*, made popular by the Weavers. Whenever I hear that song, it always brings me back to those weekends at VCB.

The VCB experience was so great that I stayed in Girl Scouts an extra two extra years just so I could participate. And I did it at a time (the late Sixties) when being a 17-year-old Girl Scout was not exactly fashionable. It gave me purpose at a time when the rest of my life seemed meaningless and confidence at a time when I felt pretty useless. I'm sure I'm not the only one who looks back at those memories at VCB with fondness and delight.

Inner Work & Outer Communion

These three events—the Equinox Gathering, the Buddhist evening at Sea World, and the weekends at VCB—are examples of what is possible when the individuals in a group harmoniously converge around a common goal, theme, or idea: how they draw into the world the kind of energy that gives us a glimpse of what is meant by the phrase "As above, so below."

But as discussed above, that energy can only be present in a group when enough individuals in that group are sufficiently integrated (both vertically and horizontally) that they are able to participate in a shared experience without either losing themselves in the process or losing their sense of shared communion.

In the case of the Equinox Gathering, the attendees were innovative but reflective community leaders with well-developed ethical values and a sense of ecological stewardship that was decades ahead of the times; these were the sort of people often referred to as old souls—the kind whose participation in a group takes nothing away from their individuality. They came together to "network," i.e., to share ideas and draw inspiration from like-minded others.

In the case of the SGI convention, the participants shared a daily spiritual practice and a uniting belief in world peace. Group efforts succeeded only when individuals were steadfast in their Buddhist practice. I saw this firsthand: when we didn't do the practices on our own, our collective efforts fell flat—often in a very public and embarrassing way![3] What we learned, collectively and individually, is that both kinds of effort are essential for a group to reach its highest potential.

And when it came to the weekends at VCB, the common thread that united its organizers was a passionate belief in the dignity of all individuals, whether old or young, blind or sighted, rich or poor. The organizers were grassroots idealists who had sought to translate their ideals into practical action and had the maturity necessary to pull it off. It was a toss-up whether they were more fiercely committed to championing the rights of the individual (especially the rights of the disabled to be recognized for their gifts) or the creation of celebratory communion. As a result, they managed to do both—and in so doing, showed people that there doesn't need to be a trade-off between the two.[4]

In terms of holon theory, we avoid trade-offs by understanding the difference between our role as an individual holon and our role as members of social holons (i.e., groups). For as both Ken Wilber and Fred Kofman have pointed out, while individual holons and social holons may co-evolve, there is a clear distinction between them, because only individual holons possess true *agency*: the ability to have an interior intention.[5] Social holons do not possess interiority; what may look like the "will of the group" is actually the will of the individuals within that group. And this is why groups have no natural authority over individuals.

At the same time, it's important for individuals to find a way to live harmoniously with one another, especially as the world becomes increasingly interdependent. But this cannot happen without the conscious cooperation of individuals—which is why individual development is critical for integral living.

In this chapter, the focus is on integral living, especially how to facilitate it in a way that supports both the individual and the community. Because it particularly involves the integration of individuals and groups, we'll start by looking at the horizontal dynamics in integral ("*win-win*") groups vs non-integral ("*win-lose*" and "*lose-lose*") groups. Then we'll add in the vertical dimension to see how *win-win* groups bring together the two dimensions in a way that connects both (a) the "one and the many" and (b) Spirit and matter. Next, we'll look at the nature of immanent spirituality (how we anchor Spirit in the world), using Jorge Ferrer's approach to look at its primary concerns and Koestler's "fixed structures and flexible strategies" model to explore the role of creativity in integral living. Finally, we'll look at receptive ascent: how the return journey to Spirit is enhanced when made from a deeply embodied perspective—and what this means for a *dharma*-based approach.

"Win-Win" vs "Win-Lose"

In a trade-off (*win/lose* or *either/or*) scenario, greater individuality means less communion and vice-versa; it's a zero sum game in which what one side wins, the other loses.[6] In systems theory, this kind of thinking gives rise to what are referred to as *closed groups*: groups with rigid structures that constrict the flow of energy and information. Closed systems focus more on restricting what is possible than promoting it. As a result, they rely on inflexible rules and regulations to maintain their existence (even when the rules are unspoken). And they have thick (non-permeable) borders both vertically and horizontally—which is why they lack both dynamism and adaptability. They also tend to have strong in-group/

out-group dynamics designed to keep members in line by punishing those who violate established norms.

Thus, although closed groups may look outwardly strong, their strength derives primarily from their rigidity. As a result, what they gain in solidity brings a loss in spontaneity, creativity, and dynamic action. And if some kind of social earthquake comes along, they quickly collapse, like buildings made out of bricks. That's what happened to North Korea from 1994–1998 after they no longer received Russian aid (due to the collapse of Soviet communism). Without it, the nation began to starve. Only its shoring up by other countries (many of which have been motivated to help because they were—and are—afraid of its nuclear capabilities) has prevented it from complete collapse.

In *open groups*, the structures may be stable but they are designed to bend when necessary so that they don't break down in the face of sudden change. There is a free flow of information up and down the levels of the holarchy, as well as within them. This gives rise to a synergistic (*win-win* or *both-and*) scenario, in which greater individuality brings greater communion and vice-versa; the two mutually enhance one another. Open groups tend to function more like associations than bureaucracies (or autocracies); they have more flexible rules, more permeable boundaries, and more energy available for creative problem-solving.

You would think that most people would prefer open groups: they are, after all, more dynamic, creative, original, and just plain fun! But open groups demand a lot in the way of personal responsibility from their partici-

pants. Also, they are not the historical norm, in that people have traditionally banded together for defensive purposes—and when the impetus for a group is based upon the need for a shared defense, this does not encourage an open-ended structure.

So the idea of open groups and free associations is a relatively recent innovation arising from the emergence of democratic values. Association-based groups can be open to the extent that they find ways to reconcile the goals of the individual with the goals of the group in a way that is mutually enhancing.

"Lose-Lose" & Political Correctness

There is a third possible scenario that we could call *lose-lose*, which arises when neither the individual nor the group "wins" because there's not enough energy present to make anything happen (good or bad), so the group gradually loses energy until it eventually dissolves. Thus, we could refer to this as a *dissipative group*.

Dissipation is a common problem in groups striving to live up to progressive ideals, i.e., those with an avowed commitment to social equality and fairness—qualities that tend to be associated in Spiral Dynamics terminology with the Green Meme. These values give rise to an extreme preoccupation with process—so much so that a group can spend almost all of its time and energy avoiding the perception of unfairness. Consensus building can become such a focus that even minor disagreements are seen as threatening to the group's integrity. As a result, little gets done beyond the repeated affirmation that everyone present is a valued member of the group.

A group like this can get so focused on pro-moting harmony that it becomes more like a *de facto* therapy group than a forum for either discussion or action. But since it is not a genu-ine therapy group (with defined therapeutic goals, trained facilitators, and members who are committed to work through their issues), it tends to devolve into rambling discussions focusing on the concerns (and too often, the emotional woes) of individual members.

The funny thing is that the taboo on con-flict creates the need for an extraordinarily rigid (if unacknowledged) social structure that does not permit the discussion of any-thing that might potentially offend any mem-ber of the group (even those who are sort of looking to be offended!). So in that sense, this is a kind of closed group. The only difference is that—due to the extreme inhibition of all those present—there are no winners.

What we are talking about often goes by the name of political correctness. While political correctness protects the individu-als within the group, it kills the spirit of the group in the process by suppressing anything that might create uncomfortable feelings. So it's not surprising that, after awhile, meetings get boring and most of the participants find something better to do.

So how does a group—especially an inte-grally-oriented group—avoid this problem? First, by looking at the focus of the group and establishing a core concept around which to focus. Second, by becoming aware of values (e.g., an overconcern with process or fairness) that might make it hard for people to express what they really feel. Third, by explicitly talk-ing about how to communicate in ways that are frank but respectful. Fourth, by recogniz-ing that conflict is bound to arise, so it won't come as a shock when it does. Fifth, by ex-ploring ways to work productively through conflicts instead of avoiding them at all costs. Sixth, by letting go and lightening up—hu-mor is a great way to help us avoid taking our-selves and our ideas quite so *seriously*!

The truth is that there is a lot of creative energy that can be liberated when conflicting ideas are exchanged in a lively but respectful manner. Groups that can "agree to disagree" from time to time are not only more produc-tive, they're more fun!

Fig. 12-1 depicts the three kinds of group dynamics we've been discussing. This ap-proach focuses on the *horizontal* interactions between the individual and the group. In an open group, interactions among members tend to strengthen both the individual and

WIN - WIN	WIN - LOSE	LOSE - LOSE
open group *(synergy)*	closed group *(trade-offs)*	dissipative group *(disappearing energy)*
MORE COOPERATION = MORE AUTONOMY	MORE COOPERATION = LESS AUTONOMY	NO COOPERATION OR AUTONOMY

Fig. 12-1. Different kinds of groups (horizontal dynamics).

the group. In a closed group, interactions among members tend to strengthen either the individual or the group but not both. In a dissipative group, interactions among members create a depletion of energy, resulting in the gradual breakdown of the group.

Vertical & Horizontal Integration

Now that we've looked at horizontal dynamics, we can add in vertical dynamics: how to think about systems not only in terms of their horizontal interactions but in terms of their relationship with other levels of life. Groups that are open in both directions are particularly dynamic and creative—like the three groups we've been discussing:

- Equinox Gathering attendees were as open to chanting *om* (opening to Spirit) as to promoting ecological stewardship (taking responsibility for the earth).

- SGI participants maintained a formal spiritual practice but their shared goal was to promote world peace.

- VCB organizers displayed that rare combination of humility and service that is the mark of those who seek to connect with something higher in order to improve the lives of those they serve.

So these three stories are examples of what can happen when the vertical and horizontal converge in a way that allows something special to happen—something that not only anchors the energy of Spirit in the world of matter (*vertical integration*) but allows that energy to transform the community (*horizontal integration*). This is the essence of immanent or embodied spirituality.[7]

Fig. 12-2 depicts the relationships discussed above. ***Version a*** depicts a scenario in

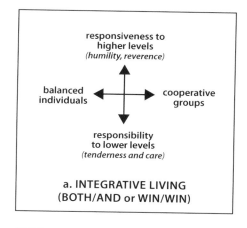

a. INTEGRATIVE LIVING
(BOTH/AND or WIN/WIN)

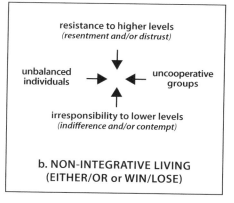

b. NON-INTEGRATIVE LIVING
(EITHER/OR or WIN/LOSE)

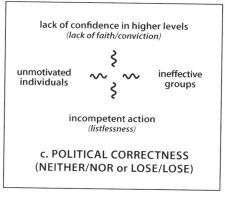

c. POLITICAL CORRECTNESS
(NEITHER/NOR or LOSE/LOSE)

Fig. 12-2. Different kinds of groups (vertical & horizontal dynamics).

which there is a synthesis involving all four directions, leading to a dynamic balance between stability and growth. *Version b* depicts a situation in which there is conflict between the opposites in both directions, which creates bad feelings and win/lose political scenarios. *Version c* depicts a situation in which the group lacks the conviction necessary to sustain itself, which leads to a gradual but steady loss of energy and motivation.

Integral living requires a balance in both directions, although not some kind of perfect, idealized balance, because that's impossible to realize in a not-quite-perfect world. Rather, the goal is to establish a "good enough" balance for something constructive to happen, especially when we get together in a group.

Fig. 12-3 depicts a hypothetical group of seven people—all well-integrated—but at somewhat different levels of development. This example is designed is introduce the somewhat daring idea that integration matters as much as level—and maybe even *more* than level—because integrated individuals are naturally predisposed to solve problems using a cooperative approach.

This idea that "integration is key" may seem a little startling to those who embrace the idea—pretty common in Integral circles—that "higher consciousness is key." While higher consciousness is wonderful, it will not automatically solve all of our problems, either individually or collectively. It is all too easy to become so focused on arriving at a more exalted level (e.g., second tier consciousness) that we pay insufficient attention to our current level—and to the opportunities for enlightened action that exist in the here and now.

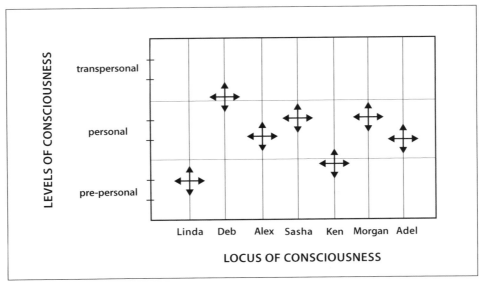

Fig. 12-3. A group of well-integrated individuals.

Thus, my goal has been to place particular emphasis on the role of integration within the transformational process, by weaving together three strands of transformational inquiry: (a) a perspective-taking approach (the personality enneagram), (b) a nine-step approach to transformation (the process enneagram), and (c) a progressively-oriented, comprehensive system for conceptualizing transformation from a bird's-eye view (Wilber's IOS). The resulting Integral Enneagram model combines features from all three models:

- a broad-based intellectual framework for conceptualizing human transformation (IOS)

- a progressive and positive philosophy of human development (IOS)

- an appreciation for diverse lines of development (IOS)

- an enhanced perspective-taking ability (personality enneagram)

- an enhanced ability to look at the relationships between perspectives and people (personality enneagram)

- an enhanced appreciation for the role of both integration and descent in the transformational process (process enneagram)

- a greater awareness of the role of cycles in transformation and how we move to a higher level in the holarchy (process enneagram)

We'll explore these features more extensively in Chapter 13. For the remainder of this chapter, the aim is look at the two main aspects of integral living: *self-immanent descent* and *self-transcendent ascent*.

Self-immanent descent means living in a way that deeply and creatively embodies Spirit in matter. Self-transcendent ascent means returning to Spirit in a way that offers up our experiences in life to the Divine by making

them part of our being, such that they're enfolded in our ascent).

We'll start by looking at the work of Jorge Ferrer, who is probably the greatest single champion of embodied spirituality currently writing on the topic.

Embodied Spirituality

Jorge Ferrer is a professor at the California Institute of Integral Studies who has written extensively (and passionately) on the nature of embodied spirituality. On p. 2 of his article, "What Does It Mean to Live a Fully Embodied Life?," he says that embodied spirituality

> views all human dimensions—body, vital, heart, mind, and consciousness—as equal partners in bringing the self, community, and world into a fuller alignment with the Mystery out of which everything arises.

Note the image of the world "arising" out of the Mystery (an entirely feminine image). Not that he is averse to referring to Spirit; he just wants to give the Mystery and Spirit equal time.

Ferrer goes on to say that fully embodied spirituality "emerges from the creative interplay of both immanent and transcendent spiritual energies"—which is an extraordinarily inclusive definition of embodied spirituality, since it even allows for the idea that transcendence has a role to play.

Ferrer sees embodied spirituality as specifically involving the resacralization of the body, sexuality, and nature; the emphasizing of creativity; the grounding of spiritual visions in lived experience; the idea that life on earth is not a mistake; the importance of social engagement; and the integration of matter and consciousness.

Not surprisingly, he also notes that embodied spirituality tends to foster *integration*, where integration is defined as the goal of promoting "harmonious participation of all human attributes in the spiritual path without tension of dissociations" (p. 5).

One of his criticisms of disembodied spirituality concerns the widely-held belief that "matter and Spirit are two antagonistic dimensions," a belief he rejects in favor of the idea that not only is Spirit innately present in matter but that it can be made *more* present, such that we have "conscious matter" and other forms of "metanormal functioning" (p. 8).

There is a lot of food for thought in Ferrer's writings. While he is obviously championing a deeply-embodied spirituality, he also acknowledges the validity of a transcendently-oriented spiritual path. But he is obviously as intrigued and awed by the feminine Mystery as the masculine Spirit. Thus, his approach is not purely descendent but integral in nature.

I especially appreciate his focus on creativity, the idea that life is not a mistake, and the importance of integrating matter and Spirit in a way that refutes the idea that "up-is-good-and-down-is-bad." Also, his work seems impeccable from a scholarly point of view.

But perhaps the single most intriguing idea he expresses in this article concerns the idea of "metanormal functioning," because it hints at the same thing I alluded to when discussing Jung's idea of synchronicity: the idea that when enough people find some semblance of inner balance, this inner reality will be reflected in outer life, creating a world which (from our current viewpoint) would seem literally miraculous, like a never-ending dance—a world in which "God is alive and magic is afoot."[8,9]

The experiences related at the chapter's beginning gave me brief glimpses of such a world, a world in which people can be themselves and at the same time experience greater communion. This is the same vision that is often evoked when I work with the nine enneagram types: a vision of a world in which we develop not only the ability to seek out different points of view but to see beyond the differences in perspective to the personhood of every individual.

The Art of Creative Living

Just envisioning a better world is not enough to make it manifest. We also need to understand the factors that facilitate integral living. We've already looked at the dynamics behind productive group interactions. But what are the factors that allow people to function more integrally as individuals, such that they come to a group with the ability to make a real contribution?

While there are many factors, most relate to the individual's ability to creatively respond to the limitations encountered in the course of embodied life. Despite the fact that most of us would say we prefer freedom to limitation, we cannot have perfect freedom on this level of reality, because there are inherent limitations that go with the experience of being incarnated in a physical body. That is one reason that transcendent spirituality so often focuses on ways to dis-identify with this level of reality (and particularly with the body).

But a more embodied approach would be to embrace the limitations of this level in order to transform them into springboards to creativity. For to the extent that we are able to work creatively within the limits we encounter, we transform them. And that is how we convert them from liabilities into assets.

To better understand the intrinsic relationship between limitation and creativity, we'll look at Koestler's concept of "fixed structures and flexible strategies"—which focuses on the interplay between the structures that limit us (especially the inner structures) and the creative strategies we can devise to use such structures to our advantage.

Fixed Structures. It can be hard to appreciate the tangible reality (or value) of psychic structures because—as Wilber has pointed out (see Chapter 10)—they are invisible and therefore easy to overlook.[10] This is one reason that "Dog Whisperer" Cesar Millan is known for his emphasis on "rules, boundaries, and limitations" in his work as an animal behaviorist: because it's the factor most easily overlooked by people who are trying to figure out why their pet is misbehaving. Many pet owners try to substitute affection for limits, and it just doesn't work. This is because without well-defined boundary conditions, there is no way to become oriented to one's surroundings.

The same principle holds just as true for humans as for animals: we need boundary conditions to stay balanced in life. But while it's easiest to envision outer rules, boundaries, and limitations, it's the ones on the inside—the psychic structures—that shape us the most. So when they are missing, incomplete, or distorted, it's hard either to get comfortable in the world or to work towards spiritual transformation.

Wilber has pointed out the importance of structures at all level of consciousness, observing that the psychic "holes" that develop during early life can become a problem in transformational work, such that—although they may start out as ego defense mechanisms—they can also screen out higher energies as well: "A rigid boundary is a rigid boundary. A wall that keeps out *id*...can keep out God as well."[11]

Psychiatrist and native healer Lewis Mehl-Madrona speaks of the importance of "holding a space," so that healing can occur, but notes that this is a "rarely-discussed concept."[12] Sufi mystic Irina Tweedie always said that her job as a Sufi teacher was simply to "hold the space," so that a certain spiritual work could be done. Her teacher Bhai Sahib (Radha Mohan Lal) taught that part of the work on the path is developing the ability to withstand higher vibrations, which obviously depends upon the ability to develop the sort of inner structures that make this possible. Llewellyn Vaughn-Lee notes that in the absence of a proper inner [spiritual] container, we simply cannot "hold" the energies of higher consciousness. Along similar lines, one of Swami Muktananda's students, Rudi (Swami Rudrananda) spoke of the difficulty he had in dealing with the powerful energies that began to flow through him as he progressed further on the path—and of the need to find students to whom he could transmit some of this energy.[13]

So whatever the level of development, we need well-formed structures to contain and channel psychic energy. This is why we've focused so much on structures in the last three chapters. In Chapter 9, when addressing the question, "How Fast Can We Grow?", I took the stance that transformation requires the alteration of inner structures—which is why it may take longer than we might like to think, especially if we want *balanced* structures.[14] In Chapter 10, we looked at the idea that psychic structures are not only vertical but horizontal in nature, citing the personality enneagram as an example of a system describing nine structurally-distinct points of view. In Chapter 11, we briefly touched upon the relationship between these nine enneagram points of view and the vertical lines of development that Wilber discusses in *Integral Psychology* (2000), focusing on how our understanding of the points of view can help us determine potentially fruitful lines of development and vice-versa. One of the points of this discussion was to demonstrate that psychic structures can be both vertical and horizontal—a thread we've been following in this chapter, as well.

What we haven't yet looked at is the role played by such structures in fostering creativity. This is where we'll head next.

Flexible Strategies. When Koestler speaks of "fixed structures and flexible strategies," it's often to stress how the structures (the *rules* of the game) give rise to the strategies (the permissible *moves*). It's the ability to devise moves that adhere to the rules, *but which are a novel adaptation* that is the mark of a creative individual.

Thus, creativity plays a central role in determining how a game, project, or artistic work turns out. The more creative we are, the more likely we are to find ways of solving seemingly intractable problems. Koestler gives the example (cited in Chapter 2) of a pianist playing variations on a theme in which the melody is the reference point (the fixed structure) that limits the kind of thematic variations (the movements) that can be de-

veloped. But within those limits, tremendous creativity is possible.

Although creativity is often associated with specific art forms, living itself can be considered a creative art form. Thus, if embodied spirituality is about how we live, it's about how we can transform conditions of limitation into opportunities for learning.

It's because there is a link between limitation and creativity that individuals interested in embodied spirituality often mention creativity as one of its defining characteristics. For example, Ferrer, Albareda, and Romero define creative spirituality as one that "integrates various dichotomies and polarities of life in very diverse ways"[15] Ferrer envisions a participatory spirituality which includes many dimensions of life (the body, instincts, heart, mind, and consciousness), noting that "the more human dimensions actively participate in spiritual knowing, the more creative spiritual life becomes."[16]

Violinist Stephen Nachmanovitch is keenly aware of the reciprocal relationship between freedom and limitations. His book, *Free Play: Improvisation in Life and Art* (1991), is about learning to see life as art, such that we can bring to our lives the same spontaneity and joy that artists bring to their work. But he too speaks of the necessity of limits, observing that

> in the I Ching, limitation is symbolized by the joints in the bamboo stalk, the bounds that give form to the artwork and to the life (p. 79).

He goes on to say that the nature of the limits shape the art produced, as the artist grapples with his paint or the violinist with his strings. But even this conflict can serve the process: "Sometimes we damn the limits, but without them, art is not possible" (pp. 80–81).

Choreographer Twyla Tharp has a very interesting way of using the idea of structure/limitation in her work. When trying to work out a new choreography, well before working out anything else (the theme, the plot, and the details), she tries to work out what she calls the "spine" of the work (i.e., its organizing principle). Once she figures that out, she knows the work will stay on track: "Having a spine lets me know where I am starting from and where I want to go."[17]

Another way to use structure is by internalizing it, so that it becomes part of our creative process. Mihaly Csikszentmihalyi's book *Flow* (1991)—considered a classic on the nature of creative consciousness—alludes to the intimate relationship between self-control (i.e., cultivated internal boundaries) and creative flow. He observes that, although we live at a time when self-control is not one of our popular ideals, "whatever the dictates of fashion,...those that take the trouble to gain mastery over what happens in consciousness do live a happier life" (p. 23).

He explains that inner order facilitates creative flow while inner disorder makes it hard to screen out unwanted distractions, thus making it impossible to focus. And without focus, we can't get into that state of deep absorption associated with *flow*—a state in which *we lose the sense of a separate self* and become one with the activity in which we're engaged: the dancer becomes the dance; the runner becomes the run; the chef becomes the meal.

Look at how similar this description is to a unitive spiritual experience—how in creative work the self "disappears." What is interesting is where it goes: not *away* but *into*. In creative work, the self becomes embodied in the work, because the work has become so big that there is no longer room for the self and the work to co-exist.

But to the artist, this disappearance of the self into the work represents a gain rather than a loss. In placing the work first, he surrenders to something greater within himself; this is the essence of self-transcendence. It is precisely the same process we encounter at Point 4 on the process enneagram, which Bernier alludes to when speaking of the need for the self to disappear so that transformation can proceed (see Chapter 7.) Nachmanovitch also talks about the same thing when saying that "for art to appear, we have to disappear," p. 51.

So it's little wonder that artists tend to regard creative work as transformational—why, for example, Julia Cameron, author of *The Complete Artist's Way* (2007), says bluntly that "creativity is a spiritual force," such that

> as we strive for our highest selves, our spiritual selves, we cannot help but be more aware, more proactive, and more creative.[18]

It is the existence of powerful but invisible structures that allows us to lose ourselves in a state of flow. It's the combination of disciplinary structures and creative energy that allows us to productively lose ourselves in the work. But it is because of the need for these structures to be constructed that we do not develop the ability to lose ourselves in creative or transformational process overnight.

Moving from Fixed Rules to Flexible Strategies. As anyone knows who takes up a new hobby, the beginning stages are often more tedious than transformational. Before we can perfect the art, we have to learn the craft. This we typically do by seeking out teachers, listening to what they say, committing it to memory, evaluating it against our own experience, and—finally—reaching the point (often after many years) that we are in a position to experience the deep absorption to which Csikszentmihalyi refers.

In their wonderful book, *Mind Over Machine* (1986), Hubert Dreyfus and his brother Stuart, give us some idea about how people get to the point in their work where deep absorption is possible, by tracing the process by which we move from being rank beginners to experts, whatever the domain. They identify five levels of expertise (novice, advanced beginner, competence, proficiency, expert) as follows:

- At the *novice level*, we simply memorize context-free rules in order to make decisions.

- At the *advanced beginner level*, we begin to get a feel for the effects of context, so that we don't apply the rules quite so mechanically.

- At the *competence level*, we are able to skillfully combine rules with our understanding of differences in context (situational variables).

(What is happening here is that what started out as externalized, decontextualized rules are gradually becoming increasingly internalized, contextualized, and embodied as structures of consciousness. With the inter-nalization of such structures, we can afford to adopt an increasingly innovative approach to decision-making.)

- At the *proficiency level*, we know how to deeply process what is happening and make decisions based on multiple inputs in a variety of complex situations. So this is a very high level of understanding, but it is not the highest.

- At the *expert level*, there is a qualitative difference in the way we make decisions. The process is no longer analytical; it's intuitive. If asked to explain our process, we can't. Like the dancer who becomes one with the dance, we have become one with the task at hand and thus *en rapport* with all that is arising in the moment.

What is actually happening is that as we become more proficient, the structures that bound our knowledge are not only becoming more elaborated but also becoming more innate (or in the words of Michael Polanyi, more *tacit*). Although the structures remain present, we notice them less and less, because they have become part of us. So the more we know, the freer we feel, which is why mastery is so often associated with a feeling of boundlessness.

Taking a closer look at these last two stages, while they both refer to advanced levels of understanding, they are qualitatively different in nature. In real life, most people in any field call themselves an "expert" when they have reached the level that these authors characterize as proficient. True expertise is something beyond mere proficiency—and involves an entirely different approach to decision-making that is hard to explain because it's not at all linear.

As I was finishing the description on the expert level, in an interesting synchronicity, I turned on the TV program *Top Chef*, just in time to see the legendary sushi chef, Katsuya Uechi talk to the contestants about what sushi-making is like. Here is what he said:

> Sushi is very simple. Rice, fish....Don't mix up too many ingredients. Always think how you [can] make people happy.

This advice sounds more like a Zen koan than a discourse on food preparation. But that's what it's like when a master speaks: much of what he says goes right over our heads, because he is seeing the activity from a completely different perspective. Instead of learning something "useful," (like maybe secret tricks of the trade), we get commentary that sounds disappointingly obvious. To appreciate it properly requires not only technical ability but the desire to see beyond the task to what it really means.

And that is precisely the point that Dreyfus and Dreyfus are trying to make in their book: that what begins as a mechanical process of rote learning can end as a meditation on living. The early stages may be tedious but they provide the framework within which to work. But the more we internalize that framework, the more we eventually transcend it. However, we transcend it not by leaving it behind but by *enfolding it within*.

Integrated Ascent

Learning to integrate our experiences during descent prepares us to do the same during ascent. While it's traditional to associate ascent with focused masculine techniques such as meditation, concentration, and discipline, techniques like these do not necessarily inte-grate our life experiences into the ascent process, especially if our spiritual practices are done to detach ourselves from worldly life.

This point was brought home to me by an interaction I saw between Andrew Cohen and a participant at a London workshop. The guy had great posture and a formal bearing. He asked an intimidatingly esoteric question about meditation—the kind you'd only hear from someone who had done a *lot* of meditation. When the questioner finally finished his complicated query, Cohen just sat there looking at him. Finally, he smiled, and—shaking his head and raising his hands—he said something to the effect of "Lord save me from long-time meditators!"

Until that moment, I'd been impressed with the guy asking the question. But Cohen's response shattered my idealized image. I realized just how dry and emotionally withdrawn the guy really was—and that while he might have acquired the ability to shut out worldly distractions, he was also shutting out the juiciness of life.

Austere practices may help us to develop higher structures but they aren't so great for helping with either integrating life experiences or cultivating an I/Thou relationship with the Divine—what Wilber has called the ability to experience "God in the 2nd Person." Christians similarly speak of this I/Thou relationship a personal relationship with God; Sufism alludes to a love affair with the Beloved. Whatever we call it, a sense of intimacy with Spirit is unlikely to develop if all our attention is on withdrawal—especially if that withdrawal is done to escape the material or social world.

But it's common for people to approach spiritual work in this way—to see transcendence not as an approach to Spirit but as an escape from flatland. It's also common to see spiritual work as *work*, i.e., in terms of effortful practices designed to bring about a particular goal. Often, the goal is person-centric, meaning that we see the whole process in terms of what we want out of the experience. As a result, it's easy to start treating spiritual energy as a commodity to be acquired, rather than a gift from the Divine. This kind of an approach can certainly get us out of flatland, but we may eventually find ourselves in a spiritual cul-de-sac, like the experienced meditator with his irrelevant questions.

There is another approach to spiritual work that is quite different. It is embodied in the well-known adage, "When the student is ready, the teacher appears." This adage embodies an approach to spiritual development that focuses not just on practices but on receptivity. Here we find Zen stories of teachers filling the cups of their students full to overflowing (because they are too "full of themselves"), stomping on students' toes (in response to falsely wise pronouncements that "the world is an illusion"), or hitting students with sticks for reporting blissful experiences in meditation. Here we also find Sufi stories of beans being boiled in order to soften them up or trickster teachers doing everything possible to throw their students into a state of confusion and despair.

From this perspective, spiritual work is not about what we do but what we *become*—and especially how we become more *receptive*. Dr. Bob Butera, writing on the Yoga Life Institute website, says of the idea that a teacher appears when the student is ready, that students begin to learn only at the point when they have a genuine "readiness to learn," such that they "choose to learn what is set before them."[19] Phillip Moffitt, founder of the Life Balance Institute, speaks of the same idea in terms of our willingness to surrender our preferences without surrendering our inner authority.[20]

So which is it: do we progress via masculine practices, focus, and work or via feminine receptivity? Probably both. But practices have traditionally had the edge. This is partly because they are geared to a male-oriented concept of spirituality (and males have been in charge for a long time) and partly because it's so much easier to focus on "doing" than "being." Practices are tangible, visible things we do to develop some ability; cultivating receptivity is a completely invisible process that nobody sees. Nevertheless, receptivity has the power to radically transform us. Moreover, as we will see, it may turn out that practices can only get us so far up the mountain: without receptivity, we may not be able to reach the top.

Receptivity During Ascent

When Russian mystic Irina Tweedie was interviewed by Andrew Cohen for the very first issue of *What is Enlightenment?* magazine, she said something very interesting—that there are two kinds of spiritual power: *yogic power* and *Divine power*. She noted that some yogis, such as Rajneesh, rely mainly on yogic powers for their spiritual attainment. And while these powers are very real, they are acquired through one's own effort, not as the result of surrender to the Divine. As a result *some self-will remains*. The highest desire, she said, must be for the Divine.[21]

According to this description, *yogic power* seems to be mainly the product of practices while *Divine power* descends in response to inner receptivity. To attract Divine power means cultivating the "desire nature" such that it can attract the energy of Spirit.

And just what is it that we attract on this path of receptivity? It is *Agape*, the quality which Wilber speaks of in *SES* (and which we talked about so much in Chapter 9): the unconditional love of the greater for the lesser. Agape is the kind of love intended to "*create value* in its object and therefore to initiate our fellowship with God" (*emphasis* mine).[22] Thus, to attract Agape means not only to attract help but to attract it in a way that brings us into greater communion with the Divine.[23]

Divine power is not something we can cultivate on our own through any sort of spiritual practice, however powerful; it is always a gift bestowed from the Above to the Below out of loving compassion. The only way to gain access to such power is to cultivate a corresponding feeling of love, to the best of our ability.[24]

And this brings up an interesting point related to our discussion of holons in Chapter 2: that the receptive attitude needed to receive Divine grace is the same attitude that allows the everyday self (as a holon) to be receptive to higher levels of its own being. And this is why self-transcendence in holon theory—the quality associated with an upward-looking holon—must necessarily be interpreted in terms of *being **receptive** to the greater,* rather than ***becoming** the greater.* For we cannot proceed to a higher level *at will*; we can only *open* to the energies of a higher level. While we can do practices designed to help us move to a higher level, there is no guarantee that this will happen.

However, the cultivation of receptivity can put us in the right mind-set for communing with higher levels, whatever our current level. That is why it's a *win-win* strategy. Conversely, putting our attention only on moving up the levels does little or nothing to enhance our communion with the Divine, because we're making the move solely (or mostly) through our own effort. There is no Agape, no relationship with the Divine. Most of all, there is no surrender—because as Tweedie points out, *some self-will remains.* This is why the yogic (self-starter) approach is unlikely to take us all the way to the top: because it lacks a way to divest us of self-will.

The problem of self-will and lack of receptivity is what may account for a lot of the problems that Wilber associates with boomeritis Buddhism (where "nobody tells *me* what to do!") or the "Mean Green Meme"—problems that seem to stem from spiritual hubris, narcissism, arrogance, and immaturity.[25]

When hubris rears its ugly head, instead of regarding "senior holons" with deference, we hate or envy them and deny their authority; instead of tenderly caring for junior holons (and exercising tolerance and patience with regard to their foibles), we view them with distaste (or even disgust) and refuse to support their growth.

A receptive approach tends to weed out qualities like these, because by asking the Divine for help with them, we receive the kind of experiences that make them hard to hang onto! While these experiences may not be pleasant at the time, they ultimately create new opportunities for both deep healing and spiritual ascent. So a receptive approach creates opportunities for ascent but does it in a way that eliminates qualities that create obstacles and heartache.

It also helps regulate the process of ascent in such a way that we ascend only when we are really ready to handle the responsibility that such a move entails. It is not uncommon for people to associate higher levels with greater freedom not necessarily with greater responsibility. But because of the nature of holarchy, the higher we move, the more responsibility we assume.

As A. G. E. Blake notes, Gurdjieff used to stress the idea that if we want to move to a higher level, we are obliged to "pull up" someone from a lower level to take our place.[26] A friend in the Sufi Ruhaniat order said something similar about the office of Sheikh: that one only rises to that level by bringing students to a high state.

Teachings such as these remind us that inner work is never done solely for our own sake but always involves a sense of spiritual responsibility; it was never intended as an escape from life. As Llewellyn Vaughn-Lee notes,

> we have tended to place meditation and prayer solely within the sphere of our personal relationship with the Divine, not recognizing its larger dimension which concerns the well-being of the whole...[The world]needs the participation of those who are awake to their own spiritual dimension and are committed to service; those whose consciousness can be aligned to something greater than their personal well-being.[27]

And upward movement is not just about taking responsibility for other people but for our own inner patterns of thinking and feeling. Irina Tweedie once remarked that at some point, she realized just how careful she had to be in her thinking and feeling because the power that now flowed through her could cause things to happen that she did not intend.

Many people would like to experience greater awareness. But how many of us are ready for the responsibility it entails? (Do we even have any real idea of what it actually is?)

One of the great advantages of cultivating receptivity is it generally prevents us from moving upward at a pace that is too accelerated for us to handle by ensuring that we will never be given more spiritual power or responsibility than we're prepared to take on. It supports our progress at a rate that does not place too much of a burden on our inner structures (so that we avoid blowing a fuse!). In addition, because it helps us learn how to listen, it helps us discover what it means to come into "right relationship" with life.[28]

Receptive Ascent on the Enneagram

Interestingly, the receptive path described by Tweedie is precisely the same transformational path described by A. G. E. Blake using the process enneagram. However, rather than discussing two ways to progress, Blake makes it clear that once we reach a certain point on the enneagram, we can *only* progress via receptivity.

You will recall from the discussion in Chapter 8 that the right-hand side of the enneagram is feminine and the left-hand side is masculine. On the personality enneagram, this describes the polarity of the types. On the process enneagram, it describes the nature of what is happening at that point in the process.

Involutionary descent, which happens from birth to mid-life, requires a striving to develop a sense of self, relationships with others, and an appropriate skill set for functioning in the physical world. So while the phase is feminine (because matter is feminine), the process we use to descend is masculine in nature: assertive, striving, and pushing forwards into life.

Evolutionary ascent, which happens from mid-life to the end of life, requires a different approach. Although it is a masculine phase (because it takes us from matter to Spirit), it requires a more feminine approach: because as our physical energy begins to wane, we gradually surrender more and more of our personal autonomy. The closer we move towards the end of life, the more we confront our physical limits and need to focus on something beyond our personal self.

Thus, our descent into the feminine world of material life is best accomplished via a predominantly *masculine* approach; our ascent into the masculine world of Spirit is best accomplished by a predominantly *feminine* approach. This is why, when speaking of the two halves of such a process, Blake speaks of "pushing" towards the goal during the first half of the cycle and "being pulled" towards the goal during the second half.[29]

This idea is congruent in holon theory with the depiction of self-transcendence as involving feminine receptivity and self-assertiveness as involving masculine responsibility (see Chapter 2). Fig. 12-4 depicts this process on the enneagram.

The core idea isn't that strange: that we balance masculine with feminine and vice-versa. So developing assertiveness is very helpful during the first half of life. However, as we approach the nadir, that assertive path of making our way in the world which worked so well between Points 0 to 3 begins to yield less satisfactory results. We continue to move forward, but with less certainty and drive—which is why Blake calls the area between 3 and 6 the "vale of soul making" in which the object is to "arrive at a capacity of dying by an act of will" (p. 152).

The dying is not literal; it is a dying to self-will. This is why it is a transitional phase often marked by a withdrawal from life: the caterpillar has entered the chrysalis and is preparing to re-emerge in a different form at Point 6, which represents the launching pad for a leap to a higher consciousness. But it's a leap that only happens if we allow ourselves to become receptive to higher energies.

So the transitional period from Points 4 to 6 represents the chance we get during each cycle to surrender self-will and become receptive to a higher will. This is a *conscious* receptivity, which is why the first shock point at Three is

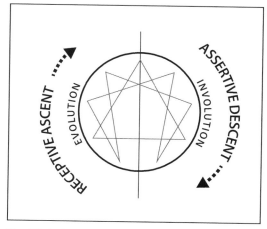

Fig. 12-4. Assertive descent & receptive ascent.

mechanical while the second at Six is not: because the decision to open to higher will is ours alone to make. When that consent is given, "the higher order can touch the lower order. A communication becomes possible" (p. 265).

When moving through Points 4 to 5, we tend to retreat in some way from life. As we approach Point 6, we begin to re-emerge into the world. But this re-emergence seldom comes without a struggle, as the remnants of self-will make it challenging to accept the shift to a new perspective.

But the sense of struggle seems to be a natural part of the process of re-emergence. A friend recently told me the story of someone watching a real-life butterfly trying to crawl out of its cocoon; it was difficult and the person felt sorry for the butterfly, so he helpfully opened the cocoon wider to make it easier. The butterfly emerged, but it was sickly and soon died. Apparently, the way butterflies develop the strength to fly is by struggling to get out of their cocoon: without that struggle, they fail to develop the wing structures needed for flight.

The butterfly's struggle is symbolic of what happens when we are approaching the point in a transformational process where we get to choose between self-will and receptivity to a greater will. It begins at Point 4, we must decide whether we can fully commit to the task at hand, whatever it may be. If the answer is yes, we become more and more identified with the work, which allows the self to step back so that the work can take precedence. That is why T. S. Eliot says that "the progress of an artist is a continual self-sacrifice, a continual extinction of personality."[30]

It also allows the beginning of an alchemical "cooking" process at the nadir that effects alchemical changes of an irreversible nature.

By Point 5, we are fully invested in the work, such that there is no "I", only an "it." This is why Point 5 on the personality enneagram is so associated with objective reasoning: because it is through objectified reasoning that we begin to understand the self-as-object.

But in order to move from Point 5 to Point 6, this intensive focus on objective development must give way to the realization that this approach has limits: it can never yield the kind of complete understanding that we seek. Only by surrendering to a higher form of Intelligence (and by moving from analyzing to acceptance) can we make the transition to a higher level of functioning.

The good news is that—to the extent that we are *fully* invested in the task—we have already surrendered the self to the work. All it takes is one more small step to surrender the task to the Divine—by realizing and admitting our limitations as taskmaster.

This is why Blake says Point 6 is where we realize that "man cannot complete self-realization from below...but requires the assistance of the Divine" (p. 61); Bennett says it is where "the unconditioned begins to work within the conditional or the spiritual within the psychological" (p. 63). As a result, once we reach Point 7 "the new man is born."

(If we cannot open to the descending energy at Point 6, we still move through the rest of the cycle, but the move is, in Blake's words, "empty," akin to the movement of people who have essentially stopped growing but still continue to go through the motions of living until the end of physical life.)

So although I earlier rejected Wilber's term Agape as a descriptor for transformational descent, it is the perfect term to describe the beneficent descent of Spirit at Point

6, where the descent occurs in response to the aspirant's willingness to open to higher energies, guidance, and standards. Spirit descends from the top of the enneagram down the left side to Point 6, where our faith, love, and trust allow it to enter us, raising us up to a higher estate (Fig. 12-5).

Notice that on Fig. 12-5, the initial part of our ascent involves the same kind of masculine "doing" process associated with the right-hand side of the enneagram (Fig. 12-4). This is the phase where the self has become identified with the task and is hence still engaged in action. But because it is now identified with the task as an object, the focus on subjective (personal) exploration at Point 4 has given way to objective exploration at Point 5.

Receptivity & Integral Living

Integral living is about bringing together unlike elements in a way that harmoniously reconciles them. The single biggest barrier to integral living is our inability to come to terms with diversity, an inability that too often causes us to splinter into opposing groups with different values. When this happens to a culture, it begins to disintegrate—and we begin to see lots of unintegrated individuals, closed groups, and a general aura of tension abroad in the land. The tension comes from the fear of what will happen with all the disharmony if we don't find a way to resolve it.

Many people like the idea of promoting diversity in theory, but cannot handle it in practice. Diversity brings change, and too much change too soon can cause us to feel shaky about our sense of identity. When this happens, we become extremely uncomfortable and seek ways to neutralize the threat, either by withdrawing, compromising, or com-

Fig. 12-5. Agape greets Eros.

peting. If we withdraw, we lose the benefits of group participation. If we compromise, we lose our sense of self-esteem. If we compete, we create schisms that destroy any sense of community within the group. So it is not easy for groups to be *win-win* instead of *win-lose*.

But a group whose members cultivate receptivity—especially receptivity to Spirit—can often overcome such obstacles, because spiritual receptivity is such a powerful force for healing and reconciliation. And it promotes the kind of healing that strengthens both the individual and the group.

Receptivity enables us as individuals to better come to terms with the limitations of life, so that we can stop seeing limits as the enemy. For despite our dislike of limits, limits provide tone and shape to life: they give us a defined space within which to work. Limits also give us a sense of personal identity, especially when we begin to internalize them in a way that transforms them into "inner limits" (inner structures). Once outer limits become internal structures, it is much easier to participate in a group without losing our sense of personal identity: because we now possess the interior stability that enables us to maintain our own worldview while experiencing that of another. We can then come together in communion without any loss of individual autonomy. And that is what integral living is all about.

We are all seeking something special in life, something that will make our lives worth living. But just what is it? What is it that calls to us when we are away from the crowd—when we are in nature, when we are alone at night, or when we have nothing else to distract us? The mysterious title of Ouspensky's book on Gurdjieff's teachings, *In Search of the Miraculous*, gives us a hint. For it speaks to the secret yearning of all human beings—even those who seem profoundly asleep—to wake up to the miraculous in life: to the awe, mystery, and wonder that makes us feel truly alive.

Even so, the first moment of awakening can come as quite a jolt. Because it's at that moment that we realize just how dimmed our consciousness has been. It's easy to react with fear—even panic—at the prospect of falling asleep again. That is why the early stages of awakening can produce a lot of reactivity, making people very keen to either transcend the world or improve it. If we transcend without including, we abandon the world to its problems. If we seek to improve what we do not love or understand, we only make things worse. So neither of these aversion-based approaches offers a *win-win* solution.

Receptivity returns us to a place of openness, so that our transformation unfolds in a way that is natural, not forced. We become (in Mark Epstein's words) *open to desire* (open to our embodied nature, so we do not use spiritual life as an escape).[32]

Receptivity can help individuals involved in transformational work to translate our desire for higher consciousness into something that allows us to see the world around us with new eyes. In personality enneagram work, it can help us see our point of view as an asset rather than a liability. In process enneagram work, it can help us see the benefits of the personality enneagram for understanding transformational processes. In integral work, it can help us see IOS from the broadest possible perspective (so we can appreciate new ideas from diverse sources).

The stories told at this chapter's beginning remind us that we don't need to be enlightened to discover the magical possibilities in life—or to participate in their unfolding. The magic is all around us, hidden in plain sight. Whatever our vertical level or horizontal point of view, we have immediate access to the Divine in life—to our higher soul's desire.

Receptivity attracts the experiences that bring us into alignment with the Divine—into alignment with the need of the moment, out of which the *dharma* flows. If we need to ascend, we ascend; if we need to descend, we descend; if we need more time or space to just hang out and digest our experiences, we get it. Life is "just so."

> *When we come to the place*
> *of inner convergence*
> *The home of the nexus,*
> *where the Two Seas meet;*
> *We find ourselves rapt*
> *in the eternal moment*
> *Where death has no meaning*
> *and life comes to greet.*[33]

Notes

1. David Armstrong & Ben H. Bagdikian *Trumpet to Arms: Alternative Media in America* (1999).

2. In the middle of writing this chapter, I took a trip to San Diego, where I visited SeaWorld for the first time since that trip back in the early 1970s. I have to say, it's really changed! It's a lot busier, noisier, and more commercial now (although my God-children still had a really good time there!).

3. An example of how a lack of shared unity can create big problems: I was involved in an SGI fife-and-drum core that marched in local parades. Objectively speaking, we weren't very skilled; few of us had ever played our instruments before we came to the group. But because we were so hopelessly outmatched, all we could do is chant together to succeed (against all odds). Amazingly, when we were really "in sync," we somehow made quite an impression, often winning top honors at parades featuring groups with much greater technical skill. But every so often, the group energy was "off"—and we experienced dramatic reversals. One time, we'd won first place in a parade and were feeling a little overconfident about the next one. To make a long story short, nothing went as planned; we had countless problems of all sorts, including getting off the beat and having our drum majorette collapse from hypoglycemia in the middle of the parade! (She was okay, fortunately, but it was sure embarrassing.) From #1 in the previous parade, our rank plummeted to #49—dead last!

4. The commitment to seek *win-win* solutions doesn't mean that we always find them. But it greatly increases the likelihood of finding an optimal solution, given the built-in limitations of the situation.

5. See Kofman's "Holons, Heaps, and Artifacts" for a discussion, Wilber's remarks on p. 72 of *SES*, and Koestler's remarks on p. 243 of *Ghost in the Machine* (1967), in which he distinguishes *integration* with a group (which is healthy) from *identification* with the group (which is not).

6. While integral theory (and specifically IOS) has many strengths, it is much better developed vertically than horizontally, for reasons discussed in Chapters 10 and 11. Thus, it is not surprising that Wilber, when discussing the relationship of individuals to groups on pp. 49–54, characterizes it in terms of two opposing drives, the drive towards *agency* (individual autonomy) and the drive towards *communion* (participatory bonding). At one point, he speaks of the "constant battle" between the two, observing that there is a trade-off between them such that "the more agency, the less communion, and vice versa." Such a characterization is true of groups we may characterize as non-integral, *win-lose*, closed, or less than optimally-functioning; it is not however true of healthy, dynamic, and open groups. While there is certainly a tension between individuality and communion in any group, in a healthy group, this tension does not give rise to trade-offs but to creative synergy. Thus, it cannot generally be said that "the more agency, the less communion."

7. It's possible to talk about horizontal integration from two perspectives: *within* an individual and *between* individuals in groups. Our focus here is on the latter.

8. From the Leonard Cohen song of the same name.

9. The topic of embodied spirituality is a big one that deserves more space than can be allocated here. It is discussed from a shamanic perspective by authors such as Mircea Eliade, Sandra Ingerman, Michael Harner, Lewis Mehl-Madrona, Joan Halifax, and Alberto Villoldo—and from a "depth psychology" perspective by Carl Jung, James Hillman, and others particularly interested in a "soul" perspective (see Chapters 1–5 of *Archetypes of the Enneagram*).

10. For a discussion on the invisibility of psychic structures, see Wilber's discussion in *Integral Spirituality* (2006), pp. 71–72, 233–234.

11. *The Eye of Spirit* (2001), p. 371.

12. *Healing the Mind Through the Power of Story* (2010), p. 61.

13. I've also had personal experiences that clued me in to the importance of psychic structures, especially in inner work. Some years ago, I had a dream in which I was with a spiritual teacher headed towards the high mountains. We stopped to spend the night somewhere along the way. I saw myself in a room full of high-voltage electrical cables that were jumbled up. I asked

the teacher what they were. She said, "It's the air conditioning." I saw an enormous electrical plug, and thought maybe I could simply pull it out, thereby removing the problem. But there was a big Danger sign next to the plug. At that point I woke up. *Air conditioning*—as soon as I awoke, I got the point: that there was some convoluted but entrenched mental conditioning that stood in the way of my spiritual journey, conditioning that could not be addressed by simply pulling the plug. The cables had to be untangled in the right way; the teacher was there to ensure the job was done properly. A year later, I had another dream in which the electrical system at an airport was being entirely revamped; until the work was done, no flights could depart. Dreams like these showed me the state of my psychic structures in symbolic form, so that I would understand why my yearning to experience higher states was insufficient for manifesting them: because I lacked the necessary structures to properly channel higher-frequency energies.

14. The appropriate attitude towards time in spiritual practice is captured in the story of two yogis who sought enlightenment. Each was told it would take several lifetimes. The first was disappointed, and said, "So long?" The second said, "So short?"—and instantly found himself enlightened.

15. Ferrer, Jose, Ramon Albareda, and Marina T. Romero (2004). "Embodied Participation in the Mystery: Implications for the Individual, Interpersonal Relationships, and Society." *Journal of Transpersonal Psychology,* 35(1): 21-42, available online at http://participatorystudies.files. wordpress.com/2011/03/embodiedparticipation-albareda-romero.pdf; accessed 1-25-13; the quotation is from p. 4 in the online version.

16. "Integral Transformative Practice: A Participatory Perspective." (2004). *ReVision*, 27-1, 10-17, available at www.integralworld.net); accessed 1-26-13, p. 7 in the online version.

17. *The Creative Habit* (2006), p. 152.

18. *The Complete Artist's Way* (2007), pp. 202–203.

19. http://www.yogalifenh.com/philosophy/teachings/29-when-the-student-is-ready; accessed 1-29-13.

20. http://www.yogajournal.com/wisdom/652; accessed 1-30-13.

21. Irina Tweedie's teacher, Radha Mohan Lal (Bhai Sahib) says that Divine power is not magic; nor is it ever sold for money. It is a form of Divine grace. Yogic powers are different, and can be acquired through yogic practices and will power (*Daughter of Fire,* 1986, p. 646).

22. Stanford University [online] dictionary of philosophy, (http://plato.stanford.edu/entries/love/; accessed 1-29-13).

23. You will recall from the beginning of Chapter 9 that when Wilber uses the word Agape, he often associates it both with self-immanence and with the process of integration during the transformational process. From that perspective, it is the embodied spiritual seeker who is the source of Agape as she reaches down to embrace the now-transcended aspects of her consciousness so that they can be integrated into the psyche as a whole (or into the *self-system*, using Wilber's terminology).

However, there needs to be a way to discern such nascent self-compassion from the descent of Divine grace that occurs in response to a human being's yearning to be loved, embraced, and lifted up by Spirit. I prefer to associate Agape exclusively with the descent of Spirit as Divine grace—the grace we draw down by our willingness to surrender to something greater than our own self-will.

24. Sufi teacher Radha Mohan Lal says that we start by cultivating feeling, then out of feeling, cultivate love.

25. In "On Mean Memes in General," Wilber makes the claim that "the MGM [Mean Green Meme] is the driving force of boomeritis, and it has dominated academia, liberal politics, and the humanities for three decades. Its damage is staggering, and only made worse by the smug self-satisfaction of these particular Inquisitors" (www.integralworld.net; accessed 1-28-13). For a lengthier exposition see Wilber's novel *Boomeritis*, 2003. (For a critique of Wilber's approach to the MGM, see Ray Harris' "Rescuing the Green Meme" at www.integralworld.net; accessed 5-9-13).

26. *The Intelligent Enneagram* (1996), p. 280.

27. www.workingwithoneness.org/articles/spiritual-responsibility-time-global-crisis; accessed 10-25-12.

28. Placing the emphasis on receptivity doesn't preclude a role for formal spiritual practices, because such practices may be necessary for various reasons, including the construction of psychic structures that enhance our ability to handle high-frequency energies.

29. See Blake's *Enneagram Monthly* article, "On Time: Only Through Time, Time is Conquered," Jan. 1998, p. 19.

30. "Tradition and the Individual Talent (1919), Part I; available at http://www.bartleby.com/200/sw4.html; accessed 2-10-13. Eliot noted in Part III that "the emotion of art is impersonal. And the poet cannot reach this impersonality without surrendering himself wholly to the work to be done." This is a very nice description of how—given the surrender of the artist to the work—the intensely emotional space at Point 4 on the enneagram gives way to the intensely impersonal space at Point 5.

31. *Autobiography of a Yogi* is now available as an e-book at no charge at Amazon.

32. Epstein, Mark. *Open to Desire: Embracing a Lust for Life* (2005).

33. In Sufi lore, the Place Where the Two Seas Meet is the nexus between Spirit and matter, life and death, the known and the unknown. It is associated with the mysterious figure of Khidr, the Green Man, who is a symbol of direct revelation. The poem is mine.

13

AN INTEGRAL VISION

Magic is making dreams real.
– David Copperfield

Freedom is attained not by escape from limitations and conditions,
but by adjusting the balance to a perfect equilibrium.
– *The Cosmic Doctrine*

I STOLE THE TITLE for this chapter from Wilber's 2007 book of the same name. In that book, Wilber introduces his integral approach to an audience who would probably never dream of picking up one of Wilber's "treatise"-style books (*SES* comes to mind)— or even his more popularized versions like *A Brief History of Everything*. *The Integral Vision* is a compact but glossy picture book in which dramatic images are used to introduce complex ideas in an accessible format.

Like Wilber, I too have an integral vision that I've tried to communicate in this book. While the images are in black-and-white— and the ideas are at times complex—the goal is similar: to make the complex ideas as accessible as possible, so that readers can explore them further.

It's fitting that this final chapter is Chapter 13, because 13 has always been the number of mystery, symbolizing the Unknown.

So while this chapter contains a summary of everything in the book, it also contains an invitation, an invitation to notice what is *not* here—all the pieces that remain missing and the explorations that have yet to be done.

We'll start with a quick summary of what we've covered until now, then compare IOS and the enneagram(s) with a focus on how each supplements the other; and finally, we'll talk about the ultimate integration: the integration of the individual with the *dharma*.

The Integral Enneagram: A Reprise

Chapter 1 set the tone for the entire book with a discussion of *dharma* and its central role in our lives and in the Kosmos. The emphasis on *dharma* (our life's path or calling) arises out of the view that life is not a random series of physical events but rather a purposeful (if mysterious) unfolding of Divine intention— an unfolding that takes place on many levels of life and many levels of the human psyche. It also presupposes a highly dynamic view of the Kosmos in which all the elements of life are in dynamic relationship with one another, whether we are talking about the physical world we see around us or the unseen world out of which the physical world arises.

This idea that life is purposeful lies in direct opposition to the mechanistic scientific model that gave rise to logical positivism and behaviorism early in the 20th century. So the first half of this chapter focused on the traditional scientific taboo against seeing life in teleological (meaningful) terms, but with an emphasis on how "meaningless science" may slowly be giving way to more "meaning-laden science," despite a lot of resistance from the forces of scientific orthodoxy. At that point, the discussion turned to the nature of purpose from the angle of spirituality, focusing especially on the *Bhagavad-Gita*, which conveys the message that life is not just purposeful in the general sense, but that each of us as individuals has a purpose in life, a purpose that only we can fulfill.

In **Chapter 2**, the focus was on the different levels of life and how they interact with one another. Arthur Koestler's theory of holarchy was introduced, a theory based on the notion that everything in life which is sentient (capable of consciousness) plays two roles: a *part* and a *whole*. As a part, it is an aspect of something larger than itself; as a whole, it is an autonomous entity capable of semi-autonomous functioning. Koestler coined the term *holon* to describe these this "Janus-faced" quality of sentient elements (which simultaneously look both up and down). He used it as the basis for a framework that could be used to contemplate the nature of living systems.

Ken Wilber picked up on the idea of holarchy and used it as the centerpiece for his most comprehensive theoretical work, *Sex, Ecology, Spirituality*; it has thus played a major role in shaping integral theory since the publication of *SES* in 1995. Wilber made certain modifications to holon theory, however, that I did not adopt (preferring to stick with Koestler's original formulation for the reasons explained in this chapter). My approach to holon theory as detailed in Chapter 2 is based on two main assumptions: that (a) in a healthy holarchy, all levels play an important and intrinsically respectworthy role; and (b) holons act as "energy nodes" for the flow of energy and information throughout the holarchy. So the emphasis in my work is on the dynamism of individual holons, their intrinsically purposeful nature, and their ability to function both as parts and wholes within a living system.

Chapter 3 provided a brief introduction to the enneagram: its geometry, introduction by Gurdjieff as a transformational symbol and system, and adaptation by Ichazo as a tool for identifying nine types of "fixated" functioning, each of which can be seen as a personality type. So this approach gives us nine personality types, each of which is associated with mental and emotional shortcomings that act as a barrier to transformation. From this perspective, the main purpose of enneagram work is to become aware of those type-related barriers, so that we can disidentify with ego (the type), which will automatically allow us to reconnect with essence (the spiritual state we were in at birth, before the type developed).

I discussed several disadvantages to this way of working and explained the key role played by Wilber's IOS in providing an alternative framework for enneagram work, one in which the types arise out of deep or core motivations that are with us from birth—and are in fact not a barrier to development but a pointer to *dharma*. The remainder of the chapter provides an overview of the features of the types as seen from a positive, *dharma*-based perspective: nine type profiles, three energy centers, 18 wing types, 27 subtypes, and 18 connecting points.

Chapter 4 introduced Wilber's IOS, starting with a brief history of how I was first introduced to Wilber's ideas, followed by a brief description of key IOS concepts: Wilber's approach to holarchy, the pre/trans fallacy and retro-Romanticism, transformation vs translation, and the five elements of IOS.

Wilber's embrace of holarchy is based on his view that the Kosmos has many levels, not just one (flatland) and that all the levels interact with one another. Wilber's pre/trans fallacy and rejection of the Romantic position embraced by many transpersonal theorists is based on the idea that transformation is progressive, not regressive—and this is very different from the retro-Romantic idea that we "progress regressively" (by shedding ego in order to return to essence). Wilber distinguishes states of consciousness from stages of consciousness by referring to the structural and irreversible nature of the latter. His current formulation of his Integral Operating System (IOS) includes five elements: states, stages, lines of development, AQAL, and types.

Both Chapters 3 and 4 presented the bare outlines of two complex systems. At that point, the goal was just to provide enough of an introduction to both systems—the enneagram and IOS—to set the stage for further explorations.

Chapter 5 focused on retro-Romanticism as it applies to the enneagram—specifically, the idea that the personality enneagram has historically been taught from a retro-Romantic perspective, one in which ego is said to displace (or at least block our ability to experience) essence: our essential state of being.

In a friendly but nevertheless sharp critique of this idea in *The Eye of Spirit* (2001) addressed to the founder of the Ridhwan psycho-spiritual school, A. H. Almaas (the pen name of Hameed Ali), Wilber provides an extremely detailed explanation as to why retro-Romanticism does not work while also addressing the main question that Romanticism is designed to answer: how people can become psychologically imbalanced—which according to Wilber is not due to the obscuration of essence by the developing ego but to the loss of specific aspects of essence that emerge at various stages of development—and which can be retrieved (which is the purpose of shadow work). Such a loss is not inevitable, he stresses, but occurs only when ego becomes over-differentiated, leading to dissociation. The solution, he says, is not to denigrate ego but to retrieve these specific aspects of our being that have been cut off.

This critique is highly relevant because of Almaas' prominent role within the enneagram community, his use of the enneagram in the School, and the many influential enneagram teachers who are also Ridhwan students. The chapter concludes with a proposal for a more integrative approach to the personality enneagram based on the work of Gurdjieff, Wilber, A. G. E. Blake, and positive psychologist Martin Seligman.

Chapter 6 introduced Gurdjieff's process enneagram, which has exactly the same geometry as Ichazo's personality enneagram. The point was made that two figures that are geometrically identical are likely to share much in common. However, the process enneagram was introduced half a century earlier by Gurdjieff and is considered by many to be the more fundamental of the two enneagram interpretations. Thus, since the process enneagram is transformationally-focused (rather than fixation-focused), linking the personality enneagram to the process enneagram justifies the development of a more transformationally-oriented approach to the personality enneagram.

The specific nature of the process enneagram was explored by looking at how a transformational process can be divided into three major transformational phases, each of which contains three of the nine enneagram points. The discussion focused on the special role of the three shock points (points at which new information is introduced into the process). The process enneagram was also depicted as a model for dramatic stories, in which there is a beginning (setup) phase, a middle ("trouble") phase, and an ending (resolution) phase. At the chapter's end, I showed how it is possible to link personality and process by linking the 18 wing types, proceeding clockwise from 9w1 all the way around to 9w8.

Chapter 7 began with a discussion about the true nature of personality—how it develops as the result of temperament, environmental factors, and personal choice—and then proceeded to use Nathan Bernier's descriptions of each process enneagram point to link each point in a transformational process with its corresponding type on the personality enneagram. We saw how linking the two enneagrams with one another allows us to understand the personality enneagram from a deeper perspective, because we can see the reasons why each type has certain characteristics (i.e., because of its position in a transformational process). We briefly looked at how this information helps us determine which life paths are associated with each of the nine types.

Chapter 8 further explored the relationship between the personality and process enneagrams by dividing the enneagram circle into zones both vertically and horizontally, based on the energy of each zone. First we looked at the personality enneagram zones, then at the process enneagram zones, and then at the interaction between the two. While the horizontal zones for both the personality and process enneagrams were characterized in terms of the same three zones (top=*spirit zone*, middle=*ego zone*, bottom=*soul zone*), the breakdown of vertical zones differed somewhat. For the personality enneagram, right=*feminine*, middle=*androgynous*, left=*masculine*; for the process enneagram, right=*descent*, middle=*stillness*, left=*ascent*.

These categorizations enabled us to further break down the enneagram into *seven zones of transformation* that depict the degree to which transformational direction on the process enneagram (ascent or descent) affect the nature of the types on the personality enneagram.

Looking at these zone combinations allowed us to take a closer look at the types, their relationship to one another, and—more broadly—the relationship of personality to transformation.

One of the key outcomes of identifying these relationships was the development of a transformational model of the life cycle which includes both an involutionary (descent) and evolutionary (ascent) phase—a model that differs from Wilber's current "ascend-only" transformational model that is described in Chapter 9). A "descend-then-ascend" (Integral Enneagram) transformational model was introduced in preparation for a more extended discussion in the following chapter.

In **Chapter 9**, we looked at ways to describe the transformational process from both an enneagram-based and IOS-based perspective. Discussing Wilber's "ascend-only" model of transformation—developed as an alternative to his previous retro-Romantic model—I discussed the disadvantages of dropping descent out of the model and proposed an enneagram-based "descend-then-ascend" transformational model that restores descent to the transformational process in a way that does not create pre/trans problems.

(The proposed Integral Enneagram model associates *self-immanence* with descent during the first half of life, depicting it as an essentially feminine process involving psychological development and the ability to adapt to life in the physical plane. It associates *self-transcendence* with ascent during the second half of life, depicting it as an essentially masculine process involving spiritual development and the ability to reconcile our psychological self with end-of-life issues and life after physical death.)

Eight potential kinds of transformational moves were identified, distinguished by *life phase* (descent versus ascent), *direction* (progressing or reversing), and *health* (integrative versus non-integrative). Then three models of transformation (retro-Romantic, Wilber's, and Integral Enneagram) were compared; seven advantages of the Rhodes Integral Enneagram model were listed.

At the chapter's end was a brief discussion of how the eight transformational moves vary by enneagram type followed by "How Fast Can We Grow?", an examination of the potential trade-offs between how fast we transform and the degree to which we can integrate our transformational experiences.

Chapter 10 focused on horizontal integration, particularly correspondences between the enneagram personality points of view and IOS quadrants, hori-zones, and the Big Three value spheres. The material presented in this chapter has particular value for IOS since it is along the horizontal dimension that the (personality) enneagram particularly shines, because those who work with the system have spent decades exploring the relational dynamics between the different energy centers (which can be mapped onto the Big Three value spheres) and the types (which can be mapped onto the eight hori-zones). Integral theorists who grasp the potential of mapping the personality enneagram onto the AQAL quadrants would find themselves with an extraordinarily powerful new tool for exploring the nature of perspective-taking.

Although my original aim in this chapter was simply to link the personality enneagram with the AQAL quadrants and hori-zones, when I got deeply into the process, I had several new insights that were discussed at the chapter's end.

The first concerns the nature of the quadrants/hori-zones. I made the point that since it is clearly possible to link them to the enneagram points of view, it is necessary to realize that one of them is sufficiently *dominant* to deeply shape our orientation to life. While having a dominant perspective/hori-zone is not a terrible problem, it does mean that we need to be aware of its influence (and to realize the impossibility of achieving the kind of aperspectival awareness that might be envisioned as an Integral ideal).

The second concerns the five elements in IOS (AQAL, types, lines, levels, and states), which can potentially be reduced to four if we see AQAL perspectives/hori-zones as akin to a type, where type refers to any kind of stable category present at any level or line of consciousness. If so, both AQAL and type can theoretically be combined into a single *individual differences* category.

The third—which arose out of my Chapter 10 explorations—concerns the nature of the perspectives described by the enneagram/AQAL, which I see as stable *horizontal structures* within the psyche, not just subsets of vertical structures defined by our current level of vertical development.

In **Chapter 11,** the aim was to look at both IOS and the enneagram from a vertical and horizontal perspective, with the intention of showing how juxtaposing each system on the other has the potential to yield new insights about both. But the chapter began with a further discussion on transformation versus translation, with the aim being to definitely demonstrate the validity of both vertical and horizontal psychic structures. As a follow-up, there was a discussion of how each of the nine enneagram types was associated with a different line of development (demonstrating the interaction of horizontal to vertical structures).

Next, several IOS constructs (AQAL, the Big Three, and Wilber's three major fulcrums of development—pre-personal, personal, and transpersonal) were mapped onto the process enneagram. Finally, the personality and process enneagrams were both mapped onto all the nine levels (fulcrums) of consciousness associated with Wilber's Spectrum model of development.

In **Chapter 12,** the focus shifted to integral living: how Spirit can become deeply integrated into our life on earth. I shared three experiences that demonstrated how integrated individuals can come together in a way that enhances both agency and communion. We then looked at the horizontal and vertical factors that help us create *win-win* groups (instead of *win-lose* or *lose-lose* groups).

The next section focused on embodied spirituality and the role of creativity in helping us anchor the energies of Spirit on earth. We then looked at the two main phases in integral living: *self-immanent descent* (where we anchor Spirit in matter) and *self-transcendent ascent* (where we return to Spirit by transcending-and-including).

The focus then turned to the key role of receptivity in transformation, starting with the counter-intuitive idea that descent tends to require a more masculine (assertive) approach while ascent tends to require a more feminine (receptive) approach. This paved the way for a discussion of how the process enneagram depicts the idea that the last third of the transformational journey comes about primarily as the result of our receptivity to the Divine. Thus, although our efforts and practices matter, we reach a point when our further development depends upon our "spiritual attractiveness," i.e., our ability to "pull down the grace." And this is where Agape re-enters the picture, as the descent of the Divine into life in response to our soul's desire.

IOS & the Enneagram Compared

Thus ends our chapter by chapter summary of *The Integral Enneagram*. Next comes a series of comparisons between IOS and the enneagram with a focus on how each system informs the other. In some cases, IOS brings insights to enneagram work that would otherwise not come into play; in others, it's the other way around.

Table 13-1 shows a point by point comparison divided into three parts: (a) IOS versus the enneagram (focusing on the enneagram from either a personality or process perspective); (b) IOS versus the process enneagram; and (c) IOS versus the personality enneagram.

IOS vs ENNEAGRAM: GENERAL CONTRASTS

> *IOS = MODERN PHILOSOPHICAL SYSTEM*
> *ENNEAGRAM = ANCIENT ESOTERIC SYSTEM*

IOS is a transformational and philosophical framework developed by Ken Wilber over the last forty years which continues to be a work-in-progress, as Wilber's ideas continue to evolve. So it has historically been an open system with room to expand. IOS represents an impressive body of work designed to address the concerns of a diverse audience of modern-day spiritual seekers, integral theorists, and transformationally-oriented philosophers, intellectuals, and academics. It thus elicits a lot of debate in diverse forums, especially online forums.

According to Gurdjieff, the enneagram is an ancient system with esoteric origins. Although it is said to explain many things about the nature of life, it is most often used to describe transformational processes. Its adaptation by Oscar Ichazo for focusing on ego types did not alter its basically mysterious origins (the sense that it is a system of revealed wisdom, rather than a system devised by human thought). As a result, the teachings of both the personality and process enneagrams tend to be seen more as spiritual "givens" than as ideas open to debate.

Implications. While both IOS and the enneagram are comprehensive, wide-ranging systems, IOS is a more open system when it comes to the public discussion of ideas. The enneagram as a system tends to be less open. Despite efforts by individuals and groups to create a more open forum for discussion, its legacy of secrecy makes it hard to initiate discussions that are more than skin-deep. Introducing IOS to the enneagram community can potentially open up the latter, so that its culture evolves in ways that tend to promote open discussion and address modern concerns. Introducing the enneagram to the IOS community can inform the latter of additional tools that support transformation—tools that are indeed based on hidden wisdom that is only now coming to light.

> *IOS = THEORETICAL SYSTEM*
> *ENNEAGRAM = ENERGETIC/GEOMETRIC SYSTEM*

IOS is an entirely theoretical system based on a conceptual view of human consciousness and transformation. Originally based on the ideas of Ken Wilber, it has in recent years incorporated ideas from other individuals,

TABLE 13-1. COMPARING IOS & THE ENNEAGRAM.

Integral Operating System	Personality Enneagram	Process Enneagram
IOS COMPARED TO THE ENNEAGRAM (OVERVIEW)		
Modern system focusing on current concerns	Ancient system w/esoteric roots	
Theoretical system	Energetic/geometric system	
A grid with levels	Perspectives within levels	Spiraling up the levels
IOS COMPARED TO THE PERSONALITY ENNEAGRAM		
Progressive (no pre/trans fallacy)	Retrogressive (ego displaces essence)*	
AQAL quadrant perspectives & hori-zones	Points of view	
Horizontal "translations" of vertical structures	Horizontal structures independent of level	
IOS COMPARED TO THE PROCESS ENNEAGRAM		
Ascend-only (all descent is prior to birth)		Descend-then-ascend (we are born half-descended)
Transcend-and-include		Transcend-and-include *plus* Include-and-transcend
Revolutionary shifts between macro levels		Evolutionary shifts within macro levels

*Retro-Romantic personality paradigm

especially those working closely with Wilber and Integral Institute.

Although the enneagram also has a theoretical component, it is in essence a *yantra*, a mystical symbol with transformative power; Fig. 13-1). It is thus part of the ancient tradition of sacred geometry, a tradition whose insights have largely been lost to Western civilization. But the power of sacred symbols remains intact. Thus, since the enneagram is a sacred symbol with an energetic core, its energy can be accessed via a variety of non-intellectual methods, such as meditation, music, or movement (which may be why Gurdjieff worked with the enneagram by incorporating it into his complex dance movements).[1]

Implications. Both IOS and the enneagram can be used for exploring the nature of human consciousness and transformative processes. However, the latter also possesses an energetic core or essence connected with its geometry, which means it has "extra" properties that can potentially be energetically accessed (although at least in the personality enneagram community, such possibilities remain largely unexplored).

IOS = A CATEGORICAL GRID WITH LINES & LEVELS

ENNEAGRAM = A SPATIAL SYSTEM WITH LINKED POINTS OF VIEW (PERSONALITY) OR A SPIRAL SYSTEM THAT LINKS THE LEVELS (PROCESS)

IOS is a categorically-based system that is organized more or less as a grid with horizontal AQAL perspectives and vertical lines of development. The focus is on making this categorical grid as complete as possible, so that it can account for all possible manifestations of human consciousness.

The personality enneagram also generates categories organized by personality type. However, it is more of a relationally-oriented system that focuses a lot on the interactions among the types. The process enneagram is similarly relational, providing a way to map the spiral path between the levels on any line of development that we can potentially envision. When we put the two enneagrams together, we can explore the relationship between individual *personality types* (and how they interact) and individual *stages of transformation* (and how they interact). While looking at so many different actions can boggle the mind, it certainly provides us with a lot of fascinating interactions to explore!

Implications. While Wilber's system is superbly suited for providing a global over-

Fig. 13-1. *Sri yantra*.

view of transformational nodes in the Kosmic network, it does not offer a great deal of information about how to connect the nodes either vertically or horizontally. Both the personality and process enneagrams help us make those connections (thereby allowing us to get a better sense of the relationships between horizontal constructs such as perspectives and vertical constructs such as lines of development).

IOS AND THE
PERSONALITY ENNEAGRAM

> ### IOS = *PROGRESSIVE*
> ### *ENNEAGRAM = RETROGRESSIVE*

The progressive thrust of Wilber's work is an area where his system particularly shines, because Wilber has not only adopted a progressive outlook but has done the theoretical work necessary to justify it. This is how he generated the pre/trans fallacy (arguably his greatest single contribution to transpersonal and integral studies). IOS theory thus supports the development of the egoic structures of personality, on the basis that such structures form the foundation for even higher structures of consciousness.

In comparison, the theory underlying the personality enneagram has been historically retrogressive, relying on retro-Romantic assumptions about the nature of transformation (which is thus viewed as a process of stripping away the ego structures that are said to obscure our original essence). The result is a model of transformation in which personality has historically been viewed as something fixated, distorted, and lacking in intrinsic value.

Implications. Focusing on transformation as a process of developing something positive is more productive than focusing on it as a process of getting rid of something negative. While it is necessary at times to strip away that which impedes one's progress (which is why reversals are sometimes necessary), to *define* transformation solely in terms of stripping something away is to take one aspect of the process (purification or shadow work) and make it the entire process. A knowledge of IOS can support a move towards the kind of progressive framework that focuses primarily on development (and that is thus an asset for attracting a new generation to enneagram work).[2]

> ### IOS = *PERSPECTIVES*
> ### *ENNEAGRAM = POINTS OF VIEW*

Both AQAL perspectives/hori-zones and enneagram points of view are horizontal constructs that delineate different stances we can take when we look at the world. In both IOS and enneagram work, we try to gain an understanding of different standpoints and how they affect us. However, IOS perspectives are presented solely as disembodied entities described in an abstract way (especially the hori-zones). There is little if any emphasis on the idea that individuals have a dominant view and what this implies about their ability to take alternative perspectives.

In enneagram work, we see perspectives both as internal points of view and as external personality types. Although this dual understanding gives us a lot of flexibility in how we choose to work with them, the historical tendency to pathologize the types makes it harder to see them simply as perspectives. But the understanding that one type is dominant is extremely helpful when we are trying to determine how to broaden our point of view.

Implications. Although Wilber's approach to the quadrant and hori-zone perspectives is informative (not to mention depathologized), it lacks the enneagram's ability to personify perspectives, identify the dominant perspective, and depict interrelationships between perspectives. However, its focus on integrating the points of view (rather than dis-identifying from them) offers a critical element that is lacking in enneagram theory. Combining both approaches gives us insights that can greatly enhance our perspective-taking ability.

> *IOS = HORIZONTAL TRANSLATIONS*
> *ENNEAGRAM = HORIZONTAL STRUCTURES*

Wilber originally started with a vertically-oriented system; horizontal processes were considered to be a function of vertical structures (mere "translations" as opposed to genuine "transformations"). Wilber thus defined structures of consciousness as vertical. Despite the fact that his system has become more horizontal (with the addition of AQAL quadrants and types), he has yet to associate horizontal processes with horizontal structures of consciousness.

In enneagram work, all the types are associated with distinctive type structures; the focus is on understanding these type structures, especially the structure associated with our dominant type. The type structures are

considered to be (a) enduring and (b) independent of our level of development.

Implications. The idea of seeing psychic structures as possessing both vertical and horizontal properties is in alignment with Wilber's own idea that types can be present at any level of consciousness (which implies that they *must* have structures that are independent of level). Thus, integral theorists can benefit by studying the enneagram, because it so clearly depicts nine stable horizontal psychic structures—the kind that persist over the course of a lifetime.

IOS VS PROCESS ENNEAGRAM

> *IOS = ASCEND-ONLY MODEL*
> *ENNEAGRAM = DESCEND-THEN-ASCEND MODEL*

Since about 1980, Wilber has been using an *ascend-only* model of transformation in order to avoid pre/trans problems. However, this approach has three disadvantages: (a) it does not account for the "trailing-clouds-of-glory" phenomenon (that babies are born with a tangible aura of holiness); (b) it makes no real provision for self-immanence in the transformational cycle; and (c) it provides no real way to account for the mid-life shift noted by Jung and others.

The process enneagram uses a *descend-then-ascend* model that both solves the above problems and avoids pre/trans problems because the re-ascent does not retrace the path of descent but takes us along a continuing arc to a new level of development at the point of origin.

Implications. Adopting an enneagram-based (descend-then-ascend) model of transformation accounts for the trailing-clouds-of-glory aura of the newly-born (by saying they arrive in a half-descended state). It makes a place for self-immanence (by locating it during the first half of life). And by introducing a two-phase model, it accounts for the mid-life shift. It avoids pre/trans problems by positing a model in which we are (a) always moving towards Spirit and (b) advancing during the life cycle.

IOS = TRANSCEND-AND-INCLUDE
ENNEAGRAM = ADDS INCLUDE-AND-TRANSCEND

Wilber's contribution to transformational theory was to add a *transcend-and-include* component to the previously pre-eminent "transcend only" model of transformation. Transcend-and-include obviously goes hand in hand with the ascend-only model discussed in the previous section.

However, transcend-and-include still focuses more on masculine ascent than feminine descent; and if we adopt a descend-then-ascend model of the transformational process, we need an *include-and-transcend* approach. We can use the process enneagram to justify a two-phase model of the process: (a) a descent in which we emphasize inclusion (psychological integration) and (b) a re-ascent in which we emphasize transcendence (spiritual ascent).

Implications. Having *include-and-transcend* followed by *transcend-and-include* gives us a model in which different things are emphasized during different parts of the transformational cycle. During the first (feminine) half of life, integration is emphasized; during the second (masculine) half of life, transcendence is emphasized. Such a model gives more

emphasis to the feminine (embodied) side of spirituality, emphasizing its potential to support the kind of transformation that is integrated rather than fragmented.

IOS = REVOLUTIONARY SHIFTS BETWEEN MACRO LEVELS
ENNEAGRAM = EVOLUTIONARY SHIFTS WITHIN MACRO LEVELS

Wilber's Spectrum model—with its nine major levels (fulcrums)—presents us with an overview of Kosmic transformation and its macrolevels of development. In addition, it describes these levels in terms of (a) balanced vs unbalanced development and (b) methodologies for becoming balanced at every level. By providing a bird's-eye view of transformation, it gives us an extremely comprehensive framework for envisioning the process of transformation. However, by focusing primarily on the macro-levels of transformation, it necessarily emphasizes revolutionary leaps (rather than evolutionary processes).

The process enneagram provides us with a transformational model that emphasizes (a) the cyclical nature of transformational processes, (b) the need to go through repeated cycles in order to effect permanent structural changes, and (c) the nine challenges we encounter during each transformational cycle. It therefore places more attention on microcycles, micro-changes, and moves within (rather than between) macro-levels, thereby emphasizing the mostly incremental nature of transformational processes.[3]

Implications. Wilber's IOS emphasizes the big but rarer shifts in consciousness while the process enneagram emphasizes the small but more common shifts. These two approaches obviously complement one other, because the former is more "macro" while the latter is more "micro." IOS provides a way to envision the transformational journey as a whole while the enneagram provides a tool for studying the process in a more moment-to-moment fashion.

Throughout this book, we've looked at parallels between IOS and the enneagram. In this chapter, the focus has been on (a) summarizing previous chapters and (b) highlighting key differences between IOS and the enneagram.

These IOS/enneagram comparisons offer yet another (more abbreviated) way to compare IOS with the enneagram. In summary, IOS's greatest strength comes from its comprehensiveness, progressive focus, and relevance to modern audiences; the enneagram's greatest strength comes from its depth, geometry (which provides a tool for analyzing relationships), and two-pronged focus (which allows us to explore the link between personality and transformation).

What the enneagram has lacked until now is a comprehensive philosophical framework that makes it possible to study it from a de-pathologized perspective (which IOS offers); what IOS has lacked is a means to account for the process by which we move from level to level (which we have in the process enneagram) and a tool for looking at the interaction between individual temperament and transformation (which we have in the personality enneagram). By bringing both systems together, we can potentially create a synthesis in which the new whole is truly more than the sum of its parts.

However, there is still one missing piece, one aspect of transformation that is not par-

ticularly stressed by either system. But if we leave it out, spiritual work too often becomes an exercise in spiritual materialism, escapism, or bypassing. Of course I am speaking of the notion of *dharma*—the idea that all of life is saturated with purpose. For humankind, it is the discovery of our life's purpose that drives all genuine inner work, whether we are consciously aware of it or not.

Fulfilling the *Dharma*

At the very beginning, I said that this is a book about *dharma*—that *dharma* is the pole around which the ideas revolve. Why is this?

Because it is the *dharma* that offers the only genuine measure by which to determine what belongs in our lives and what does not. As esoteric writer Elizabeth Haich bluntly puts it, "each man must know what God wishes of him." She then points out that "if a person feels called by God to follow a certain path, he will then acquire all possible means to follow that path" (p. 95). Thus does "the call compel the answer."

The God to which she refers, however, cannot be known through doctrine alone but manifests interiorly in the form of our "deepest conviction." And it is thus this deep sense of conviction that provides us with the impetus to transform, an impetus that extends beyond the personal desire to experience higher states (because they are pleasant) or to get out of flatland (because it is not). In the end, transformation is not about higher consciousness *per se*; it's about doing whatever brings our personal intentions into alignment with those of the greater Kosmos. For it's then and only then that we feel genuinely fulfilled.

Andrew Cohen has expressed a similar-sounding idea in two of his five teaching tenets, the first of which states that in seeking enlightenment, we need as individuals to want freedom more than anything else. The fifth tenet states that we pursue enlightenment not for ourselves, but for "the sake of the whole." Potentially, this means starting out with a desire for personal freedom but gradually coming to realize that transformation is never just about personal gratification but about some greater purpose.

From my perspective, the fulfillment of *dharma* allows us to do both, for it brings together the unique destiny of the individual with the need of life for our particular contribution. *Dharma* fulfillment is thus never really a *win-lose* scenario (where we either fulfill our own destiny or sacrifice it in order to serve the whole). It is by nature a win-win scenario in which we learn how to relate to life as a partner rather than an adversary.

The only rub here is that I'm not sure this is the way that Tenets 1 and 5 are normally interpreted by those who follow them. When I attended a three-week retreat in 2000 sponsored by Cohen's organization EnlightenNext in Rishikesh, India, where we studied these tenets in depth, many participants (most of them his students) seemed to believe that Tenet 1 is eventually superseded by Tenet 5, such that our personal goals ultimately come to be set aside in favor of superordinate goals.

I found the idea of a trade-off scenario unsettling. From a vertical perspective, it can mean transcendence without inclusion; from a horizontal perspective, it can mean that groups matter more than individuals.

I sought clarification from Cohen in a public discussion, but he didn't answer the question directly. Instead, he posed a hypothetical in which he asked me to imagine myself in some situation in which some act of personal sacrifice (nothing too daunting, as I recall) would benefit others in a big way. Would I make that sacrifice?

Well, there was only one acceptable answer, and I gave it. But what, I wondered, does he really think? That Tenet 5 does in fact trump Tenet 1? Or did he just want to avoid answering in a way that might be used as a justification for ducking out on personal responsibility?

I don't know. What I *do* know is that this interchange made me think deeply for the next several years about the relationship between our individual destiny and the larger purposes of life—and to ultimately arrive at the conclusion that there is no such thing as a tradeoff between the two: what is good for the individual is good for the group, and vice-versa.

What actually determines the rightness of our actions is *how attuned we are to the need of the moment.* Because it is that need which determines "right action." There are moments when right action means asserting our needs as individuals and moments when it means allowing the needs of others (or the needs of life) to take priority. From this perspective, the Golden Rule might be stated as "Be attuned!"

This principle of attunement is beautifully illustrated in my two favorite Star Trek films, *The Wrath of Khan* (2002) and *The Search for Spock* (2004). In the first film, Spock sacrifices his life in order to save the crew of the Enterprise; as he lays dying, he pragmatically observes to Kirk that "the needs of the many outweigh the needs of the few." In the second film, the Enterprise crew (realizing at some point that Spock's soul can potentially re-animate his body) goes to extraordinary lengths to retrieve the sealed capsule containing the body and to once again re-connect it to his soul, making many personal sacrifices in the process. When Spock asks why they did it, Kirk replies, "Sometimes the needs of the few outweigh the needs of the many."

This pair of films sends a powerful message: that *right action cannot ultimately be determined by any predetermined rule*, because life is too dynamic for that. Circumstances arise that offer opportunities for growth, opportunities that we can learn to recognize and grasp, if we so chose. When we choose rightly, our actions invite reciprocation, such that the unselfish act of one party may encourage others to respond in kind.

But the sacredness of a genuinely sacrificial act arises out of its voluntary nature. Because personal sacrifice is never an obligation but an act of generosity that invites (but does not demand) reciprocation. As such, it represents an expansion of consciousness, such that our personal "needs" are perceived to include the needs of others, such that it becomes natural to think of their welfare as an extension our own. And this is why those whom we call heros never see themselves as exceptional: because their acts always flow out of this expanded sense of concern, such that the child drowning in an icy river evokes their desire to save the *child*, not to save *themselves*.

If we try to save our own arm or leg from injury, this is not considered to be a heroic act; similarly, if we care about others the way we care about ourselves, then we are moti-vated to look out for them as we would for ourselves. This kind of caring does not pre-suppose a denial of self but an *extension* of self (i.e., our sense of self), a form of real life transcendence-and-inclusion. The more we expand our sense of self, the more we promote a "pay-it-forward" ethos that ripples outwards into the Kosmos. Thus, from my perspective, the goal of an integrally-oriented life is never to deny the self but always to integrate it—so that we can reconcile the opposites within our nature.

Visually, this process of moving from partial awareness to a more integrated view can be depicted as the process we engage in when confronted with a "stereogrammatic ("Magic Eye") image (Fig. 13-2).[4] Initially, the image looks flat and uninteresting, like a pattern of dots bereft of meaning. But if we learn how to look at the image—a process that is hard to describe but which involves "relaxing our gaze"—a new three-dimensional image begins to emerge, an image that is not only 3D in its shape but which seems luminous and somehow scintillating with energy.

Not many people immediately grasp how to "see" the image in a way that creates the 3D effect; most of us find it difficult. But once we catch on, it becomes easy; the image pops out every time. And what do we come to realize? *That the image has been there all the time*—but we can only perceive it after we learn how to *see*.

This is what discovering the *dharma* is like: learning how to look at life in a way that allows us to see what really matters. There are some people who seem to do this intuitively; they instinctively move through life knowing pretty much where to go and what to do. But many of us struggle to get in sync with

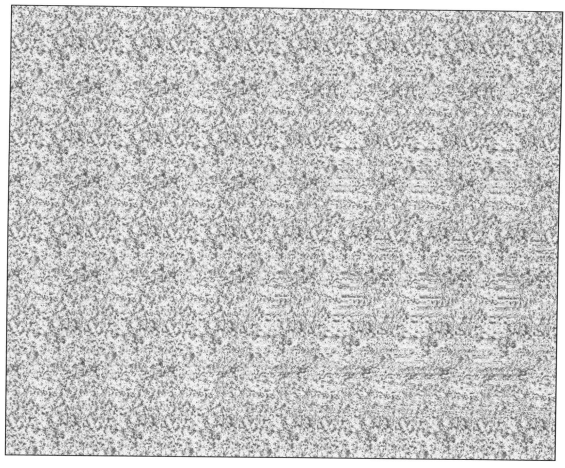

Fig. 13-2. Stereogram example. Can you see the hidden figure?

life, bumbling around a lot and skinning our shins a lot in the process!

That was me, as related in Chapter 1. For years, I lived in a state of disconnect between myself and life. One of my main misapprehensions was that I had to be a "well-rounded person"—that I had to be good at everything to be worth anything. So I spent an inordinate amount of time trying to make myself into the kind of person that I saw as well-rounded. Then one day, I had a dream (previously related in my *Archetypes* book).

The dream was about taking care of books; the level of care needed was expressed in terms of a grade I needed to earn. Some of the books needed very special (A+) handling; others needed enough care to earn a B or even a C. There were even books that could almost be entirely neglected; a mere D would suffice.

But what mattered was that I correctly identified which books were which: that I gave high priority to the "A" books and low priority to the "D" books.

Previously, I had unconsciously thought that doing pretty well (say, earning a B- or C+) in most areas of life would be enough. But this dream was telling me that life has little or nothing to do with "satisficing" (doing okay at a lot of things but excelling at none of them). It has to do with pursuing the things that matter to *me*, given my unique nature and circumstances in life. And what matters to me is not the same as what matters to my parents, my neighbors, or anybody else. That's why I had gotten confused: I was trying to be "all things to all people" and was losing myself in the process.

But the dream also helped me realize that this tactic of satisficing was also a way to avoid facing my fear of failure. For as long as I didn't fully invest myself in my dreams, it wouldn't really matter if I failed. But what if I really went for it—really invested myself in my dreams—and then failed? That would be awful! But getting in touch with the "awful truth" helped me pinpoint my fears, which was a step in the right direction.

I had another significant dream just before embarking on a new spiritual path. This dream too was about books. I was in a magnificent library; across the room was a wizard whose face I could not see. I awoke realizing that my path had something to do with that library, but I didn't know what. Some years later, I began writing books and articles about the enneagram which necessitated a lot of study—and perhaps a little wizardly assistance from sources I could not fully see.

The first dream alerted me to my mistaken belief that life is about avoiding mistakes; the second obliquely pointed to my future work as a writer, work that seems to be central to my *dharma*.[5] These dreams helped me separate the wheat from the chaff in my life. They also helped me see that what is wheat to me may be chaff to somebody else and vice-versa—that to be integrated does not mean seeking to do a little bit of everything but to do the *right things* from an integrated perspective.

What these dreams did not reveal—or at least not in detail—was the core motivation (i.e., the Type 4 perspective) that informs my writing. It was only when I found the enneagram that I realized why I was so drawn to meaning-making systems and creative work: because it is innate to my temperament. And this understanding helped me bring my inner self into alignment with my outer work, so that I could work from a place of greater authenticity.

But I could not have stuck with the enneagram had I not found an approach that gave me an integrally-oriented way of working with the nine types: Wilber's Integral Operating System. Wilber's approach provided the framework I needed at exactly the time that I needed it. And that is how I came to work interactively with both systems and to write about those interactions in my books and articles.

The focus on *dharma* emerged as I realized that the only way I could unreservedly support ego development is for the purpose of achieving holarchic balance. For the ego, like all holons, can only fulfill its purpose in life when it can strike a balance between self-transcendence (responsiveness to higher levels) and self-assertiveness (responsibility for lower levels). When it functions holarchically, it becomes integrated. And the integrated ego becomes the vehicle for *dharma* fulfillment.

But to embrace the *dharma* is seldom easy. It means accepting everything about it, not just the parts we like. While it may be inspiring to speak of a sacred calling, it can nonetheless bring us face to face with our greatest fears and avoidances. That's why it can seem pretty scary.

But it's interesting how close the word *scared* is to the word *sacred*. They're anagrams. Just by moving one little letter, we transform fear into faith—and faith can move mountains.

Notes

1. See Peter Brooks' beautifully choreographed film *Meetings with Remarkable Men* (1997) to view both examples of the movements and an account of Gurdjieff's lifelong search for truth.

2. Interestingly, the process enneagram, like Wilber's system, is progressively-oriented. This may be why there is not as much overlap between people in the process and personality enneagram communities as we might expect—because the Gurdjieff (Fourth Way) groups that work with the enneagram focus on the role of the nine points in a transformational process. This is a very different than seeing them as points of fixation.

3. While the process enneagram emphasizes evolutionary change via cyclical progression, it does not lack the ability to describe revolutionary shifts, as well. These kinds of shifts tend to be associated with its three shock points, which constitute places of discontinuity where we must leap from one level to another to continue our journey (see Chapter 6). But much of the time, these leaps are small, like a two-foot leap we make to clear a small stream. However, it is these ordinary, everyday leaps that prepare us for the much greater leaps necessary to produce revolutionary shifts in consciousness—the kind that completely change our lives.

4. Image generated at www.easystereogram-builder.com/3d-stereogram-maker.aspx.

5. When I contemplated writing my first book, *The Positive Enneagram*, I had serious misgivings about whether the time was ripe for such a project. Then one night, I dreamed I was in a noisy office where people were engaged in all sorts of important activities. But my office was apart from all the hubbub, and consisted of a little room with a table. On the table, there was one item: my book. This dream gave me the confidence to proceed.

EPILOGUE

MY PURPOSE IN WRITING THIS BOOK was to compile all the individual articles I'd written linking the enneagram and Wilber's IOS into a single book. Although I have indeed included all that material, the final product turned out to be more than the sum of its parts.

The writing of the book took me on a journey I did not anticipate, a journey that compelled me to spend much longer in the writing phase than I'd originally planned. There were three reasons for this.

The first was that I felt compelled to do a lot more research on Wilber's ideas than I had originally done in order to make sure that I knew his material pretty well (I say "pretty well," rather than "thoroughly," because given the depth and breadth of his work, I don't know that I'll ever be 100% sure that there's not some obscure endnote containing "buried treasure" or answers to my unanswered questions; such is the scope of Wilber's writing).

The second was that when I actually went to integrate the ideas—looking for interrelationships both between the two enneagrams and between the enneagram(s) and IOS—these interactions turned out to be extremely complex; Chapter 8 alone took me six months to complete (and Chapters 9 and 10 weren't much bet-

ter)! First I had to work out what I wanted to say and then devise a way to convey the ideas that was relatively straightforward. Given the nature of the material, this was not easy.

Third—and most challenging—was the fact that once I got really deep into the analysis, I encountered both unexpected problems and realizations that forced me to do more than simply compile the material generated in previous articles.

For example, differences in Wilber's and Koestler's approach to holon theory meant that I had to choose one and justify the choice in a convincing way (see Chapter 2). Another example concerns my comparison of two transformational models (IOS vs the process enneagram), which made me realize that the latter offered a more compelling model of the transformational process—a realization that was impossible to ignore and which therefore became incorporated into my discussion of transformation in Chapters 8 and 9. A third example concerns the three implications of pairing the personality enneagram with Wilber's IOS which are discussed in Chapter 10: that (a) IOS hori-zones = enneagram types; (b) psychic structures are not just vertical but horizontal; and (c) Wilber's IOS can potentially be described by reference to only four elements. These are controversial ideas that may be hard to accept from an Integral point of view.

However, the intention in this book was always to link IOS with the enneagram, not to critique Wilber's work *per se*, which I highly respect (despite his taste for invective, which is not mine).

But as a theorist, I had to take the ideas that flowed out of my work and find a way to intelligently incorporate them. The fact that I ended up suggesting a couple of significant changes to integral theory takes away nothing from my admiration for Wilber as a theorist; he himself has been reworking and revising his ideas for four decades.

One of the biggest surprises was how the book came to focus so much on immanent spirituality: on inclusion, integration, and immanence. This was not really part of the plan, either, when I started out; it just sort of happened as I went along, somehow spiraling out of the creative process. It's only now, towards the end, that I realize why this theme arises again and again: because without a deep, creative, and passionate involvement in embodied living, material life turns into flatland and spiritual life becomes just another way of refusing to feel the pain. If so, then what does it really mean to transform? What real purpose does it serve?

Many inner doors opened for me during the writing of this book. These openings made me realize how passionately committed I am to a more feminine and embodied approach to transformation. It's not that I want to replace transcendence with immanence, because I've never seen them as opposites. It's just that the deeper I delve into this material, the more I see the necessity of dignifying the role of embodied spirituality, the necessity of making it an equal partner with transcendent spirituality. For me, this is not a belief but a discovery.

It is discoveries like this that make the writing process worthwhile for the writer: whatever your original idea, it inevitably changes when you set pen to paper. This is especially true when generating a book that attempts to mesh two complex systems. When the final image comes together, it's a "just so" moment. But until you get there, you don't quite know where you're headed or what it will take to arrive.

These ideas aren't set in stone. They're just ideas. But I love ideas, so I hope that love will give them wings.

I want to end with the image of an open door, not fully open but slightly ajar. What will happen if you open it and walk through? Close your eyes and see.

Appendixes

Appendix A
Resources for Self-discovery

Books that explore individual differences, especially in terms of life themes, life paths, personality types, or career paths, can be useful for helping people get a sense of what kinds of paths are associated with different ways of being in the world. Caroline Myss' *Sacred Contracts* provides an excellent introduction to focusing on life from a *dharmic* perspective, as well as specific methodologies for understanding the archetypes that are influential in our lives.[1]

Sylvia Browne's *Adventures of a Psychic* (1990) is similarly useful for its list of 45 potential life themes based on Browne's work with past life regressions. Whether or not you believe in reincarnation, the themes themselves are compelling, providing any reader with ample food for thought.[2]

Psychological aptitude tests such as the Kuder Test or Strong-Campbell Interest Inventory can be useful for identifying work-related aptitudes and ruling out unsuitable options. When I initially took the Kuder in high school, I was an agnostic with little self-insight and was shocked that the highest score for interest was for "religious educator"—which made me think the test was crazy. Decades later, I realized that this was one instance where the test unearthed an interest in spirituality that I had yet to discover myself.

The MBTI (Myers-Briggs Type Indicator), which identifies 16 personality types from a Jungian point of view, has been used extensively to look empirically at the relationship between personality and career.[3] It helped me understand why I find office work (and any sort of regimentation) very difficult, relieving me of the burden of trying too hard to "fit a square peg in a round hole."

But of all the systems I used for self-assessment, I found the enneagram the most useful, due to both its depth and flexibility. This is probably because the enneagram is not the product of some psychologist's imagination, but is rooted in ancient teachings about human nature and transformation. Thus, it is particularly helpful for looking at the link between personality and *dharma*, because its nine personality types are based on inner motivation, not just outer behavior.

Elizabeth Wagele's *The Career Within You: How to Find the Perfect Job for Your Personality* (2009) explores the relationship between the nine enneagram types and various career paths. It's very detailed in scope and offers excellent insights to people trying to figure out how to find a career that's a good match for their type-related goals and talents.

My second book, *Archetypes of the Enneagram: Exploring the Life Themes of the 27 Subtypes from the Perspective of Soul* (2010), explores some of the same territory but from a less specific and more transformationally-oriented perspective. It focuses on the relationship between the 27 subtypes and our *dharma* in life,[4] using examples from film and TV to explore the life paths/life themes associated with each subtype. It relies mainly on the insights of Jungian psychology (and other soul-oriented depth psychologies) to offer an alternative perspective on the nature of the nine types. And it not only lists the 27 life paths we can follow (along with their many variants), but provides an assessment tool at the end for life path discovery.

Notes

1. My only reservation about Myss' work is the way in which she approaches both her material and her reader, in that she presents her ideas as though they are facts and addresses her reader as though he or she is Myss' student (and perhaps a recalcitrant student, at that!). To get the most out of Myss' material, I find I have to overlook the tone and focus on the ideas, which are quite useful.

2. See Chapter 10, "Why Am I Here?", especially pp. 190–201.

3. See especially *Gifts Differing*, by Isabel Briggs Myers with Peter Myers. Palo Alto: Consulting Psychologists Press, 1980.

4. Each of the nine types can be broken down into three variants—self-preservation, sexual, and social—each of which has a somewhat different perspective on life. *Self-preservation types* tend to be cautious, solitary, and independent-minded; *sexual types* tend to be spontaneous, volatile, and intense; and *social types* tend to be relationally-oriented, status conscious, and diplomatic (see Chapter 3).

APPENDIX B

ARTHUR KOESTLER'S HOLARCHIC TENETS

SOME GENERAL PROPERTIES OF SELF-REGULATING OPEN HIERARCHIC ORDER (1969)

THE FOLLOWING TEXT is the Appendix to *Beyond Reductionism* (1969), on the Alpbach Symposium, edited by Arthur Koestler and J. R. Smythies.

1. THE HOLON

1.1 The organism in its structural aspect is not an aggregation of elementary parts, and in its functional aspects not a chain of elementary units of behaviour.

1.2 The organism is to be regarded as a multi-leveled hierarchy of semi-autonomous sub-wholes, branching into sub-wholes of a lower order, and so on. Sub-wholes on any level of the hierarchy are referred to as holons.

1.3 Parts and wholes in an absolute sense do not exist in the domains of life. The concept of the holon is intended to reconcile the atomistic and holistic approaches.

1.4 Biological holons are self-regulating open systems which display both the autonomous properties of wholes and the dependent properties of parts. This dichotomy is present on every level of every type of hierarchic organization, and is referred to as the "Janus phenomenon."

1.5 More generally, the term "holon" may be applied to any stable biological or social sub-whole which displays rule-governed behaviour and/or structural Gestalt-constancy. Thus organelles and homologous organs are evolutionary holons; morphogenetic fields are ontogenetic holons; the ethologist's "fixed action-patterns" and the sub-routines of acquired skills are behavioural holons; phonemes, morphemes, words, phrases are linguistic holons; individuals, families, tribes, nations are social holons.

2. DISSECTIBILITY

2.1 Hierarchies are "dissectible" into their constituent branches, on which the holons form the nodes; the branching lines represent the channels of communication and control.

2.2 The number of levels which a hierarchy comprises is a measure of its "depth", and the number of holons on any given level is called its "span" (Herbert Simon).

3. RULES AND STRATEGIES

3.1 Functional holons are governed by fixed sets of rules and display more or less flexible strategies.

3.2 The rules - referred to as the system's canon - determine its invariant properties, its structural configuration and/or functional pattern.

3.3 While the canon defines the permissible steps in the holon's activity, the strategic selection of the actual step among permissible choices is guided by the contingencies of the environment.

3.4 The canon determines the rules of the game, strategy decides the course of the game.

3.5 The evolutionary process plays variations on a limited number of canonical themes. The constraints imposed by the evolutionary canon are illustrated by the phenomena of homology, homeoplasy, parallelism, convergence and the *loi du balancement* (Geoffroy de St. Hilaire).

3.6 In ontogeny, the holons at successive levels represent successive stages in the development of tissues. At each step in the process of differentiation, the genetic canon imposes further constraints on the holon's developmental potentials, but it retains sufficient flexibility to follow one or another alternative developmental pathway, within the range of its competence, guided by the contingencies of the environment.

3.7 Structurally, the mature organism is a hierarchy of parts within parts. Its "dissectibility" and the relative autonomy of its constituent holons are demonstrated by transplant surgery.

3.8 Functionally, the behaviour of organisms is governed by "rules of the game" which account for its coherence, stability and specific pattern.

3.9 Skills, whether inborn or acquired, are functional hierarchies, with sub-skills as holons, governed by sub-rules.

4. INTEGRATION AND SELF-ASSERTION

4.1 Every holon has the dual tendency to preserve and assert its individuality as a quasi-autonomous whole; and to function as an integrated part of an (existing or evolving) larger whole. This polarity between the Self-Assertive (S-A) and Integrative (INT) tendencies is inherent in the concept of hierarchic order; and a universal characteristic of life.

The S-A tendencies are the dynamic expression of the holon's wholeness, the INT tendencies of its partness.

4.2 An analogous polarity is found in the interplay of cohesive and separative forces in stable inorganic systems, from atoms to galaxies.

4.3 The most general manifestation of the INT tendencies is the reversal of the Second Law of Thermodynamics in open systems feeding on negative entropy (Erwin Schrödinger), and the evolutionary trend towards "spontaneously developing states of greater heterogeneity and complexity" (C. J. Herrick).

4.4 Its specific manifestations on different levels range from the symbiosis of organelles and colonial animals, through the cohesive forces in herds and flocks, to the integrative bonds in insect states and Primate societies. The complementary manifestations of the S-A tendencies are competition, individualism, and the separative forces of tribalism, nationalism, etc.

4.5 In ontogeny, the polarity is reflected in the docility and determination of growing tissues.

4.6 In adult behaviour, the self-assertive tendency of functional holons is reflected in the stubbornness of instinct rituals (fixed action-patterns), of acquired habits (handwriting, spoken accent), and in the stereotyped routines of thought; the integrative tendency is reflected in flexible adaptations, improvisations, and creative acts which initiate new forms of behaviour.

4.7 Under conditions of stress, the S-A tendency is manifested in the aggressive-defensive, adrenergic type of emotions, the INT tendency in the self-transcending (participatory, identificatory) type of emotions.

4.8 In social behaviour, the canon of a social holon represents not only constraints imposed on its actions, but also embodies maxims of conduct, moral imperatives and systems of value.

5. Triggers and scanners

5.1 Output hierarchies generally operate on the trigger-release principle, where a relatively simple, implicit or coded signal releases complex, preset mechanisms.

5.2 In phylogeny, a favourable gene-mutation may, through homeorhesis (Conrad Waddington) affect the development of a whole organ in a harmonious way.

5.3 In ontogeny, chemical triggers (enzymes, inducers, hormones) release the genetic potentials of differentiating tissues.

5.4 In instinctive behaviour, sign-releasers of a simple kind trigger off Innate Releasive Mechanisms (Lorenz).

5.5 In the performance of learnt skills, including verbal skills, a generalized implicit command is spelled out in explicit terms on successive lower echelons which, once triggered into action, activate their sub-units in the appropriate strategic order, guided by feedbacks.

5.6 A holon on the n level of an output-hierarchy is represented on the (n + 1) level as a unit, and triggered into action as a unit. A holon, in other words, is a system of relata which is represented on the next higher level as a relatum.

5.7 In social hierarchies (military, administrative), the same principles apply.

5.8 Input hierarchies operate on the reverse principle; instead of triggers, they are equipped with "filter"-type devices (scanners, "resonators", classifiers) which strip the input of noise, abstract and digest its relevant contents, according to that particular hierarchy's criteria of relevance. "Filters" operate on every echelon through which the flow of information must pass on its ascent from periphery to centre, in social hierarchies and in the nervous system.

5.9 Triggers convert coded signals into complex output patterns. Filters convert complex input patterns into coded signals. The former may be compared to digital-to-analogue converters, the latter to analogue-to-digital converters (Miller, G. A., Galanter, E. and Pribram, K. H., *Plans and the Structure of Behaviour*, 1960).

5.10 In perceptual hierarchies, filtering devices range from habituation and the efferent control of receptors, through the constancy phenomena, to pattern-recognition in space or time, and to the decoding of linguistic and other forms of meaning.

5.11 Output hierarchies spell, concretize, particularize. Input hierarchies digest, abstract, generalize.

6. Arborization and reticulation

6.1 Hierarchies can be regarded as "vertically" arborizing structures whose branches interlock with those of other hierarchies at a multiplicity of levels and form "horizontal" networks: arborization and reticulation are complementary principles in the architecture of organisms and societies.

6.2 Conscious experience is enriched by the cooperation of several perceptual hierarchies in different sense-modalities, and within the same sense-modality.

6.3 Abstractive memories are stored in skeletonized form, stripped of irrelevant detail, according to the criteria of relevance of each perceptual hierarchy.

6.4 Vivid details of quasi-eidetic clarity are stored owing to their emotive relevance.

6.5 The impoverishment of experience in memory is counteracted to some extent by the cooperation in recall of different perceptual hierarchies with different criteria of relevance.

6.6 In sensory-motor coordination, local reflexes are short-cuts on the lowest level, like loops connecting traffic streams moving in opposite directions on a highway.

6.7 Skilled sensory-motor routines operate on higher levels through networks of proprioceptive and exteroceptive feedback loops within loops, which function as servo-mechanisms and keep the rider on his bicycle in a state of self-regulating, kinetic homeostasis.

6.8 While in S-R theory the contingencies of environment determine behaviour, in O.H.S. theory they merely guide, correct and stabilize pre-existing patterns of behaviour (P. Weiss).

6.9 While sensory feedbacks guide motor activities, perception in its turn is dependent on these activities, such as the various scanning motions of the eye, or the humming of a tune in aid of its auditory recall. The perceptual and motor hierarchies are so intimately co-operating on every level that to draw a categorical distinction between "stimuli" and "responses" becomes meaningless; they have become "aspects of feed-back loops" (Miller et al.).

6.10 Organisms and societies operate in a hierarchy of environments, from the local environment of each holon to the "total field", which may include imaginary environments derived from extrapolation in space and time.

7. Regulation channels

7.1 The higher echelons in a hierarchy are not normally in direct communication with lowly ones, and vice versa; signals are transmitted through "regulation channels", one step at a time.

7.2 The pseudo-explanations of verbal behaviour and other human skills as the manipulation of words, or the chaining of operants, leaves a void between the apex of the hierarchy and its terminal branches, between thinking and spelling.

7.3 The short-circuiting of intermediary levels by directing conscious attention at processes which otherwise function automatically, tends to cause disturbances ranging from awkwardness to psychosomatic disorders.

8. Mechanization and freedom

8.1 Holons on successively higher levels of the hierarchy show increasingly complex, more flexible and less predictable patterns of activity, while on successive lower levels we find increasingly mechanized, stereotyped and predictable patterns.

8.2 All skills, whether innate or acquired, tend with increasing practice to become automatized routines. This process can be described as the continual transformation of "mental" into "mechanical" activities.

8.3 Other things being equal, a monotonous environment facilitates mechanization.

8.4 Conversely, new or unexpected contingencies require decisions to be referred to higher levels of the hierarchy, an upward shift of controls from "mechanical" to "mindful" activities.

8.5 Each upward shift is reflected by a more vivid and precise consciousness of the ongoing activity; and, since the variety of alternative choices increases with the increasing complexity on higher levels, each upward shift is accompanied by the subjective experience of freedom of decision.

8.6 The hierarchic approach replaces dualistic theories by a serialistic hypothesis in which "mental" and "mechanical" appear as relative attributes of a unitary process, the dominance of one or the other depending on changes in the level of control of ongoing operations.

8.7 Consciousness appears as an emergent quality in phylogeny and ontogeny, which, from primitive beginnings, evolves towards more complex and precise states. It is the highest manifestation of the Integrative Tendency (4.3) to extract order out of disorder, and information out of noise.

8.8 The self can never be completely represented in its own awareness, nor can its actions be completely predicted by any conceivable information-processing device. Both attempts lead to infinite regress.

9. EQUILIBRIUM AND DISORDER

9.1 An organism or society is said to be in dynamic equilibrium if the S.A. and INT tendencies of its holons counter-balance each other.

9.2 The term "equilibrium" in a hierarchic system does not refer to relations between parts on the same level, but to the relation between part and whole (the whole being represented by the agency which controls the part from the next higher level).

9.3 Organisms live by transactions with their environment. Under normal conditions, the stresses set up in the holons involved in the transaction are of a transitory nature, and equilibrium will be restored on its completion.

9.4 If the challenge to the organism exceeds a critical limit, the balance may be upset, the over-excited holon may tend to get out of control, and to assert itself to the detriment of the whole, or monopolize its functions - whether the holon be an organ, a cognitive structure (idée fixe), an individual, or a social group. The same may happen if the coordinate powers of the whole are so weakened that it is no longer able to control its parts (C. M. Child).

9.5 The opposite type of disorder occurs when the power of the whole over its parts erodes their autonomy and individuality. This may lead to a regression of the INT tendencies from mature forms of social integration to primitive forms of identification and to the quasi-hypnotic phenomena of group psychology.

9.6 The process of identification may arouse vicarious emotions of the aggressive type.

9.7 The rules of conduct of a social holon are not reducible to the rules of conduct of its members.

9.8 The egotism of the social holon feeds on the altruism of its members.

10. REGENERATION

10.1 Critical challenges to an organism or society can produce degenerative or regenerative effects.

10.2 The regenerative potential of organisms and societies manifests itself in fluctuations from the highest level of integration down to earlier, more primitive levels, and up again to a new, modified pattern. Processes of this type seem to play a major part in biological and mental evolution, and are symbolized in the universal death-and-rebirth motive in mythology.

APPENDIX C
COMPARING VERTICAL SCALES

IN CHAPTER 11, I discussed the parallels between Wilber's nine-level Spectrum Model, the nine-level process enneagram, and the nine point-of-view personality enneagram. I also noted that I see the process enneagram as the basis for many developmental models, e.g., Jane Loevinger's nine-level ego developmental model, Suzanne Cook-Greuter's more recent modification of that model, as well as personality enneagram theorists Don Riso and Russ Hudson's Strata model to uncovering the true self.[1] For a discussion of the Strata approach in the context of my approach to enneagram work, see my article, "Personality, Process, & Levels of Development," originally published in the *Enneagram Monthly* (Dec. 2011–Jan. 2012; now available on my website (www.enneagramdimensions.net).[2]

Most of the discussion in this appendix centers on the correspondence between characteristics of each point on the enneagram and each level of ego development described by the Loevinger/Cook-Greuter models; see Table C-1. There is another table (C-2) at the end that includes all six approaches, for ease of comparison.

The following discussion comparing the two approaches (the enneagram and Loevinger/Cook-Greuter) is brief because to go into greater depth would be beyond the scope of this book, which is primarily designed to link the enneagram with Wilber's IOS. This appendix is included in part because the Loevinger/Cook-Greuter approach is becoming very influential in integral work. So the goal here is to provide at least a bare-bones approach for linking the enneagram with these related developmental models.

One thing to note is that there are two ways to conceptualize a developmental model: using an (a) cyclical approach or (b) linear approach. The former focuses on the transformational processes and their repetitive nature, with secondary emphasis on the stages within each cycle; the latter focuses more on how we "climb the ladder" from stage to stage (and how to tell one stage from another).

The process enneagram is primarily a cyclical model, in that it invites us to look at each of its nine points from a cyclical perspective (as a temporary state through which we pass during a repeated transformational cycle,

TABLE C-1. PARALLELS BETWEEN ENNEAGRAM & LOEVINGER/COOK-GREUTER APPROACH.

		ENNEAGRAM		LOEVINGER/COOK-GREUTER	
		Process Stages	**Personality Challenges**	**Loevinger's Nine Levels**	**Cook-Greuter's Nine Levels**
Transpersonal	9	Final synthesis	Presence & integration	Integration	Unity
	8	Unified awareness	Mastery & leadership	Autonomy	Construct-awareness, Alchemy
	7	Expanded awareness	Freedom within limits	Individualism	Individualism, Pluralism
Personal	6	Fear & intuition	Transmuting fear into trust	Conscientiousness	Conscientiousness
	5	Cognition	Understanding	Self-consciousness, Conscientiousness	Self-consciousness, Conscientiousness
	4	Self-identity	"Role me vs real me"	Self-awareness	Self-consciousness
Pre-personal	3	Competency	Concrete adaptation	Self-protectiveness/ Conformity	Conformity
	2	Connecting	Bonding & self-mirroring	Impulsiveness	Impulsiveness
	1	Orientation	Making sense of reality	Pre-social	Infancy

such as a 24-hour day). We can also use it to identify structure-stages in development (i.e., permanent changes that occur over a lifetime). However, the geometry encourages "thinking cyclically" rather than "thinking vertically."

The Loevinger/Cook-Greuter scales are more naturally linear in nature, in that they present us with a nine vertically-arranged structure-stages, each of which describes an irreversible level of ego development. The emphasis is on (a) identifying the stages and (b) promoting upward advancement. In terms of practical applications, the focus of those who employ these scales is usually on organizational management and leadership (and hence, on ego development during adulthood; see, e.g., Maureen Metcalf & Mark Palmer's *Innovative Leadership Fieldbook* (2011) for a discussion.)[3] These models do, however, cover the entire gamut of ego development, from infancy onwards, as we can see in Tables C-1 and C-2. In the discussion below, both models are mapped onto the process enneagram for purposes of comparison.

Point by Point Comparison

At *Point 1* on the process enneagram, we are getting oriented to the world, developing standards that allow us to evaluate what the world (or a given transformational cycle) is about. On both the Loevinger and Cook-Greuter models, it points to the earliest stage of development, the point at which we have yet to internalize external standards of value.

At *Point 2* on the process enneagram, having begun the orientation process, we want to bond, both for the sake of comfort and in order to see ourselves emotionally mirrored in others; we begin to acquire "emotional intelligence." According to Loevinger/Cook-

Greuter, this is the impulsive phase, where our emotional impulses are active but we have not yet learned to develop self-control. In both cases, this stage involves learning how to work with emotions and develop healthy relations with others, especially those close to us.

At *Point 3* on the process enneagram, we are developing competencies and receiving new information from the outer world. The focus is on adaptation to outer standards and the development of a cohesive ego self able to operate in a social environment. According to Loevinger/Cook-Greuter, it is where we find the "conformist"; Loevinger also speaks of a self-protective stage that I would broadly associate with the early stages of Point 3, where an individual is first coming to grips with the bigger world outside the family. The term "conformist" would not be used in personality enneagram circles; however, everyone would recognize this appellation as associated with the Point 3 (who are usually more politely called Achievers). But the impetus is the same: to adapt to and succeed within the existing social environment.

At *Point 4* on the process enneagram, we are getting fully (emotionally) committed to whatever we are involved in—looking beyond surfaces to see what lies beneath. According to Loevinger/Cook-Greuter, it is where we become self-aware (Loevinger) or self-conscious (Cook-Greuter). Interestingly, those at Point 4 on the personality enneagram are hyperaware of the self and therefore self-conscious both in the sense of "self-aware" and "emotionally naked."

At *Point 5* on the process enneagram, we shift from self-focus and deep self-awareness in the emotional sense to an entirely new awareness in which life is foregrounded and the self is backgrounded. So it's a momentous shift—one that requires us to re-locate the self in relation to everything else, which is why it is associated with a self that is detached from the social world: the detachment is what enables us to eventually reattach at a higher (more conscientious, i.e., humanitarian) level. But its very nature makes it hard to see from either a personal or social point of view. And this is why it may not be clearly represented on the Loevinger/Cook-Greuter scale: because this stage is more like a withdrawal from self rather than the assertion of self.

Point 6 represents a reassertion of self but within the larger context of community—and the understanding that community has a valid claim on our time, resources, and emotional energy. On the Loevinger/Cook-Greuter scale, it represents the emergence of genuine conscientiousness; on the enneagram, interestingly enough, if we can't meet the challenge, we will likely fall back into conformity (connecting point to Three). To the extent that this challenge is met, it paves the way for more open, spontaneous ways of relating at Point 7.

Loevinger/Cook-Greuter associate both objectivity and conscientiousness with the same stage, but I would argue (using both the personality and process enneagrams as a basis) that although they are related, they are two separate stages, with subjective self-consciousness emerging first (Point 4) followed by objective self-consciousness (Point 5) followed by a sense of duty, obligation, or service at Point 6.

As discussed in both Chapters 7 and 8, Points 4–6 on the process enneagram are particularly associated with the process of individuation and transformation, i.e., moving from emotional independence at Point 4 to intellectual independence at Point 5 to the potential for complete individuation at Point 6, in the sense that Point 6 is the place where we either accept who we really are (once and for all) or fall back into a conventionalized persona (basically regressing to Point 3).

At *Point 7* on the process enneagram, if we come to terms with the issues at Point 6, we find ourselves in a space of expanded awareness and new possibilities for growth. According to Loevinger, we become an individualist, which is associated with freedom and expansion; according to Cook-Greuter, we become pluralistic in orientation—just like Type 7 on the personality enneagram!

At *Point 8* on the process enneagram, we fully embody all that we are or have ever been at any point in life; this point represents the culmination of the current cycle of transformation. According to Loevinger, it is where we achieve true autonomy; according to Cook-Greuter, it is where we find the "construct-aware" strategists or alchemists (individuals who act as catalysts or transformers). "Strategist" is a word often used to describe Eights on the personality enneagram; "alchemist" would be an equally apt term, considering their natural leadership and mastery.

At *Point 9* on the process enneagram, we move beyond the current cycle (or lifetime) to become part of something larger, more universal or integrative. Loevinger describes this as the integrated phase of development while Cook-Greuter describes it in terms of unitive consciousness, and equates it with acceptance, interconnectedness, and timelessness.

TABLE C-2. PARALLELS BETWEEN SIX DEVELOPMENTAL MODELS.

	Process Enneagram Stages	Personality Enneagram Challenges	Wilber's Stages/Levels	Loevinger's Levels	Cook-Greuter's Levels	Riso-Hudson Strata Model
9	Final synthesis	Presence & integration	Causal	Integration	Unity	Universal Being
8	Unified awareness	Mastery & leadership	Subtle	Autonomy	Construct-awareness	Personal Being
7	Expanded awareness	Freedom within limits	Psychic	Individualism	Individualism, Pluralism	The Void
6	Fear & intuition	Transmuting fear into trust	Vision-logic	Conscientiousness	Conscientiousness	Dark Night of the Soul
5	Cognition	Understanding	Formal-reflexive mind	Self-consciousness, Conscientiousness	Self-consciousness, Conscientiousness	Libidinal energies
4	Self-identity	"Role me vs real me"	Script/role thinking	Self-awareness	Self-consciousness	Underlying affects
3	Competency	Concrete adaptation	Representational-mind	Self-protectiveness/ Conformity	Conformity	Motivations
2	Connecting	Bonding & self-mirroring	Emotional-sexual	Impulsiveness	Impulsiveness	Behavior
1	Orientation	Category definition	Sensori-physical	Pre-social	Infancy	Habitual attitudes

Transpersonal (9, 8, 7) — Personal (6, 5, 4) — Pre-personal (3, 2, 1)

Such a brief analysis cannot really do justice to the possible parallels between the process enneagram and these two related developmental models. But it can serve to open the door to future explorations.

Notes

1.   The Riso-Hudson Strata model is described most fully on pp. 372–377 in Riso and Hudson's *Wisdom of the Enneagram* (1999). Briefly, it delineates the process by which we move from lack of awareness regarding our true nature to an illumined state of awareness. Because it describes the stages through which we pass as our awareness develops, it is a true hierarchical model that can be compared to other models describing the development of human consciousness, as shown in Table C-2.

2.   "Personality, Process, & Levels of Development" served as the basis for the discussion in the last part of Chapter 11.

3.   The information on Loevinger's nine stages is derived from Wikipedia and "Exceptional Maturity of Personality: An Emerging Field," by Angela H. Pfaffenberger and Paul W. Marko, available at http://www.sunypress.edu/pdf/62108.pdf; accessed 11-15-12; the information on Cook-Greuter's stages comes from Cook-Greuter's "Ego Development: Nine Levels of Increasing Embrace," available from http://www.cook-greuter.com/9%20levels%20of%20increasing%20embrace%20update%201%2007.pdf; accessed 11-15-12.

APPENDIX D

LINES OF DEVELOPMENT AT EACH ENNEAGRAM POINT

CHAPTER 11 INCLUDES a discussion of how we might link the nine enneagram points of view with various lines of development, especially (but not exclusively) those listed by Wilber at the end of *Integral Psychology* (2000); see Fig. 11-3. This material was a late addition to the book, which means that it was not possible to explore these ideas as extensively as I would have liked. I had to either include the material in brief or leave it out. I chose to include it and to add this appendix for purposes of clarification.

There are a few things to point out before briefly discussing these mappings between lines and points. First of all, they are intended to be suggestive rather than definitive. I am not trying to prove that a certain line of development is invariably associated with a certain point of view or personality type. This would be premature, given that virtually none of the scales discussed below was constructed with the enneagram in mind. While the enneagram points of view arise out of specific kinds of inner motivation, developmental scales may or may not focus on inner motivation (or even inner states). The more empirically-oriented the scale, the more likely it is to focus solely on measurable behavior.

It is nevertheless useful to match the lines to the points, because the fit is "good enough" to constitute a starting point for thinking about the relationship between horizontal points of view and vertical lines of development.

Second, as discussed in Chapter 11, just because a certain line is associated with a type doesn't mean this is the main line along which a person of that type could or should develop. We can each develop along virtually any line—and sometimes, developing along unusual lines can provide unusual opportunities for growth. However, discovering our type can help us understand why some lines may seem easier, more natural, or more productive than others. This can thus help us "work smart"—in a way that makes the developmental process easier rather than harder.

Last, it is a fact that some enneagram points are currently associated with numerous well-known lines of development (e.g., moral development at Point 1 or ego development at Point 3) while other points are associated with lesser-known, more obscure, or harder-to-measure lines of development (e.g., esoteric or shamanic development at Point 5, the development of authenticity or emotional depth at Point 4, and the development of courage at

Point 6). Even leadership at Point 8 turns out to be associated with no well-known vertical scale (perhaps because it involves diverse developmental factors related to the other eight points).

Whatever the reasons, the fact that some enneagram points seem to have more lines than others (or seem to be associated with better-known lines) should not be taken to mean that those types have more developmental potential. All this tells us is that some attributes are (a) easier to formally measure using currently available methods or (b) of greater interest to investigators (perhaps because they promote the type of development most esteemed within the culture).

With these factors in mind, let's take a brief look at how we might pair various developmental clusters with each of the nine enneagram points of view based on the groupings depicted by Fig. 11-3 in Chapter 11. Please note that *for each line of development listed in* Integral Psychology, *I've provided a page number in that book for easy reference.* For scales not listed in *Integral Psychology*, I've provided an alternative reference whenever possible.

Point 1: ethical/activist/religious/ idealistic/self-disciplinary/law- & justice-oriented development. Examples include Lawrence Kohlberg's stages of moral development (p. 206), Carol Gilligan's hierarchy of feminine moral development (p. 206), John Rawls' moral positions (p. 208), and Scott Peck's moral motivations (p. 207). All of these scales relate to the development of moral standards and lawful action, which is a central concern at Point 1.

Point 2: empathic/emotional/social/ communicative/erotic development. Examples include Daniel Goleman's stages of emotional development,[1] Marie Fortune's

erotic relationships (p. 212), Wilber's [emotional]Affects scale (p. 212), Suzanne Benack's empathy scale (p. 212), and Turner/Powell's social role-taking (p. 207). The scales listed here describe the development of emotional differentiation (Goleman, Wilber), empathy (Benack), the ability to ethically engage in erotic relationships (Fortune), and the ability to socially interact with others (Turner/Powell).

Point 3: development of ego/practical skills/adaptability/team-oriented values. Examples include ego development scales developed by Jean Piaget (p. 201), Suzanne Cook-Greuter (p. 205), Jane Loevinger (p. 203), and Robert Kegan (p. 205). These are but a handful of the scales that can be used to describe our ability to develop the kind of solid ego identity that enables us to become psychologically stable while at the same time skillfully adapting to our environment.

Point 4: development of aesthetics/depth psychology/authenticity/individuality/ the ability to stand alone. Examples include the stages involved in Jung's individuation process,[2] the hero's journey (descent) into the unknown, and Wilber's Art[istic] development (p. 213). It is difficult to find truly formal measures by which to assess the development of many Point 4 attributes, especially emotional authenticity. Although I have assigned Wilber's Art scale to this point, this is not because Fours are more artistic than other types but because the art they create is so often central to their transformational process.

Point 5: rational/philosophical/esoteric/ shamanic development. Examples include the development of cognitive abilities as determined by IQ tests such as the Stanford-Binet, academic degrees in philosophy and related fields, the acquisition of "deep wisdom" via shamanic initiations or tests given to those seeking esoteric wisdom (reflected, e.g., in the 33 Masonic degrees of the Freemasons). While Point 5 is strongly associated with intellectual development (and with measures designed to assess cognitive abilities of all stripes), it is these hidden measures of wisdom that may better capture the true nature of Point 5 development.

Point 6: development of faith /conviction /courage/stewardship /duty /enlightened empiricism; overcoming fear via high-risk /daredevil /counterphobic paths. Examples include James Fowler's Stages of Faith (p. 209), military rankings, and medals for heroic acts. Aside from Fowler's Stages of Faith, there are few if any scales that directly measure the development of faith, courage, or stewardship. However, there are many less direct forms of recognition, taking the form of ranks given to firefighters, police, or military personnel.

Point 7: egalitarian /transpersonal / visionary /revolutionary /futuristic/ systems-oriented development. Examples include Beck & Cowan's Spiral Dynamics (p. 204) and Wilber's variant on Spiral Dynamics (SD).[4] Point 7 paths would also include those that rely upon the ability to imagine unconventional or visionary outcomes (although examples are hard to come by, because of their very uniqueness and unconventionality!). I've placed Spiral Dynamics at Point 7 because it represents the attempt to synthesize many different streams of development in a single but integrally-oriented scale that focuses on both individual and cultural transformation.

Point 8: development of mastery /leadership/ expertise /unity consciousness. Examples include Sri Aurobindo's stages of Integral Yoga (pp. 200 and 202), Dreyfus & Dreyfus' five levels of expertise,[5] Qabalistic levels linked to the 10 Sephiroth (p. 200), C. W. Leadbetter's theosophical levels (p. 200), and the seven levels of alchemical development.[6]

Although the development of leadership is obviously of great interest, there is surprisingly little in either the academic or popular literature about a generic path of leadership development (the focus being more on leadership styles or the situational variables that determine the efficacy of different styles). The concept of mastery also remains relatively undiscussed, I suppose because it often involves the kind of hands-on involvement that is hard to describe in theoretical terms (e.g., the development of a master craftsmen, mechanic, or builder)—although the Dreyfus & Dreyfus model is pretty good for describing the development of expertise (see Chapter 12). However, if we focus on spiritual development, we can include all paths designed to lead to spiritual realization, especially those will a comprehensive orientation, such as Sri Aurobindo's Integral Yoga.

Point 9: mystical /integrative /harmony-oriented /organic development. Examples include Evelyn Underhill's stages of mystical development (p. 209), St. Teresa of Avila's seven stages of interior life (p. 211), and the Sufi stations on the path of the heart.[7]

As the most naturally mystical point on the enneagram, Point 9 is associated with paths that are innately natural, unforced, and inward rather than outward. Such paths tend to "blend into the background" in a way that makes them hard to pin down and analyze, but they direct our attention to the value of acting in accordance with whatever is arising in the present moment.

The above summary is designed to clarify Fig. 11-3 in Chapter 11 and to flesh out the brief discussion on the relationship between enneagram points of view and vertical lines of development in that chapter. It is obviously not intended to provide a comprehensive list of all possible lines of development that could be associated with each enneagram point of view. (Interested readers can take a look at my second book, *Archetypes of the Enneagram*, 2010, for ideas about the different archetypes associated with each type, because these give rise to different paths of development.)

This discussion also provides a jumping off point for future explorations into not only the relationship between our horizontal point of view and the vertical lines along which we develop, but the role of culture in determining which lines of development are formally recognized and encouraged and which lines are disparaged, ignored, or even prohibited by law.

Notes

1. http://danielgoleman.info/growth-stages-of-ei/; accessed 6-4-13.

2. See, e.g., http://www.goertzel.org/dyna-psyc/2005/Whitlark.htm; accessed 6-4-13.

3. See, e.g., http://www.journeyccs.com/blog/2011/09/27/myth-and-personal-development-the-story-eros-and-psyche-in-depth-psychology/; accessed 6-4-13.

4. See Wilber's Fig. 2-4 on the inset after p. 68 in *Integral Spirituality* (2006) and the discussion of using the colors of the rainbow as an alternative to Spiral Dynamics' color scheme (which relies on linking the color of each level to the theorized properties associated with that level), such that beige is associated with "grassland survival," purple with the first dyes used in early civilizations, red with aggressive emotional energy, etc.; for a complete list of the correspondences between color and level, see http://www.spiraldynamics.ua/Graves/colors.htm; accessed 6-4-13.

5. See the "Art of Creative Living" section in Chapter 12.

6. See Maurice Aniane's article, "Alchemy: the Cosmological Yoga, Part 2: Phases of the Work," for a breakdown on seven alchemical stages of development, available at http://www.alchemylab.com/; accessed 6-3-13. (The same website has an interesting quiz that enables you to locate yourself on the alchemical spectrum of development; see http://www.alchemylab.com/quiz.htm).

7. Different Sufi schools and lines describe these stations in related but slightly different ways; see, e.g., the seven stages as described by one Qadiri source at http://www.sufiway.net/sec3=PRINsuf=maqm811326.html; accessed 6-3-13.

REFERENCES

Almaas, A. H. (1986). *Essence: The Diamond Approach to Inner Realization.* Newburyport, MA: Red Wheel Weiser.

Almaas, A. H. (1998). *Facets of Unity: The Enneagram of Holy Ideas.* Berkeley: Diamond Books.

Almaas, A. H. (2000). *The Pearl Beyond Price: Integration of Personality into Being: An Object Relations Approach.* Berkeley: Diamond Books.

Armstrong, David, & Ben H. Bagdikian (1999). *Trumpet to Arms: Alternative Media in America.* Cambridge, MA: South End Press.

Avinov, Marie, & Paul Chavchavadze (1968). *Marie Avinov: Pilgrimage Through Hell.* Englewood Cliffs, NJ: Prentice-Hall.

Baron, Renee, & Elizabeth Wagele (1994). *The Enneagram Made Easy.* New York: HarperCollins.

Beauregard, Mario, & Denyse O'Leary (2007). *The Spiritual Brain: a Neuroscientist's Case for the Existence of Soul.* San Francisco: HarperOne.

Begley, Sharon (2007). *Train Your Mind, Change Your Brain.* New York: Ballantine.

Bem, D. J. (2011). "Feeling the Future: Experimental Evidence for Anomalous Retroactive Influences on Cognition and Affect," *Journal of Personality and Social Psychology,* 100, 407-425.

Bennett, J. G. (1983). *Enneagram Studies.* York Beach, ME: Samuel Weiser.

Bernier, Nathan (2003). *The Enneagram: Symbol of All and Everything.* Brasilia, Brazil: Gilgamesh.

Blake, A. G. E. (1983). Preface to *Enneagram Studies,* by J. G. Bennett. York Beach, ME: Samuel Weiser.

Blake, A. G. E. (1996). *The Intelligent Enneagram.* Boston: Shambhala.

Blake, A. G. E. (1998). "On Time: Only Through Time, Time is Conquered," *Enneagram Monthly,* Jan. issue.

Briggs Myers, Isabel, with Peter Myers (1980). *Gifts Differing.* Palo Alto: Consulting Psychologists Press.

Broad, William J. (2012). *The Science of Yoga: The Risks and the Rewards.* New York: Simon & Schuster.

Browne, Sylvia (1998). *Adventures of a Psychic.* Carlsbad, CA: Hay House.

Bruner, Jerome (1990). *Acts of Meaning.* Cambridge: Harvard University Press.

Caplan, Marianna (1999). *Halfway Up the Mountain: The Error of Premature Claims to Enlightenment.* Prescott, AZ: Hohm.

Conquest, Robert (1986). *Harvest of Sorrow: Soviet Collectivization and the Terror-Famine.* New York: Oxford University Press.

Csikszentmihalyi, Mihalyi (1990). *Flow: The Psychology of Optimal Experience.* New York: HarperCollins.

Daniels, Michael (2005). *Shadow, Self, Spirit: Essays in Transpersonal Psychology.* Charlottesville, VA: Imprint Academic Philosophy Documentation Center.

de Becker, Gavin (1989). *A Gift of Fear: Survival Signals that Protect Us from Violence.* New York: Dell.

Deci, E. L., R. Koestner, & R. M. Ryan. (1999). "A Meta-analytic Review of Experiments Examining the Effects of Extrinsic Rewards on Intrinsic Motivation," *Psychological Bulletin,* 125, 627–668.

Doidge, Norman (2007). *The Brain That Changes Itself.* New York: Penguin.

Dossey, Larry (2009). *The Power of Premonitions: How Knowing the Future Can Shape Our Lives.* New York: Dutton.

Dreyfus, Hubert, & Stuart Dreyfus. (1986). *Mind Over Machine: The Power of Human Intuition and Expertise in the Era of the Computer.* New York: Free Press.

Eliade, Mircea (1964/2004). *Shamanism: Archaic Techniques of Ecstasy.* Princeton: Princeton Univ. Press.

Epstein, Mark (2005). *Open to Desire: Embracing a Lust for Life, Insights from Buddhism & Psychotherapy.* New York: Gotham.

Ferrer, Jorge (2004). "Integral Transformative Practice: A Participatory Perspective," *ReVision,* 27(1), 10-17.

Ferrer, Jorge (2008)."What Does It Mean to Live a Fully-Embodied Spiritual Life?" *International Journal of Transpersonal Studies,* 27, 1–11.

Ferrer, Jorge (2011). "Participation, Metaphysics, and Enlightenment: Reflections on Ken Wilber's Recent Work," *Transpersonal Psychology Review,* 14(2), 3–24.

Ferrer, Jorge, Ramon Albareda, and Marina T. Romero (2004). "Embodied Participation in the Mystery: Implications for the Individual, Interpersonal Relationships, and Society," *Journal of Transpersonal Psychology,* 35(1), 21–42.

Ford, Debbie (2010). *The Darker Side of Light Chasers.* New York: Riverhead.

Fortune, Dion (1949/1995). *The Cosmic Doctrine.* London: Society of the Inner Light.

Fortune, Dion (1962/2000). *Applied Magic.* York Beach, ME: Samuel Weiser.

Fortune, Dion (1987). *Sane Occultism & Practical Occultism in Everyday Life.* London: Aquarian.

Fortune, Dion (1987/1995). *Esoteric Orders and Their Work & The Training and Work of an Initiate.* London: Thorsons.

Fortune, Dion (2000). *The Mystical Qabalah,* York Beach, ME: Weiser.

Fox, Matthew (2004). *Creativity: Where the Divine and the Human Meet.* New York: Jeremy P. Tarcher.

Graves, Clare (1974). "Human Nature Prepares for a Momentous Leap," *The Futurist,* April issue, 72–87; revised and available at www.claregraves.com.

Gray, Kurt, & Daniel M. Wegner (2008). "The Sting of Intentional Pain," *Psychological Science,* 19, 1260–1262.

Haich, Elizabeth (1982). *Sexual Energy and Yoga.* Santa Fe, NM: Aurora Press.

Halifax, Joan (1979). *Shamanic Voices: A Survey of Visionary Narratives.* New York: E. P. Dutton.

Hall, Manly P. (1977). *The Secret Teachings of All Ages.* Los Angeles: The Philosophical Research Society.

Hanh, Thich Nhat (1998). *The Heart of the Buddha's Teaching: Transforming Suffering into Peace, Joy, and Liberation.* New York: Broadway Books.

Hurley, Kathleen, & Theodore Dobson (1993). *My Best Self: Using the Enneagram to Free the Soul.* New York: HarperCollins.

Ichazo, Oscar (1988). *Letters to the School.* New York: Arica.

Interviews with Oscar Ichazo (1982). "Breaking the Tyranny of Ego." Interview of Oscar Ichazo by Sam Keen. New York: Arica, 3–24.

Jenny, Hans (1967/2001). *Cymatics: A Study of Wave Phenomena & Vibration.* Eliot, ME: Macromedia.

Johnson, Robert (1998). *Balancing Heaven and Earth.* San Francisco: HarperOne.

Jung, C. G. (1954/1981). "The Development of Personality," in *The Development of Personality: Papers on Child Psychology, Education, and Related Subjects.* R. F. C. Hull, trans. Princeton: Princeton Univ. Press.

Jung, Carl (1971). "The Stages of Life," in *The Portable Jung*, Joseph Campbell, ed. New York: Penguin.

Jung, Carl (1971/1976). "Dream Symbolism in Relation to Alchemy," in *The Portable Jung*, Joseph Campbell, ed. New York: Penguin.

Jung, Carl (1989). *Memories, Dreams, and Reflections.* Aniela Jaffe, ed. New York: Vintage.

Ken Wilber in Dialogue (1998), Don Rothberg & Sean Kelly, eds. Wheaton, IL: Quest.

Kennedy-Moore, Eileen, & Jeanne C. Watson (1999). *Expressing Emotion: Myths, Realities, and Therapeutic Strategies.* New York: Guilford Press.

Koestler, Arthur (1954/1998). *The Invisible Writing.* New York: Macmillan.

Koestler, Arthur (1964/1990). *The Act of Creation.* New York: Penguin.

Koestler, Arthur (1967). *The Ghost in the Machine.* New York: Macmillan.

Koestler, Arthur (1969). *Beyond Reductionism: New Perspectives in the Life Sciences (The Alpbach Symposium).* Boston: Beacon Press.

Koestler, Arthur (1978). *Janus: A Summing Up.* New York: Random House.

Koestler, Arthur (1980). *Bricks to Babel.* New York: Random House.

Kofman, Fred [no date given]. "Holons, Heaps, and Artifacts (And their corresponding hierarchies)"; available at www.integralworld.net.

Kornfeld, Jack (1993). *A Path With Heart.* New York: Bantam.

Krechevsky, I. (later known as David Krech) (1932). "Hypotheses in Rats," *The Psychological Review*, 39 (6), 316–332.

Lakoff, George, & Mark Johnson (1980). *Metaphors We Live By.* Chicago: Univ. of Chicago Press.

Lazar, Sara. "Growing the Brain through Meditation" (2006); available at www.hms.harvard.edu/hmni/ On_The_Brain/Volume12/OTB_Vol12No3_ Fall06.pdf.

LeShan, Lawrence (1990). *The Dilemma of Psychology.* New York: Dutton.

Loftus, E.F., E. Greene, & K. H. Smith (1980). "How deep is the meaning of life?" *Bulletin of the Psychonomic Society*, 15, 282–284.

Long, Jeffrey, & Paul Perry (2010). *Evidence of the Afterlife: The Science of Near-Death Experiences.* San Francisco: Harper One.

Luke, Helen (1975). *Dark Wood to White Rose.* Pecos, NM: Dove.

Mackenzie, Vicki (1998). *Cave in the Snow: Tenzin Palmo's Quest for Enlightenment.* New York: Bloomsbury USA.

Maharishi Mahesh Yogi (1966/1975). *The Science of Life and Art of Living.* Livingstone Manor, NY: MIU Press.

Maitri, Sandra (2000). *The Spiritual Dimension of the Enneagram.* New York: Tarcher.

Maitri, Sandra (2005/2009). *The Enneagram of Passions and Virtues: Finding the Way Home.* New York: Tarcher.

Masters, Robert P. (2010). *Spiritual Bypassing: When Spirituality Disconnects Us from What Really Matters.* Berkeley: North Atlantic Book.

Mayer, Elizabeth Lloyd (2007). *Extraordinary Knowing: Science, Skepticism, and the Inexplicable Powers of the Human Mind.* New York: Bantam.

McNab, Peter (2012). "Towards an Integral Enneagram," *Enneagram Journal*, 5, 79–114.

McTaggart, Lynne (2008). *The Intention Experiment: Using Your Thoughts to Change Your Life and the World.* New York: Free Press.

Mehl-Madrona, Lewis (2010). *Healing the Mind Through the Power of Story: The Promise of Narrative Psychiatry.* Rochester, VT: Bear & Co.

Meins, Elizabeth (1997). *Security of Attachment and the Social Development of Cognition.* New York: Psychology Press.

Metcalf, Maureen, & Mark Palmer (2011). *Innovative Leadership Fieldbook*. Tuscon, AZ: Integral Publishers.

Meyerhoff, Jeff (2010). *Bald Ambition*: Inside the Curtain Press; available at www.integralworld.net.

Mitchell, John, & Alan Brown (2009). *How the World is Made: The Story of Creation According to Sacred Geometry*. Rochester, VT: Inner Traditions.

Moore, Richard K. (1997). "Inventing Enneagrams: The 'Dramatic Story' and Two-Force Analysis," *Enneagram Monthly*, August issue.

Muller, Herbert J. (1943). *Science and Criticism: The Humanistic Tradition in Contemporary Thought*. New Haven: Yale University Press.

Myss, Caroline (2003). *Sacred Contracts: Awakening Your Divine Potential*. New York: Three Rivers Press.

Nachmanovitch, Stephen (1990). *Free Play: Improvisation in Life and Art*. New York: Jeremy P. Tarcher.

Naranjo, Claudio (1994). *Character and Neurosis: An Integrative View*. Nevada City, CA: Gateway Books.

Naranjo, Claudio (2004). *The Enneagram of Society: Healing the Soul to Heal the World*. Nevada City, CA: Gateway Books.

O'Brien, Justin (1998). *Walking with a Himalayan Master: An American's Odyssey*. St. Paul, MN: Yes International Publishers.

Ooten, Deborah, & Beth O'Hara (2010). "Levels of Consciousness," *Enneagram Journal*, 3, 33–53.

Ouspensky, P. D. (1949/2001). *In Search of the Miraculous: The Teachings of G. I. Gurdjieff*. New York: Harvest.

Palmer, Helen (1995). *The Enneagram in Love & Work*. San Francisco: Harper.

Pearsall, Paul (1998). *The Heart's Code: Tapping the Wisdom and Power of Our Heart Energy*. New York: Broadway Books.

Pfaffenberger, Angela H., & Paul W. Marko (2011). "Exceptional Maturity of Personality: An Emerging Field"; available at www.sunypress.edu/pdf/62108.pdf.

Plato, Timeus, 29/30; 4th century B.C.

Polanyi, Michael (1965). "On the Modern Mind," *Encounter*, 24, 12–20, cited in *Michael Polanyi*, by Mark T. Mitchell (2006). Wilmington, DE: ISI Books.

Radin, Dean (2006). *Entangled Minds: Extrasensory Experiences in a Quantum Reality*. New York: Paraview Pocketbooks.

Reynolds, Brad (2006). *Where's Wilber At? Ken Wilber's Integral Vision in the New Millennium*. St. Paul, MN: Paragon House.

Rhodes, Susan (2006). "On The Nature of the Enneagram Subtypes"; available at www.enneagram-dimensions.net.

Rhodes, Susan (2007). "Reconciling Personality with Process: Linking Two Views of the Enneagram," *Enneagram Monthly*, April issue.

Rhodes, Susan (2009). *The Positive Enneagram*. Seattle: Geranium Press.

Rhodes, Susan (2010). "The Retro-Romantic Ideal and the Enneagram," *Enneagram Monthly*, September issue.

Rhodes, Susan (2010). *Archetypes of the Enneagram*. Seattle: Geranium Press.

Rhodes, Susan (2011). "Integral Living and the Enneagram," *Enneagram Monthly*, October issue.

Rhodes, Susan (2011). "Ken Wilber's 8 Hori-zones & 9 Enneagram Types," *Enneagram Monthly*, June issue.

Rhodes, Susan (2011/2012). "Personality, Process & Levels of Development," *Enneagram Monthly*, Dec. 2011–Jan. 2012 issue.

Rhodes, Susan (2012). "An Enneagram-based Model of Integral Transformation," *Enneagram Monthly*, June issue; an updated version is available at www.integralworld.net.

Riso, Don, & Russ Hudson (1999). *Wisdom of the Enneagram*. New York: Bantam.

Riso, Don, & Russ Hudson (2000). *Understanding the Enneagram*. Boston: Houghton-Mifflin.

Rodman, F. Robert (2003). *Winnicott*. Cambridge: Perseus.

Sansonese, J. Nigro (1994). *The Body of Myth: Mythology, Shamanic Trance, and the Sacred Geography of the Body*. Rochester, VT: Inner Traditions.

Scammell, Michael (2009). *Koestler*. New York: Random House.

Schaef, Anne Wilson (1994). *Beyond Therapy, Beyond Science: A New Model for Healing the Whole Person*. New York: HarperCollins.

Schwartz, Gary, & Linda Russek (1999). *The Living Energy Universe: A Fundamental Study that Transforms Science and Medicine*. Newbury Port, MA: Hampton Roads.

Searle, Judith (1997). "The Gap at the Bottom of the Enneagram," *Enneagram Monthly*, September issue.

Seligman, Martin (2011). *Flourish: A Visionary New Understanding of Happiness and Well-being*. New York: Free Press.

Shah, Idries (1994). *The Commanding Self*. London: Octagon Press.

Shakespeare, William. *Hamlet* (1.5.166-7).

Sharf, Richard S. (2000). *Theories of Psychotherapy & Counseling: Concepts and Cases*, 2nd ed. Belmont, CA: Wadsworth.

Sheldrake, Rupert (1981/1995). *A New Science of Life*. South Paris, ME: Park Street Press.

Sheldrake, Rupert (2012). *The Science Delusion: Freeing the Spirit of Enquiry*. London: Coronet.

Siegel, Daniel (1999). *The Developing Mind: How Relationships and the Brain Interact to Shape Who We Are*. New York: Guilford Press.

Smuts, Jan (1999). *Wholism and Evolution*. Sherman Oaks, CA: Sierra Sunrise.

Stark, Rodney (2008). *What Americans Really Believe*. Waco, TX: Baylor Univ. Press.

Stern, Daniel N. (2000). *The Interpersonal World Of The Infant: A View From Psychoanalysis And Developmental Psychology*. New York: Basic Books.

Stone, L. Joseph., Henrietta T. Smith, & Lois Barclay Murphy, eds. (1973).*The Competent Infant*. New York: Basic Books.

Swami Prabhupada (1989). *Bhagavad-Gita, As It Is*, 2nd ed. Los Angeles: Bhaktivedanta Book Trust.

Swami Yogananda (1959). *Autobiography of a Yogi*. Los Angeles: Self Realization Fellowship; available as an Amazon kindle book at no charge.

Tart, Charles (2009). *The End of Materialism: How Evidence of the Paranormal is Bringing Science and Spirit Together*. Oakland: New Harbinger Publications.

Taylor, Jill Bolte (2009). *My Stroke of Insight*. New York: Plume.

Tharp, Twyla (2006). *The Creative Habit: Learn It and Use It for Life*. New York: Simon & Schuster.

Three Initiates (2009). *The Kybalion: A Study of The Hermetic Philosophy of Ancient Egypt and Greece*, e-book ed.: The Kybalion Resource Page.

Tolman, Edward C. (1931/1964). *Purposive Behavior in Animals*. Berkeley: Univ. Cal. Press.

Tweedie, Irina (1991). "A Sufi Should Never Give a Bad Example: Interview with Irina Tweedie," *What Is Enlightenment?*, 1(1), 9-11.

Tweedie, Irina (1995). *Daughter of Fire: The Diary of a Spiritual Training with a Sufi Master*. Inverness, CA: The Golden Sufi Center.

Van Bertalanffy, Ludwig (1950). "The Theory of Open Systems in Physics and Biology," *Science*, 111, 23–29.

Visser, Frank (2003). *Ken Wilber: Thought as Passion*. Albany: SUNY Press.Wallace, Robert Keith (1993). *The Physiology of Consciousness*. Fairfield, IA: MIU Press.

Welwood, John (2000). *Toward a Psychology of Awakening: Buddhism, Psychotherapy, and the Path of Personal and Spiritual Transformation*. Boston: Shambhala.

Wesselman, Hank (2011). *Bowl of Light*. Boulder: Sounds True.

Wilber, Ken (1977/1993). *The Spectrum of Consciousness*. Wheaton, IL: Quest.

Wilber, Ken (1979/1981). *No Boundary: Eastern and Western Approaches to Personal Growth.* Boston: Shambhala.

Wilber, Ken (1980). *The Atman Project: A Transpersonal View of Human Development.* Wheaton, IL: The Theosophical Publishing House.

Wilber, Ken (1980)."The Pre/Trans Fallacy," *ReVision,* 3(2), 51–73.

Wilber, Ken (1981). *Up from Eden: A Transpersonal View of Human Evolution.* Garden City, NY: Anchor/Doubleday.

Wilber, Ken (1983/1996). *Eye to Eye: The Quest for the New Paradigm.* New York: Anchor/Doubleday.

Wilber, Ken (1983/2005). *A Sociable God: A Brief Introduction to a Transcendental Sociology.* New York: McGraw-Hill.

Wilber, Ken (1990). "Two Patterns of Transcendence: A Reply to Washburn," *Journal of Humanistic Psychology,* 30(3), 113–116.

Wilber, Ken (1995/2000). *Sex, Ecology, Spirituality: The Spirit of Evolution.* Boston: Shambhala.

Wilber, Ken (1996). *A Brief History of Everything.* Boston: Shambhala.

Wilber, Ken (1998). *The Essential Ken Wilber: An Introductory Reader.* Kendra Crossen Burroughs, ed. Boston: Shambhala.

Wilber, Ken (1998). *The Marriage of Sense and Soul: Integrating Science and Religion.* New York: Random House.

Wilber, Ken (2000). *Integral Psychology: Consciousness, Spirit, Psychology, Therapy.* Boston: Shambhala.

Wilber, Ken (2000). *One Taste: the Journals of Ken Wilber.* Boston: Shambhala.

Wilber, Ken (2001). *A Theory of Everything.* Boston: Shambhala.

Wilber, Ken (2001). *The Eye of Spirit: An Integral Vision for a World Gone Slightly Mad.* Boston: Shambhala.

Wilber, Ken (2002). *Boomeritis: A Novel That Will Set You Free.* Boston: Shambhala.

Wilber, Ken (2003). *Kosmic Consciousness* [CD set]. Louisville, CO: Sounds True.

Wilber, Ken (2004). *The Simple Feeling of Being: Visionary, Spiritual, and Poetic Writings.* Boston: Shambhala.

Wilber, Ken (2006). *Integral Spirituality: A Startling New Role for Religion in the Modern and Post-Modern World.* Boston: Shambhala.

Wilber, Ken (2007). *The Integral Vision: a Very Short Introduction to the Revolutionary Integral Approach to Life, God, the Universe, and Everything.* Boston: Shambhala.

Wilber, Ken, Jack Engler & Daniel P. Brown (1986). *Transformations of Consciousness: Conventional and Contemplative Perspectives on Development.* Boston: Shambhala.

Wilber, Ken, Terry Patten, Adam Leonard & Marco Morelli (2008). *Integral Life Practice: A 21st-Century Blueprint for Physical Health, Emotional Balance, Mental Clarity, and Spiritual Awakening.* Boston: Integral Books.

Williams, Meg Harris. "The Chamber of Maiden Thought," Chapter 4, 82–94, from *Wordsworth: The Visionary Gleam* [no date given]; available at www.artlit.info/pdfs/Chamber-Wordsworth.pdf.

INDEX

3135999R00195

Made in the USA
San Bernardino, CA
09 July 2013